Ennius Noster: Lucretius and the Annales

Ennius Noster: Lucretius and the *Annales*

JASON S. NETHERCUT

OXFORD
UNIVERSITY PRESS

OXFORD
UNIVERSITY PRESS

Oxford University Press is a department of the University of Oxford. It furthers
the University's objective of excellence in research, scholarship, and education
by publishing worldwide. Oxford is a registered trade mark of Oxford University
Press in the UK and certain other countries.

Published in the United States of America by Oxford University Press
198 Madison Avenue, New York, NY 10016, United States of America.

Library of Congress Cataloging-in-Publication Data
Names: Nethercut, Jason S., author.
Title: Ennius noster : Lucretius and the Annales / Jason S. Nethercut.
Other titles: Lucretius and the Annales
Description: New York, NY : Oxford University Press, 2021. |
Includes bibliographical references and index.
Identifiers: LCCN 2020024409 (print) | LCCN 2020024410 (ebook) |
ISBN 9780197517697 (hardback) | ISBN 9780197517710 (epub)
Subjects: LCSH: Lucretius Carus, Titus. De rerum natura. | Ennius, Quintus—Influence. |
Ennius, Quintus. Annales. | Epic poetry, Latin—History and criticism.
Classification: LCC PA6485 .N38 2020 (print) | LCC PA6485 (ebook) | DDC 871/.1—dc23
LC record available at https://lccn.loc.gov/2020024409
LC ebook record available at https://lccn.loc.gov/2020024410

1 3 5 7 9 8 6 4 2

Printed by Integrated Books International, United States of America

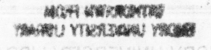

Patri Amatissimo, Magistro Optimo

"*. . . And yet one word*
Frees us of all the weight and pain of life:
That word is love. Never shall you have more
From any man than you have had from me.
And now you must spend the rest of your life without me."

—Sophocles, *Oedipus at Colonus*, 1615–1619

Contents

Acknowledgments

THIS BOOK IS the work of many years and many conversations. Behind the words that fill its pages lie the hands of so many others who have helped bring it into the light. It seems appropriate here to take proper account of this debt. First and foremost, I must thank my colleague, professionally and domestically, Sarah Scullin, who looked over every word in this book with her characteristically rigorous and loving eye. Those who have worked with Sarah will know that anything that lives up to her standards is something worth protecting. It is the greatest honor of my life that she has chosen to share her life with me. Joe Farrell has served as midwife to every argument in this book and has commented on every draft of it I have sent him. I have had the great fortune to be the student and friend of one of our best Latinists and certainly one of our best humans; his influence permeates everything I do. I am also grateful to my two anonymous readers, whose penetrating and constructive feedback forced me to recalibrate important arguments in this book; the final product is much better for it. Cynthia Damon, Matt Farmer, Sander Goldberg, Philip Hardie, James Ker, Damien Nelis, and Ralph Rosen have all read through individual chapters of this book. I am grateful to have had such generous and erudite readers. I owe more general thanks to a great teacher, John Henderson, whose influence on my work I could never hope to account for adequately. I am sure that all those who have worked with John will understand my predicament. He shifts your assumptions and challenges your orthodoxies, and I shall always cherish the hours spent in his rooms conversing about the nature of things. I owe special thanks to Stefan Vranka, Isabelle Prince, and the entire production team at OUP, who at every turn simplified a complicated process.

Others have offered their expertise, and, although their names appear in the footnotes of this book, I think it is appropriate to single them out here as well: Frederik Bakker, Sam Beckelhymer, Seth Bernard, Caroline Bishop, Pramit Chaudhuri, Jessica Clark, Ginna Closs, Lesley Dean-Jones, Casper De Jonge, Jackie Elliott, Virginia Fabrizi, Denis Feeney, Ayelet Haimson-Lushkov, John Marincola, Andrew Morrison, Donncha O'Rourke, Dan-el Padilla Peralta,

Christoph Pieper, Bettina Reitz-Joosse, Christiane Reitz, Andrew Riggsby, Barney Taylor, and Antje Wessels.

Friends and family have all assisted the gestation of this project. My three sons, Isaac, Freddie, and Nicky, fill my world with a contagious joy that has always made the writing of this book bittersweet; I would have preferred to spend all my time with them. This book would not have been written without the support (both practical and psychological) of Bettie Scullin. I would not have made it to a point where I could finish this project without Cate Denial, Danielle Fatkin, Jeremy LaBuff, Nick and Sunshine Regiacorte, and Alison Traweek. My colleagues in Florida—Buddy Hedrick, Hip Kantzios, Anne Latowsky, Eleni Manolaraki, David Rohrbacher, and Stephan Schindler—have all given me helpful advice and professional assistance. Their contributions to this book are fundamental.

The research for this book was subsidized by the Loeb Classical Library Foundation, the Fondation Hardt, the Department of World Languages and the Humanities Institute at the University of South Florida, and, at the invitation of Ineke Sluiter, Leiden University, where I served as Spinoza Visiting Researcher in Classics. I am especially grateful to Ineke, who provided me with time and space (the two most precious gifts) to finish this manuscript.

Finally, I want to thank my dad, Bill Nethercut, who, at the time of my writing this, has just died, having faced a terminal illness with his characteristic *ataraxia*. The world would be infinitely more joyful, infinitely more positive if we all could see it through Bill Nethercut's eyes. Throughout my life, he was my biggest supporter and my most loving teacher. My first encounters with the ancient world and with Latin and Greek took place in our living room. He modeled for me the value of constant diligence and a curious mind; both lessons continue to serve me well, especially in my professional activities. In him, I always experienced the embodiment of Lucretius' *lucida tela diei*. He was the first to encourage me (before I was ready for it, perhaps) to make sense of the opening lines of Lucretius' poem: "tolle, lege" he said "maxima cum cura." I dedicate this book to him for the many lessons he taught me, and as a testament to the love and wonder with which he infused everything he cared for, especially his children. *Maxima cum cura*, indeed.

Introduction

ENNIUS' *ANNALES* WAS one of the most important hexameter epics written before Vergil's *Aeneid*, and perhaps *the* most influential Latin poem of *any* period. Writing during the Republic, and covering Roman history from the fall of Troy through his own lifetime, Ennius was the first to write Latin hexameters. His *Annales* was hugely popular, and its use as a school text only cemented its popularity in the Roman imagination.

This is not a book about Ennius' *Annales*.

If this were a book about Ennius' *Annales*, it would be doomed from the start, as we have only fragments of this influential text, and cannot generalize even about some of its most important aspects. This is not to say that much early work on Ennius did not focus on reconstructing—sometimes with reckless creativity—the original text. In a corrective move, recent work on Ennius, especially by Jackie Elliott, has shown us how little we can securely say about this original form of the *Annales*,[1] given that Ennius' epic is always presented to us through the lens of later citation sources, most of whom have their own reasons for citing the *Annales*. The current resurgence in Ennian studies, in addition to offering deconstructions—or destructions, in some cases—of older *recon*structions of the *Annales* has, perhaps paradoxically, also given rise to many new large-scale ideas about the poem, while generally remaining attentive to the pitfalls involved in working with fragments.[2] Although the result has not been the formation of a clear consensus about these matters, we do now have a number of well-argued interpretive approaches, each of which serves to some extent as a useful check on the others.

---

1. Elliott 2013.

2. In addition to Elliott 2013, see Breed and Rossi 2006; Fitzgerald and Gowers 2007; Fabrizi 2012; Goldschmidt 2013; Fisher 2014; Goldberg 2018; and Damon and Farrell 2020.

Ennius Noster: Lucretius and the Annales. Jason S. Nethercut, Oxford University Press (2021). © Oxford University Press. DOI: 10.1093/oso/9780197517697.001.0001.

But, as I said, this book does not provide a reconstruction of the *Annales* in this vein; rather, it capitalizes on the fruits of this new situation in Ennian studies in order to analyze the reception of Ennius' *Annales* in Lucretius' *De Rerum Natura* (*DRN*). When Lucretius set out at the end of the Republican period (probably in the 50s BCE[3]) to write a didactic poem about atomic physics, the foundation of the Epicurean system of philosophy, he chose to make frequent overt gestures to the fact that he was writing in the same tradition of hexameter poetry as Ennius' *Annales*. He even went so far as to single out Ennius' epic as especially influential for the kind of poetry he himself writes *de rerum natura*.

For the reader interested in Lucretius, this book offers a systematic analysis of the primary Latin poetic model of the *DRN*, and so fills a long-standing and sizeable gap in our understanding of Lucretian poetics and his allusive program. For the reader interested in Ennius, this book offers, at best, an excavation of Lucretius' version of the *Annales*, a version that must have been foundational for many subsequent receptions of the *Annales*, not the least of which was Vergil's in the *Aeneid*. What emerges upon this excavation is evidence that Lucretius' engagement encompasses a comprehensive revision of the entire Ennian value system, on literary as well as philosophical grounds, and in terms of form as well as content. What emerges from this excavation is the sense that Lucretius appears to have selected Ennius as a model not because it was the expected or inevitable thing for any hexameter poet to do, not because he admired Ennius as a poet more than he did any other predecessor or contemporary, and not because some part of Lucretius agreed with Ennius in spite of himself. Rather, he chose Ennius as a model precisely in order to dismantle thoroughly what he considered (or constructed as) Ennian values: the importance of history as a poetic subject in general, the importance of Rome's historical achievement in particular, and an innovative, quasi-philosophical conception of literary history. In fundamental opposition to this thought-world of Ennius' *Annales*, Lucretius articulates an Epicurean account of the universe and its history.

This book thus builds on what has become a central observation of Lucretian scholarship, articulated most forcefully by Monica Gale and Philip Hardie: that Lucretius goes to great lengths to criticize the heterodox philosophical views of other poets.[4] In this sense, Lucretius' critical treatment of Ennius' conception of poetry and history largely mirrors his engagement with the traditions

---

3. On the date of the *DRN*, see Hutchinson 2001 (followed by Schiesaro 2007: 53–54 and Farrell 2020: 227–228) along with the responses of Volk 2010 and Krebs 2013 who reaffirm the traditional dating; cf. Morgan and Taylor 2017; Rebeggiani 2019; and Trinacty 2020.

4. Hardie 1986 and Gale 1994.

of mythological poetry. But Ennius is special, I suggest, and was a particularly important poetic target for such revisionism because his entire (implied) world-view, to a greater extent than that found in any other poetic tradition, represents ideas about Rome and its place in the cosmos that are indefensible when one accepts the truths of Epicureanism. This pride of place is not surprising, given that we have ample evidence that Ennius came to represent a growing sense of general Roman entitlement to empire and self-aggrandizement, especially as one moves from the (apparently) nonpartisan presentation of figures like Romulus or Pyrrhus of Epirus in the earlier books of the *Annales* to the jingoistic satire of Philip V or the highly partisan representation of Romans like Fulvius Nobilior in the later books of the epic.[5] In other words, we can safely infer that for Romans of the first century BCE, the *Annales* offered a perspective on Roman power that could be used to support and extend Roman hegemony in the Mediterranean.

Now, regardless of what may actually have been written in the *Annales* itself, I argue that Lucretius goes to great lengths to set the poem up in just this way—and he does this in order to create a foil for his own articulation of the Epicurean universe; it proves, therefore, peculiarly advantageous for Lucretius to confront Ennius' worldview with a revisionist agenda.[6] Yet Lucretius' correction of the Ennian perspective does not derive solely from the fact that Epicureanism stands directly opposed to the system of values given poetic form in the *Annales*. Recent scholarship on Ennius has suggested that Ennius makes a number of universalizing claims for the significance of his poetic achievement and that he conceived of the *Annales* as a kind of universal history.[7] Against this background, I argue that Lucretius' own universalizing claims contrast with those of Ennius and with the troubled condition of the Roman state in the years when he was writing the *DRN*. One of the major arguments advanced in this book is that Lucretius implies that his poem transcends not just the Ennian conception, but *all* traditional concep-tions of poetry, whether mythological or historical. Lucretius' engagement with Ennius is thus fundamental to his argument, because Lucretius represents Ennius as his most conspicuous poetic target. Ennius effectively stands in as *pars pro toto* in Lucretius' revisionist poetics; if we extend the implications of Lucretius' dis-mantling of the Ennian perspective to their logical conclusions, then the logic of the *DRN* would appear to dismantle all other poetic value systems, too. As a microcosm, the *DRN* reflects the only real system and the only meaningful

---

5. See especially Fabrizi 2012.

6. Compare Gee 2020: 201 on Lucretian "intertextual polemic" and specifically his revisionist engagement with the Stoicism of Cicero's *Aratea*; cf. Gee 2016.

7. Elliott 2013: 233–294.

values—namely, those that are reflected in the physical universe as interpreted by
Epicurean philosophy.

Ennian Form, Ennian Content

The drastically revisionist appropriation of the *Annales* that I argue for does
not, at first glance, appear to comport with the unmistakable and wide-ranging
Ennian idiom that Lucretius adopts in writing Latin hexameters—why would
Lucretius, who seemingly worships at the altar of Ennian poetics, practice such
heresy when it comes to the content of Ennius' poem? Indeed, Lucretius' Ennian
obsession has long been marked by a critical consensus that regards Lucretius as
a self-consciously Ennian poet. This is understandable. Lucretius writes in an
insistently Ennian style, and traces of Ennian language appear scattered through-
out the *DRN*. But the reader interested in trying to make sense of the Ennian
aspects of Lucretius' poem is confronted with major difficulties in the scholarly
literature. The only comprehensive studies of the relationship between Ennius
and Lucretius simply present catalogs of verbal correspondences between the two
poets without any sort of analysis of such parallels as are adduced.[8] While these
works are valuable for the information they contain, they do not seek to interpret
this information. A second difficulty is that actual analysis of the relationship
between Lucretius and Ennius is quite superficial and usually begins and ends
with what Lucretius says about Ennius' *Dream of Homer* in the proem to the
DRN (1.102–135)—namely Lucretius' assertion that Ennius' claim to be Homer
reincarnate was false.[9] The standard interpretation of this passage is that Lucretius
is announcing his own Homeric and Ennian pedigree, while at the same time dis-
tancing himself from the misguided philosophical principles upon which Ennius'
own boast are founded. This interpretation rests on the fact that the proem to
the *Annales* seems to have characterized Ennius as *Homerus redivivus*—Homer

---

8. Pullig 1888; Wreschniok 1907; Merrill 1918; Marx 1927: 191–195.

9. Norden 1927: 369–372, esp. 371; Skutsch 1985: 12; Gale 1994: 106–109; Gale 2000: 68
n. 34 and 239 n. 29; Kenney 2007: 96; cf. Murley 1947: 336–346; West 1969: 23–34; Gigon
1978: 167–196; Hardie 1986: 193–219; Mayer 1990: 35–43; Volk 2002: 87–88, 114–115. On the
use of Ennius in the proem to the *DRN*, see Harrison 2002; Volk 2002: 114–115; Goldberg
2005: 131–136; Taylor 2016: 145–150; and Taylor 2020a: 79–82. For the sophisticated nature of
Lucretius' allusion to Ennius as a poetic source, see now Gellar-Goad 2018 and 2020: 51–54;
Kronenberg 2019: 287 n. 42; and Hanses (forthcoming). Most recently, Elliott (2013: 115–117)
reminds us that "no ancient source ever quotes Ennius directly in explanation of Lucretius'
language" (116), and, again, "[o]ur perception today of the relationship between the *Annales*
and the *DRN* is the product of Lucretius' heavy imitation of Ennian word-forms and hexamet-
ric cadences (against the developing neoteric trend of his day), which we can match with the
linguistic and metrical forms of the fragments of the *Annales*" (117).

reborn—through the process of metempsychosis.[10] Because Lucretius explicitly attacks Ennius' idea of metempsychosis as misguided philosophy in that passage, and offers in its stead an Epicurean rebuttal, Lucretius, the standard argument goes, appears to align himself with Ennian poetic *form* while rejecting Ennian philosophical *content*, an interpretation that certainly stands in harmony with the fact that Lucretius' own poetic style (form) is "Ennian" in many ways. And so Lucretius has long been assumed to be an archaizing poet in the Ennian tradition.

According to the *status opinionis*, therefore, the relationship between Lucretius and Ennius is primarily a function of form, not content. Earlier studies focus on the verbal texture of this relationship, while the more penetrating analyses that more recent scholars have offered focus uniformly on Lucretius' repudiation of Ennian philosophical content, a repudiation that also entails, paradoxically, an emphatic affirmation of Ennian poetic form. In both instances, the relationship between Lucretius and Ennius is treated quite superficially and in a way that reinforces the form/content binary. In effect, the current orthodoxy maintains that Lucretius' Ennian idiom is an inert marker of his comprehensive adherence to an Ennian aesthetic, and that the only minor deviation from this adherence concerns Ennius' embrace of metempsychosis. One of the primary objectives of this book is to put pressure on the way we conceive of Lucretius' relationship to both Ennian form *and* Ennian content. Not only do I show that Lucretius' embrace of Ennian stylistics is dynamic and strategic (and certainly transcends our current emphasis on Lucretius' desire to be an "Ennian poet"), but I also underscore Lucretius' wide-ranging engagement with Ennius as a philosophical poet on many other topics in addition to psychology. In fact, I show that Lucretius often uses his Ennian stylistics (form) to highlight places where he is critiquing Ennian philosophy (content). This synergy between form and content in Lucretius' reception of Ennius' *Annales* builds on another central observation of Lucretian scholarship, namely that, on the basis of the metaphor of the honeyed cup, Lucretius programmatically announces his subsequent procedure in the *DRN* of using form in the service of content, of poetry in the service of philosophy.[11]

---

10. Articulated most explicitly by Gale 2007a, though scholars have frequently argued that Lucretius goes to great lengths to associate himself with the tradition of epic poetry represented by Ennius and Homer (e.g. Murley 1947; West 1969: ch. 3; Hardie 1986: 193–219; Mayer 1990; Gale 1994: 99–128), often with specific reference to the fact that he simultaneously distances himself from these two poets philosophically.

11. The scholarship here is vast. The most important contributions are Gale 1994: esp. 46–48 and Volk 2002: 96–98. See most recently, Nethercut 2018b; Morrison 2020; and O'Keefe 2020 with further bibliography.

One major criticism that can be directed at the *status opinionis* regarding Lucretius' relationship to Ennius as I have described it is that it oversimplifies the "Ennius" that Lucretius engages with, in terms both of content and form. On the one hand, it treats the philosophical Ennius that Lucretius constructs, the poet whose Homer discourses on *rerum natura* (1.126), as essentially concerned with only one major philosophical topic—metempsychosis. Yet whenever Lucretius' deploys the phrase *rerum natura* elsewhere in his poem, it always covers much more expansive philosophical terrain. Why should we arbitrarily narrow the parameters of Lucretius' engagement with Ennian philosophy, when Lucretius himself refuses to do so? On the other hand, one often finds discussion of Lucretius' Ennian poetic form or Ennian style.[12] But these discussions regularly speak in imprecise generalizations that often invoke "archaism" without adducing any sort of focused criteria upon which Lucretius' style can justly be considered Ennian. To the extent that any sort of argument is ever made on this front, it goes like this: Lucretius and Ennius both exhibit "archaism," and, by virtue of such archaism, Lucretius is an Ennian poet. The conceptualization of Lucretius' Ennian style is excessively narrow, then, paradoxically because it is discussed in quite general terms that do not permit of any more focused analysis. No wonder that no such focused analysis exists for the reader interested in understanding how, or according to what criteria, Lucretius should be taken as writing in an Ennian style.

Lucretius' Ennian Style

To be fair, the reason that the *status opinionis* has focused so closely on Lucretius' Ennian form is that his form *is* unmistakably Ennian throughout much of the *DRN*; but we are still in serious need of nuance when we make such claims. Such nuance can be found in detail in Appendix 2, which contains my raw data and my interpretations of it, but for now I want to highlight what I consider the five unambiguous markers of Ennian style in Lucretius (Table 1). Such an identification, combined with a consideration of distribution in the *DRN*, will allow me to make better account of the effect of Ennian stylistics in Lucretius. I want to stress upfront also that our sense of Lucretius' Ennian style will never be able to

---

12. Many important studies of Lucretian style have been written, all offering their own unique perspective on his peculiarities: Holtze 1868; Munro 1886: 2.8–20; Sellar 1889: 384–407; Cartault 1898; Bailey 1947: 72–171; Boyancé 1963: 288–315 (with further bibliography at 343–346); Leonard and Smith 1965: 129–186; Maguinness 1965; Kenney 1971: 14–29; and Kenney 2007. See more in Appendices 2–5 at the back of this book and Taylor (forthcoming).

be reduced finally to quantification and data-sets alone, even as these certainly advance our understanding.

Now on a first impression, several (perhaps all) of the items in Table 1 might look like elements that are typical of pre-Lucretian poetry *in general* rather than necessarily of Ennius in particular. One might be justified in asking whether our sense of what counts as an Ennianism is inflated by the disproportionate representation of Ennius in the citations that populate our body of fragments of Republican epic poetry. Another way to frame this issue would be to ask when are Ennianisms, as I define them in Table 1, Ennianisms, and when are they just archaisms. This book remains alive to these issues , especially in Appendix 2, and it takes seriously the need to exhibit how these five markers of Ennian style represent a set of fine discriminations *within* the overall category of archaic-looking patterns.

Table 1 Markers of Ennian Style in Lucretius

1. The alliteration of the same word-initial sound at least three times in the same line or sense unit
2. The use of the genitive ending in *-ai*
3. Hexameter lines that end in one word of just one syllable
4. Hexameter lines that end in one word of five syllables
5. The elision of word-final *-s* in order to make position metrically (sigmatic ecthlipsis)

One general observation at the outset helps to establish the especially Ennian association of these phenomena: the frequency of all five of these markers follows a similar trajectory over the course of Republican Latin, reaching a high point in the poetry of Ennius, only gradually to decrease in use until Lucretius' *DRN*, where all five of these markers peak again, sometimes at an even higher frequency than they had occurred in Ennius, and almost always at a significantly higher frequency than in any earlier poet except Ennius. In post-Lucretian Latin these markers either disappear entirely or decrease in frequency to such an extent that their appearance often serves as a sort of reflexive annotation of an author's allusion to Ennius.

THE INTERESTED READER will find a more thorough and technical discussion of these five markers of Ennian style in Appendix 2, which is supplemented by raw data in Appendices 3–5.

In terms of unpacking what might be meant when one speaks of Lucretius' style as Ennian, I want to note first of all that none of these five Ennianisms appear with any sort of consistency or regularity in all parts of the *DRN*. Instead, Lucretius' formal Ennianisms tend to conglomerate at points, then to disappear for long stretches, only later to reappear in concentration again. In other words, Lucretius can be shown to combine these five effects with one another in clusters at specific points in his poem, even as it can be shown that long stretches of the *DRN* do not contain a single Ennian effect. I have provided a map of all the Ennianisms in Lucretius in Appendix 5, where I have broken the poem down by Bailey paragraphs to show the location of such clusters. I have also identified what I call "anti-clusters," or paragraphs in which the frequency of Ennianisms is significantly lower than in the rest of the poem.[13] On the basis of these data, the first three books of the *DRN* are much more "Ennian" than the last three books. Moreover, one-third of the paragraphs in Bailey's edition have clusters or anti-clusters of Ennianisms, and so deviate significantly from the average frequency of Ennianisms in the poem as a whole. Ten Bailey paragraphs contain no Ennianisms at all, while the longest continuous stretch of the poem without an Ennianism is 36 lines (5.1343–1380).

Cumulatively, these data prove that while Lucretius' style was definitely and markedly "Ennian" (i.e., characterized by poetic effects, morphology, and metrical phenomena either invented by or closely associated with Ennius' *Annales*), Lucretius deploys these Ennianisms not uniformly, but strategically, clustering them at various points in his poem, and, just as importantly, omitting them entirely at other points. We must, therefore, recognize that Lucretius' Ennian style, which has received so much surface attention in the scholarly literature, is not an inert phenomenon, but a versatile component of his overall poetics. This book takes this aspect of Lucretian poetics seriously. It is thus the first study to make suggestions as to why Lucretius makes the choices he makes with regard to his adoption of an Ennian stylistic register.

My collection of this data affords many opportunities for evaluating the *DRN* in a new light, the most tantalizing, if also the most precarious, of which is the possibility of using Ennian clusters in the *DRN* to look for imitation of Ennius in places where we cannot otherwise identify securely an allusion to the fragments that remain of the *Annales*. In order to account fully for this possibility, consider the opening of *DRN* 3 (1–8), where Lucretius combines allusion to Ennius with clustering of Ennian stylistic features (Key: <u>alliteration</u>; **monosyllabic line-endings**):

> *e <u>t</u>enebris <u>t</u>antis <u>t</u>am clarum extollere lumen*
> *qui primus potuisti inlustrans commoda vitae,*

---

13. I define a "cluster" as a passage containing 50% more Ennianisms per ten lines than the average throughout the poem and an "anti-cluster" as one containing less than half of the average frequency of Ennianisms per ten lines throughout the poem.

te sequor, o Graiae gentis decus inque tuis **nunc**
ficta pedum pono pressis vestigia signis,
non ita certandi cupidus quam propter amorem
quod te imitari aveo; quid enim contendat hirundo
cycnis, aut quidnam tremulis facere artubus haedi
consimile in cursu possint et fortis equi **vis?**[14]

You who first were able to lift such a bright light
out of such great darkness, illuminating the joys of life,
I follow you, O glory of the Greek race, and now
in your prints, pressed firmly, I place my own fashioned footprints
not so much desiring to vie with you as on account of love,
because I long to imitate you; for how could a swallow rival
swans, or what could kids on trembling limbs accomplish
in a race to compare with the strong force of a horse?

In these eight lines Lucretius includes a cluster of six Ennianisms (alliteration: 3.1, 3.4, 3.5, 3.6; monosyllabic line-endings: 3.3, 3.8). This frequency (.75 per line) is almost three times higher than the rest of the poem (.26 per line). Not surprisingly, these lines also feature two clear verbal allusions to Ennius' *Annales* that are generally regarded as such in the scholarly literature (*pedum pono pressis=premitur pede pes, Ann.* 584 Sk, and *tremulis . . . artubus=Ann.* 34 Sk).[15] Other examples like this abound (e.g. *DRN* 8.830–869, with allusion to *Ann.* 309 Sk; 4.615–632, with allusion to *Ann.* 417 Sk; and 4.1007–1014, with allusion to *Ann.* 2 Sk and *Ann.* 428 Sk). These passages all contain clusters of Ennianisms as well as identifiable and generally accepted allusions to the extant fragments of the *Annales*.

I should stress that I am not going to be making any arguments about Lucretius' reception of Ennius that are based only on clusters of Ennianisms in the *DRN* unless these clusters also appropriate Ennian language that appears in the very few extant fragments of the *Annales*. As a thought experiment, though, I do want to highlight the potential for recognizing heretofore unattested allusions to the *Annales* fragments that may have slipped under the radar, but which present themselves when we recognize Lucretius' practice of clustering Ennianisms in certain passages. Consider, for example, the following lines from Lucretius' description of atomic motion at the beginning of Book 2 of the *DRN* (2.142–146):

---

14. Throughout this book I use Deufert's new Teubner edition of Lucretius' text, and any disagreements with his text are duly noted with my own justifications. All translations are my own.

15. See, e.g., Bailey 1947 ad loc. Merrill 1918: 256 also includes *equi vis=equos vi, Ann.* 465 Sk.

nunc quae mobilitas sit reddita materiai
corporibus, paucis licet hinc cognoscere, Memmi.
primum aurora novo cum spargit lumine terras
et variae volucres nemora avia pervolitantes
*aera **per tenerum** liquidis loca vocibus opplent . . .*

Now, what speed of movement has been given to the bodies of matter,
Memmius, you may understand in a few words from this example:
When first dawn sprinkles the lands with its first light,
And the diverse birds flying through the pathless groves
***Through the soft air** fill these places with their clear voices . . .*

This passage comes from a section of the *DRN* that displays a heightened frequency of Ennianisms.[16] Outside of such a cluster, the collocation *per tenerum* might not strike the reader as especially Ennian, but in the context of this Ennian cluster, where Lucretius is writing in his most Ennian vein, one can read this Lucretian collocation as an allusion to *Ann.* 18 Sk (*transnavit cita **per teneras** caliginis auras*). This collocation may seem unremarkable on the surface, but these are the only two instances of *per* and *tener, -a, -um* in pre-Vergilian Latin, and, after Lucretius we only have two more examples (*Aen.* 9.699 and Apul. *Met.* 5.13.8–9).[17] It is relevant also that in both Lucretius and Ennius, this collocation involves a description of something flying through the air: Venus (probably) in Ennius, birds (definitely) in Lucretius.

I have purposely chosen this example because I consider it to be liminal—as such, I assume that many readers might not be prepared to accept that there is here, in fact, an allusion to Ennius. But this is precisely the point I am trying to make, namely that the phenomenon of Ennian clusters in Lucretius draws our focus to Ennian language that might escape our notice, were we not alerted to the fact that Lucretius wants us to read a passage with Ennius in mind. While my analysis in what follows will never depend on such speculation, this possibility remains open. In this context, one could appeal to the unbounded application of Kristevan intertextuality, and say that the collocation *per tenerum* is just one element in a "mosaic of quotations" of Ennius' *Annales* that reflects the complete

16. The lines that initiate Lucretius' discussion of atomic motion (2.80–166) contain roughly .44 Ennianisms per line, or almost 60% more Ennianisms per line than the baseline frequency of .26 Ennianisms per line that Lucretius uses in the rest of his poem.

17. Cf. *teneras . . . per herbas*, Lucr. 1.260 and Ov. *Met.* 15.14 and *teneros . . . per artus*, Val. Flac. 6.670.

absorption of the earlier text into the fabric of Lucretius' poem.[18] There is power
in this approach, especially because I do think (and I will argue in this book)
that Lucretius goes to great lengths in the *DRN* to subsume and destroy Ennius'
Annales as he represents it. I myself embrace the idea of "allusion," and I do so
with Stephen Hinds' adumbration of the valences of this term specifically in
mind, so I am not usually going to approach Lucretius' appropriation of Ennius'
Annales in a Kristevan way.[19] In any case, I want to emphasize the fact that many
Lucretian passages marked in this way—showcasing significant Ennian clusters
with no clearly identifiable allusions—recall Ennius in general, or an Ennian
theme, rather than any specific passage on every occasion.

The inverse, or passages marked by their *absence* of Ennianisms ("anti-
clusters"), may also reveal interesting aspects of Lucretius' reception of the
Annales, and may even suggest that Lucretius writes in such a way that might
discourage the reader from thinking about Ennius, although Ennius will always
be an absent presence in this situation, available for the reader "under erasure," as
Heidegger and Derrida have it. While almost all such anti-clusters do not appear
to contain allusions to the *Annales*, we do have a few counter-examples. Most glar-
ingly, we find this situation in the Anthropology at the end of *DRN* 5, the section
of Lucretius' poem whose style is marked proportionally with the least amount
of Ennianisms, yet the one that is filled with the highest frequency of identifiable
allusions to Ennian language in the *Annales*. I discuss this phenomenon in much
more detail in chapter 3, but I can say here generally that in this passage of the
DRN, Lucretius would appear to be trying to differentiate himself from Ennius
with respect to both content *and* form; this section may even function as a way
of underlining the differences between himself and Ennius. Lucretius provides
his own Epicurean account of human history in the Anthropology; as such, this
passage represents the closest Lucretius ever comes to writing on the same subject
as Ennius himself wrote in the *Annales*. That he does so in a consistently and
decidedly (by Lucretian standards) un-Ennian style is striking, indeed. In fact,
it suggests that Lucretius wants to indicate how historical epic *should* be written,
and that it should be written in a way that is very different from the way Lucretius
implies Ennius wrote it in the *Annales*. In any case, the Anthropology clearly rep-
resents the exception that proves the rule regarding anti-clusters of Ennianisms
in the *DRN*. Taken this way, Lucretius' anti-clusters may provide a powerful

---

18. See Kristeva 1969 (quote on 85).

19. Hinds 1998: 17–51, esp. 21–25 and 47–51. See more in the next section.

demonstration of the broader anti-Ennianism that characterizes the reception of the *Annales* in the *DRN*.[20]

A Note on Methodology and Fundamentalism

I have already described the reception of the *Annales* in Lucretius as "allusion." Throughout my argument, I choose this word purposefully, and I do so specifically with Stephen Hinds' discussion of the term in mind.[21] In adopting this theoretical premise, I assume with the intertextualists that the ultimate intention of the author (in this case, Lucretius) is unknowable and not part of the text I am analyzing (the *De Rerum Natura*). I will regularly emphasize, along with the intertextualists, that the *Annales* is not simply a text that inserts itself in the *DRN*, but rather that it is a text that is created by the *DRN* itself. This book, then, is fundamentally about Lucretius' *Annales*, and I want to emphasize upfront that I assume not only that Ennius' *Annales* is as unrecoverable as recent work on Ennius has shown, but that, even if an entire edition of Ennius' *Annales* were discovered tomorrow, such a hypothetical *Annales* would "always already" be a reflection of Lucretius' *Annales* anyway.[22]

On the other hand, I will describe the process of appropriation in this book as a fairly straightforward one, in which the (implied) reader is meant to recognize the presence of Ennius' *Annales* in Lucretius' text; I usually offer one specific avenue of interpretation when confronted by the *Annales'* presence. My argument will thus de-emphasize the complex process of allusion, which involves, as Hinds argues, "indirection as much as direction, concealment as much as revelation;"[23] this does not mean, however, that I deny that allusion is a complex process. In adopting such an approach, I am also insisting on more discipline in adducing literary influences. In order to argue convincingly

---

20. Other examples of allusions to the *Annales* embedded in anti-clusters of Ennianisms in the *DRN*: Lucr. 1.688=*Ann.* 193 Sk; Lucr. 1.882=*Ann.* 79 Sk; Lucr. 1.1064=*Ann.* 48 Sk; Lucr. 4.820=*Ann.* 3 Sk; Lucr. 5.235=*Ann.* 6 Sk; Lucr. 5.1098=*Ann.* 298 Sk; Lucr. 6.144=*Ann.* 434 Sk; Lucr. 6.155=*Ann.* 451 Sk; Lucr. 6.508=*Ann.* 391 Sk; Lucr. 6.708=*Ann.* 167 Sk; Lucr. 6.728=*Ann.* 376 Sk; Lucr. 6.1197=*Ann.* 265 Sk; Lucr. 6.1228=*Ann.* 48 Sk.

21. Hinds 1998: 17–51, esp. 21–25 and 47–51; cf. Farrell 2005. The debate between advocates of intertextuality and those of allusion or reference appears now to have cooled. For helpful points of triangulation, see Thomas 1982; Zetzel 1983; and Thomas 1986 (for "reference"); Pasquali 1942; Conte 1986; Farrell 1991: ch. 1; Hinds 1998: esp. 17–51 (on "allusion"); Conte 1986; D. Fowler 1997; Edmonds 2001 (on "intertextuality").

22. See especially Martindale 1993.

23. See the criticisms of intertextuality in Hinds 1998: 49–50. On Lucretian intertextuality, see Fowler 2000b and Morrison 2020.

that reception is taking place, I assume that one must show that verbal parallels are combined with thematic elements or motifs, and that one can interpret this combination. "Allusion" understood in the way I have advocated can more efficiently address these criteria for reception than "intertextuality" can. When appropriate, in what follows I will associate the evidence I adduce with these criteria for reception.

Chapter Overview

Ennius has traditionally been regarded as the largest influence on Latin poetry until the time of Lucretius and the Neoterics, but in chapter 1 I argue that Lucretius' choice of Ennius as a model was more novel than most traditional accounts maintain. In order to appreciate more clearly the literary terrain into which Lucretius was entering, I analyze the remains of Republican epic before Lucretius, but without the benefit of the Lucretian hindsight that most such accounts assume. This approach proves especially important, since it is precisely because of Lucretius and his overt and insistent Ennianizing poetics that many scholars have suggested that Ennian aesthetic principles dominated Latin poetry, until being rejected by Catullus and the other New Poets. But a survey of the fragments of Republican epic between Ennius and Lucretius only rarely turns up evidence of an overtly Ennianizing poetics; where Ennianisms can be found, so too can be found much more nuanced literary strategies at play than traditional accounts of this material maintain. In fact, the evidence of allusive play, both in terms of style and content, in the extant fragments of Republican epic permits of a sophisticated, at times eristic, tradition of Ennius-reception in the period between the *Annales* and Lucretius.

Having established that Lucretius' wholesale appropriation of the *Annales* was unprecedented at the time he was writing the *DRN*, I turn in chapter 2 to an analysis of this appropriation. One might not think of Ennius' poem as primarily a work of natural philosophy, yet that is precisely how Lucretius represents the *Annales* in the proem to the *De Rerum Natura*. Chapter 2 approaches Lucretius' engagement with Ennius on Lucretius' own terms and explores how the *Annales* serves Lucretius as a model (or a foil, rather) for poetry about the universe. Lucretius makes clear his identification of Ennius and Ennius' Homer as poets who also write on "the nature of things" when he singles them out by name in the proem to the *DRN* (1.117–126). Obviously, the whole tradition of interpreting epic poetry from Homer onward as allegorical philosophy is behind these lines. Throughout the *DRN*, Lucretius recurrently figures his universe as a direct response to the Ennian cosmos in a procedure that involves philosophical polemics as much as poetic polemics. In so doing, Lucretius articulates a universe whose philosophical dynamics are anti-Ennian, precisely because they are emphatically Epicurean.

Whereas the preceding chapter met Ennius on Lucretius' terms, chapter 3 meets the *Annales* on its own narrative terms, arguing that Lucretius responds to the *Annales*' conceptualization of history and time in a comprehensively revisionist way. Lucretius alludes repeatedly to historical episodes and personalities from Ennius' *Annales* that would appear to valorize Roman hegemony and exemplarity, only to strip them of whatever value they may have had in their Ennian context. This procedure is, of course, tendentious because Lucretius both suggests what value these elements had in the *Annales* and then strips them of it. Lucretius implies that the *Annales* presents universal history as diachronic and teleological, and that individual historical episodes like the wars with Pyrrhus of Epirus and the Carthaginians all build cumulatively to Rome's *imperium sine fine* over the cosmos itself. The Epicurean explanations of natural history in the *DRN* regularly reject this implied Ennian perspective.

In chapter 4, I build on these conclusions to show that Lucretius' rejection of Ennian historiography extends into a rejection of Ennian poetology. I argue that, for Lucretius, the primary example of Ennius' misguided notions of the past is the narrative of the Punic Wars in the *Annales*. Lucretius alludes extensively to Ennius' version of these events, but only in the context of rejecting the possibility of metempsychosis. Here I adduce Ennius' own metaphors for literary tradition and affiliation, specifically metempsychosis and the heart, in order to suggest that one of Lucretius' central aims in the *DRN* is to undermine Ennius' literary-historical claims by appropriating and destroying the psychological metaphor that Ennius insisted upon. Lucretius complicates this metaphor while making constant reference to Epicurean physics, thereby literalizing Ennius' metaphors to show that they are incompatible with the nature of things. As a consequence of investigating how Lucretius goes about correcting Ennius, I argue that Lucretius rejects conventional ideas of literary affiliation and poetology and that he articulates this rejection in terms of the physical first principles of Epicureanism. For example, a standard reading of Lucretius' lines on Ennius at *DRN* 1.112–135 is that, unlike Ennius, who flaunted his connection with Homer, even claiming to be *Homerus redivivus*, Lucretius insists that such a claim violates the laws of nature, insofar as souls cannot be reborn. Lucretius argues that even if souls could be reborn, such a reconstituted soul would have no memory of its previous existence, showing that Ennius' claim, even when taken on its own terms, is impossible and should be rejected. Lucretius is rejecting, I argue, not only Ennian/Pythagorean psychology, but also the literary-historical claims involved with Ennian psychology. This rejection of the literary implications of Ennius' Dream, which itself imitates Callimachus' Hesiodic Dream in the *Aitia*, stands in direct opposition to the fetishization of literary affiliation that we find in so many poets, from Callimachus' acknowledgement of Aratus' Hesiodic credentials to Horace's genealogy of satire and well beyond. In short, Lucretius uses Ennius against himself in order to assert the insignificance—and, if we extend Lucretius' arguments to their logical conclusions, the unreality—of any conventional notion of literary tradition.

In the Conclusion, I offer an overview of what we might imagine the *Annales* looked like according primarily to Lucretius' reconstruction of Ennius' *magnum opus*. Here I suggest that it is very possible that the elements that characterize Lucretius' version of Ennius' poem were also interrelated in the *Annales* itself, to an extent beyond which we can now determine in the fragments. I do not insist on this suggestion, however.

After all, this is not a book about Ennius' *Annales*.

I

Ennius and the Tradition
of Republican Epic

Ennius in Literary History

I HAVE BEFORE me the very difficult task of rewriting received wisdom. In doing so, I will be swimming against the tide of what everyone thinks they know about Republican epic poetry, and against what everyone before us, for the past century, assumed about Latin epic of this period.[1] But such a project is necessary if we are to approach the topic of Ennius in Lucretius' *De Rerum Natura* (*DRN*), for, as I will soon show, our understanding of Ennius, of Lucretius, and of the form and content of Latin Republican epic and hexametric poetry has all been tainted by uncorroborated conjecture that has snowballed into sweeping generalizations. And so, naturally, before I begin my study of Lucretius' reception of Ennius, I must first reconstruct what the reception of Ennius likely would have suggested to readers at the time Lucretius was writing the *De Rerum Natura*.

The traditional view of Ennius' accomplishment in the *Annales* and its effect on subsequent poetry maintains that Ennius revolutionized the nascent tradition of Latin epic by writing a comprehensive narrative of Roman history titled *Annales*, and by means of the various idiosyncratic poetic effects he employed in his originary use of the dactylic hexameter. The effect of Ennian form and content was so great that virtually all poets after him copied his style and subject matter, and many even copied his title. A few basic facts about our primary evidence

---

1. The material contained in the first five sections of this chapter was originally accepted for publication in the volume *Ennius' "Annals": Poetry and History*, published by Cambridge University Press and appears there as Nethercut 2020a. The copyright in the material on these pages is owned by or licensed to Cambridge University Press, or reproduced with permission from other third-party copyright owners. It is reprinted with permission in the current chapter, having also been altered at various points.

Ennius Noster: Lucretius and the Annales. Jason S. Nethercut, Oxford University Press (2021). © Oxford University Press.
DOI: 10.1093/oso/9780197517697.001.0001.

from this period have encouraged this inference about the influence of Ennius' *Annales*. First, we have the entirety of Lucretius' *De Rerum Natura*, which, on its own, would appear to provide evidence of an insistently Ennian style in post-Ennian hexameter poetry. Second, we can tell that Lucretius writes in an Ennian idiom because we do possess a number of fragments from the *Annales* that corroborate this perspective. Third, we have only a few fragments of Latin hexameter poetry between the *Annales* and Lucretius, yet despite this dearth we know of a few epic poems with the title *Annales*. The traditional view, as I have been calling it, bases its inference of the widespread, reflexive influence of Ennius on subsequent Latin epic on the combination of Lucretius' insistent Ennian idiom and the existence of these post-Ennian *Annales* epics.

Yet in drawing this inference they overstate the case for a number of reasons. Not only are there problems with the titles of the lost epics from the period between the *Annales* and Lucretius, but also the fragments we do have from that period do not actually exhibit a consistently Ennian style. One can easily recognize how this narrative took hold, because we are naturally drawn to periodization and linear developments; one of my aims in this chapter is to suggest precisely where this traditional view first took form.

In any case, this chapter is primarily meant to clear the deck, as it were, so that we can appreciate more clearly the literary terrain into which Lucretius was entering when he wrote the *DRN* in an emphatically Ennian idiom. To do this, I need to investigate the remains of Republican epic without the benefit of Lucretian hindsight. As already suggested, it is this very hindsight that runs the risk of creating a dangerous feedback loop of analysis; in fact, it is precisely because of Lucretius and what has been perceived as his overt and insistent Ennianizing poetics that many scholars have suggested that after Ennius, Latin poetry, and especially epic poetry, was dominated by Ennian aesthetic principles until these were finally rejected by Catullus and the other New Poets writing around the time of Lucretius. Lucretius thus serves as a contemporary foil for these so-called Neoterics. These New Poets appear to have deviated purposefully from what is taken to be Ennius' style, on the one hand, by adopting a different linguistic texture characterized by "refinement," and they opposed Ennian content, on the other, by prizing different thematic subjects written in non-epic genres. Additionally, it seems that they conflated the principle of continuous epic narrative with the Callimachean concept of *hen aesima dienekes* or *carmen perpetuum*. And so, in order to correct this circular view, one must work to rebuild an image of pre-Lucretian Republican epic that does not depend on Lucretius' view of this period.

I am not the first to be suspicious of this circular argumentation, however. Jackie Elliott has recently sounded the alarm against assuming that Ennius'

Annales was structured as a continuous and complete narrative of Roman history; although she does not prove that it was *not* structured this way, her opening of this question has implications that extend beyond Ennius to later Republican epic.[2] It is fair to say that Elliott has made it difficult, and perhaps impossible, to infer that these epics all offered continuous narratives like that of the *Annales*, because we can no longer be as sure as we thought we could about the *Annales* itself. To put it another way, we really should not be inferring *any* larger narrative structures for Republican epic, given its extremely fragmentary condition, and we especially should not import onto Republican epic our false assumptions about Ennian narrative features.

Rather, if we look at the style and content of the fragments of Republican epic, and focus especially on the role of allusive poetics in what we find, a different picture emerges. This is not to say that the assumptions that have usually been made about this poetry are impossible, but more to show that any arguments that have actually been made in their favor, such as they are, are very far from conclusive. The evidence, on this view, permits of other inferences—inferences that are more plausible than the traditional narrative. This new picture that emerges suggests two reasons why we ought to reject the notion that subsequent Latin epicists reflexively imitated Ennius. In the first place, many of the extant fragments of these poets show no apparent evidence of Ennian influence or imitation; and, secondly, in the places where we *can* detect engagement with Ennius, we find not inert imitations, but rather the kind of sophisticated, self-conscious allusive gestures that characterize much of Hellenistic and Latin poetry.

Received Wisdom Regarding Post-Ennian Republican Epic

Beginning with Friedrich Leo's *Geschichte der römischen Literatur*, Ennius' *Annales* has been assumed to have been so influential that all subsequent Roman epics before the Neoteric revolution took the *Annales* as a model in terms of both style and content. Regarding the form that Ennius introduced to the Latin hexameter, Leo claims that "the foundations established by Ennius remained intact. This applies to his verse as it does broadly to his entire epic art."[3] Later, in the same

---

2. Elliott 2013: esp. 18–74.

3. Leo 1913: 187: "Die ennianische Form des Hexameters blieb länger als Jahrhundert nach seinem Tode in voller Geltung; für die Satire hat Horaz sie von neuem festgelegt. Alle Reformen nach der modernen Technik und nach den Einsichten von Künstlern wie Vergil und Ovid verhielten sich doch zum ennianischen Hexameter wie die spätere griechische Technik zur

work, he even says that "Ennius...must have had his Homeridae."[4] Half a century later, Brooks Otis echoes Leo's position, writing in *Virgil: A Study in Civilized Poetry* that "Ennius had many followers. We probably lack even the names of most of them but we have enough to show the trend."[5] Note that Otis, in an especially bold claim, generalizes in such a way as to include poems that may never even have existed. Conte, in his history of Latin literature, similarly says that epic in this period was "completely dominated by the example of Ennius," and that the New Poets regarded this genre as a "static survival, dusty and empty."[6] Even more recently, Adrian Hollis refers to post-Ennian epic as a "very traditional category," and concludes apropos of Furius Bibaculus' fragments that "the style is what we might expect, showing strong influence from Homer and Ennius. By this time the old epic tradition had fallen into some disrepute; everyone knows what Catullus (poem 36) said about the 'Annales Volusi' (of which not a word survives!)."[7] Lastly, and perhaps in its most extreme formulation, Suerbaum writes in the first volume of Herzog-Schmidt that "[t]he variety (and in part the nature) of the citations indicates that the *Annales* was the representative epic (*das repräsentative Epos*) in Rome during the Republican period."[8] Suerbaum applies no stipulations to this claim, so we must infer that he has in mind both the *Annales'* style and its content when he calls the work "the representative epic of the Republic." In so doing, Suerbaum would appear to be reworking and expanding what appears in the original *Geschichte der römischen Literatur* by Schanz, who, in a discussion of Ennius' influence on Roman poetry, writes, "(Ennius') poem remained the main

---

homerischen; **die von Ennius gezogenen Grundlinien sind bestehen geblieben. Dies gilt für seinem Vers wie in weitem Masse für seine ganze epische Kunst.**"

4. Ibid. 407: "Von den vielen Poeten, die in einer so stark literarisch vordringenden Zeit für ihren Tag etwas gegolten haben, kennen wir nur weinge Namen. Man fragt natürlich nach dem Epos. **Denn Ennius, obgleich und grade weil er so entschieden das Feld behauptet, muss doch seine Homeriden gehabt haben**; und die römischen Feldherren müssen sich auch nach Fulvius um Sänger ihrer Taten bemüht haben. Von einem Epiker Hostius hören wir aus Vergilkomentaren und durch ein paar gelehrte Zitate gerade genug, um die typische Figur zu erkennen. Er hat den istrischen Krieg besungen, das heisst den Feldzug des Tuditanus vom Jahre 129. Das war ohne Zweifel eine dem Konsular und Gönner direkt erwiesene poetische Gunst, ein rechtes Feldzugepos von hellenistischer Art, aber römisch nach dem Muster des Ennius."

5. Otis 1964: 24.

6. Conte 1994b: 110.

7. Hollis 2007: 128–129.

8. Herzog-Schmidt 2002: 140: "Die Vielzahl (und teils die Art) der Zitate zeigt, dass die *Annales* **das repräsentative Epos Roms** in der republikanischen Zeit waren."

epic (*Hauptepos*) of the Republic."[9] Schanz does not nuance this claim, so there is no way to know if he meant, for example, "the main *stylistic* model for Republican epic" or "the Roman national epic, until the *Aeneid* appeared." Given, however, that Schanz explicitly juxtaposes the fortune of the *Annales* in eclipsing Naevius' epic, we may infer that Schanz's term *Hauptepos* is used in an expansive way that includes both style and content.

Scholarly discussions of the individual Republican epicists include similarly sweeping conclusions. Of Accius' *Annales*, Otis writes that they "were certainly historical epic in the Ennian vein," on the grounds merely that both works have the same title.[10] On similar grounds, Conte asserts that Accius' title provides "a clear programmatic link to Ennius."[11] In an even more breathtaking claim, Stärk in Herzog-Schmidt writes that Accius' work "derives its title, its architecture and the style of its verses" from Ennius and the genre of historical epic.[12] These are the starkest examples of such tenuous connections, but that is not to say that we do not find more nuanced articulations of essentially the same idea. Sander Goldberg offers the most balanced perspective that I have found, when he states that while "the aims and expectations of this motley group [i.e., Republican epic poets after Ennius] must remain unclear, their fragments nevertheless preserve sure signs of the continuing tradition within which they worked. The subject, vocabulary, and very sound of a line like Hostius' 'percutit atque hastam pilans prae pondere frangit' . . . produce a distinctly Ennian ring . . . It is hard to read Accius' line, 'fraxinus fixa ferox infensa infinditur ossis'. . . without recalling the trees of Ennius' funeral pyre (177, cf. 620) . . . Epic diction had clearly achieved a stability that gives these scattered remains an air of consistency, if not cliché, and the limited range of their effects may also in part explain their failure to maintain a readership. Certainly none of these poets came close to rivaling Ennius' achievement."[13]

Students of Latin poetry, it is fair to say, have tended to see post-Ennian Republican epic as thoroughly Ennian. What is more, with the exception of Goldberg, most proponents of this perspective have presented superficial and unsystematic appraisals of the fragments, given that most of their statements are

---

9. Schanz 1890: 57.

10. Otis 1964: 24.

11. Conte 1994b: 110.

12. Herzog-Schmidt 2002: 164: "Auf Ennius und das hist. Epos führen der Titel, der Bau und der Stil der Verse, ihr Inhalt jedoch nur zum Teil."

13. Goldberg 1995: 135–136.

sweeping generalizations based on very little evidence.[14] In fact, I have come to
suspect that each of these sweeping generalizations all derive from Leo's original
Homeridae claim. This is the most likely reason why so many of the scholars I have
quoted here cite Leo specifically, but no earlier authority. If this is true, then the
entire scholarly conceit about Ennius' influence on subsequent Republican epic
derives from Leo; and although Leo was undoubtedly a very great scholar whose
opinion has to carry weight, because some of his key points are merely supposi-
tions, and because he does not support his claims with rigorous analysis of the few
fragments that we actually have, we would do better to start from scratch.

As if this damning scholarly stemma were not enough to cast doubt on the tra-
ditional Ennianizing narrative for Republican epic, most of the statements above
also display a number of argumentative fallacies. First, their authors assume that
the second and first centuries BCE witnessed the production of many historical
epics in Latin, even though we have evidence for a scant few. Second, these schol-
ars seem to imagine that Ennius' influence was so pervasive that it dominated not
only the many unattested historical epics that have been supposed into "indubi-
table" existence, but it also extended into other genres and subgenres. To take the
example of Accius' *Annales*, Conte does not place this poem in the epic genre,
but he does insist that it was thoroughly Ennian. Third, scholars assert that this
putative Ennian tradition operated on a pretty low stylistic level, and, beyond
this, that the poems as a whole were repetitive and monotonous. But, to use the
example of Accius again, such an assessment does not agree with what we know
of his work as a whole, and he is the only author concerned whose work survives
beyond a handful of fragments. Finally, these scholars assume that the degree of
Ennian engagement to be found in the very few lines we have from the very small
number of poems titled *Annales* is typical rather than unusual. That is to say, they
take these lines to support the idea that these poems were repetitive and unimagi-
native Ennian imitations. But these last two assumptions are not convincing if we
consider these fragments carefully and without prejudice.

It is important at this point to emphasize that the continued acquiescence to
the assumptions of Friedrich Leo about Republican epic replication of Ennian
form and content represents a striking critical anachronism. It should be push-
ing at an open door for a modern Latinist to argue that when a later poet imi-
tates Ennius, the objective is active engagement rather than inert replication.
I assume most modern Latinists would accept the idea that poetic imitation is

---

14. See now Goldberg 2020 for further nuance: he shows that Ennius' *Annales* was not espe-
cially well represented in later Republican citations of earlier poetry and awareness of the epic
was confined to only a small number of its books. More generally, see Goldschmidt 2013: ch.1,
esp. 18–28.

always active with regard to any Latin poet's imitation of any other literary predecessor. Yet, as I have shown in this section, there remains resistance to this idea in the scholarly literature on post-Ennian Republican epic. For now, I want to leave this observation here, and I will return to it again at various points in what follows.

Varieties of Epic Poetry in Rome, c. 250–c. 50 BCE

Upon closer examination, and scrubbed of the tenuous conclusions of the traditional accounts given in the previous section, the remains of epic poetry written in the third, second, and first centuries BCE do not, in fact, present as predominantly Ennian, either in terms of style or content. We have substantial evidence for a number of epics, written in both Greek and Latin, between the time of Ennius and that of Lucretius, though their remains are woefully fragmentary. Nevertheless, this evidence (compiled in Appendix 1), undermines the traditional view of post-Ennian epic.

In the first place—and this may seem too obvious a point to make, but I say it for the sake of destabilizing the sweeping generalizations of traditional accounts of epic written in this period—there was a large amount of Republican epic, and most of it was written in Greek, which naturally would necessarily mean that it would not reflect Ennian influence in any fundamental way. Of course, it is difficult to say anything entirely definitive about such fragmentary material as what remains of Greek epic between Ennius and Lucretius. Just as a thought experiment, and to test the strength of my assertion, one could imagine that a Greek epic about a recent Roman war—for example, the lost epics that Archias wrote on the wars between the Cimbri and Mithradates—could have been written in an "Ennian" style, particularly if such an epic were offered in praise of the Romans. But it is not clear that we know enough about Ennius to say what features of his style were sufficiently distinctive—and not themselves derived from earlier Greek epic (Homer or otherwise)—that we could prove that a post-Ennian Greek poet was channeling Ennius. Potential "Ennian" features such as compound adjectives or pentasyllabic line-endings could easily derive from Homer, for example, without Ennian mediation. It is hard to imagine how a writer of Greek epic would attempt to imitate Ennius, and even more difficult to imagine that many of them would have wanted to do so.

To continue this thought experiment, however, and consider content rather than form, one could certainly imagine that one of these Greek epics might have covered a typical "Ennian" subject, although, again, one cannot say that Ennius was the inventor of this type of epic, not even in Latin, since Naevius wrote the *Bellum Poenicum* before Ennius. Choerilus of Samos, for example, wrote an epic on the Persian wars long before the *Annales* were written, while the *Iliad* presents itself as a model for an epic of the sort I am imagining. Thought experiment aside, what we *do* have evidence for is not monographic treatments of individual wars (i.e., what people assume Ennius' followers wrote); rather, most of the Greek epics we know about from this period are of the *ktisis* (foundation) sort, so there are many reasons to suppose that Ennius was not influential on subsequent Greek epic, either in content or in style.[15]

So much for Greek epic, but what about Latin? Where the content of most epic written in Greek focused on the *ktisis*-type, on the Latin side there was, by contrast, a good deal of variation in the kinds of epic that poets wrote. In addition to the definitive evidence for historical epic after Ennius, we also know of mythological epics, including at least one (the *Carmen Priami*) that was written in Saturnians. In hexameters, we know of a reworking of Livius Andronicus' *Odusia*; new translations of Homer by Mattius, Ninnius Crassus, and the later Naevius; and what appear to be hexameter experiments by Cicero and Julius Caesar. All of this is to say that mythological epic and other forms of hexameter continued—and one might even more accurately say, began— to be written after Ennius. This is a point that may seem obvious, but it does need to be made. One cannot make sweeping claims about Republican epic without taking into account the vast amounts of Greek epic and the varied types of Latin epic; Ennius' influence, therefore, was not so great that all epic poetry from this period was subsequently written only on historical themes or in Ennian style.

The Title Annales

I have until now been admittedly pedantic in pushing back against the notion of "Republican epic" as used in traditional accounts of Ennius' influence on this period. But leaving aside epics written in Greek, Latin epics on mythological themes, and translations, and narrowing the focus considerably, one can still ask how thoroughly Ennian style permeated *historical epic written in Latin hexameters* (which is the category that surely some of these scholars must have at least been imagining when they overstated their case). This is indeed a narrower focus. Let me divide this subset into those poems that would appear, on the surface, to be explicitly aligned with Ennius' *Annales*, by virtue of the fact that they

---

15. I think in this context of the more overt Homerizing fragments of Ennius, some, even, with Homerisms that are not Latin (e.g., *Mettoeoque Fufetioeo*, *Ann.* 120 Sk). This suggests that if there were any relationship between the *Annales* and Greek epic, the influence is unidirectional from Greek to the *Annales*.

share the same title. I will discuss the other historical epics from this period, not titled *Annales*, below, in the section "Ennian Influence on Other Fragments of Republican Historical Epic."

We know of only four poems between Ennius and Lucretius that were titled *Annales* or that may have had the word *Annales* in their titles. In presumed chronological order, these are:

- Accius' *Annales*, written sometime before 100 BCE, of which 12 lines survive from different sources;
- the *Annales* of Furius Antias, written around 100 BCE, 6 lines of which are preserved in Gellius;
- the *Annales* of Volusius immortalized by Catullus around 50 BCE as *cacata charta*, of which nothing survives; and
- Furius Bibaculus' *Annales Belli Gallici*, to which 14 lines are traditionally ascribed, again from various sources; it is assumed that this poem dealt with Julius Caesar's exploits in Gaul, making it more or less contemporary with Volusius' poem.

The fact that *Annales* is found in the title of four Latin hexameter poems out of roughly twenty that survive or are attested from this period must be one reason that scholars have assumed that there existed a veritable cottage industry of historical epics after Ennius, many of them called *Annales* and all of them resembling Ennius' poem in their style, subject matter, and general ethos. But let me repeat: *four* out of twenty poems. That is very far from a majority. What is more, these poems were not clustered together in such a way as to suggest a trend; Accius' poem, the second such to be called *Annales*, appeared nearly seventy years after the first *Annales* by Ennius, and the final two did not appear until the Neoteric revolution was already under way. So, scarcity and chronological distance alone provide enough reasons to cast doubt on the traditional Ennianizing narrative. But, even putting these facts aside, the surviving evidence suggests that the *Annales* poems that were written after Ennius were less Ennian, or perhaps Ennian in a different way, than is usually assumed.

I have already shown how many scholars have inferred that a work like Accius' *Annales* must have been very much like Ennius' *Annales*, with some going so far as to suggest Accius' poem presented as a self-conscious continuation of Ennius' epic. As far as I can tell, these inferences derive completely from Leo's original (overstated and possibly inaccurate) conjecture and depend mainly or even solely on the fact that the two works share the same title. In the first place, even if we assume that Accius' title does refer in some way to the title of Ennius' masterpiece, in the wake of Jackie Elliott's work, we now have good reason to wonder exactly what Ennius' title meant, as well.[16] But even if we assume, for the sake of argument, that, to Ennius, *Annales* meant "an account of Roman history," it is perfectly possible—and in view of the material that does survive, it is hardly unlikely—that Accius offered his own, innovative conception of *Annales* in deliberate *contrast* to Ennius. Identical titles aside, Accius' and Ennius' poems have been connected *in spite of* the fact that some fragments, like the one that deals with the origin of the Roman Saturnalia in the Athenian Cronia festival (fr. 3 Courtney), have suggested to some that Accius' poem was more like Ovid's *Fasti* than Ennius' *Annales*. The surviving fragments, to the extent that they offer a glimpse of Accius' poem, do not unambiguously suggest a historical work similar to Ennius' epic.

In fact, the surviving fragments of Accius' *Annales* do not reveal Ennian influence in any consistent way, apart from a single obviously Ennianizing line, which is, unsurprisingly and inevitably, adduced as evidence that Accius *generally* employed an Ennian style. There is no reason to suppose that this fragment is typical of Accius. In fact, this fragment makes the most sense if we regard it as a pointed engagement with an equally famous passage of Ennius. The line in question, which is given by Priscian, has been connected to fragments 175–179 in Skutsch's edition of Ennius' *Annales*:

> (*hoc ossum*) Accius . . . in Annalibus
> **fraxinus** *fixa ferox infensa infinditur ossis.*

> (*this "bone"*) Accius . . . in the Annales
> *the ash tree, pierced through, haughty, hostile,*
>   *is split in its bones.*   (Accius, 4 Courtney)

> *incedunt arbusta per alta, securibus caedunt*
> *percellunt magnas quercus, exciditur ilex,*
> **fraxinus** *frangitur atque abies consternitur alta*
> *pinus proceras pervortunt, omne sonabat*
> *arbustum fremitus silvai frondosai.*

> *They advance through the deep woods; they cut with axes;*
> *they strike down the tall oaks; a holm-oak is cut down;*
> *an ash is broken and the high fir is laid low;*
> *they overturn lofty pines. The whole wood echoes*
> *the roaring of the leafy forest.*   (Ennius, Ann. 175–179 Sk)

---

16. Elliott 2013: 18–38.

Here we can see multiple elements shared between Accius and Ennius: the theme of tree-felling, the unusual word *fraxinus*, and some pronounced alliteration. That these elements converge on both these passages is not surprising when we consider that Accius may be alluding specifically to Ennius' *Annales* and to the epic programmatics involved in the Ennian passage. In the first place, episodes of heroic felling and gathering of timber have a long epic pedigree that ultimately derive from the description of Patroclus' Funeral in *Iliad* 23. Ennius no doubt imitates this famous episode as part of his program of Homeric intertextuality, and Accius surely would have recognized this fact. Second, the word *fraxinus* occurs for the first time in surviving Latin literature in the Ennian passage, and for the second time here in this fragment of Accius; it is not found again before Vergil. *Fraxinus*, therefore, would seem to be a distinctively Ennian coinage. Lastly, the theme of lumberjacking seals the allusion to Ennius, before one ever considers the matter of alliteration. And when one moves to consider alliteration, the similarities between the passages are thrown into relief.

Before moving on, however, I should say a few words about this alliterative similitude, because although the two fragments both display this effect, this similarity does not negotiate a relationship between the two works in the way most critics have believed. Alliteration alone is not enough to declare a passage "Ennian," even if many scholars of Latin poetry often invoke alliteration as an especially Ennian effect when it is deployed by subsequent poets. But alliteration is commonly deployed in all varieties of early Latin poetry, be it in Saturnians, hexameters, or in dramatic meters. For that matter, when the Neoteric revolution finally arrives, it does not banish alliteration from the Latin poet's repertoire. Given the ubiquity of alliteration, we can hardly consider alliteration to be an exclusively Ennian effect. It is true, however, that Ennius appears to have had a penchant for repeating the same word-initial sound three times or more in the same line, and that he deploys this specific effect with more frequency than all other Republican poets, regardless of meter. The data suggests that this specific kind of alliteration was practiced especially by Ennius, and that its frequency declines gradually throughout the rest of Republican poetry.[17] And we should note that on occasion Ennius deploys this effect with gusto, as in lines like *o Tite, tute, Tati, tibi tanta, tyrrane, tulisti* (*Ann.* 104 Sk) and *at tuba terribili sonitu tarantara dixit* (*Ann.* 451 Sk).

If we return to the tree-felling passage, with these two examples in mind, you can see that here Ennius employs a different kind of alliteration, one that is more general, and one that cannot be held as a specifically "Ennian" stylistic

---

17. See Appendix 4 for comparative data on alliteration in Republican Latin poetry.

feature. There, Ennius does not insistently repeat a single, percussive sound (as in 104 and 451 Sk), but uses variation, both between different particular sounds, and between different kinds of sound, including harder and softer ones, shifting the repetition of *c* first to *f*, then to *p*, and then back to *f*, and generally not confining the repetition of sounds to the word-initial position, but often reducing their effect by placing the repeated sounds in medial position. Meanwhile, Accius, while himself no stranger to alliteration, displays what I have argued *is* a specifically Ennian effect: the repetition of the same word-initial sound (*f*) three times in the same line.[18] With this insistent repetition of word-initial *f*, this line's alliteration is actually more extreme than the Ennian passage, resembling, in fact, the other Ennian lines cited above more than it does the timber-felling passage.

As we have seen, this fragment certainly encourages the reader to think about this passage of Ennius in particular, but Accius' treatment of it is such that one has to wonder whether, far from giving us an example of the way Accius himself usually writes, the line is meant to invoke instead some sort of parody of Ennius.[19] If so, then Accius' choice of this particular Ennian passage makes sense, inasmuch as the source text offers multiple opportunities for parody, including Ennius' Homeric pretensions, his characteristic lexical inventiveness, and his occasional readiness to deploy decorative or onomatopoetic alliteration to a high degree. On this last point, we see more evidence of parody, as Accius not only alludes to this Ennian tendency at its most blatant, but actually misrepresents the comparative sophistication of the alliteration in the passage that he is ostensibly imitating. If, as I believe, Accius overemphasizes alliteration purposefully in an Ennian context in order to parody Ennius at his most extreme, the correct inference from this passage would not be that Accius always writes like this (i.e., like Ennius), but that he wants his audience to read this particular passage with certain pretensions and tendencies of Ennius specifically in mind.

I want to underscore this point, and to be as clear about it as possible, because I will return to it in my discussion of Lucretius' Ennian style throughout this

---

18. We do find this exact type of alliteration in two other tragic fragments at *Armorum Iudicium* 150 (*in quo salutis spes supremas sibi habet summa exerciti*) and at *Atreus* 200 (*maior mihi moles, maius miscendum est malum*), although, again, these are exceptional cases, rather than representative. See the data in Appendix 4.

19. In a different context, namely the penultimate poem in the collection of Catullus' poems (115), similar arguments regarding alliteration have been made to suggest that Ennius is the object of allusion. For example, Ross 1969: 103 n. 243 argues that the triple alliteration of word-initial *m-* in Catullus' *mentula magna minax* (115.8) "makes the reference [to *Ann.* 620 Sk) perfectly clear," while Zetzel 1983: 256 adds the further consideration that "the alliteration of the final words (*mentula magna minax*) alone would lead one to suspect parody."

book. Again, I do not suggest that alliteration is an inherently Ennian character-istic, that Accius used alliteration because he normally and deliberately cultivated an Ennian style, or that alliteration is to be regarded as an Ennian characteristic in post-Ennian poetry. What I infer from the passage under discussion here is that Accius regards *Ennius* as willing to employ rather extreme forms of alliteration that were open to parody as hyper-alliteration. I suggest that Lucretius learned this technique from Accius and deploys it in the *DRN* at various points when he wants his reader to read a particular passage through an Ennian lens.

Leaving aside whether or not actual parody is involved in this Accius frag-ment, there is another angle we ought to take when considering why Accius might allude to Ennius here specifically, rather than everywhere generally: the logging *topos* in Vergil as discussed by Stephen Hinds.[20] After Accius, so far as we know, no one had used *fraxinus* until the *Eclogues* and *Georgics*, where it occurs four times. But in the *Aeneid*, it is found twice in the context of gathering wood for heroic funerals.[21] Hinds, like most interpreters, regards this deployment of the word not as a symptom of pathological Ennianism, but as a signal of Vergil's self-conscious manipulation of the logging *topos*, which ultimately highlights the innovative nature of Vergil's own treatment. This poetic technique, which has been called "window reference" or "two-tier allusion," is very familiar to students of Latin poetry. It is usually interpreted not as a symptom of unimagi-native repetition, but as evidence of creative engagement with—and even mas-tery over—the literary past. The belated poet, therefore, represents himself as the culmination of a tradition that he himself creates. Most would say that this is manifestly true of Vergil, but many might balk if I were to suggest that the same is true of Accius. Accius is probably thought to be too early or too primi-tive for such things. However, I would point out that Ennius himself employed two-tier allusion to situate earlier Latin poets in the Homeric tradition he constructs in the *Annales*, as in his famous evocation of Livius Andronicus' *Odusia* proem (*Ann.* 322–323 Sk). There, in addition to offering a sort of trib-ute to Livius, Ennius most obviously demonstrates his innovative superiority to Livius as a Homeric poet.[22] Not only is it possible, it is probable, even, that Accius deploys the tree-felling *topos* in a similar way, perhaps with a measure of

---

20. Hinds 1998: 10–16; see now Nethercut 2019: 201–206.

21. *E* 7.65, 7.68; *G* 2.66, 2.359; *Aen.* 6.181, 11.136. Around the same time as the use of *fraxinus* in the *Aeneid*, Horace uses the word at *Carm.* 3.25.16, undoubtedly as part of an allusion to Ennius' logging fragment (cf. Nisbet and Rudd 2004 ad loc).

22. Again, see Hinds 1998: 58–62.

tribute to Ennius, but also one of active *aemulatio*, and not uninspired *imitatio* alone.[23]

With that possibility in mind, we should remember that the only reason we even have this fragment preserved is that it includes the unusual form *ossum, -i* (as opposed to *os, ossis*), "bone." Such a coinage looks more like one of the many eccentric linguistic experiments that fill the fragments of Accius, rather than like a characteristically Ennian element. In fact, we know that Accius himself was no traditionalist, but that he was self-consciously innovative and independent in matters of language. Ennius himself was innovative and experimental; but as Hinds, again, points out with regard to Ennius' stance toward Naevius, this innovation was all part of the belated poet's way of representing himself as "innovative," and anything but "derivative," by making his predecessor appear "archaic."[24] In short, it seems quite likely that Accius is adopting a certain posture toward Ennius, just as Ennius had done toward Livius and Naevius, a posture that I would call provocative *in this particular passage*; but it is not so obvious that we can or should read any of the other surviving fragments of Accius in quite this way. And so, we should resist drawing the conclusion that Accius' poem was consistently "Ennian." His title, *Annales*, is not against this: to the extent that it does make Ennius' poem a point of reference, it does so not because this is what poets had been doing since Ennius' *Annales* appeared. On the contrary, no poet that we know of had done this during the seventy intervening years. It is a reasonable inference that Accius is pointing to Ennius, but the evidence suggests that he is doing so deliberately and not reflexively. As for the fragments, both passages that allude to Ennius directly, like the logging fragment, and those that do not, like the one on the Saturnalia, could just as easily be meant to measure the differences between Accius and his predecessor, rather than the similarities.

In the case of Accius, scholars have had at least *some* evidence for Ennian tendencies that helped form the basis of sweeping claims about the influence of Ennius. In the case of the *Annales* ascribed by Catullus to a certain Volusius (c. 36), however, they have drawn similar conclusions based on literally *just the title*. In general, *Annales* is unstable when used as a title. The case of Ennius' epic is unusual, because we are quite confident of its title, since we find *Annales* as early as Lucilius (343 Marx) without any competition until Diomedes lists the undoubtedly

---

23. This seems particularly likely here, because Ennius appears to be activating the frequent metaphor of poetic ὕλη/*silva*—that is to say, lumber—as poetic material. For a discussion of this passage along similar lines, see Hinds 1998: 12–14 with further bibliography. The metaphor is certainly active in Hellenistic poetry, if not even earlier, so there is no reason to doubt that Ennius and his successors would have had access to it.

24. Hinds 1998: 63–74.

corrupt *Romais*. In the historiographical tradition, on the other hand, there is no example of the title *Annales*, which is not in competition with *Historia*. Tacitus is, perhaps, the most famous example of the slippage between these terms. We have no MS authority for the title *Annales*, the title deriving ultimately from Beatus Rhenanus, who in his 1533 edition referred to all major historical writings as *Annales*. Subsequently Lipsius would differentiate between Tacitus' *Annales* and *Historiae*, presumably on the basis of the ancient opinion, put forward by, for example, Servius (*Aen.* 1.373), that *historia* applies to events that the writer actually lived to see, while *annales* applied to earlier events.[25] The two terms *historia* and *annales*, of course, were regularly used interchangeably (see Verbrugghe 1989 and *FRHist* 3.277–281). Moreover, as Jackie Elliott has reminded me *per litteras*, we have no evidence for the title *Annales* that is internal to the tradition of *annales* itself, and our earliest witnesses are Cato (*FRHist* 80=*Orig.* 4.1 Chassignet) and Sempronius Asellio (*FRHist* 1–2=Gellius, *NA* 5.18.8–9), neither of whom is sympathetic to *annales*, as each aims to distance himself from it. The basic complaint of Asellio, as preserved in Gellius, is that those who write *annales* simply list events without explaining how things happened. We generalize at our peril about the title *Annales* and what it tells us about any Ennian tradition of epic poetry.

Volusius' *Annales* is arguably, after Ennius, the most famous poem to bear this title, but we know nothing at all about it in terms of either style or content, besides its title and the fact that Catullus did not care for it. It has been reasonably inferred on the basis of Catullus' contempt that Volusius' poetry must have been antithetical to that of Catullus in both style and content. It has further been assumed, solely on the basis of its title, that it must resemble Ennius' *Annales*. And on the basis of these inferences, the further inference has been drawn that Catullus must have regarded Ennius as equally antithetical to his own poetic ideals.[26] A thorough dismantling of these connected inferences is beyond the scope of my analysis here; briefly, I would cite the important piece of circumstantial evidence that Catullus does not seem to have held Ennius himself in contempt: for it is generally agreed that Catullus engages with Ennius (e.g., with the *Medea Exsul* in c. 64) in creative and sophisticated ways.[27] Even if the *Medea* is a specimen of Ennian tragedy, and not epic, this in itself is a positive indication that runs counter to the traditional view of Catullus' attitude toward Ennius and the tradition that he putatively founded. Moreover, in

---

25. For further discussion of this issue as it relates to Tacitus, see Goodyear 1972: 85–87.

26. For example, witness the discussion at Hollis 2007: 128–129.

27. Fundamental are Thomas 1982 and Zetzel 1983. See, most recently, and with further bibliography, Timpanaro 2005: esp. 23–25; Maggiali 2008; Mastandrea 2008; Pavlock 2013; and Adamik 2014.

c. 64 Catullus engages with Ennius in a context where he also alludes to poets like Euripides, Apollonius, and others, whom Catullus at least regarded as worthy of his attention and imitation, and who were held in high esteem by Catullus' contemporaries and their Augustan followers. We may remember in this context, too, that when Cicero speaks of the *cantores Euphorionis* in the *Tusculan Disputations*, it is Ennian tragedy, not epic, that we infer is the object of their scorn. But perhaps it is not really necessary to go into the degree to which Catullus would have wanted to insult a poet who may or may not have composed in an Ennian style or on an Ennian subject. For again, in regard to a putative Ennian tradition, and Volusius as a representative of it, the point is that we have no direct evidence at all. We do know the poem's title, but, as the case of Accius suggests, we cannot really be certain what either the form or the content of a poem titled *Annales* actually was.[28]

We have nothing of Volusius' *Annales*, but we do have a few lines from the *Annales* of a certain Furius Antias. Gellius, who preserves these lines, reports the fact that the grammarian Caesellius Vindex upbraided Furius for his insistent neologisms, especially the creation of inceptive verbs. Ennius, too, was of necessity a linguistic innovator, and perhaps Furius admired and emulated him in this; but to emulate an author in this way is the exact opposite of imitating his most typical or characteristic features. In any case, scholars also regularly note the specifically un-Ennian character of the fragments of Furius' *Annales*,[29] a fact which itself is strong evidence that poets could write poems called *Annales* without necessarily following Ennius. We should be careful, however, because the only lines we have are contextually bound to what Gellius reports: the chastisement of Caesellius Vindex regarding Furius' use of inceptive verbs. The specificity of the Gellian context suggests a priori that we have nowhere near a representative sample of Furius' *Annales*, and does not preclude that Furius might have followed Ennius elsewhere in his *Annales*. But that is a purely speculative point, and there is nothing—again, apart from the problematic title *Annales*—to support it. In short, we simply do not have enough data to make any sort of generalizing conclusions about Furius' literary relationship with Ennius' *Annales*, nor can we say anything definite about the subject of Furius' poem. All that can be affirmed with certainty is that Furius wrote a hexameter poem, which Gellius calls *Annales*.

From the positive evidence we have, one might actually conclude that the title *Annales* was purposefully adopted in the spirit of rivalry with Ennius, since in the

---

28. Jackie Elliott suggests to me that the word *annales* itself in Catullus 36 is at least as easily read as an insult as an actual title. See, further, Elliott 2013: 18–19, 28–32, and 58–60.

29. Most directly, Batstone 1996: 391–392. There is no mention of Ennius in Courtney's edition of the fragments, and Franz Skutsch was the first to suggest that Antias shows no Ennian imitation (*RE* 1910: VII 322).

lines we do possess, scholars have been unable to find any Ennian influence in terms of allusion, style, or metrics, and since Furius appears to have been innovative in matters of diction. The very freedom from Ennian influence in a poem that takes its title from Ennius' magnum opus could be read as an attempt to re-establish Roman epic as un-Ennian (or even anti-Ennian), or at least as a claim that the influence of Ennius does not exert control over what a poem titled *Annales* might look like. We may think in this context back to Accius' *Annales*, and my suggestion above that Accius may have chosen the title *Annales* purposefully as a sort of riposte to Ennius. If polemics were involved in Accius' choice of title, we might speculate that Furius could be following Accius in some way, or even alluding back to Ennius through Accius. We cannot determine Furius' poetic intentions with certainty, of course, owing to the paucity of our fragments. And the evidence we do have does not support the conclusion that a tradition of *Annales* poems was moving forward by a kind of irresistible Ennian momentum.

To conclude my overview of the Republican epics we know of that shared their title with Ennius' epic, I turn now to the complicated case of the putative *Annales Belli Gallici*, generally thought to have been written by Catullus' contemporary, Furius Bibaculus. Unfortunately, both points are uncertain: we cannot be sure either that Furius Bibaculus did write an epic or that there was an epic, by any poet, that bore the title *Annales Belli Gallici*. Since this is quite a thorny issue, and because my purpose is to re-examine the most widely held opinions about Republican epic, I want to accept for a moment, and for the sake of argument, the *communis opinio* that Furius Bibaculus *did* write an epic poem titled *Annales Belli Gallici* and that its subject matter was Caesar's Gallic campaigns.[30] Regardless of the title of the work or the name of its author, we do, in fact, have some fragments that permit of analysis. Regarding this actual evidence, fragments

---

30. The arguments against Furius Bibaculus having written an epic were carefully presented by Jessica Clark in excellent papers at the annual meetings of CAMWS (2015: "Who am I? Style and Identity in Poetic Fragments") and the SCS (2016: "Fragmentary Furii and Latin Historical Epic"), arguing ultimately that these fragments belong to Furius Antias. Her work will appear as Clark (forthcoming). I summarize the most salient data here: (1) Macrobius gives eight hexameter quotations of a certain Furius from a work he calls *Annales* in at least eleven books; (2) elsewhere, including in Macrobius himself, Furius Bibaculus is *always* identified with his cognomen, and never is referred to as simply Furius (see Hollis 2007: 125); (3) the Verona scholiast to Vergil includes a reference to a work called *Annales Belli Gallici*, though we have a lacuna where the author's name should have appeared (at Verg. *Aen.* 9.379); (4) Porphyry attributes the line parodied at Hor. *Sat.* 2.5.40 to Furius Bibaculus and Pseudo-Acro on the same line says it comes from a work by Furius Vivaculus called the *pragmatia belli Gallici*. To believe that Furius Bibaculus wrote an epic titled *Annales Belli Gallici* whose fragments are preserved in Macrobius, one has to accept a number of interrelated suppositions, namely (1) that the *pragmatia belli Gallici* attributed to Furius Vivaculus in Pseudo-Acro is the same work as the authorless *Annales Belli Gallici* attested in the Verona scholiast to Vergil,

7–10 in Courtney's text (which correspond to 72–75 in Hollis' edition) all show marked Homerisms, perhaps even more than Ennianisms. That is to say, some features appear to gesture toward Homer through Ennius, while others find no specific parallel in Ennius at all.

Courtney's fragment 8 exemplifies most fully the sophisticated nature of Bibaculus' engagement with Homer and Ennius. If we juxtapose the Homeric original with similar lines in Ennius, we can see Furius using the same technique of window reference or two-tier allusion that I identified in the Accius fragment above. In the first tier, Furius alludes to Ennius:

> *ille gravi subito devictus volnere habenas*
> *misit equi <u>lapsusque</u> in humum defluxit et <u>**armis**</u>*
> <u>*reddidit*</u> <u>***aeratis***</u> <u>*sonitum*</u>.   (*8 Courtney=73 Hollis*)

> *Conquered by a serious wound, that one of a sudden let go of the horse's reins*
> *and, having slipped, he fell down onto the ground,*
> *and he returned a sound from his bronze weapons.*

> *concidit et <u>sonitum</u> simul insuper arma <u>dederunt</u>*   (*Ennius, Ann. 411 Sk*)

> *He collapsed and at the same time the weapons produced a sound on top of him*

Courtney and Hollis cite fragment 411 from Skutsch's edition of the *Annales* as a model for Furius' fragment, and I agree that Furius is influenced by Ennius here, and in interesting ways. For example, Furius' *reddidit sonitum* recalls Ennius' *sonitum dederunt*, not just lexically and sonically, but metapoetically as well: while Ennius' arms "produce the sound," Furius "returns" it. The *re-* prefix of Furius' *reddidit* thus serves as a sign of doubling or iteration, and, perhaps, of re-storation of the *topos* to its ultimate Homeric, and not just its immediate Ennian, source.[31]

---

(2) that the *Annales Belli Gallici* in the Verona scholiast is the same work as the *Annales* referenced in Macrobius, and (3) that the Furius who wrote the *Annales* quoted by Macrobius is Furius Bibaculus and not some other Furius (e.g., Furius Antias). I think it is quite unlikely, therefore, that Furius Bibaculus wrote an *Annales Belli Gallici*, and I agree completely with Clark that it is much more probable that the Furius quoted by Macrobius is the same Furius quoted by Gellius, namely Aulus Furius Antias, the subject of whose *Annales* is unrecoverable from the extant fragments. The major implication of her argument, of course, is that we now have more than double the amount of material for Furius Antias' *Annales*, and, as a result, we have much more evidence for *his* engagement with Ennius' epic.

31. Vergil appears to link himself to this poetic chain, as Macrobius adduces this fragment as a parallel for *Aen.* 11.500.

In addition to this Ennian allusion, commentators also frequently adduce as the object of Furius' allusion a line that is repeated five times in the *Iliad*:

> δούπησεν δὲ πεσών, ἀράβησε δὲ τεύχε᾽ ἐπ᾽ αὐτῷ
>
> (Il. 4.504, 5.42, 13.187, 17.50, 17.311)

> *and he fell with a thud, and his weapons clanged upon him*

Indeed, the combination in Furius of a participle *lapsusque*, with two verbs, *defluxit* and *reddidit sonitum*, looks like a conflation of Homer's δούπησεν δὲ πεσών with Ennius' *concidit et sonitum dederunt*. Moreover, the nexus of allusion in Furius may be even more Homeric, considering this line occurs only once in the *Odyssey*, where it describes the death of Eupeithes at Laertes' hands less than twenty-five lines from the end of the poem:

> καὶ βάλεν Εὐπείθεα κόρυθος διὰ <u>χαλκοπαρήου</u>.
> ἡ δ᾽ οὐκ ἔγχος ἔρυτο, διαπρὸ δὲ εἴσατο <u>χαλκός</u>.
> δούπησεν δὲ πεσών, ἀράβησε δὲ τεύχε᾽ ἐπ᾽ αὐτῷ.   (Od. 24.523–525)

> *and he struck Eupeithes through his helmet that had bronze cheek-pieces*
> *and this did not withstand the spear, but the bronze passed through*
> *and he fell with a thud, and his weapons clanged upon him.*

The emphasis here on the bronze weapons of both combatants, an element absent in all the instances of this line in the *Iliad*, suggests that Furius' adjective *aeratis*, which of course is not in Ennius, contains an implicit boast of his textual command over both Homeric epics, as well as evidence that he is conflating them in these lines.[32]

Elsewhere in the fragments of the *Annales Belli Gallici* we find strange, and one might say, "un-epic" phrasing.[33] We might consider such eccentricities as

---

32. There may be even more to it than that, if we consider Furius' use of *aeratis* as a *contaminazione a distanza* of *Annales* fr. 411 with fr. 393, the only instance of the adjective *aeratus -a,-um* in Ennius, and a fragment in which Skutsch sees a model for the Furius fragment I have been discussing (Skutsch 1985: 560–561).

33. Courtney 1993: 197–198 discusses the evidence, including the use of the "tasteless word *iugulare*" to describe the killing of Memnon by Achilles. In fr. 8 Courtney, we can also note the peculiar genitive *habenas . . . equi*, which is further highlighted by the enjambment of lines 1–2. Most famously, perhaps, Furius uses the image of Jupiter "spitting snow" over the Alps (*Iuppiter hibernas cana nive conspuit Alpes*, 15 Courtney=80 Hollis, "Jupiter spit on the wintry Alps with white snow"). This line was famous enough that Horace could mock it in the *Sermones* in a pretty offhand way, by calling Furius simply *Alpinus* at 1.10.36.

evidence that Furius grapples with Ennius in his own idiosyncratic way. Furius brings Ennius to mind, both by virtue of putting *Annales* in the title of his poem and by alluding to him at various points in the fragments, as we have seen; he evokes Ennius in this way in order to showcase his own Homeric style, which appears to have involved a certain amount of linguistic experimentation. In short, the evidence suggests that Furius, just like Accius before him, engages with Ennius actively as part of a sophisticated allusive program.

On the basis of the fragments that remain, the poems between Ennius and Lucretius titled *Annales* exhibit some positive evidence that the title *Annales* was adopted at times as a mantle of *aemulatio* with Ennius' epic. The very few fragments from these poems that are usually adduced as evidence of insipid Ennian *imitatio* often reveal a sophisticated interaction with Ennius' claim to be the Roman Homer. In the next section, I will continue this analysis by investigating the fragments from historical epic after Ennius' *Annales* from poems that were not titled *Annales*.

Ennian Influence on Other Fragments of Republican Historical Epic

Other historical epics were written between Ennius and Lucretius that were not called *Annales*. Presumably our interpretation of these fragments has been the most prone to distortion from Leo's view of an Ennianizing tradition, since these fragments are even further removed from Ennius by virtue of their different titles and their monographic treatments of specific wars. We should remain open to the fact that it may be precisely because of Leo's view of the evidence that scholars have been keen to point out Ennianisms in their fragments. Even when we can be relatively certain of Ennian influence in these poems, however, we must continue to resist the traditional sweeping generalizations about what this influence indicates. In this section, I will move from the most secure evidence of engagement with Ennius' *Annales* to the least secure.

The earliest of these epics is that of Hostius, who dates from the generation after Ennius himself. In his *Bellum Histricum* scholars have argued, not surprisingly, for the influence of Ennius. For example, Courtney's fragment 1 has been seen as highly Ennian both because of its alliteration and because of shared Ennian vocabulary:

percutit atque hastam pilans prae pondere frangit   *(Hostius, 1 Court.)*

he struck through and he broke the spear fixing it firm before his weight

nam me gravis impetus Orci

percutit *in latus*   *(Ennius, Ann. 564 Sk)*

For the heavy attack of Orcus strikes me through in my side

aut permarceret paries **percussus** *trifaci*   *(Ennius, Ann. 548 Sk)*

or a wall struck through with a missile should crumble

As already noted, alliteration per se is not inherently Ennian, especially at this early date. While we do have here the specifically Ennian penchant for insistent repetition of a word-initial consonant in the same line, and while this looks very similar to what we saw in Accius' reception of the logging fragment from the *Annales*, we have parallels with this fragment in Hostius from non-Ennian sources. The verb *percutit*, the one word in this line that is sufficiently rare and attested for Ennius, also appears in Plautus (*pectus mihi pedibus* **percutit**, *Casina* 930, "he strikes my breast with his feet") and Caecilius Statius—in both cases with the same insistent alliteration (**percutias** *pavidum, postremo a parco patre*, fr. 204 Ribbeck, "may you strike him fearful, finally from your frugal father"). This evidence makes it much more difficult for us to assume that Hostius, like Accius would later do, is using this Ennian alliterative effect to highlight his engagement with Ennius. But even if Hostius had no reason to think these features in this fragment were unique to Ennius, it is possible that he was interested in the Ennian passage in particular as an imitation of Homer. This reading is supported by the fact that commentators have also emphasized its Homeric pedigree, in spite of their interest in linking this line specifically to Ennius. Vinchesi, for example, argues that the succession of two movements in the duel (the striking of a blow followed by the broken spear) approximates most closely to similar type scenes in Homer more than it does to anything in Ennius.[34] Such evidence suggests, once again, that Hostius is employing two-tier allusion in a spirit of emulation, as Hostius outdoes Ennius in the specificity of his Homeric allusion.

Hostius' version of the many-mouths *topos* is another fragment that has been seen as especially Ennian:

Non si mihi *linguae*
<u>centum</u> *atque* <u>ora sient</u> *totidem* **vocesque liquatae**   *(Hostius, 3 Court.)*

Not if I were to have one hundred tongues
and mouths and the same number of purified voices

---

34. Vinchesi 1984: 41–43. See *Iliad* 11. 234–235; 13.160–163; 17.606–607.

non si lingua loqui saperet quibus, <u>ora decem sint</u>
*in me, tum ferro **cor** sit pectusque revinctum*   (*Ennius, Ann. 469–470 Sk*)

Not if there were ten mouths in me from which my tongue knew how
*to speak, nor if my **heart** and breast were bound up with iron*

πληθὺν δ᾽ οὐκ ἂν ἐγὼ μυθήσομαι οὐδ᾽ ὀνομήνω
οὐδ᾽ εἴ μοι δέκα μὲν γλῶσσαι, δέκα δὲ στόματ᾽ εἶεν,
φωνὴ δ᾽ ἄρρηκτος, χάλκεον δέ μοι ἦτορ ἐνείη   (*Il. 2.488–490*)

But I could not speak of nor name the common masses
Not if I had ten tongues, and ten mouths,
and an unbreakable voice, and the heart inside me were bronze

In analyzing Hostius' employment of this many-mouths *topos*, we would do well to keep in mind Hinds' discussion of *topoi* and poetic innovation as outlined above with respect to Accius' use of the logging *topos*. Courtney's fragment 3 has been connected, explicitly and rightly, to Ennius' many-mouths *topos*.[35] But, just as I argued regarding the Homeric pedigree of the *topos* of logging in Accius' *Annales* (fr. 4 Courtney), the *topos* of many-mouths derives ultimately from Homer. In fact, Hostius' line opening matches Homer's version more closely than it does Ennius' (*non si mihi*=οὐδ᾽ εἴ μοι at *Il.* 2.489). Additionally, Hostius' phrase *vocesque liquatae* recalls Homer's ἄρρηκτος φωνή (*Il.* 2.490), although not without differences: ἄρρηκτος seems to agree with the brazen material of which Homer's voice is made, whereas *liquatae* seems related to the clear sound of the voice, rather than the material that produces it.[36] In any case, this element is absent in Ennius. The adjective *liquatae* may, in fact, imply a poetics that has been "purified" of allusion to Ennius, in touch with Homer and unadulterated by any other intermediate sources.[37] So, to this extent, the passage looks like what we must now understand as a typical instance of beating Ennius at his own Homeric game.

---

35. See Pascucci 1959; Vinchesi 1984: 46–48; Courtney 1993: 53; and Hinds 1998: 36–38.

36. Hostius also changes the phrase from singular to plural.

37. Vinchesi has even suggested that the context in Hostius is the same as in Homer. While this suggestion is, of course, speculative, it is true that Macrobius, who provides us with this fragment, also tells us that Hostius "follows" Homer in deploying this *topos* in Book 2 of his poem, and not in Book 6, as seems possible for Ennius. This ascription has been suggested by Kleve 1990, on the basis of his reading of a Herculaneum papyrus. See also Suerbaum 1995.

Courtney's fragment 4 also displays such Homerizing: *Dia Minerva, simul
<simul> autem invictus Apollo / arquitenens Latonius* ("Now bright Minerva,
now unconquered Apollo, the bow-holder, Son of Latona"). Vinchesi's sug-
gestion that these lines are modelled on *Il.* 7.58–61, where Athena and Apollo
appear together to watch the fighting at Troy, suggests that once again Hostius
engages in window allusion with multiple sources.[38] If this is true, Hostius' use
of *dia* to describe Minerva is likely an acknowledgment of the fact that Ennius
likely imported the form into Latin from the Homeric epics. That said, *arquite-
nens* is not Ennian, as it first appears in Naevius as one in a string of epithets
describing Apollo (*dein pollens sagittis inclutus arquitenens / sanctus . . . Pythius
Apollo*, 20 Strzelecki, "then powerful with arrows, famous, the bow-holder, holy,
Pythian Apollo"), and it is one of Naevius' most successful inventions, having
long remained in use.[39] Most scholars believe that Naevius in turn is gesturing to
an epithet found in Homer: ἀργυρότοξος Ἀπόλλων, *Il.* 7.58.[40] And so one could
reasonably conclude that Hostius is offering a tour-de-force of allusivity, per-
haps acknowledging Ennius' linguistic innovation in *dia*, while also alluding
to Homer through Naevius. In doing so, Naevius may be signaling that not only
was Ennius *not* the only Homeric poet ever to write in Latin, but also that he was
not even the first, nor the last. On this reading, therefore, the same evidence that
has been traditionally mobilized to argue that Hostius' epic is "Ennian" actually
helps build a plausible case that Hostius is trying to be both *more* Homeric and
more Naevian than he is trying to be Ennian.

While there is much we can say about Hostius, Accius, and Furius, the hex-
ameter fragments of Gannius, Varro Atacinus, and Sueius simply do not permit of
any definite conclusions regarding their engagement with Ennius' *Annales* or their
relationship to any putative tradition of Ennian historical epic. From Gannius, for
whom we have no date, we have three lines quoted by Priscian for their use of the
strange word *ador, adoris*, a grain used for making *mola salsa* in sacrifices. We can
plausibly infer that these three lines come from some sort of description of sacrifice
(*illam sponte satos adoris stravisse maniplos*, 3 Courtney, "willingly she spread out the
sown bundles of grain"), but they show no signs of Ennian influence. It is true that
they contain alliteration, but yet again we will do well to remember that alliteration
alone is an unreliable marker of Ennian influence.

---

38. Vinchesi 1984: 49.

39. Accius 167 Ribbeck; Cic. *Aratea.* 34.272, 34. 405 Soubiran; Verg. *Aen.* 3.75; Sen. *Phaed.* 709;
Statius *Theb.* 4.756; and *Achil.* 1.682.

40. Vinchesi 1984: 49–50, with further bibliography, and Courtney 1993: 54. The Homeric
epithet τοξοφόρος found only at *Il.* 21.483 approximates most closely to *arquitenens*.

We have at least one line from the *Bellum Sequanicum* of Varro Atacinus, who also translated the *Argonautica* into Latin hexameters and wrote small-scale didactic on the model of Aratus. When we look at the two fragments that Courtney ascribes to the *Bellum Sequanicum*, we note first of all that one (*semianimesque micant oculi lucemque requirunt*, 2 Courtney=11 Morel, "and eyes, half-alive, flash and they seek the light") is not just Ennian, it is literally lifted wholesale from the *Annales* (*Ennii est=Ann.* 484 Sk); or, as Servius says (*Aen.* 10.396), Varro took this line as it stood (*ita ut fuit*) over into his poem.[41] In either case, however, we have no information beyond the allusion itself to determine the nature of Varro's engagement with Ennius' *Annales*, and therefore we are simply not justified in making any sort of sweeping claims about the *Bellum Sequanicum* as a specimen of Ennian historical epic.[42] As for the second fragment of the *Bellum Sequanicum*, (*deinde ubi pellicuit dulcis levis unda saporis*, Courtney 1, "then when the light wave of sweet flavor enticed") the arrangement of the line and the diction point us to the poets Laevius and Cinna, neither of whom has traditionally been seen as especially Ennian.[43] Absent any positive evidence regarding the narrative context of this line in the *Bellum Sequanicum*, and given that this is the only line we can securely ascribe to this poem, we simply cannot assume that Varro saw himself as continuing in Ennius' footsteps.

Finally, all that exists of Sueius are two hexameter fragments in Macrobius (frs. 7–8 Courtney) that commentators have assumed must come from an epic, on the grounds that Ennian phrases appear in both lines (*rumore secundo*, 7 Courtney=*Ann.* 244 Skutsch "with favorable rumor," *volatile telum*, fr. 8, "flying spear," which Courtney reconstructs as an Ennian phrase in dialogue with Pease at *Aen.* 4.71). But we have no title for this poem, and, even if we did, we have seen time and again how deceptive titles can be with regard to our broader interpretation of fragments. We also have no notice as to the subject matter of Sueius' poem, and no context given for these lines. Given that we do not even have a date for Sueius, it may be that his lines do not even belong in the group of post-Ennian Republican epics. As in the case of so much of the fragmentary material I have

---

41. See Courtney 1993: 238. Because Servius does not name the poem of Varro in which this line appears, many scholars have actually assumed that fr. 2 Courtney comes from Varro's *Argonautae* (cf. Ap. Rhod. 4.1524–1525).

42. Caesar cannot help clarify this fragment or its relationship to Ennius, because we have no means of determining any sort of narrative context for this fragment in Varro. I do, however, discuss Lucretius' engagement with this fragment in Chapter 3 (pp. 91–94).

43. Courtney 1993: 238 suggests that this line's ending with two adjectives and two nouns reminds us of Cinna fr. 2 Courtney, while the verb *pellicuit* directs the reader back to Laevius fr. 18 Courtney.

been covering, we generalize at our peril, and we certainly should not use these meager and problematic hints of Ennian influence to reconstruct a dominant tradition of Ennian historical epic.

Cicero's De Consulatu Suo

It would take much more space and focus to account adequately for Cicero's use of Ennius' *Annales* in the *De Consulatu Suo*—in fact, such a project would be its own book. What I can show here, however, is that while there are definite and significant points of contact (allusion, diction, even metrics to some extent) between Cicero and Ennius' *Annales*, we can safely assume that whatever Cicero's relationship to Ennius' *Annales* was in the *De Consulatu Suo*, it was not primarily a function of an Ennian tradition of historical epic. While we do possess more lines of Cicero's poem on his own consulship than of all other Republican Latin epics after Ennius combined, evidence of Ennian influence in the fragments of *De Consulatu Suo* is not as widespread as one might assume, given Cicero's obsession with Ennius elsewhere in his corpus.[44]

Scholars often speak of Cicero's use of Ennian language and metrics, but rarely do they point to specific allusions, and almost nowhere do they interpret the allusions that are adduced.[45] Nevertheless, we do find a number of allusions to Ennius in the long fragment quoted in *De Divinatione* (10 Courtney). Perhaps the most secure allusion to Ennius here is the line-ending *sanctusque senatus* (10.57 Courtney), which surely recalls the Ennian line-ending *sanctoque senatu* (*Ann.* 272 Sk).[46] In context, Cicero has Urania recount the omens of 65 BCE, and he emphasizes that belief in providence is sanctioned by traditions like the Senate. The original Ennian context to which Cicero alludes is the "Good Companion" fragment, in which Ennius describes how the consul Servilius Geminus would spend his time in friendly conversation after he had completed his civic duties for the day. One interpretation of this allusion is to suggest that, as is typical of Cicero's response to Ennius elsewhere in his corpus, this allusion appears to

---

44. See especially Cole 2006 and Zetzel 2007.

45. See, most extensively, Goldberg 1995: 142–143 and 146–147, with a more overarching assessment of Cicero's debt to Ennius; on Cicero's Ennian metrics, see esp. Courtney 1993: 150–151.

46. Both Ewbank and Courtney cite this as an allusion to Ennius. The only other occurrence of the collocation of *sanctus* with *senatus* is at *Aen.* 1.426, when Aeneas surveys Dido's growing city in Carthage. It seems difficult to deny that Vergil is alluding specifically back to Cicero and Ennius in that passage, and so would offer corroboration that Cicero is working with Ennius here.

fortify the basic point being made by citing Ennius as an authority regarding Roman civic affairs. Cicero implies that the Senate has always been *sanctus*, and Ennius provides evidence for this fact. In effect, this literary continuity reinforces the basic point of Urania's speech that the Romans are right to keep the traditions of their ancestors sacred (10.66–70 Courtney).[47]

Despite such examples of Ennian allusions, however, the general consensus maintains that Cicero's hexameters approximate more to those of Catullus than to those of Ennius, even if Cicero does sometimes write in an archaizing idiom by, for example, eliding word-final -*s* in order to make position.[48] When Cicero does allude to Ennius, he has his own programmatic reasons to do so, and such allusion reflects Cicero's use of Ennius' epic elsewhere in his writings. In any case, where Cicero does employ overt Ennianism, he does so in such a way as to signal poetic innovation and creative engagement—deploying Ennius in precisely the same way, and to the same effect, as I have argued Hostius, Accius, and Furius Bibaculus do.

Conclusion

I have made four interrelated claims in response to the traditional view that there was an Ennian tradition of epic poetry that dominated the period between the *Annales* and the Neoteric revolution: (1) articulations of this traditional view often take the form of sweeping generalizations that are unsupported by our evidence; but in fact, (2) there were really only a few epic poems written during this period that might plausibly have been Ennian; (3) of the four poems that may have been called *Annales*, we cannot even be sure that any of them was an historical epic; and (4) the passages we actually have, which have been taken to be evidence of an uninspired, routine imitation of Ennius, actually look more like attempts at virtuoso responses to Ennius as an imitator of Homer. These engagements express each poet's own sense of style and of literary history; as such, they

---

47. Other, less secure allusions may be involved in this passage. For example, *nam pater alti-tonans stellanti nixus Olympo* (10.36 Courtney) makes use of the Ennian line-ending *Olympo* (*Ann.* 1 Sk) and the epithet *altitonans* (*Ann.* 554 Sk). Even less securely, *terribili . . . tremefecit . . . tellus* (10.23–25 Courtney) may recall Ennius' *Africa terribili tremit horrida terra tumultu* (*Ann.* 309 Sk).

48. The bibliography on the history and the development of the Latin hexameter is vast, but especially helpful analysis can be found in Christ 1879; Hardie 1907; Sturtevant 1919 and 1923; Wilkinson 1940 and 1963: 118–134 and 193–202; Hellegouarc'h 1964; Raven 1965; Pearce 1966; and Duckworth 1969. For a more recent and interpretative discussion of the Latin hexameter, see Morgan 2010: 284–377.

are likely to be exceptional rather than typical in comparison to most narrative passages in these poems.

I said at the beginning of this chapter that Lucretius himself is partly to blame for the traditional sweeping generalizations regarding an "Ennian tradition." But in the chapters that follow I will marshal evidence that suggests that Lucretius is really better regarded as invoking Ennius for very specific reasons of his own, and not because doing so was the normal, inevitable, or expected thing to do. It is also the case that Lucretius' Ennian style is hardly as inert as that of Volusius is imagined to have been; on the other hand, neither, as Ennian as it is, would one mistake most of Lucretius' poetry for Ennius' own. But in any case, without Lucretius the case for a continuous tradition of Ennian writing might not look as strong as it does. And so, I can now add this as a fifth argument (5) against the traditional view of this issue. Cumulatively, these five arguments do not invalidate the traditional view of Ennius' influence altogether, but they do call into question how implicitly we can believe in it.

In addition to pushing back against the traditional narrative of an Ennianizing vogue for Republican epic, I should also make note of the positive aspects of the *Annales* to which poets, in the period between the *Annales* and Lucretius, responded, because this will provide an important context for my analyses of Lucretius' engagement with Ennius in the following chapters of this book. It is clear especially from the fragments of Hostius, Accius, and Furius that the *Annales* was the target of allusion because of its engagement with Homer and its linguistic innovations. All three of these poets acknowledge the Homeric aspirations of the *Annales*, and all three of them seem to innovate on Ennius' Homeric program. Hostius and Accius do so through their appropriations of Homeric *topoi* (e.g., the many-mouths theme, the tree-felling motif), which show clear allusion to Ennius, but also show their own innovations. Furius features a compound allusion that incorporates both Homeric poems and Ennius' *Annales*.

The effect of these fragments' engagement with Ennius and Homer appears to be one of poetic rivalry, in which the question of who will be the Roman Homer is still very much open. The fact that we have fragments of a poem in Saturnians that treats of Homeric subject matter (the *Carmen Priami*) reinforces this idea: Ennius' claim in the *Annales* to be literally *Homerus redivivus* certainly did not preclude subsequent Latin epic poets from developing different and novel ways of engaging with Homer. If anything, it actually suggests that there was already at the time of the *Annales* competition for the chair. Moreover, when these poets allude to Ennius and Homer, we regularly find engagement with Ennius' innovative use of the Latin language in crafting a poetic vocabulary for the hexameter. Accius creates new noun forms, a regular feature of his poetry across genres, Hostius alludes back to Naevius' coinage of epithets, and

Furius experiments with images and turns of phrase that, while novel, were considered unfortunate by subsequent critics. This all suggests that, in the wake of the *Annales*, Ennius did not have the last word on how Latin could be made to adapt to the hexameter.

If, then, we have reason to question the traditional view of an inert Ennian tradition of Latin epic poetry, when it comes to Lucretius, who obviously adopts an Ennian idiom in the *DRN*, it is clear from the foregoing analysis that Lucretius was not simply following the path of least resistance in this regard. This inference opens up the possibility that Lucretius imitates Ennius for strategic purposes, just as we must now assume Hostius, Accius, and Furius had done before him. Even if we grant the possibility that there were many more poets churning out poems called *Annales* in imitation of Ennius, on the basis of the fragments I have canvassed above, we cannot really evaluate whether these were more or less Ennian than Lucretius is. In fact, it seems probable that they were less so, and that Lucretius' language struck contemporary readers as much more obviously and deliberately archaizing than that of other "Ennian" poets. It is also quite clear that the poets of the next generation admired Lucretius even more, perhaps, than they admired Ennius, and, in any case, that they did not ignore Lucretius in the way that they evidently did ignore most other late Republican poets, on stylistic or any other grounds. The hypothesis that Lucretius does not represent most of the lost poetry of the Republic, but that he was a deliberately and strategically archaizing poet, may actually be a bit stronger than the case that he was out of step with his Neoteric contemporaries.[49] In any case, my concern hereafter is not to delineate precisely into which period of the literary canon Lucretius falls—whether he is affecting Ennius because he was the last of the pre-Neoterics or whether he was one of the first Neoterics and so deliberately archaizing—so much as to evaluate *why* Lucretius adopted a hyper-Ennian style in the first place. As will become clear in the chapters that follow, my inference is that by alluding so forcefully to Ennius, Lucretius sought to throw into greater relief his subversion of Ennian values.

---

49. Scholarly consensus maintains that Lucretius was engaged with the poetic sophistication of the so-called Neoterics: Kenney 1970; Brown 1982; King 1985; Farrell 1991: 291–299; Donahue 1993; Gale 2007a; and Nethercut 2018a; *contra*, though cautiously, Knox 1999. Even if Lucretius *were* out of touch with Neoteric developments, and were just writing in an Ennian idiom along with so many lost Republican epigones, this could still be a subversive affectation.

2

Lucretius on the Ennian Cosmos

ONE MIGHT NOT think of Ennius' *Annales* as primarily a work of natural philosophy, but that is precisely how Lucretius describes it in the *De Rerum Natura*. It makes sense, therefore, to begin my study of Lucretius' engagement with Ennius' *Annales* on Lucretius' own terms and explore how the *Annales* serves Lucretius as a model for poetry about the universe. Lucretius makes clear his identification of Ennius as a poet who also writes on "the nature of things" when he singles him out by name in the proem to the *DRN*. In that famous passage, he programmatically associates the poetry of Homer and Ennius with his own poem, by describing Homer's discourse in the proem to the *Annales* as concerning "the nature of things" (*rerum natura*, Lucr. 1.126), which is, of course, both the subject matter and the title of his own poem. This passage echoes an earlier one in which Lucretius asks Venus to lend him assistance as he writes "on the nature of things" (*de rerum natura*, Lucr. 1.25), titling his poem as well as announcing its subject matter. Some circumstantial evidence may, in fact, suggest that Ennius did use the phrase *rerum natura* in the *Annales* to describe Homer's discourse. Lucretius uses the Ennian verb *pangere* (Lucr. 1.25; cf. *pangit melos*, *Ann.* 293 Sk) to describe his versifying of *rerum natura*. Moreover, Lucretius' description of the Dream itself frequently appropriates Ennian language (*Acherusia templa*=Lucr. 1.120; *Andromacha* fr. 24 Manuwald; *dictis*=Lucr. 1.126; *Ann.* 130, 246, 250, 533 Sk). The fact remains, however, that we simply do not have enough positive evidence to extend *rerum natura* back into the *Annales*-proem, and, even if Ennius did use the phrase *rerum natura*, he almost certainly did not mean the same thing as what Lucretius indicates. Still, one cannot deny the Ennian terms of the discussion in Lucretius. According to Lucretius, Ennius' Homer—and, therefore, Ennius himself—writes the same kind of poetry as Lucretius does, that is to say, poetry on natural philosophy.

Ennius Noster: Lucretius and the Annales. Jason S. Nethercut, Oxford University Press (2021). © Oxford University Press. DOI: 10.1093/oso/9780197517697.001.0001.

These connections—between Lucretius, Ennius, and Homer—have not gone unnoticed, and many commentators have long argued that Lucretius incorporates epic elements into the *DRN*.[1] But most efforts to make sense of these epic elements have focused solely on what they tell us about Lucretius' poem, and have failed to consider how Lucretius might be making a generic claim *about* Ennius, rather than or in addition to "importing" Ennius' epic pedigree into his own didactic poem on natural philosophy. In other words, these epic elements are taken as evidence for a thoroughgoing effort on Lucretius' part to present his *DRN* as an epic—or at least to highlight the generic similarities between didactic and epic. But what if Lucretius is instead (or also) establishing, however tendentiously, Homer and Ennius as didactic poets? After all, when Lucretius identifies Homer's discourse in the Dream that opens the *Annales* as an exposition *de rerum natura*, one way to understand this phrase is to realize that Lucretius implies that Ennius' *Annales* is the same kind of poem as Lucretius' own. Since Lucretius then goes on to explain the physical dynamics of the entire cosmos in his own *De Rerum Natura*, Lucretius would seem to affirm with this implication that the *Annales* similarly offers a philosophical account of the universe and its working apparatus. We have many reasons to assume that here Lucretius may be misrepresenting what Ennius actually wrote as part of his narrative of his Dream. Regardless of what Ennius may have had Homer say as part of his *somnia Pythagorea*, Lucretius certainly represents Ennius as articulating a developed philosophy of nature, and he insists that this articulation serves as a model for the poem he himself is writing *de rerum natura*.[2]

This programmatic moment has other consequences beyond merely redefining Homeric and Ennian poetry as philosophical didactic rather than mythological or historical epic. When Lucretius juxtaposes his own version of *rerum natura* with those of these other poets, but especially with that of Ennius, he is not just announcing his poetic and philosophical forebears; he is also marking out his targets.[3] For, throughout the *DRN*, Lucretius articulates his own vision of the

---

1. See especially Murley 1947; Sallmann 1968; West 1969: 23–34; Hardie 1986: 193–219; Mayer 1990; Farrell 1991: 305–307; Conte 1994a: 1–3; Gale 1994: 99–128, 2000: 235–238, 2004, and 2005; Piazzi 2008; and Roy 2013. For a contrary view, see Volk 2002: 69–118, especially 69–73.

2. The fact that there existed in antiquity a robust tradition of allegorical criticism of Homer as a poet of natural science bolsters this internal evidence. See Buffière 1956; Innes 1979; Murrin 1980; Lamberton 1986; Hardie 1986; Feeney 1991: 5–33; Farrell 1991: 326–332 and 2014: 78–83. On allegory in Lucretius, see Buglass 2019. On the importance of Ennius' Dream in Latin literary history, see Suerbaum 1968: 46–113; Hardie 1986: 76–83; Aicher 1989/90; and Barchiesi 1995.

3. On Lucretius' engagement with Ennius in the proem to the *DRN*, see esp. Harrison 2002; Goldberg 2005: 28–38; Taylor 2016 and 2020a: 79–82.

Epicurean universe through revisionary allusion to moments in the *Annales*. Not only do these allusions insinuate a cosmic background for Ennius' narrative of Roman history, they also function uniformly and implicitly to correct or criticize this Ennian cosmic perspective. Viewed this way, then, Lucretius' construction of a literary tradition that comprises poetry *de rerum natura* is primarily polemical, even as it incidentally gives Lucretius *qua* hexameter poet an illustrious pedigree.

Moreover, when Lucretius redefines the father of Latin epic as a natural philosopher, he does not just mark him—or mark *just* him—as an ideological opponent, but also sets his own Epicurean lineage against (what Lucretius implies is) Ennius' Empedoclean poetry. For implicated in Lucretius' claim to write *rerum natura* are not just Homer and Ennius, but also Empedocles—the natural philosopher who himself wrote a poem titled *On Nature* (*peri physeos*, a phrase that is effectively translated into Latin as *de rerum natura*). The connections with the cosmos compound when one considers that Ennius famously represented ur-poet Homer as himself expounding a possibly Pythagorean theory of metempsychosis, a theory that prior to Ennius found its most articulate poetic testimony in Empedocles.[4] Lucretius' inclusion of Empedocles further muddies the water: on the one hand, Empedocles forms a foundational component of what seems like a quite solid tradition in which heroic and philosophical epic coexist; but on the other, Empedocles is the poet-philosopher whose reception has generated some of the thorniest issues of generic divisions, given that Aristotle (*Poetics* 47b13–20) famously and problematically called into question the genre of his poetry, and proceeded to question whether he is even to be regarded as a poet at all. Another way of looking at the presence of epic elements in the *DRN*, however, is to recognize that Lucretius, rather than trying to epicize his own philosophical poem, may be suggesting that epic is already inherently philosophical. By associating the poetry of Homer, Ennius, and Empedocles with the *DRN*, then, Lucretius actively problematizes the genre of this tradition he has constructed and into which he positions his own work—or perhaps he exploits Aristotle in this regard.[5]

In any case, these poetic connections are strong, and they recur throughout the first book of the *DRN*, where Lucretius regularly uses verbal echoes to associate

4. Much recent work has focused on Lucretius' intense engagement with Empedocles throughout the *DRN*. Fundamental is the comprehensive study of Garani 2007, but see also Nethercut 2017: 85–87, with further bibliography.

5. This possibility is consonant with more recent scholarly trends in the interpretation of epic and didactic, going back at least to the work of Lamberton 1986 and Hardie 1986; cf. Innes 1979. Other important contributions in this respect are Clausen 1987: 29–32; Farrell 1991: esp. 326–332; Feeney 1991: 5–33; Nelis 1992; Hunter 1993: 175–179; and Gale 2005.

his activity (both poetic and philosophical) with that of his poetic-philosophical forebears. For example, Lucretius uses the verb *exponere* exclusively in Book 1 to describe the activity of the poets involved in the tradition *de rerum natura* he constructs in the proem (Ennius and Homer: 1.121; Empedocles: 1.732; and Lucretius: 1.833 and 1.946). This tradition is further developed in Book 1 when Lucretius speaks of Empedocles' *divinum pectus* (1.731), a phrase that previously only Ennius had used at *Ann.* 1.16 Sk, where it describes the prophetic abilities of Anchises.[6] Relatedly, Lucretius says that Ennius' Homer speaks of how metempsychosis involves divine agency (*pecudes alias divinitus insinuet se*, 1.116) in a line that scholars have suspected alludes to metaphysical descriptions both in Ennius' Dream (*Ann.* 8–10 Sk) and in Empedocles (*pecudes alias*=ἄλλων ἔθνεα θηρῶν, DK 26.4).[7] Lucretius later uses the same phrasing to explicitly reject Empedoclean pluralism (*divini pectoris eius*, 1.731; *divinitus*, 1.736). Finally, as Monica Gale has shown, Lucretius implies that Ennius is an Empedoclean poet with an etymological pun that hints at Empedocles' own name.[8]

By representing Ennius as an Empedoclean poet who writes poetry *de rerum natura* just as Homer had done before him, Lucretius encourages the reader to envisage a tradition of hexameter poetry on the subject of natural philosophy, a tradition that includes Homer, Ennius, *and* Empedocles, that takes shape in the pivotal moment of Ennius' Dream, and that culminates in Lucretius' *DRN*.[9] We do not know what Ennius may have actually had Homer say in the proem to the *Annales* beyond the subject of metempsychosis; this lacuna makes it difficult to extend these Empedoclean connections in Lucretius back to the *Annales* itself.[10] This evidence does show us, however, that for Lucretius, all of these poets in this tradition function primarily as natural philosophers. When Lucretius recurrently figures his universe as a direct response to the Ennian cosmos, philosophical

---

6. The only other occurrences of this phrase in Latin literature are found at Catullus 64.383 and Petronius 138.7.2, both of which have to do with prophetic utterances; cf Volk 2002: 106–107.

7. The Empedoclean context of this line-ending is a description of how the four roots exist and come together to form human beings and "the races of other animals" (cf. Wright 1995: 181–184 and Inwood 2001: 53). Bailey 1947: 619 adduces the Empedoclean line and the Dream of Homer from the *Annales* as parallels for Lucr. 1.116. See also, Farrell 1988.

8. Gale 2001b connects Lucretius' assessment of Ennius (*perenni fronde coronam... quae clara clueret*) with the component parts of Empedocles' name (ἔμπεδος + κλέος), suggesting that both poets win "un-ending fame" through their poetry.

9. Skutsch restores his fragment 5 to Homer's discourse in the Dream and suggests that the discourse included a description of the water cycle, in addition to the transmigration of souls. On Lucretius' possible engagement with this fragment, see chapter 4 (pp. 134–139).

10. On Empedocles in the *Annales*, see Norden 1916: 10–18 and Bignone 1929: esp. 10–11; less speculatively: Nelis 2000; Fabrizi 2020; and Glauthier 2020.

polemics are perhaps more involved than poetic polemics. Lucretius articulates a universe whose philosophical dynamics are anti-Ennian, precisely because they are emphatically Epicurean.

Ennius (and Homer and Parmenides and Empedocles) v. Epicurus

Lucretius activates these polemics earlier in the proem, when he constructs a generically complex literary ancestry for Epicurus, the "protagonist" of his poem, through allusion to Homer, Parmenides, Empedocles, and Ennius' *Annales* (*DRN* 1.62–79). In this episode, he describes Epicurus' "Triumph of the Mind," in which the Greek philosopher breaks through the borders of the cosmos with sure information about the nature of the universe.[11] He brings this information back to humanity as a weapon against religious superstition. Once again, the effect of such allusion is polemical: Lucretius repeatedly states that Epicurus' teaching is the only correct version of how the universe operates, and, as any reasonably well-informed reader will understand, Epicurus' philosophy is not fundamentally compatible with what we find in Homer, Parmenides, Empedocles, or Ennius. In addition to establishing a literary ancestry for Epicurus, Lucretius also constructs a convoluted and paradoxical temporal loophole, in which Ennius' poetry is presupposed in the description of Epicurus' philosophical activities. This anachronism becomes fundamental to the interpretation of the philosophical polemics in the *DRN*.

Conte was the first to draw attention to the Homeric valences of this passage, though he does not pursue the implications of the allusion. Nevertheless, he adduces verbal parallels between Epicurus' confrontation with *religio* and Glaucus' reproach against Hector for not having faced Ajax that suggest we are to understand a martial undertone for Lucretius' conception of philosophical history:[12]

> *primum Graius homo <u>mortalis tollere contra</u>*
> *est <u>oculos</u> **ausus** primusque* obsistere contra   (*Lucr. 1.66–67*)

> First a Greek man **dared** <u>to lift mortal eyes</u>
> and he was the first to stand against *(it)*

---

11. Generally, see Buchheit 1971, but see most recently O'Rourke 2020b: 108–110, 118; cf. Asmis 2020: 257–258; Kennedy 2020: 279–280; Shearin 2020: 146–148; and O'Keefe 2020: 187–188.

12. Originally, at Conte 1966: 356 n. 43, but more extensively at Conte 1994a: 1–3.

ἀλλὰ σύ γ᾽ Αἴαντος μεγαλήτορος οὐκ ἐτάλασσας
στήμεναι ἄντα κατ᾽ ὄσσε ἰδὼν δηΐων ἐν ἀϋτῇ　　(Il. *17.166–167*)

> But **you did not dare** to stand against *great-hearted Ajax,*
> <u>looking him in the eyes</u> *amidst the enemy's battle cry*

Here, we can see that Lucretius compares his Epicurus to Hector, the greatest Trojan hero, even though Epicurus is identified as a *Graius homo,* a phrase that Ennius uses in referring to Pyrrhus (*Ann.* 165 Sk), who in the *Annales* is frequently identified as a descendant of Achilles (167 and 197 Sk).[13] This allusion does more than just confirm that, for Lucretius, epic and philosophy are intertwined or indistinguishable; it also shows that Lucretius' Homer is usually Ennius' Homer. That Lucretius' allusion to Homer here is couched in Ennian language implies once again that Lucretius accesses Homer through the *Annales.* That the hero whom Hector does not dare face is Ajax, also a relative of Achilles, implies that Lucretius thus pits Trojan against Greek, recasting, as it were, the Iliadic confrontation between Hector and Achilles as the battle between Epicurus, the "hero" of his own poem, and *Religio.*[14]

More than just an Iliadic hero, however, Lucretius' Epicurus also would appear to be a sort of Homeric Odysseus, his achievement depicted as a journey of intellectual discovery (Lucr. 1.72–74):[15]

> *ergo vivida vis animi pervicit, et extra*
> *processit longe flammantia moenia mundi*
> *atque omne immensum peragravit mente animoque.*

> *And so, the lively force of his mind won out, and*
> *he advanced far beyond the fiery walls of the world*
> *and, in mind and heart, he wandered through the boundless entirety.*

The telos of Epicurus' journey is knowledge, specifically knowledge of how the universe works. The fact that he, just like Odysseus, is introduced without a name

---

13. On this phrase see now Taylor 2020a: 79–82, who focuses on the unease this juxtaposition should engender in the reader; cf. Harrison 2002: 9.

14. If we follow Fabrizi 2012: 125–150, Lucretius also thus conflates the dichotomy Ennius had set up between the Achillean Pyrrhus and the Greek (Odyssean) Romans; cf. Dench 2005: 58, Fantham 2006: 551–552.

15. Schrijvers 1970: 18–20; Hardie 1986: 194–195; Gale 1994: 119–120; Fowler 2000a; and Gale 2004: 56–57.

(*Graius homo*, Lucr. 1.66; ἄνδρα . . . πολύτροπον, *Odyssey* 1.1) further cements Epicurus' representation as an Odysseus figure.[16]

Additional complexity arises when we recall that Epicurus is again programmatically praised anonymously as the Greek man who first brought the illumination of atomic physics to humankind (in the proem to *DRN* 3, esp. *qui primus*, at 3.2). Here, however, in addition to alluding to Homer, Lucretius appears to be following Empedocles, who introduced his own latter-day Odysseus—Pythagoras—without a name in *On Nature* (DK 129):[17]

ἦν δέ τις ἐν κείνοισιν ἀνὴρ περιώσια εἰδώς,
ὃς δὴ μήκιστον πραπίδων ἐκτήσατο πλοῦτον,
παντοίων τε μάλιστα σοφῶν <τ'> ἐπιήρανος ἔργων·
ὁππότε γὰρ πάσηισιν ὀρέξαιτο πραπίδεσσιν,
ῥεῖ' ὅ γε τῶν ὄντων πάντων λεύσσεσκεν ἕκαστον
καί τε δέκ' ἀνθρώπων καί τ' εἴκοσιν αἰώνεσσιν.

*There was among them **a man of extraordinary knowledge***
who indeed possessed a vast wealth of understanding,
a master of all kinds of wise deeds.
For whenever he reached out with all his understanding,
he easily saw everything that exists,
over ten and twenty generations of men.

Both Lucretius and Empedocles leave their respective philosophical masters unnamed (*Graius homo*, 1.66 and *o Graiae gentis decus*, 3.3; ἀνὴρ περιώσια εἰδώς, DK 129.1).[18] All of this evidence implies that Lucretius forges a connection (by way of Ennius and Homer) between his own Epicurus and Empedocles' Pythagoras.

---

16. Shearin 2015: 118–124 argues that the anonymity of Epicurus functions as a sort of materialist antonomasia.

17. First pointed out by Furley 1970. See also Burkert 1972: 137; Hardie 1986: 39 n. 17; and Sedley 1998: 29–30; cf. Schiesaro 2014: 76–77.

18. Moreover, according to Skutsch 1985: 331, the Lucretian and Ennian periphrasis *Graius homo* likely ultimately derives from the Homeric Δάρδανος ἀνήρ, which occurs only twice in Homer (*Il.* 2.701 and 16.807); on one occasion this Homeric periphrasis describes Euphorbus (*Il.* 16.807). This is the same man whose soul passed into Pythagoras himself through metempsychosis, and we have evidence that Ennius cited this occurrence as parallel to the migration of Homer's soul into his own body (Tert. *de an.* 34.1 and *de resurr.* 1.5, Schol. Pers. 6.11, Ps.-Acro Hor. *Carm.* 1.28.10, and Lactantius Placidus on Stat. *Theb.* 3.484; cf. Burkert 1972: 137–145).

Furthermore, as I have noted, Empedocles apparently represented Pythagoras as an Odysseus figure who makes an intellectual journey.[19] In addition to the anonymity that Pythagoras and Odysseus share, one can adduce the similar form in which additional information about them is brought in (i.e., the relative clauses introduced by ὅς μάλα, *Od.* 1.1 and ὅς δὴ, Empedocles, DK 129.2; cf. *qui primus*, Lucr. 3.2), as well as the emphasis on the knowledge both of the characters possess (ἀνθρώπων ἴδεν ἄστεα καὶ νόον ἔγνω, *Od.* 1.2 and περιώσια εἰδώς, Empedocles, DK 129.1). In this respect, a further allusion may present itself, namely the opening of Parmenides' poem in which he describes himself as knowledgeable, referring to "(the highway which) carries a knowledgeable man throughout all the towns" (κατὰ πάντ᾽ ἄστη φέρει εἰδότα φῶτα, DK 1.3). Not only does Parmenides allude to the opening of the *Odyssey* here (e.g., he leaves himself unnamed; cf. κατὰ πάντ᾽ **ἄστη** εἰδότα φῶτα and πολλῶν ἀνθρώπων ἴδεν **ἄστεα** καὶ νόον ἔγνω, *Od.* 1.3), but it is probable that in describing Pythagoras as an ἀνὴρ περιώσια εἰδώς (DK 129.1), Empedocles alludes to Parmenides, himself an εἰδότα φῶτα (Parmenides, DK 1.3), in the spirit of rivalry.[20] Empedocles obviously is formally and generically indebted to Parmenides, but his Pythagoras—and hence, he himself—is philosophically superior to Parmenides. In any case, Lucretius' characterization of Epicurus as an anonymous Odysseus figure situates him at the head of this Odyssean strand of archaic philosophy.[21]

From this evidence, then, one could build a persuasive case that Lucretius represents Epicurus as an epic figure who exhibits better than Hector himself the characteristics of an Iliadic warrior as well as those of Odysseus, which are filtered through a tradition of philosophical poetry. Moreover, this connection may be amplified by the possibility that Lucretius characterizes Epicurus as an Odysseus figure, specifically because the anonymity that Epicurus shares with Odysseus is couched in language that resembles Ennius' introduction of Pyrrhus in *Annales* 6 (*Graius homo, DRN* 1.66=*Ann.* 165 Sk). Here once again the Iliadic and Odyssean aspects of Epicurus appear to combine, given that Ennius' Pyrrhus, initially

---

19. Diogenes Laertius (8.54) suggests that Parmenides is the ἀνὴρ περιώσια εἰδώς whom Empedocles here describes. Were this the case, the relevance of the journey in characterizing this man as a latter-day Odysseus would take on special significance, given the opening of Parmenides' poem.

20. Diels 1956 notes many motifs common to Parmenides' poem and the *Odyssey*, while subsequent scholars have expanded on his insights: Havelock 1958; Mourelatos 1970: 1–46, esp. 17–25; Hershbell 1972; and Gale 1994: 51–55. Given that there is some textual difficulty regarding the phrase κατὰ πάντ᾽ ἄστη in v. 3 of Parmenides (see Coxon 1986 ad loc.), it may be that the allusion to the proem to the *Odyssey* relies, as Gale 1994: 52 implies, on the parallel phrases εἰδότα φῶτα and ἄνδρα . . . πολύτροπον.

21. On Odysseus in ancient philosophical discourse, see Montiglio 2011.

presented anonymously (and so as an Odysseus type), is clearly aligned through genealogy and intertextuality with the Iliadic Achilles.[22] The phrase *Graius homo*, therefore, does similar work for Lucretius as the subsequent discussion of Ennius' Dream of Homer, by outlining a tradition of hexameter poetry; this outline works backward from Ennius' *Annales* to include Empedocles, Parmenides, and Homer. Lucretius' Epicurus—that is, the poetic creation who serves as a sort of protagonist in the *De Rerum Natura*—is figured as directly descended from, and effectively culminating, this tradition. After all, Epicurus was the first (*primum*, 1.66; *primus*, 1.66) to battle down *religio* and bring real knowledge of *rerum natura* to humanity. Obviously, Epicurus actually lived in an earlier period than Ennius, but, by the logic of Lucretius' allusive gestures here, the reader is meant to recognize that the Epicurus encountered in Lucretius' poem, whose cosmic vision Lucretius versifies, inhabits a post-Ennian poetic universe. This chronological paradox lies at the heart of Lucretius' engagement with Ennius, who appears to have written the *Annales* without reference to the Epicurean system that had been articulated almost a century before he composed his epic.

Having established Ennius and Epicurus as the culmination of two different knowledge systems, Lucretius later connects Epicurus' parallel achievements explicitly back to those of Ennius by referring to both as "the first" with respect to their poetic and philosophical achievements. In the only two instances of the collocation *qui primus* in Lucretius, Epicurus was the first to bring illumination to mankind regarding the workings of nature (*qui primus*, 3.2), just as Ennius was the first to bring the garland of the Muses to Italy (*qui primus*, 1.117).[23] When Lucretius then goes on to describe Ennius (via the Dream of Homer) as a poet who presents *rerum natura*, he implies that his reader should juxtapose Ennius with Epicurus and, hence, Ennian natural philosophy with Epicurean natural philosophy. With his principal players thus set against each other, Lucretius is able to undertake a sustained revision of the Ennian cosmos, in Epicurean terms. Whereas Lucretius represents the *Annales* as establishing a cosmos whose physical, temporal, and conceptual center was situated in Rome, Lucretius insists on an anti-Ennian vision: an unbounded universe decentered from Rome and a cosmos inevitably prone to dissolution.

---

22. For instance, he is pointedly referred to as *Aiacida* (*Ann.* 167 Sk; cf. *genus Aiacidarum*, *Ann.* 197 Sk), an overdetermined epithet for a man from Epirus. Achilles was frequently referred to in Greek literature as Αἰακίδης (e.g. *Il.* 2.860, 2.874, 9.184, 9.191, 10.402, 11.805, 18.222, 21.178, 23.28; *Od.* 11.471, 11.538; Aeschylus fr. 229.3 Mette; Euphorion fr. 40 Powell; Mnaseas fr. 7.6 Müller). Fabrizi 2012: 140–149 further complicates these polygeneric associations of Ennius' Pyrrhus via his literary ancestors in tragedy and Pindar.

23. See Nethercut 2020c for the natural philosophical valences of *qui primus* in the first line of Vergil's *Aeneid*.

The Cosmic Setting of the Annales *in Lucretius*

The Ennian vision of the cosmos, which begins with Homer's discourse in the Dream and carries on throughout the rest of the poem's narrative of Roman history, has now been described by Jackie Elliott. In juxtaposing the cosmological account of the origins of the universe with an account of Roman history in the *Annales*, Ennius, Elliott suggests, "implies, first, chronological continuity between the origins of the universe and Roman history," and that as a result, the reader infers a reciprocity "between the history of the cosmos given by 'Homer' and the history of Rome given in the poem's main narrative voice."[24] Lucretius, I will argue, alludes to many of these "Ennian cosmic moments" in the *Annales* only to undercut them. Remembering that Lucretius (as noted in the first section of this chapter) establishes a fundamental antithesis where to be Epicurean is to be anti-Ennian, Lucretius can further be seen to reject the cosmic significance of the Roman past as presented in the *Annales*, and thus emphasize an anti-Ennian cosmic perspective. For Lucretius, the cosmos is mortal; this fact necessarily makes it an unreliable or unstable backdrop against which to elevate specifically Roman events. Whereas Ennius imagines Roman history as universal history by providing an elevated, cosmic setting for the narrative he relates about the past, Lucretius alludes to this very procedure in the *Annales*, but redeploys it in his own poem so as to emphasize the inevitable destruction of the cosmos and all its components. Rome and its past, present, and future are insignificant in the infinite Epicurean universe.[25]

The cosmic framework of the *Annales* is especially prominent in lines such as *interea fugit albus iubar Hyperionis cursum* (*Ann.* 571 Sk) and *vertitur interea caelum cum ingentibus signis* (*Ann.* 205 Sk). Lines like these originate in Homer, even if Ennius is not necessarily alluding to any specific passage in Homer when he writes them. Whatever their original context may have been, one can draw the inference that lines like these serve a transitional function (*interea*), and therefore fill the narrative interstices of the *Annales* with a reminder of the great cosmic mechanism against which, and as part of which, the action of the poem takes

---

24. Quotations from first Elliott 2013: 246, then 255. Fundamental for all that follows, and in Elliott's analysis, is Hardie 1986.

25. This is in addition to other instances where Lucretius alludes to this cosmic setting in the *Annales* as part of the larger texture of his argument, but not necessarily in his arguments about the nature or disposition of the Epicurean universe (e.g. *Ann.* 414 Sk=Lucr. 5.1190; *Ann.* 419 Sk=Lucr. 2.331, 2.591, 3.272; *Ann.* 33 Sk=Lucr. 6.856; *Ann.* 160 Sk=Lucr. 5.986; *Ann.* 264 Sk=Lucr. 1.788; *Ann.* 428 Sk=Lucr. 4.1014; *Ann.* 545 Sk=Lucr. 5.521, 5.931, 5.1189; *Ann.* 205 Sk=Lucr. 5.915).

place.[26] Such a juxtaposition elevates and ennobles this narrative action, as "from the contemplation of a cosmic setting," according to Hardie, "the buoyant spirit derives pride in the immediate and particular object of interest, to which is transferred something of the grandeur of the setting; there is an irrational feeling that the whole exists only for the sake of the small part."[27] Where Ennius' cosmic setting was just that, in Lucretius the cosmic setting becomes, in effect, the narrative, insofar as Lucretius' primary aim is to give an Epicurean account of the universe and its operations.[28] That Lucretius collapses the Ennian setting into his own narrative makes sense in the context of my earlier suggestion that Lucretius presents Ennius as a poet whose subject matter is in direct competition with the ideas of Epicurus.

A note of caution is warranted at this point. While it is undoubtedly clear that the fragments of the *Annales* contain such cosmic moments of which Jackie Elliott makes very much, it is not at all clear that lines such as the ones I have been discussing represent anything more than decorative or ornamental transitions to mark the temporal movement in the *Annales*. In other words, it is not clear that these lines would have had any wider philosophical or thematic significance, especially as most of them are presented to us removed from their original context in the *Annales*. Moreover, we have some positive indication in the fragments that such lines precisely were poetic decorations. Take, for example, the line *interea sol albus recessit in infera noctis* (*Ann.* 84 Sk). In this case, we do have a wider context, as this line is used to describe the narrowest possible narrative interstice, namely the passage of time as Romulus and Remus wait on their respective hills watching for birds. This line turns out to be a fanciful way of saying, in effect, "meanwhile, the sun (or possibly the moon?) set."[29] Although it is striking that such lines regularly establish such transitions by appealing to the wider cosmic

26. We know from Macrobius that *Ann.* 205 Sk occurred in *Annales* 6, and so would have served as a transitional device in Ennius' account of the war with Pyrrhus. Priscian quotes *Ann.* 571 Sk without any book ascription, though he does say it came from the *Annales*.

27. Hardie 1986: 68; cf. Elliott 2013: 255, who suggests that "these lines set the narrative in its fullest context, dignifying the contents and lending them grandeur, in a manner familiar to us from the works of Homer and Vergil."

28. On Lucretian "narrative," see Gale 2004.

29. I thank Sander Goldberg for raising this possibility for me. If we really should not view lines like these as any more than poetic decorations, we have abundant examples of this sort of feature also in Ennian tragedy. So, e.g., *Iphigeneia* fr. 83 Manuwald (*quid noctis videtur? in altisono / caeli clipeo temo superat / stellas sublimen agens etiam / atque etiam noctis iter*) is adduced by Varro (*Ling.* 7.73) with the observation *hic* [Ennius] *multam noctem ostendere volt a temonis motu*. In other words, this passage is just an elaborate way to say "it was late at night."

apparatus, we should resist claiming more about the original function of such lines in the *Annales* than the evidence permits.

When it comes to Lucretius, however, he regularly reads these lines as part of a comprehensive cosmic vision in the *Annales*, regardless of what original function they may have served in Ennius' epic. Such a reading in Lucretius, of course, is tendentious, because he alludes to these lines as part of his own corrective explanation of the Epicurean universe. So, in what follows, I will be focusing on Lucretius' reading of the Ennian cosmos in the *Annales*, rather than on what Ennius actually wrote about the cosmos in the *Annales*. And I note here in passing that Lucretius' reading of Ennius' cosmos corroborates what Hardie and now Elliott may be turning into a new orthodoxy.

We can see Lucretius appropriating the Ennian cosmos most explicitly when he adduces the traditional cosmic triad, well known in the hexameter tradition, of earth, sea, and heaven.[30] We find this cosmic structure established at *Ann.* 555–556 Sk:

> *qui fulmine claro*
> *omnia per sonitus arcet, terram mare caelum*

> *Who, with brilliant lightning,*
> *contains everything—earth, sea, sky—through the sound*

Ennius' structuring of the cosmos in the *Annales* in this way likely would have lent his poem the cosmological authority that came with this tradition, an authority that Lucretius, it would seem, was all too willing to grant him, if only for the purpose of then tearing it down.[31] Ps.-Probus, who preserves this fragment for us, explicitly cites Lucretius for this tripartite view of cosmic origins (*plane trinam esse mundi originem . . . Lucretius confitetur*, Verg. *Ecl.* 6.31), and even implies an original cosmogonical setting for this fragment in the *Annales*, offering as evidence Lucr. 5.92–96:

> *principio maria ac terras caelumque tuere;*
> *quorum naturam triplicem, tria corpora, Memmi,*
> *tris species tam dissimilis, tria talia texta,*
> *una dies dabit exitio, multosque per annos*
> *sustentata ruet moles et machina mundi.*

---

30. See Elliott 2013: 260–261.

31. Hardie 1986: esp. 313–325.

> *First look upon seas and lands and sky*
> *the threefold nature of these, their three bodies, Memmius*
> *their three forms so different, their three textures, each in its kind,*
> *one single day will send to destruction, and held up through the many years,*
> *the massive form and apparatus of the world will collapse headlong.*

These lines assuredly allude to the Ennian conception of cosmic order, as they correspond in terms of subject, and perhaps they even allude to the terms Ennius uses specifically (*terram mare caelum=maria ac terras caelumque*). These Lucretian lines also contain many Ennian stylistic elements (e.g., the hyper-alliteration of the same letter in *tria talia texta* and *moles et machina mundi*; cf. *machina multa minax minitatur maxima muris*, *Ann.* 620 Sk). Moreover, the line-ending *per annos* (5.93) may serve as a reflexive annotation of *Ennius perennis* and his *Annales*.[32] For my immediate purposes, I want to stress that this allusion to the Ennian cosmos would appear to be polemical. Lucretius adduces this tripartite framework, the *machina mundi*, which he takes over specifically from the *Annales*, only to emphasize its impermanence. Such emphasis would also seem to be the point of the allusion to the famous pun of *Ennius perennis* in Lucretius' line-ending *per annos*: by actively breaking down the elements of the adjective *perennis* and separating it into its component parts, Lucretius provides the reader with an object lesson in cosmic destruction, performed at the level of atoms and "atomology." We witness Lucretius actively dismantling the permanence of the Ennian cosmos with his verses.[33]

This kind of engagement with the mechanism of cosmic framing in the *Annales* appears elsewhere in the *DRN*, sometimes with interesting side effects. For example, in his frequent description of the sun as a "wheel" (*rota solis*), Lucretius brings forward the Ennian framework to describe in Epicurean terms the atomic tempest that must have given rise to the cosmos as Ennius describes it in the *Annales*; in other words, Lucretius alludes to a fixture in the Ennian cosmos as part of his own cosmology, rewriting the cosmic apparatus he reads in the *Annales* in Epicurean terms. The commentators remind us that, in Greek,

---

32. See, Lucr. 1.118, along with Gale 2001b; cf. Feeney 1999.

33. For more examples of Lucretius' use of this sort of verbal deconstruction to reinforce the meaning in his lines, see Hinds 1987 and P. Fowler 1997: 135; more generally, see Friedländer 1941. Of course, these are much more violent linguistic disruptions than *perennis→per annos*, but the point remains that Lucretius uses this sort of linguistic procedure to mirror the content of his poem. For a more speculative example of this sort of polemical engagement with the Ennian cosmos, see 5.560 with *Ann.* 415–416 Sk.

ἡλίου κύκλος belongs to pre-Socratic cosmological speculations, and it is likely
that Ennius develops them in lines such as this (*Ann.* 572 Sk):[34]

> *inde patefecit radiis* rota candida *caelum*

> *thereupon* the shining white wheel *opened the sky with its beams*

This fragment has been connected to a number of Lucretian passages that describe
the sun bringing daylight into the heavens. Most explicitly, we can compare some
lines from Lucretius' account of cosmology in *DRN* 5 that describe the origins of
the heavenly bodies (Lucr. 5.432–442):

> *hic neque tum* solis rota *cerni* lumine largo
> *altivolans poterat nec magni siderà mundi*
> *nec mare nec* caelum *nec denique terra nec aer*
> *nec similis nostris rebus res ulla videri*
> *sed nova tempestas quaedam molesque coorta*
> *omne genus de principiis, discordia quorum*
> *intervalla vias connexus pondera plagas*
> *concursus motus turbabat proelia miscens,*
> *propter dissimilis formas variasque figuras*
> *quod non omnia sic poterant coniuncta manere*
> *nec motus inter sese dare* convenientis.

> *At this point in time, neither could the* wheel of the sun *be seen,*
> *flying on high* with abundant light, *nor the stars of the huge world,*
> *nor the sea, nor the* sky, *nor finally the earth nor air*
> *nor anything at all like the things we know,*
> *but only a kind of new storm, a mass gathered together,*
> *every kind of thing made of first-beginnings, whose discord*
> *was throwing into confusion interspaces, pathways, interlacings,*
>   *weights, blows,*
> *comings-together, and movements, waging war*
> *because, on account of their different forms and diverse shapes,*
> *all things were not able to remain joined, as they are now,*
> *nor were they able to give amongst themselves harmonious motions.*

---

34. Skutsch 1985: 712; Flores et al. 2009: 395. It also belongs to tragedy: Aesch. *PV* 91; *Pers.*
504; Soph. *Ant.* 416.

These lines allude not only to Ennius' line on the sun's wheel bringing the dawn, but also feature an Ennian pentasyllabic line-ending at Lucr. 5.442. Here again, Lucretius alludes to a description of the cosmos in the *Annales* in order to clarify the cosmology it implies, and in this case he describes a time *before* the Ennian line happens, a time filled with the incessant movement of the atoms, which are figured as a storm (*nova tempestas*). This allusion, then, functions almost archaeologically: Lucretius alludes to what he finds in Ennius, so that he can provide a proper Epicurean account of what came before the Ennian cosmos. The cosmic setting in the *Annales* may magnify the narrative of Roman history, but in Lucretius it exists primarily as a foil for *Epicurean* cosmology (which is emphatically anti-Ennian). Lucretius shows his reader what is logically and temporally anterior to any cosmic setting in Ennius.[35]

Nowhere is the explanatory inadequacy of Ennius' cosmic backdrop highlighted more than in *DRN* 6, where Lucretius explains why lightning occurs most frequently in the autumn and the spring (Lucr. 6.357–363):

> *autumnoque magis stellis fulgentibus apta*
> *concutitur caeli domus undique totaque tellus*
> *et cum tempora se veris florentia pandunt.*
> *frigore enim desunt ignes, ventique calore*
> *deficiunt neque sunt tam denso corpore nubes.*
> *interutrasque igitur cum caeli tempora constant,*
> *tum variae causae concurrunt fulminis omnes.*

> *And more in autumn is the house of heaven, fitted with shining stars,*
> *shaken on all sides, and the whole earth*
> *and again when the flowery season of spring spreads itself open.*
> *For in the cold fires are lacking, and in the heat winds fail,*
> *nor are there clouds of so dense a body.*
> *Therefore, when the season of heaven stands between these two,*
> *then do all the diverse causes of lightning run together.*

---

35. Skutsch 1985: 712 also cites Lucr. 5.564 (*solis maior rota*) as a parallel for *Ann.* 572 Sk, while Flores et al. 2009: 394 add Lucr. 5.659 (*caelum radiis*), Lucr. 1.10 (*species patefactast verna diei*), and Lucr. 5.683 (*imparibus currens anfractibus aetheris oras*). The fact that Lucretius returns to this fragment of the *Annales* so frequently in the *DRN* in his descriptions of the cosmos and its workings is a testament to how important the Ennian cosmic setting is to Lucretius' Epicurean account of the cosmos, even as it underscores how polemical Lucretius' response is to what he finds in the *Annales*.

These lines contain allusions to multiple fragments of Ennius (*Ann.* 27, 45, 348, 586 Sk):

> *qui caelum versat* stellis fulgentibus aptum
> *caelum prospexit* stellis fulgentibus aptum
> *hinc nox processit* stellis ardentibus apta

> *he who twists the sky,* fitted with shining stars
> *he looked at the sky,* fitted with shining stars
> *night advanced from here,* fitted with burning stars

> *divom* domus, *altisonum* cael

> The house *of the gods, the high-sounding* sky

Lucretius' *stellis fulgentibus apta* conflates three different Ennian line-endings (of *Ann.* 27, 145, 348 Sk). These lines served Lucretius well in his engagement with whatever cosmic orientation he reads into the *Annales*. A cosmic focus is especially prominent in these lines, and it is no surprise that these are the very fragments that Elliott adduces to demonstrate how Ennius stakes "a serious claim to transmit crucial knowledge about the way the world works."[36] Jackson (in Flores et al. 2006) connects these fragments to Empedocles (πύρινα [sc. εἶναι τὰ ἄστρα] ἐκ τοῦ πυρώδους, A53), who follows Anaximenes (ὁμοίως δὲ καὶ ἥλιον καὶ σελήνην καὶ τὰ ἄλλα ἄστρα πάντα πύρινα ὄντα, 13A7.4, and πυρίνην μὲν τὴν φύσιν τῶν ἄστρων, 14); in the Hellenistic period, these cosmological speculations found their way into Aratus (ἔσχατος ἀστηρ/ . . . αἰθομένης γένυος, *Phaen.* 211–212, and ὑπ' αἰθομένῳ κέντρῳ . . . μεγάλοιο/Σκορπίου, *Phaen.* 402–403).[37] The line-endings *stellis fulgentibus aptum* and *stellis ardentibus apta* ultimately derive from the Homeric formulae εἰς οὐρανὸν ἀστερόεντα (*Il.* 15.37, 19.128; *Od.* 9.527, 11.17, 12.380; cf. Skutsch 1985: 301), καὶ οὐρανῷ ἀστερόεντι (*Il.* 4.44; cf. Flores et al. 2006: 257), and καὶ οὐρανοῦ ἀστερόεντος (*Il.* 5.769, 6.108, 8.46, 19.130; *Od.* 20.113; cf. Flores et al. 2006: 257).[38] All of these connections led Jackie Elliott to suggest that we can trace in this related collection of Ennian fragments a developed tradition of hexameter poetry that contains cosmological speculation. Ennius places himself in this tradition, while at the

---

36. Elliott 2013: 262.

37. Flores et al. 2006: 257–258.

38. It is intriguing that from the fragments available, Ennius seems to imitate the fact that this formula exists in three Homeric variants.

same time offering his own innovation; as Elliott writes, "what was above all new in Ennius' vision is that the heavenly bodies, as described in language that carried all the authority of the various Greek hexametric traditions of 'scientific'-*cum*-heroic poetry behind it, now presided over action unambiguously centered at Rome."[39]

This Lucretian passage reads such cosmic overtones into the *Annales* while simultaneously implying a correction of any Ennian cosmic perspective by juxtaposing the line-ending *stellis fulgentibus apta* with the phrase *caeli domus*.[40] Here Lucretius combines two allusions to Ennius' *Annales*.[41] This section appears even more polemical—hostile, even—when one considers its context: these lines occur in the extended section of *DRN* 6 where Lucretius emphasizes the importance of giving an Epicurean explanation for lightning, since, more than any other natural phenomenon, humans use lightning as justification for their misguided understanding of the cosmos and the gods (Lucr. 6.68–91). By mentioning the gods explicitly, Lucretius opens up the possibility that this allusion seeks to correct *Ann.* 586 Sk, where Ennius implies a (causal?) connection between the heavenly reverberations from natural phenomena (*altisonum cael*) and the gods' presence (*divom domus*).

This is not the only place where Lucretius' correction of Ennian "cosmology" can be found in the context of Epicurean "atheism." Earlier, in Book 5, the poet excoriates humans for their tendency to ascribe natural phenomena to the gods' actions when such phenomena all have perfectly reasonable, Epicurean explanations (Lucr. 5.1198–1210):

> *nec pietas ullast velatum saepe videri*
> *vertier ad lapidem atque omnis accedere ad aras*
> *nec procumbere humi prostratum et pandere palmas*
> *ante deum delubra, nec aras sanguine multo*
> *spargere quadrupedum, nec votis nectere vota*
> *sed mage placata posse omnia mente tueri.*
> *nam cum suspicimus magni caelestia mundi*
> *templa super stellisque micantibus aethera fixum,*
> *et venit in mentem solis lunaeque viarum*

---

39. Elliott 2013: 262; Elliott's argument here is analogous to the observation at Feeney 1991: 127–128 about the importance of Ennius making the supreme being of the Greek pantheon, who is politically neutral, into the chief and very partisan divinity of the Roman state.

40. On domestic metaphors for the sky in Greek poetry with respect to their use in Ennius, see Skutsch 1985: 203. The metaphor of the *caeli domus* does not appear in Latin literature before Lucretius except in Ennius; cf. Lucr. 2.1110 and Cic. *Tusc.* 1.24.12, 1.51.7; *Nat. D.* 2.90.8–9.

41. This allusion is further corroborated by the fact that the subject of the Lucretian passage may also imply the Ennian adjective *altisonum*.

tunc aliis oppressa malis in pectora cura
illa quoque expergefactum caput erigere infit,
ne quae forte deum nobis inmensa potestas
sit, vario motu quae *candida* sidera verset.

Nor is it piety at all to be seen often with covered head
turning towards a stone and to approach every altar
nor to lie prostrate on the ground and to stretch out one's palms
before the shrines of the gods nor to sprinkle the altars with abundant blood
of beasts nor to link vows with vows
but rather to be able to contemplate all things with a calmed mind.
For indeed when we look up at the heavenly tracts of the great world,
and the ether above fitted with twinkling stars,
and it comes to our mind to think of the wanderings of the sun and moon,
then into our breasts weighed down by other evils that concern
also begins to raise its wakened head,
that there may be by chance some boundless power of the gods over us,
which twists *about the shining white* stars *in their diverse motions.*

This passage shares not only a common theme, but also much common phrasing, with 6.357–363. At 5.1198–1210 Lucretius identifies the widespread misconception that he actively works to correct at 6.357–363, then links the two passages verbally (*stellisque micantibus . . . fixum*, Lucr. 5.1205=*stellis fulgentibus apta*, Lucr. 6.356), using phrasing that alludes directly back to *Ann.* 27 Sk (*stellisque micantibus . . . fixum*, Lucr. 5.1205=*stellis fulgentibus aptum*, and *quae . . . sidera verset*, Lucr. 5.1210=*qui caelum versat*). Lucretius' explicit rejection of the notion of divine activity in our world includes many allusions to the *Annales* in such a way as to suggest that when he rejects divine activity he also rejects Ennius' ideas.

We have already seen that Ennius serves Lucretius as a good source for this misguided notion of the gods, as in *Ann.* 586 Sk, where thunder and divine activity share an implicit association. The divine in Ennius is even further connected to material reality in *Ann.* 51 Sk (*cenacula maxuma caeli*), which presents the abode of the gods in the sky as analogous to a human house.[42] Similarly, Lucretius literalizes

42. Tertullian who gives us this fragment, mockingly connects it to the end of *Iliad* 1. Certainly Lucilius' adaptation of the gods' assembly could be seen to mock metaphors like this in Ennius, and the use of *cenaculum* at Plautus, *Amph.* 863 further emphasizes the comedic valences of this metaphor in Ennius. Skutsch 1985: 203 lists Hor. *Sat.* 1.5.103 and Ov. *Met.* 1.176 as similar metaphors that figure heaven as a human habitation. On this fragment as part of the *Annales'* cosmic setting, see Elliott 2013: 258.

Ennius' metaphor of the *caeli templa* (e.g., *quamquam multa manus ad caeli caerula templa, Ann.* 48 Sk) in order to correct the Ennian perspective on divinity. Lucretius says that early humans decided that the gods lived in the sky (*in caeloque deum sedis et templa locarunt*, 5.1188), and so established temples to them on earth (*qui delubra deum nova toto suscitat orbi*, 5.1166). Of course, this Ennian idea of *templa* in the sky also implies that there are divine residences in the sky, so one major effect of Lucretius' allusion is to explain in Epicurean terms how misunderstandings about the gods come to appear in Ennius' poem. Lucretius thus excavates Ennius' metaphor for the ultimate source of a harmful idea that Epicurean philosophy aims to correct. Lucretius later, in *DRN* 6, mocks this notion, perhaps even alluding to this metaphor specifically, when he disproves the idea that it is Jupiter, and not nature, who sends lightning. There, Lucretius cites the many instances of lightning-struck temples on earth (*sancta deum delubra*, Lucr. 6.417) asking why Jupiter destroys his own house (*suasque / discutit infesto praeclaras fulmine sedes*, Lucr. 6.417–418), as if to underscore the absurdity of the Ennian notion that the gods inhabit a house. Similarly, where Ennius attributes the cause of favorable weather to Jupiter smiling (*Iuppiter hic risit* **tempestates***que serenae / * **riserunt** *omnes risu Iovis omnipotentis, Ann.* 445–446 Sk), Lucretius removes the divine activity from his allusive treatment of this passage. His unmistakable allusion to this Ennian fragment retains the metaphor of "smiling weather," but removes any mention of Jupiter (*praesertim cum* **tempestas ridebat** *et anni / tempora pinguebant viridantis floribus herbas*, 5.1395– 1396; cf. *praesertim cum* **tempestas adridet** *et anni / tempora*, 2.32–33). Lucretius engages Ennius this way because the notion that the gods have any role in the workings of nature is fundamentally at odds with the Epicurean perspective.

Another example of how Lucretius uses the divine machinery from the *Annales* as a foil for his own Epicurean cosmos comes from the discussion of the origin of species (*nam neque* **de caelo** *cecidisse animalia possunt / nec terrestria de salsis exisse lacunis*, Lucr. 5.793–794), where, according to Lucretius, it is impossible for animals simply to fall *de caelo*. Here Lucretius alludes to at least two places in the *Annales* where this phrase is used to describe prodigies and omens, divine acts which in the Ennian narrative are regularly interpreted as literally deriving from the gods. We can compare to these lines a passage of Ennius that occurs in the context of the *auspicium* fragment in *Annales* 1 (*cedunt* **de caelo** *ter quattuor corpora sancta / avium, Ann.* 88–89 Sk), as well as another, definitely ascribed to *Annales* 3, but whose original narrative context is unclear (*olli* **de caelo** *laevom dedit inclutus signum, Ann.* 146 Sk).[43] Both of these Ennian fragments imply the providential

---

43. Skutsch 1985 ad loc. suggests that this fragment concerns the flames above Servius Tullius' head (followed by Flores et al. 2002: 88), although he notes that most editors, beginning with Colonna, suggest that it describes the eagle that takes Tarquin's hat. Additionally, we can note

activity of the gods in the universe and affirm an interactive relationship between the gods and humans, including one that involved the founding of Rome itself. Lucretius, by contrast, rejects with the same phrase the idea that any providential hand played a role in the origin of animal life on earth. But this rejection may go further, as, to the extent that Rome's foundation may also be implicated, Lucretius may be offering a more pointed refutation of Ennius' presentation of the role of the gods in the expansion of Roman hegemony. In effect, this allusion could encourage a reader to conclude that, given that the gods had nothing to do with the creation of animal species, surely they would not worry themselves over the specific events that pepper the history of one group of one single species.

I have been arguing in this section that Lucretius alludes to fragments of the *Annales* both in order to imply a cosmic framework in Ennius' epic and in order to correct the assumptions implicit in the universalizing perspective implied by this cosmic framework. This argument is supported by the fact that Lucretius singles out the cosmic frame in Ennius' *Annales* as the poetic mechanism through which he generalizes about humans' misunderstanding of cosmic phenomena. This suggests that, for Lucretius, what he reads into the *Annales* functions as the perfect instantiation of a more general problem he aims to address, and the cosmic backdrop of the *Annales* thus serves as the lens through which he articulates his argument. This lens gains even more focus when Lucretius sets his gaze upon Roman hegemony.

The Roman Cosmos of the Annales *in Lucretius*

A fundamental part of the universalizing aspect of the *Annales* is that Ennius regularly associates Rome and its citizens with elements of the cosmos itself. This procedure effectively forges an identity between Rome and the wider cosmos, and Rome becomes easily, in some sense, coextensive with the cosmos.[44] For example, Festus provides us with *Ann.* 127 Sk (*Cael>i caerula prata*) specifically in order to highlight Ennius' verbal play between the Caelian Hill and the tracts of heaven. Part of Rome becomes, then, literally identical with a fixture of the cosmos, and we can see in this pun how Ennius maps Rome through synecdoche onto the cosmic mechanism featured in the *Annales*.[45]

---

that Lucretius' *salsis . . . lacunis*, would appear to allude to an Ennian use of the adjective *salsus, -a, -um* (cf. *Ann.* 370 Sk, with commentary ad loc.).

44. On this phenomenon in the *Annales*, see Elliott 2013: 257–260 and Feeney 2016: 186–187.

45. It is worth emphasizing that even though Ennius was punning, in whatever spirit, on *caelum* and *Caelius mons*, most later poets (e.g. Ovid, *Met.* 14.814) respond primarily to *Ann.* 54–55.

This connection between Rome and the cosmos is underscored by the many similes that unite Ennius' actors with the cosmos. Most directly, Ennius connects the potential of Roman hegemony with the unbounded expansion of the heaven above (*fortis Romani sunt quamquam caelus profundus, Ann.* 559 Sk, "The Romans are as brave as the heaven is high").[46] Similarly, more traditional epic similes connect Roman soldiers with natural phenomena (e.g. *Ann.* 266, 432–434 Sk). Lucretius consistently responds to this type of simile by inverting its terms.[47] For example, Ennius follows the Homeric precedent of comparing activity on the battlefield to the various meteorological elements—such as when he compares the barrage of missiles sent by the Istrians against a Roman tribune to a rainstorm (***undique conveniunt*** *velut imber tela tribuno, Ann.* 391 Sk, "from all sides the missiles converge like a rainstorm on the tribune"). Lucretius instead uses the same collocation (*convenere undique*) to describe the action of rain itself (Lucr. 6.506–512):

> *consimili ratione ex omnibus amnibus umor*
> *tollitur in nubis. quo cum bene semina aquarum*
> *multa modis multis* convenere undique *adaucta*
> *confertae nubes imbris demittere certant*
> *dupliciter; nam vis venti contrudit, et ipsa*
> *copia nimborum turba maiore coacta*
> *urget et e supero premit ac facit effluere imbris.*

> In like manner moisture from all rivers
> is raised to the clouds. And when many seeds of waters
> in many ways have duly come together there, increased from all areas,
> the packed clouds battle to let out their showers
> for two reasons; for the violence of the wind pushes it on and
> the very forces of clouds, driven together in a greater group,
> presses on it and weighs it down from above and makes the showers flow out.

This collocation is rare in Latin literature before Lucretius, and only appears in poetry in this fragment of Ennius' *Annales* (cf. Lucr. 5.600).[48] We find

---

46. Elliott 2013: 257 writes, "this line expresses the limitlessness of Rome's capacity to achieve dominion."

47. On similes in Lucretius, see Townend 1965: 95–114; West 1969: 74–78 and 1970; Pasoli 1970: 367–386; Leen 1984; Hardie 1986: 219–223; Schiesaro 1990; Gale 1991: 416–417 and 1994: 63–65.

48. In prose the collocation appears only rarely, and most of these instances come after Lucretius (Cic. *Verr.* 1.1.54.6, *Luc.* 144.6, *ad Att.* 4.1.4.13; Caes. *BG* 2.10.4.8, 4.27.7.2, 5.17.5.2, 6.34.9.1,

other Ennianisms in this Lucretian passage, as well. For example, *tollitur in nubis* appropriates the Ennian opening *tollitur in caelum* (*Ann.* 428 Sk), the only two pre-Vergilian instances of this collocation,[49] and we also find hyper-alliteration of the sort that is a marker of Ennianism in Lucretius (*multa modis multis*). Given these features, then, it would appear likely that Lucretius wants his reader to recognize an allusion to the *Annales*. Unlike Ennius, however, who had compared human military action to a storm, Lucretius compares the *forces of nature* to a sort of battle, as the activity of the winds and rains is described in language taken from the military lexicon. The clouds battle (*certant*) to release the water inside of them, while the forces of the clouds (*nimborum copia*) press on from above (*urget et e supero premit*; cf. in an explicitly military context, *scandit et instat*, Lucr. 3.651). Lucretius thus inverts the simile he finds in the *Annales*, upturning the association Ennius had made between the actions of his narrative and the wider cosmos.[50] By retaining the image of a cosmic battle, Lucretius thus positions the forces of nature as superior to those of Ennius' humans. In this way, Lucretius can be seen to detach from the cosmos the Roman elements with which Ennius had imbued it and lay bare the Epicurean reality that the cosmos is not "Roman," despite what Ennius implies with his similes.

Lucretius' rejection of Ennius' Romanized cosmos is on display at other points, as in his description of Epicurus' philosophical triumph in the proem to the *DRN*. There, Lucretius combines both generally Roman and specifically Ennian elements in such a way as to acknowledge that the cosmos is "Roman" according to the model he reads into the *Annales*. At the same time Lucretius also appears to reject the validity of this implied Ennian perspective. For example, Lucretius presents Epicurus as a general who bursts through the *moenia mundi* (1.73) to survey the great infinity (*omne immensum*, Lucr. 1.74) of the universe. Kennedy highlights the fact that this triumph is presented in specifically Roman terms, with Epicurus presented as "a Roman general celebrating a formal

---

7.63.6.1, and *BC* 3.47.3.4). Skutsch 1985: 560 dismisses allusion here because the collocation is "so easy and natural that Ennian influence cannot be postulated." Skutsch is likely influenced by the fact that Vergil deploys the phrase with some frequency (Verg. *Aen.* 2.799, 4.417, 5.293, 9.720), but, actually, the collocation is not common outside of Vergil in post-Lucretian poetry, occurring only at Silius Italicus, *Pun.* 12.485.

49. Elliott 2013: 257 has connected this line to Ennius' cosmic apparatus in the *Annales*.

50. This move is exactly analogous to when Vergil recycles elements from the *Georgics* into similes in the *Aeneid* (see West 1969; Ross 1987: 51; Farrell 1991: 211–213, 240–253). On the tendency in Lucretius to use similes to represent the wider truth of Epicurean physics, see Hardie 1986: 221.

triumph."[51] As we have seen, however, Epicurus is also associated with Ennius' Pyrrhus by virtue of the phrase *Graius homo* (1.66=*Ann.* 165 Sk). In this passage, therefore, Lucretius underscores the infinity of the universe (*omne immensum*) by repurposing language from the *Annales* (*Graius homo*).

This passage in the proem opens up a more sustained philosophical rebuttal of the Ennian perspective of a cosmos centered in Rome. Jackie Elliott has argued persuasively that Ennius regards Rome as the center of things, and in some sense he does.[52] But to be clear, as Ennius does not actually say in the fragments of the *Annales* that the universe has a center located in Rome, we should not treat Elliott's argument as a fact, even as her reading does provide a useful way to conceive of the conceptual world of the *Annales* in spatial terms. But this conceptual world of the *Annales* is fundamentally un-Epicurean. Centers and midpoints, after all, are not important concepts in Lucretius' conception of the universe, as infinity precludes the notion of centrism.[53] Rather, since the universe is boundless for Lucretius, the concept of a middle actually has no relevance.[54] But Lucretius does use this Ennian conception as a foil in his own most explicit articulation of the infinite universe (Lucr. 1.958–1117).[55] There Lucretius argues that the universe is absolutely without limit, an idea that is fundamentally oppositional to one centered in Rome, because an infinite universe cannot have a center. In fact, Lucretius argues that, if there were a center to the universe, and if all things pressed toward this center, cataclysm would ensue. Time and again, Lucretius seems to distance his own exposition of universal infinity from the conceptual point of reference

---

51. Kennedy 2013: 57. See now Taylor 2020a: 79–82, with further bibliography.

52. Elliott 2013: 252–263.

53. For an example of this lack of interest, note how cagy Lucretius is regarding the shape of the *orbis terrarum* and of our world, the *mundus*, such that we cannot assume that he thinks that the earth is spherical or that it is situated at the center of the *mundus*, as it does in the Aristotelian or Eratosthenic conception. Bakker 2016: 162–254 has, however, conclusively shown that Lucretius does not conceive of the earth as flat. In general, see Shearin 2019.

54. The closest Lucretius ever comes to putting anything in the middle of anything is when he complains that the temperate zones occupy so small a section of the earth at 5.195–234 (see Bakker 2016: 180–254, esp. 220–223), and, in the context of his cosmogony, he seems to imply a conception of planet earth at the center of the cosmos (5.534–538), when actually he is only speaking of earth-qua-soil (**terraque ut in media mundi regione quiescat**, 5.534), and, besides, this would appear specifically to counter Empedocles' ideas about the origin of the cosmos. In other words, *terra* in that passage does not mean "the Earth," but rather the Empedoclean element "earth" (cf. Nethercut 2017: 98–100).

55. On Epicurean infinity, see the primary texts at Long and Sedley 1987: 1.44–46; Morenval 2017; Bakker 2018; and O'Rourke 2020b.

provided by the idea of centrism, and he regularly couches this procedure in identifiably Ennian language.[56]

If Ennius had conceived of the cosmos as centered in the city of Rome, Lucretius conceptualizes our world itself as a city via the metaphor of the *moenia mundi*.[57] Scholars have often remarked on the way in which Lucretius' conceptualization of the cosmos and its contours reflects certain aspects of cities.[58] Elsewhere in the *DRN*, we find *machina mundi* (5.96), *regio mundi* (5.534), and the Lucretian metaphors of *fines* and *alte terminus haerens* (1.75–77, 594–596, 670–674, 792–797, 3.519–524); all of these imply the urban aspects of the cosmos.[59] Outside of Lucretius, *moenia* is almost always used to describe the defensive fortifications that surround a city, and the noun can even denote the city itself.[60] In the extant fragments of the *Annales*, *moenia* is used only once, and there it describes the walls of Rome in a fragment that specifically alludes to the one time Rome's walls were breached (*Ann.* 227–228 Sk):

> qua Galli furtim noctu summa arcis adorti
> moenia *concubia vigilesque repente cruentat*

> *When the Gauls attacked in secret the highest walls of the citadel*
> *in the middle of the night and slaughtered the guards suddenly*

In the Lucretian passage about Epicurus' "Triumph of the Mind," Epicurus is presented, in Ennian language (*Graius homo*), as a Roman general who breaks

---

56. One wants to avoid circular argumentation, but a case could be made that Lucretius' opposition to Ennius' perspective in these passages tends to confirm Elliott's idea that centrism is important to Ennius, because it does seem to be the concept that Lucretius is implicitly rejecting in explicitly Ennian language.

57. *moenia mundi*: 1.73; 1.1102; 2.1045; 2.1144; 3.16; 5.119; 5.371; 5.454; 5.1213; 6.123. For the most comprehensive treatment of this aspect of Lucretius' poetic vision, see Hardie 1986: 157–240, esp. 168–172, 187–193 and Gale 1994: 122–124. See, generally, Atack 2019 and Sauron 2019.

58. In Roman culture, we frequently encounter the idea that the walls of the city of Rome were coextensive with the limits of the cosmos, that the *urbs* was equivalent, in some sense, to the *orbis terrarum*. For explicit etymology of the two words, see Varro *Ling.* 5.143. For the deployment of the pun, see, for example, Cic. *Cat.* 1.4.9, *Cat.* 4.6.11, *Fam.* 4.1.2; Prop. 3.11.57; Ov. *Fast.* 2.683–684 and *Ars am.* 1.174. Fundamental for universalism in the Roman imagination is Hardie 1986 (see 364–366 for a discussion of *urbs/orbis* with further bibliography).

59. In general, see Nethercut 2020b. On *machina mundi*, see now Galzerano 2018 and Taylor 2020a: 109–111.

60. For *moenia* as synecdoche for a city, see, e.g., Lucil. 104 Marx; Cic. *Verr.* 5.160; Verg. *Aen.* 6.541; Luc. 1.248.

down the walls of the cosmos. Lucretius uses the same language to describe the borders of the cosmos that Ennius had used to describe the breach of Rome's own walls in the *Annales*. Obviously, the noun *moenia* is quite common, and therefore insufficient evidence by itself to anchor an allusion to the *Annales*.[61] But if we are meant to extend the Ennian associations of Lucretius' *Graius homo* over onto the *moenia mundi*, then we might say that Lucretius alludes to Ennian language for the walls of Rome, the city that had served as the conceptual center of the cosmos in the *Annales*, to describe the walls of the Epicurean cosmos itself. The spoils of triumph that this Ennian *Graius homo* brings back is the knowledge that the Epicurean universe, unlike the Ennian cosmos, is infinite and certainly not coextensive with Rome or with Roman rule. In other words, Ennius was wrong, and Lucretius suggests that the Ennian conception of a "Roman" cosmos is itself being deconstructed in this passage on Epicurus' philosophical achievements.

This deconstruction is again operative later in *DRN* 1, when Lucretius offers proof that the universe is infinite.[62] Lucretius primes the reader to think specifically of the *Annales* when contemplating the proofs of an infinite universe by alluding to Ennius' epic in the lines leading up to his argument for infinity (Lucr. 1.951–957):

> *sed quoniam docui solidissima materiai*
> *corpora perpetuo volitare invicta per aevom,*
> *nunc age, summai quaedam sit finis eorum*
> *necne sit,* evolvamus; *item quod inane repertumst*
> *seu locus ac spatium, res in quo quaeque gerantur,*
> *pervideamus utrum finitum funditus omne*
> *constet an immensum pateat vasteque profundum.*

> *But since I have taught that the most solid bodies of matter*
> *fly around forever unconquered through the ages*
> *now come on, whether there be a certain limit to their sum total*
> *or not,* let us unroll; *and likewise the void that has been discovered*
> *or room or space, in which each and every thing is moved about,*
> *let us see clearly whether it is altogether bounded*
> *or spreads out measureless and endlessly deep.*

---

61. In addition to this instance in the *Annales*, *moenia* appears seventeen times in pre-Lucretian Latin (Lucilius, 104 Marx; Plautus, *Mil.* 228, *Rud.* 692, *Stich.* 695, *Trin.* 687; Accius, fr. 273, 385, 597 Ribbeck; Cic. *Verr.* 2.5.50.18, 2.5.77.1, 2.5.95.8, 2.5.96.11, 2.5.160.4, *Cat.* 1.5.4, 2.1.7, *Mur.* 6.2 and 33.7). One assumes that Ennius would have used this noun elsewhere in the *Annales*, but we have no other positive evidence to support this assumption.

62. On the connection between these two passages, see Galzerano 2019: 29–38.

This passage is one of the most stylistically Ennian passages in the entire *DRN*,
containing effects such as the genitive singular inflection of *materiai* at 1.951 (also
a pentasyllabic line-ending) and *summai* at 1.953.[63] These Ennian stylistic effects
highlight the possibility that Lucretius alludes to the *Annales*, so it comes as no
surprise that commentators regularly connect the verb *evolvamus* at 1.954 back to
Ennius' singular use of this verb in *Ann.* 164 Sk (*oras evolvere belli*), and regularly
suggest that Lucretius alludes specifically to this fragment of the *Annales*.[64] From
Quintilian (6.3.86), we can be almost certain that *Ann.* 164 Sk opened *Annales*
6, meaning that this fragment would have described the work involved in nar-
rating the confrontation with Pyrrhus. Lucretius thus implicitly juxtaposes his
own proof that the universe is infinite with Ennius' narrative of the war against
Pyrrhus. As I have just been arguing, Lucretius had figured Epicurus as a latter-
day Pyrrhus (*Graius homo*, 1.66) who was able to win for humanity the certain
knowledge of cosmic infinity (*omne immensum*, 1.74). It is also worth remem-
bering in this context that it was with the war against Pyrrhus that the *Annales*
effectively may have begun to present the universe as centered in Rome, not least
because Ennius was able to counter the Hellenocentric visions of human history
by presenting the war with Pyrrhus in a thoroughly Homeric manner.[65] When
Lucretius thus figures himself as a latter-day Ennius, now providing a "narra-
tive" of Epicurus' "Pyrrhic" discovery of the unbounded universe, he is, in fact,
engaging implicitly with Ennius' conception of the Roman cosmos. Of course,
the main point of the proofs that will follow is to show how conceptions of the
universe as bounded or centered are completely inaccurate.

   After reactivating here his engagement with the Roman cosmos of the *Annales*
from the passage in the proem about Epicurus' Triumph of the Mind, Lucretius
then reworks a thought experiment found first in Archytas (DK A24), but he
amplifies his proof by implying the infinity of the universe and of space (Lucr.
1.968–983):

> *praeterea si iam finitum constituatur*
> *omne quod est spatium, si quis procurrat ad oras*
> *ultimus extremas iaciatque volatile telum*

---

63. See Appendix 2, where I argue that the use of this ending on adjectives is especially Ennian.
The frequency of Ennianisms in these lines (.57 per line) is more than twice that in the poem as
a whole (.26 per line) and in Book 1 (.28 per line).

64. See, e.g., Wakefield 1813 ad loc. and Skutsch 1985: 330. On *evolvere* in Lucretius, see
O'Rourke 2020b: 119–120.

65. Elliott 2013: 279–281. See Feeney 2007: 24–25 for the evidence that the war with Pyrrhus
was widely recognized as the moment Rome came online in Greek accounts of universal time.

id validis utrum contortum viribus ire
quo fuerit missum mavis longeque volare
an prohibere aliquid censes obstareque posse?
alterutrum fatearis enim sumasque necessest.
quorum utrumque tibi effugium praecludit et omne
cogit ut exempta concedas fine patere.
nam sive est aliquid quod probeat officiatque
quominus quo missum est veniat finique locet se
sive foras fertur, non est a fine profectum.
hoc pacto sequar atque, oras ubicumque locaris
extremas, quaeram: quid telo denique fiet?
fiet uti nusquam possit consistere finis
effugiumque fugae prolatet copia semper.

Moreover, assume now that all space were finite,
if one were to run all the way to the end,
to its furthest borders and throw a flying spear
do you prefer that that spear hurled with strength advances
where it has been sent and flies afar
or do you think that something prevents it and is able to block it?
For you have to admit and choose one or the other option.
Each one shuts off your escape and
forces you to admit the universe spreads out with boundaries removed.
For if there is something which curbs it and blocks it
from arriving at the point it was directed and placing itself in its goal
or if it is carried onward and outward, it has not departed from a boundary.
In this way I shall pursue you and, wherever you establish the furthest
borders,
I shall ask: what then will happen to the spear?
It will come to pass that nowhere can a boundary be established
and room for flight always prolongs the chance for flight.

Allusions to Ennius proliferate in this proof. For example, Lucretius' *iaciatque volatile telum* (1.970) recalls *tela . . . iacientes* (*Ann.* 398 Sk), which Paladini and Salvatore explicitly cite as an allusion.[66] The collocation of *iacere* with *telum* may seem too unexceptional to be read as a specific verbal allusion to the *Annales*. But the fact that this collocation occurs only one other place in all of Latin before

---

66. Flores et al. 2006: 398.

Lucretius (Cic. *Cael.* 21.1), and does not proliferate even after Vergil incorporated the Ennian formulaic line opening *tela manu iaci-* into the *Aeneid* (10.264, 10.886, 11.893; followed in epic only at Ov. *Met.* 8.389 and Sil. *Pun.* 6.559) suggests otherwise. More obviously allusive is *validis . . . viribus* (Lucr. 1.971), which Lucretius takes over from the *Annales* (298 Sk).[67]

The allusion to Ennius here functions, once more, as a pointed refutation of what Lucretius represents as Ennian cosmology. It is something of a scholarly commonplace to point out that Lucretius presents himself in this passage as the Fetial priest.[68] In Lucretius' proof the universe is figured as Roman territory, insofar as the spear hurled by the Fetial priest was meant to fly across the boundary from Roman into non-Roman territory. Lucretius' thought experiment in this passage, therefore, would seem to be an affirmation of the Ennian Roman cosmos, especially because, as the distribution of the fragments that remain in the *Annales* suggests, Ennius' narrative treated events at the fringes of Roman territory disproportionately more frequently in comparison to domestic events located in the city. For example, Elliott takes this distribution as evidence that the *Annales* "faced primarily outward from the central standpoint of Rome," an orientation that results from the fact that Roman hegemony required both a moral and historical explanation.[69] Moreover, insofar as Lucretius' proof also insists that there are not, finally, any boundaries in the universe, this could be seen as a powerful affirmation of—perhaps even inspiration for—the later Vergilian idea of *imperium sine fine*, an idea that may appear in a nascent form in the *Annales*. Lucretius thus alludes extensively to Ennius in this passage. One could argue from this evidence that Lucretius accesses the Roman cosmos of Ennius, then amplifies these Roman associations by incorporating the religious image of the Fetial spear. Lucretius' procedure could even be seen to reinforce metatextually the spatial expanse of the universe that he insists upon in this passage. Lucretius, in other words, both extends the contours of the cosmos as he reads it in the *Annales* and articulates this extension in Roman terms, exactly as he regularly implies that Ennius had done.

---

67. The other Ennianisms in this passage (e.g., a pentasyllabic line-ending at 1.968 and a monosyllabic line-ending 1.978) and the fact that the frequency of Ennianisms in this section is higher than the average for the rest of the poem both suggest that Lucretius alludes specifically to the *Annales* and alerts his reader to this allusion with this heightened use of Ennian effects.

68. Wakefield on *percurrat* at 1.969 saw a military valence (cf. Verg. *Aen.* 12.266), and he cites Bentley for the suggestion that the "Fetial" declaration was being alluded to in Lucretius (followed by Bignone 1945: 230; Bailey 1947: 769; Mayer 1990: 37; O'Rourke 2020b; cf. Kennedy 2013: 54 n.7).

69. Elliott 2013: 274–275; quotation at 274.

Yet in the context of Lucretius' affirmation of the boundlessness of space, Rome, both as abstract concept and as concrete locality, is figured as insignificant in the scheme of Lucretius' wider universal vision. I say "insignificant" because Lucretius' proof of the infinity of the universe—and consequently his hyper-Roman language—is what leads him directly to conclude that the idea of cosmic centrism necessitates cataclysm. By positing an infinite universe with an infinite number of cosmoi, in other words, Lucretius destroys any Ennian conception of a cosmos centered in one location. In fact, *DRN* 1 ends with Lucretius insisting that any putative cosmic center, toward which all things might be directed, would cause the cosmos to tear itself apart. (Lucr. 1.1102–1117):

> *ne volucri ritu flammarum moenia mundi*
> *diffugiant subito magnum per inane soluta*
> *et ne cetera consimili ratione sequantur,*
> *neve ruant caeli tonitralia templa superne*
> *terraque se pedibus raptim subducat et omnis*
> *inter permixtas rerum caelique ruinas*
> *corpora solventes abeat per inane profundum,*
> *temporis ut puncto nil extet reliquiarum*
> *desertum praeter spatium et primordia caeca.*
> *nam quacumque prius de parti corpora desse*
> *constitues, haec rebus erit pars ianua leti,*
> *hac se turba foras dabit omnis materiai.*
> *haec sic pernosces parva perductus opella:*
> *namque alid ex alio clarescet, nec tibi caeca*
> *nox iter eripiet quin ultima naturai*
> *pervideas: ita res accendent lumina rebus.*

> *Lest in the winged manner of fire the walls of our world*
> *suddenly fly apart, dissolved through the great void,*
> *and lest everything else in similar manner follow them;*
> *lest the thundering regions of the sky rush upward,*
> *and the earth hastily withdraw itself from under our feet and,*
> *amidst all the mingled ruin of things on earth and of the sky*
> *loosening their atoms, it depart through the deep void,*
> *so that in an instant of time nothing of what remains should exist*
> *beyond deserted space and the unseen first-beginnings.*
> *For from whatever side you maintain that the atoms first fail,*
> *this side will be the doorway of death for things,*
> *by this path will all the crowd of matter send itself abroad.*

These things will you learn in this way, led on with little trouble:
  for one thing will become clear from another and blind
    night will not snatch the path from you, preventing you from seeing the
    utmost truths of nature: so shall things kindle a light for other things.

We find many allusions to the *Annales* in this passage. Lucretius' *caeli . . . templa*
(1.1105) comes from Ennius (*multa manus ad caeli caerula templa / tendebam,*
Ann. 48–49 Sk, which comes from Ilia's Dream), as does the collocation *se . . .*
foras dabit (1.1113; cf. *exin candida se radiis dedit icta foras lux, Ann.* 85 Sk, which
comes from the *augurium* fragment). Both of these Ennian fragments provide a
cosmic setting for the *Annales* as they figure the cosmos and the heavenly bodies
as a backdrop to the narrative action in the poem.[70] The effect of these allusions
to the Ennian cosmic setting, in an argument about how the centering of the
cosmos in any given spot necessarily entails cataclysm, is devastatingly decon-
structive.[71] In fact, one could scarcely imagine a more powerful way for Lucretius
to reject the Ennian conceptualization of Rome's central position in the cosmos
than to use Ennius' own cosmic language against itself in this way. The Ennian
perspective would be fundamentally impossible because it would violate the
physical laws that Epicureanism affirms. That the result of Lucretius' affirmation
of Epicurean reality is a profoundly anti-Roman conception of the universe is
merely a secondary effect; of primary importance is the positive articulation of
an Epicurean universe that has no room for a centrist conceptualization of the
cosmos like the one that Elliott argues is present in the *Annales*.[72] It is important
here to note again that, in all of this, Lucretius may be misrepresenting what he

---

70. Additional Ennianisms further cultivate an Ennian setting for Lucretius' allusion (e.g., pen-
tasyllabic line-endings at 1.1109 and 1.1113; hyper-alliteration at 1.1114 (*pernosces parva perduc-*
tus); and the genitive ending -*ai* at 1.1113 and 1.1116), and the frequency of Ennianisms in these
lines is higher than the average for the rest of the poem and the rest of Book 1.

71. Munro 1886 ad loc. takes these lines after the lacuna to entail a reaffirmation of the Epicurean
position (as opposed to the Stoic perspective), where the boundary of the cosmos limits neither
space nor matter, and hence is effectively abolished. This position has been adopted recently
by Bakker 2016: 203–205, to whom I am grateful for discussing these issues with me both in
person and *per litteras*. On this passage generally, see now Galzerano 2019: 29–68.

72. cf. Schiesaro 2007: 41–42, who zeroes in on Lucretius' basic procedure here: "There is
no need to wait for Anchises, or for Virgil's tantalizing references to *imperium sine fine*
(*Aen.* 1.279), to recognise that such a view of the cosmos entails a radical disruption of deep-
seated assumptions about Rome and its position. A belief in the contemporaneous existence
of multiple worlds destroys any illusion about the uniqueness, let alone the centrality, of our
own, just as in a random world floating in a random universe Rome's pre-eminence must by
definition be transient: neither its destiny nor that of the world is in the providential hands of
a divine agent."

actually found in the *Annales*. Even if the cosmic moments in the *Annales* fragments did not originally amount to a comprehensive cosmic perspective out of which Rome's rise to power was narrated, *Lucretius* reads the *Annales* in precisely this way, and he does so always with the purpose of correcting or of repudiating what he reads in(to) Ennius. A primary component of Lucretius' presentation of the infinite, Epicurean universe is the dismantling of the Rome-centered, Ennian cosmos that he implies was the backdrop for the narrative of Roman history in the *Annales*.

Conclusion

When Lucretius designates Homer's discourse in the proem to the *Annales* as *rerum natura*, he invites his reader to compare the cosmological perspectives that inhere in the Dream and the *Annales* at large with what he will go on to present in the *DRN*. This is his primary motivation for singling out Ennius' Homer (and Ennius and Homer) as narrating *rerum natura* in the middle of the proem to his own poem *de rerum natura*. If Lucretius found in the *Annales* a vision of the cosmos with which his own philosophical system fundamentally disagreed, or especially if he read such a cosmic vision into the *Annales*, it remained for him systematically to deconstruct this Ennian cosmos in his own presentation of the Epicurean universe. Implicated in his revisionist appropriation of the Ennian cosmos, however, is also an emphatic rejection of the political and historical implications of the cosmological aspects of the *Annales*, especially the idea that Rome had its own manifest destiny as literal center of the cosmos. At every point in this revision, Lucretius anticipates these political and historical implications, and disarms them by incorporating and insinuating them into his own revisionary presentation: whereas Ennius gave us the *Caeli caerula prata*, Lucretius figures himself as the Fetial priest of the universe; whereas Ennius supplied a fixed cosmic frame for the rise of Roman power, Lucretius insists on the eventual cataclysm of everything in our world. Lucretius provides for us, finally, an account of the *rerum natura* that is as fundamentally anti-Ennian as it is Epicurean. In the next chapter, I turn from context to text, as it were, focusing in on the historical narrative itself of the *Annales*, and leaving behind the cosmic background for this narrative.

3

Ennian Historiography in Lucretius

Ennius on the Past

WHERE LUCRETIUS' CHARACTERIZATION of the *Annales* as *rerum natura* is of necessity tendentious, his response to Ennius' conception of the past is more straightforward, given that Ennius' historicizing would appear to have been much more central to the narrative of the *Annales* than its cosmic setting. In this chapter, I sketch out the concept of history that Lucretius attributes to the *Annales*. Although we might also attribute this concept of history to Ennius' *Annales* itself, or at least reasonably assume Lucretius' contemporary readership would have attributed it to Ennius, my approach in this chapter primarily highlights what Lucretius reads into Ennian historiography, rather than what Ennian historiography actually emphasized in the *Annales*. Lucretius alludes time and again to historical episodes and personalities in Ennius' *Annales* that would appear to valorize Roman hegemony and exemplarity, only to strip them of whatever value these elements may have had in their Ennian context. Regularly, then, we witness Lucretius setting up an Ennian straw man that he effortlessly destroys in his exposition of Epicurean *vera ratio*.

Recent work on the historiography of the *Annales* can serve as a frame of reference for understanding this tendentious reception of Ennian historiography in the *DRN*. In contrast to the earlier scholarly notion that the *Annales* was just a chronicle of Roman history, Jackie Elliott has argued that Ennius presented a sort of universal history.[1] The *Annales*, in her view, laid out a temporal and geographical framework that structured the universe as centered in Rome, with Rome becoming "the hub of space and time, the primary focus of the cosmos in all its aspects."[2] Ennius' narrative very well could have started by establishing this framework in the Dream of Homer, with a cosmological explanation of the

---

1. Elliott 2013: 233–294. Feeney 2016: 186–187 advances Elliott's position; cf. Gildenhard 2003.

2. Elliott 2013: 234.

Ennius Noster: Lucretius and the Annales. Jason S. Nethercut, Oxford University Press (2021). © Oxford University Press.
DOI: 10.1093/oso/9780197517697.001.0001.

origins of the universe immediately followed by a narrative of Roman history down to the poet's own time. Such an arrangement would have established a chronological continuity, therefore, between the beginning of the universe and Rome's claim to dominion over it. The past, in other words, would have been presented as both cause of and sanction for present realities in the *Annales*.[3]

This idea that the *Annales* situated Rome as the center and culmination of the universe does not, I think, run counter to the ethos that would have been represented in a straightforward chronicle of Roman history. Elliott's point is that Ennius was not simply versifying the pontifical record, and that the design of the poem reflects larger ideas about historical discourse than the principles of chronological order and comprehensiveness. Either conception—that the *Annales* was precisely annalistic or Elliott's theory that the poem was a sort of universal history—suggests that Ennius placed a very high value on history itself, and especially on Rome's place in history.[4]

Virginia Fabrizi's work contributes to the picture of the *Annales* as focused on history.[5] For Fabrizi, Ennius presents Roman history as not predominantly bellicose, but one with moral and ethical dimensions. Ennius' *Annales* shows us that Roman hegemony is established because the Romans observed the *pax deorum*, practiced appropriately honest diplomacy, and cultivated a shrewd and expansive approach to politics just as much as they excelled at military force.[6] Fabrizi builds on the work of Gildenhard, as she is most interested in the *Annales* as a mode of sociocultural memory.[7] She concludes that Ennius presented the past as a justification for the contemporaneous hegemony Rome enjoyed at the time Ennius was writing. Fabrizi's conclusions corroborate those of Elliott, especially insofar as the *Annales*' perspective on the past is concerned: both scholars see in Ennius a response to the Roman past that marshals long distant events in defense of the Roman present; these events thus hold explanatory and legitimizing power.[8] Moreover, according to Fabrizi, major figures from Rome's past provide

---

3. Elliott 2013: 246–247.

4. In this regard, it is worth noting that if the arguments about the Italic tradition in the *Annales* in Fisher 2014 are correct, the Romanization of the past in Ennius' poem is on display wherever Ennius inflects ritualized language into his descriptions of past events.

5. Fabrizi 2012.

6. Summarized well at Fabrizi 2012: 205–208.

7. Gildenhard 2003.

8. See also now Biggs 2020 and Damon 2020; Haimson Lushkov 2020 shows how this aspect of the *Annales* was fundamental for Livy's reception of Ennius.

paradigms of action that serve as *exempla*, both positive (e.g., Romulus) and negative (e.g., Pyrrhus), from which Ennius meant his audience to learn.[9]

Triangulating between the analyses of Elliott and Fabrizi—assuming, of course, that they are both basically correct—we might be justified in inferring that Lucretius' contemporaries could read in the *Annales* how for Ennius the past was primarily a means to explain the present, and how there was a causal connection between past events and their effects in the present, and between the origin of the cosmos and contemporary Roman hegemony. In this way, the *Annales* established Rome's powerful position at the center of the cosmos by appealing to the teleology of the past.[10] Regardless of whether or not this was actually a feature of the *Annales* as Ennius wrote them, it is precisely this sort of historical teleology that figures into Lucretius' response to the past generally, and to Ennius' version of the past as narrated in the *Annales* specifically.

Lucretius on the Past[11]

That Lucretius was interested in Ennius' poem at all should surprise us. After all, Lucretius and Epicureans in general do not value the events of the past highly, and Ennius wrote an entire poem devoted to narrating Roman history.[12] This Lucretian disdain for history is most famously found in his marshaling of the Punic Wars as proof that historical events do not have any effect on the present (Lucr. 3.830–869). Even earlier in the *DRN*, Lucretius argues that the past does not actually exist—at least not in the fundamental way that atoms and void exist. In his discussion of "properties" (*coniuncta*) and "accidents" (*eventa*), Lucretius argues that nothing exists per se except atoms and void; everything else is only either a property or an accident of these two ontological foundations (Lucr. 1.418–458). History is implicated in this ontological destruction, for, included among the many accidents of body and void that Lucretius lists, are slavery, poverty, riches, freedom, war, civic harmony, and time. Amplifying this last example, he argues that time does not exist except as an accident of body, while past events

9. Romulus: Fabrizi 2012: 73–117; Pyrrhus: Fabrizi 2012: 119–150.

10. On Ennius as a universal historian, see Gildenhard 2003: 97; Elliott 2010, 2013: ch. 5, and 2015; Biggs 2015: 716–717; Sciarrino 2015: 425; Feeney 2016: 186–187. For dissenting opinions, see Goldschmidt 2015: 425; Clark 2015: VI–VII; Gildenhard 2016: 511; cf. Damon 2020: 125–128.

11. The following five sections of the current chapter represent an updated and expanded version of Nethercut 2014. Brill has graciously allowed this material to be reprinted here with permission.

12. For Epicurean apathy regarding the value of antiquity, see Ramelli 2014: 495.

are accidents of the regions in which they took place (Lucr. 1.459–470). To illustrate this point, Lucretius introduces the example of the Trojan War, an event that conventionally marked the boundary between the mythical heroic and the historical periods, but that Lucretius clearly treats as historical (Lucr. 1.471–482):[13]

> denique materies si rerum nulla fuisset
> nec locus ac spatium, res in quo quaeque geruntur,
> numquam Tyndaridis forma conflatus amoris
> ignis, Alexandri Phrygio sub pectore gliscens
> clara accendisset saevi certamina belli
> nec clam durateus Troiianis Pergama partu
> inflammasset equos nocturno Graiiugenarum;
> perspicere ut possis res gestas funditus omnis
> non ita uti corpus per se constare neque esse
> nec ratione cluere eadem qua constet inane,
> sed magis ut merito possis eventa vocare
> corporis atque loci, res in quo quaeque gerantur.

> And so, if there had been no substance of things
> nor place nor space in which all things are borne about,
> never would the fire, inflamed by the beauty of his love,
> Tyndareus' daughter, swelling in the Phrygian breast of Alexander,
> have kindled the famous contests of savage war
> nor, unknown to the Trojans, would the wooden horse
> with its nocturnal birthing of Greek sons have set fire to Pergama.
> So that you can see that all events from first to last
> do not exist nor are by themselves just like body,
> nor can they be said to exist in the same way as void exists,
> but rather so that you can correctly call them "accidents"
> of body and void, in which all things are borne about.

Despite the fact that Lucretius regards historical events such as the Trojan War as "accidents" (eventa), he nevertheless describes such events in epic terms—note the epicizing forms "of the daughter of Tyndareus" (Tyndaridis, Lucr. 1.473) and "of

---

13. On the Trojan War as a marker of the separation between these two periods, see Clarke 2008, with further bibliography. On this ancient view of Homer as a historian, see Kim 2010: 22–46, with further bibliography. On the historicity of the Homeric poems, Finley 1954 is fundamental, but see too Snodgrass 1974; Geddes 1984; Morris 1986; Sherratt 1990; Crierlaard 1995; and Brown 2016.

the Greek-born men" (*Graiiugenarum*, Lucr. 1.477). Moreover, he may also characterize such accidents as specifically Homeric: the transliteration of the Greek adjective δουράτεος (Lucr. 1.476), which is found only here in Latin, would appear to be taken over from Homer's version of the wooden horse at *Odyssey* 8.493 and 8.512.[14] This transliteration is especially striking given that Lucretius rarely uses Greek vocabulary—the only two examples of transliterated philosophical technical terms in the *DRN* are *homoeomeria* (Lucr. 1.830) and *harmonia* (Lucr. 3.131).[15]

Lucretius' treatment of the Trojan War in a later passage about the history of the universe reinforces its status as a historical event. There, Lucretius asserts that the earth and the sky had to have some beginning, and thus that our world is mortal and will one day be destroyed. Lucretius introduces an overdetermined example to prove his point. Were our world immortal, existing from time everlasting, he writes, surely we would have stories older than the epic poems on the Theban and Trojan wars (Lucr. 5.324–331):[16]

> *Praeterea si nulla fuit genitalis origo*
> *terrarum et caeli semperque aeterna fuere,*
> *cur supera bellum Thebanum et funera Troiae*
> *non alias alii quoque res cecinere poetae?*
> *quo tot facta virum totiens cecidere neque usquam*
> *aeternis famae monimentis insita florent?*
> *verum, ut opinor, habet novitatem summa, recensque*
> *naturast mundi neque pridem exordia cepit.*

---

14. The connection is drawn in the Aldine edition of Avancius in 1500. Given that Calepino's *Cornucopia* of 1502, which basically served as a collation of the entire lexicographical tradition up to that point, does not include this connection, it would seem that Avancius was the first to make this claim. Before Avancius, it may be that Pontanus or Marullus made such an observation; these, at least, would be the most likely candidates, since they were the most prominent humanist scholars who wrote on Lucretius before the *editio princeps* in 1473. I cannot say anything definitive about Pontanus, however, because I have not been able to look at his emendations. Regarding Marullus, no one has seen his emendations with complete certainty, and most attributions of readings to him were made by Lachmann. Many recent scholars (see especially Reeve 1980: 44–46; Deufert 1999; Baier 2008; and Brown 2010: 116–117, 120–122; but cf. *contra* Flores 2002: 33), however, argue that they have detected Marullus' hand in certain manuscripts, and, on the basis of Baier 2008, who has provided the fullest account to date of Marullus' working habits, it would be surprising if Marullus located specific textual references to Homer, or if the nature of his emendations were overly philological.

15. Sedley 1998: 48–51 discusses Lucretius' use of Greek terminology, concluding that the point is always to highlight the strangeness of what is so described. See now Taylor 2020a: 147–171.

16. For this point, see Schrijvers 1999: 112–113.

> *Moreover, if there was no origin that gave birth*
> *to the earth and sky and they were always eternal,*
> *why beyond the Theban war and the funerals of Troy*
> *have not other poets sung of other events as well?*
> *Whither have so many deeds of men so often passed away and why*
> *are they nowhere flourishing enshrined in the eternal memorials of fame?*
> *But indeed, as I think, our whole world has newness and the nature*
> *of the universe is fresh nor long ago did it receive its beginning.*

Lucretius here again appears interested in epic poetry—he specifically cites the *poetae* who have sung about Thebes and Troy (Lucr. 5.327)—*qua* historiography, implying that the sagas he cites offer reliable information about the early history of humanity (the earliest history of humanity, in fact). Lucretius thus considers these events historical in the sense that they are the earliest human affairs of which he believes we have reliable records.[17]

By adducing mythological epic as an example of historiography, Lucretius recasts the epic tradition according to his own tendentious motives. By mentioning a "Theban War" (*bellum Thebanum*, Lucr. 5.326), Lucretius may also be pointing to epic poetry, specifically one of the cyclic epics *Thebaid* or *Epigoni*, given that these two parts of the Theban cycle are the only ones to narrate a war.[18] This addition of Thebes suggests that Lucretius thinks that *all* epic, not just the Homeric poems, treats of historical events—or at least thinks that the events celebrated in epic poetry could be read as history.[19] This suggestion would seem to imply that Lucretius characterizes epic not only as philosophical, but also as historiographical. In this regard, Lucretius may be introducing this example at the very beginning of his own Epicurean historical narrative of the cosmos and civilization, the narrative that occupies him for the rest of *DRN* 5, as a means of undermining the historical authority of epic.[20] After all, Lucretius rejects the authority of poets in the course of his own account of history, doing so explicitly

---

17. It seems clear enough that he is pointing to Homer in mentioning the Trojan War (see Schrijvers 1999: 113).

18. The other two cyclic epics on the Theban saga, *Oedipodea* and *Alcmeonis*, did not treat of war. On the Theban epics, see Davies 2015.

19. See Nethercut 2019: 197 for further discussion.

20. See Gale 2004 on the narratological aspects of the *DRN*, with special reference to *DRN* 5. See also my discussion on Lucretius' anthropology as a response to Ennian historiography, in the section below on "Ennian Historiography in Lucretius' Anthropology," pp. 101–106.

in the case of events like the primeval flood and conflagration (Lucr. 5.380–415) and perhaps implicitly in his account of the origins of human civilization.[21]

From Lucretius' historiographical reading of the epic tradition, we must understand two important gestures. First, Lucretius represents the Trojan War as the paradigmatic example of a historical event by singling it out for discussion and even citing epic poetry about the war as a historical source—a move that suggests that for Lucretius epic may be inherently historiographical, and that epic's most useful explanatory power for Lucretian philosophy may have to do with its status as a historical genre.[22] But secondly, and perhaps paradoxically, Lucretius adduces this historical example with the main purpose of illustrating his ontological contention that "history"—which in this connection is perhaps better called "the past"—does not actually exist. This contention does not have to mean that the codification of "the past" in epic poetry has no existence for Lucretius, but it certainly calls into question any value that epic *qua* historiography may have, at least as historiography is traditionally conceived and written (e.g., *res gestae* or *de viris illustribus*). On the other hand, when Lucretius subverts the aims and values of traditional historiographical writing, it may be in order to amplify the value that he does place on *natural* historiography throughout *DRN* 5, a possibility that I will return to later in this chapter.

Lucretius on the Ennian Past: The Punic Wars

That the Roman poet who influenced Lucretius perhaps most profoundly—both in terms of form and content—wrote a historical epic comes as no surprise, then, given Lucretius' interest in complicating traditional epic historiography. Indeed, Ennius' *Annales* represents the perfect model for the type of epic Lucretius appears to be characterizing in the lines from *DRN* 5 above.[23] Moreover, by far the majority

---

21. I am thinking here especially of Lucretius' response to Hesiod's metal races *qua* historical account of human progress implied by the account of metallurgy at Lucr. 5.1241–1280, on which see Gale 1994: 171–174 and, more generally, Gale 2013. Throughout his historical narrative in *DRN* 5, Lucretius relies solely on analogical reasoning (see, Kenney 1972 and Schiesaro 1990: 140–168).

22. On the topic of possible generic mixing in this regard, we should also note that Lucretius represents the Trojan War as having been caused by Paris' lust, much as the elegists were later to do. Herodotus does this also by implication (Hdt. 1.3–4; cf. 2.112–114), even if there is no indication that Lucretius has Herodotus specifically in mind here.

23. For the *Annales* as historiography, see Elliott 2013: 154–171 and 176–195, and see section below on "Ennian Historiography in Lucretius' Anthropology," pp. 101–106.

of historical *exempla* and digressions in the *DRN* allude to Ennius' *Annales*.[24] That
we can establish this point is remarkable, given the highly incomplete nature of
the *Annales* as we have it. In fact, it would hardly overstate the situation to say
that the historical record with which Lucretius seems to engage most pointedly is
defined in its most important aspects by Ennius (and, as we have seen, by Homer).
At the same time, however, Lucretius always activates such historical material with
one purpose: to show that the traditional form of written commemoration of
historical events—which, remember, have no existence in the present—is (there-
fore) irrelevant to our existence in the present. Lucretius thus regularly appears to
engage allusively with Ennian historical epic in order to comment, paradoxically,
on the *lack* of value that such epic historiography has for our lives.

Perhaps the most prominent example of this practice is Lucretius' appropria-
tion of the Punic War narrative from Ennius' *Annales* as evidence that the past
has no effect on the present (Lucr. 3.830–842):

> *nil igitur mors est ad nos neque pertinent hilum,*
> *quandoquidem natura animi mortalis habetur.*
> *et velut ante acto nihil tempore sensimus aegri,*
> *ad confligendum venientibus undique Poenis,*
> *omnia cum belli trepido concussa tumultu*
> *horrida contremuere sub altis aetheris oris,*
> *in dubioque fuere utrorum ad regna cadendum*
> *omnibus humanis esset terraque marique,*
> *sic, ubi non erimus, cum corporis atque animai*
> *discidium fuerit quibus e sumus uniter apti,*
> *scilicet haud nobis quicquam, qui non erimus tum,*
> *accidere omnino poterit sensumque movere,*
> *non si terra mari miscebitur et mare caelo.*

> *Death, then, is nothing to us nor does it matter one bit,*
> *inasmuch as the nature of the soul is held to be mortal.*
> *And just as in the time that has passed we felt nothing ill,*
> *when the Carthaginians came from all sides to raise a martial conflict,*
> *when all things shaken by the trembling tumult of war*

---

24. This does not mean that Ennius is the only lens through which history can be seen in the
DRN. The major exception to this Ennian rule of course is Lucretius' narrative of the Athenian
plague (Lucr. 6.1138–1286), which clearly takes Thucydides' account at 2.47–52 as inspira-
tion, on which see especially Lück 1932: 175–190; Bailey 1947: 1723–1744; Commager 1957;
Stoddard 1996; and Foster 2009.

bristled and shook under the high coasts of the ether,
and they were in doubt to which people's kingdoms the lot
of all humans had to fall both on land and by sea;
in this way, when we will be no more, when there will come
a severance of body and soul out of which we are made one,
you may know that nothing at all will be able to happen to us,
who will not exist at that time, nor arouse our sensation;
not even if the earth will be mixed up with the sea and the sea with the sky.

Most agree that this passage follows Ennius' account of the Punic Wars.[25] Bailey
and Kenney both believe that a temporal clause in Lucretius recalls a fragment of
Ennius that evidently belongs to his narrative of one of the Punic Wars:[26]

> *omnia cum belli trepido concussa <u>tumultu</u>*
> <u>*horrida*</u> *con<u>tremu</u>ere sub altis aetheris oris*   *(Lucr. 3.834–835)*

> *when everything quaking with the trembling tumult of war*
> *trembled and shook under the high coasts of heaven*

> *Africa terribili <u>tremit</u> <u>horrida</u> terra <u>tumultu</u>*   *(Ann. 309 Sk)*

> *Africa, a quaking land, trembled with the terrible tumult*

This passage contains many of the characteristic Ennianisms that Lucretius
deploys regularly throughout his poem to give a generally Ennian patina to a pas-
sage, such as a monosyllabic verse-ending (*non erimus tum*, 3.840), insistent allit-
eration (3.830, 834–835, and 842), and the genitive singular *-ai* (*animai*, 3.838). In
general, the Bailey paragraph (3.830–869) exhibits markedly more Ennianisms
per line than the frequency in the poem as a whole, and in *DRN* 3 specifically,
so Lucretius is writing in a concertedly more Ennian way in this passage than

25. On Ennius in the lines, see Mayer 1990: 40; Gale 1994: 110–111; Fabrizi 2012: 153–155; Elliott
2013: 116; and Goldschmidt 2013: 25–26. Gee 2020: 207–211 emphasizes the rich intertextual
background in these lines, analyzing them for anti-Stoic polemics via Lucretius' appropriation
of Cicero's *Aratea*.

26. See, e.g., Bailey 1947 ad loc. and Kenney 2014 ad loc., who further notes the similarity
between Lucr. 3.832–842 and Livy 29.17.6 and conjectures that the correspondence is due to
the use of a common source, namely Ennius. Even Elliott 2013: 116, who is always cautious not
to infer too much about our fragments beyond what appears in their sources, seems to accept
Skutsch's attribution of this fragment to the Punic War narrative in the *Annales*.

he usually does.[27] That the parallel may reference Ennius' Punic War narrative is both attractive and tantalizing, especially since so little of it survives.

The commentators have provided different explanations for the fact that Lucretius singles out the Second Punic War in particular as a past event that is of no concern to us. Bailey stresses the importance of pre-existence as well as survival in the arguments in antiquity for immortality, emphasizing that the Punic Wars were viewed as the greatest conflict that Rome ever faced.[28] The point, then, is that Lucretius makes his argument *a fortiori* here: if the most consequential event in all of Roman history does not leave its mark on our souls, surely nothing can. This argument is hammered home at the end of the *exemplum*, where Lucretius imagines the end of the world brought about by cosmic upheaval (Lucr. 3.838–842). Kenney, on the other hand, focuses on the poetic possibilities that this example offers Lucretius, suggesting that here Lucretius imitates, or even parodies, the high epic style in order to bolster his argument, a move that he favors. As we saw above, Lucretius appropriates epic elements earlier in his poem (Lucr. 1.462–482), when he adduces the example of the Trojan War to make the point that the past no longer exists in a way that makes it directly relevant to us; in the course of that description he alludes to Homer and deploys a range of epicisims.[29] Here, Lucretius presents the Second Punic War in the high epic style and infuses his own account of the conflict with Ennianisms as part of an argument that the past does not affect the present.[30] In this passage, then, Lucretius implies that

---

27. For these features as especially Ennian, see my discussion in Appendix 2.

28. Bailey 1947: 1134–1135.

29. As discussed above, the most prominent among the epic elements of this passage is the transliteration of the adjective *durateus*—not technically a Latin adjective, but taken over from Homer's version of the wooden horse at *Odyssey* 8.493 and 8.512. Similarly we notice the proliferation of epic forms of proper nouns (*Tyndaridem*, Lucr. 1.464 (cf. Lucr. 1.473); *Troiiugenas*, Lucr. 1.465; *Graiiugenarum*, Lucr. 1.476). It is also suggestive that this passage is introduced with *dicunt* (Lucr. 1.465), which can be read as an example of the so-called Alexandrian footnote; cf. Nethercut 2018a.

30. The rejection of the importance of the Second Punic War here is even more pointed if we see an allusion to Ennius' description of the crowd watching Romulus and Remus vie for the rule over Rome (*sic expectabat populus atque ore timebat / rebus **utri** magni victoria sit data regni, Ann.* 87–88 Sk) in Lucretius' description of the uncertainty surrounding the contest with Carthage (*in dubioque fuere **utrorum** ad **regna** cadendum / omnibus humanis esset terraque marique,* Lucr. 3.836–837). Lucretius could be seen to conflate the founding of Rome with its victory over Carthage, implying a teleological evolution from Rome's beginning to its Mediterranean hegemony. That this frame is focused through allusions to Ennius' narrative of both pivotal moments in Roman history suggests that such a teleological understanding of Roman dominion was already implicit, or maybe even explicit, in the *Annales* (see, Fabrizi 2012: 151–177; Elliott 2013: 233–294; and the section below on "Ennian Historiography in Lucretius' Anthropology," pp. 101–106).

Ennius writes history in such a way as to draw a connection between the past and the present, but Lucretius immediately denies that this implied Ennian position is philosophically viable.

Lucretius on the Ennian Past: The Value of Historical Exempla

Similarly, later in *DRN* 3, Lucretius produces the examples of prominent historical personalities to illustrate the truth that even the best men must die (Lucr. 3.1024–1052). The three properly military and political figures whom he names— later Lucretius adds lists of poets and philosophers—are Ancus Marcius, Scipio, and Xerxes. Remarkably, Lucretius characterizes all three of these figures with language used in the *Annales*. Lucretius begins this section by quoting Ennius' assessment of Ancus Marcius:[31]

> *lumina sis oculis etiam bonus Ancus reliquit*　　　　　(Lucr. 3.1025)

> Even good Ancus lost the lights from his eyes

> *postquam lumina sis oculis bonus Ancus reliquit*　　　　　(Ann. 137 Sk)

> After good Ancus lost the lights from his eyes

A few lines later, Lucretius similarly alludes to Ennius' *Annales*. This time he includes this allusion in a description of Scipio, regardless of the original context this fragment may have had in the *Annales*:[32]

> *Scipiadas, belli fulmen, Carthaginis horror,*
> *ossa dedit terrae, proinde ac famul infimus esset*　　　(Lucr. 3.1034–1035)

---

31. On the use of Ennius here in the *DRN*, see Gigon 1978: 187–188; Gale 2007a: 63; and Elliott 2013: 116.

32. Scholars have tried to restore the fragment to Hannibal's address to Scipio before the Battle of Zama. This ascription was proposed initially by Hug 1852: 30, but taken further by Skutsch 1985: 489–493, who compares Livy 30.30 and Polyb. 15.6.8. Nonnus tells us that this fragment appeared in *Annales* 9, but beyond that we can only speculate. Others have suggested that the fragment is voiced by Scipio regarding the fate of Syphax (e.g., Kvičala 1906: 116; cf. Sil. *Pun.* 17.143–145), a fact that underscores the evidentiary uncertainty of the fragment's original context in the *Annales*.

The son of the Scipios, thunderbolt of war, terror of Carthage,
<u>gave</u> his bones to the earth just as though <u>he had been the lowliest house-slave</u>

mortalem summum Fortuna repente
re<u>did</u>it †summo regno <u>famul</u> †ut †<u>optimus esset</u>   (*Ann. 312–313 Sk*)

Fortune of a sudden <u>brings it about</u> that the loftiest mortal
removed from the loftiest seat of regal power <u>becomes the best house-slave</u>

While we cannot know the context of this Ennian fragment in the *Annales*, we can safely say that Lucretius uses Ennian language and applies it to Scipio. The connection between the two passages would seem to be clinched by the form *famul*, the only occurrence of this nominative form—and perhaps in the same metrical *sedes*—in Latin aside from the Ennian fragment.[33] The Ennian atmosphere is furthered by the use of the phrase *Carthaginis horror*, "the terror of Carthage," which recalls the use of Ennius' Punic war narrative earlier (Lucr. 3.834–835).

Finally, Lucretius' description of Xerxes may allude to Ennius' own description of Xerxes at the beginning of *Annales* 13:[34]

Ille quoque ipse, viam qui quondam per mare magnum
stravit iterque dedit legionibus ire per altum
ac pedibus salsas docuit super ire lacunas
et contempsit equis insultans murmura ponti
lumine adempto animam moribundo corpore fudit.   (*Lucr. 3.1029–1033*)

Even he himself, who once through the huge sea
paved a way and provided a path for his legions to go through the deep
and he taught them to cross the salty lakes on foot
and he despised the roarings of the ocean, prancing upon it with his horses,
with the light removed he breathed out his soul from his dying body.

---

33. It seems possible that *famul* is the genuine nominative, developed from *famulos* by regular syncope, and replaced at a later point by *famulus* (the first appearance of this form is at Hor. *Ars P.* 239). The *sedes* of the noun is complicated by the presence of *ut*, which Skutsch 1985: 491 notes could be either omitted or transposed to precede *famul*. In either case, *famul* would share its metrical *sedes* with the Lucretian line. That the Lucretian use of this Ennian fragment has proved central to many analyses of its provenance in the *Annales* should encourage a restoration of *famul* in Ennius to the same *sedes* as in Lucretius.

34. Skutsch 1985: 535–537.

Isque Hellesponto pontem contendit in alto
Salsas ... lamas   (*Ann. 369–370 Sk*)

And he stretched a bridge in the deep Hellespont
the salty ... lakes

Uncertainties abound in this example. Servius provides the notice for us that Ennius used the adjective *salsus, -a, -um* to describe the very rare word *lama* (*Aen.* 2.173), but says nothing further. We have no idea regarding the work, meter, or even the inflection of the phrase in Ennius' corpus. While we know *Ann.* 369 Sk obviously refers to Xerxes (Varro corroborates this for us, as if we needed his help), we do not know the Ennian context, let alone the work, from which this line is taken. Moreover, *Ann.* 369 Sk does not share any language with the Lucretian lines except *altum* (*in alto*; *per altum*, Lucr. 3.1030), which is too common to anchor any sort of definitive allusion. Skutsch, in an almost perfectly circular argument, uses Lucretius' lines to prove that his ascription of these Ennian fragments is correct. We should be cautious, therefore, about claiming more than the evidence permits.

What can be claimed, however, is that *Lucretius* wants the reader to read his Xerxes as Ennian. Xerxes is adduced in a pointedly Ennian context between the *exempla* of Ancus Marcius and Scipio. Lucretius is the only Latin author after Ennius to use the striking phrase "salty lakes" to signify the sea,[35] and Ennian language appears throughout these lines (*mare magnum*, Lucr. 3.1029=*Ann.* 434 Sk; *animam ... corpore fudit*, Lucr. 3.1033=*animam de corpore mitto, Ann.* 193 Sk). This whole passage exhibits heightened Ennian effects compared to the rest of the poem. We should be cautious about reading Lucretius' Xerxes back into the fragments of the *Annales*; it *is* clear, however, that Lucretius' wants his readers to recognize his own Xerxes as Ennian.

That Lucretius inflects the *exempla* of these three political leaders with Ennian associations suggests that Lucretius reads history through an Ennian lens again in this passage. That these leaders are adduced as examples of the inevitability of death shows, once again, Lucretius redirecting Ennian historiography to his own Epicurean ends, here deflating the importance that he implies Ennian historiography attaches to historical events. It may be that Lucretius, in the process of revising the historical perspective he attributes to Ennius, also develops ideas that are latent or even implied in the *Annales*. For example, Lucretius applies the idea of the vicissitudes of human fortune to Scipio, while reference to Xerxes

---

35. We do find *lacu salso* much later in Curtius Rufus (9.10.1.2).

usually involves the price he pays for his hubris.[36] It could be, then, that Lucretius is reactivating a humanistic strain in Ennius against a tendency to interpret him in a more simplistic way, as, for example, Cicero appears to have done. In this very process of reactivation, however, Lucretius denies the philosophical legitimacy of this perspective by insisting that these figures from the past only help us as proof of the finality of death. For again, the point in Lucretius is that the most prominent historical protagonists died, despite their renown; they have value for us, then, only insofar as they are just three of the countless people who have died, exactly as we all must. This belief would seem to stand in direct opposition to Ennius' focus on memorializing the deeds of men and on the positive value of such *exempla* as seen, for example, in an idea like "the Roman state is founded on its ancient morals and its men" (*moribus antiquis res stat Romana virisque*, *Ann.* 156 Sk).[37]

Shortly after this passage, Epicurus himself is adduced in the exact same context. While Lucretius certainly would not deny that Epicurus' discoveries have value for us, it would seem, in this passage at least, that the man himself *qua* human does not offer us any value except to illustrate the certainty of death. Of course, later in *DRN* 5, Lucretius will say that Epicurus was a "god" (*deus*, Lucr. 5.8) because of his discoveries. When it comes to Epicurus, therefore, Lucretius is clearly comfortable with a degree of ontological ambiguity. Perhaps we would do better to conceptualize Lucretius' Epicurus as the ultimate, indeed the definitive, Epicurean *exemplum*, on the one hand superseding traditional (Ennian) historical *exempla*, and, on the other, taking on the polysemantic function that these *exempla* traditionally perform.

Obviously, there is a kind of paradox in the fact that Lucretius, by writing about the past, even indirectly, helps it to survive. But the fact that *exempla* keep their power as *loci communes* in many different contexts, while remaining susceptible of (and susceptible to) many different readings, proves advantageous for Lucretius, who is able to redirect these Ennian *exempla* to his own Epicurean ends, while at the same time implying that Ennius has read them incorrectly. In so

---

36. Feeney 2016: 246–247 weighs in on this nexus and its historiographical possibilities as the closing vignette in his study of the beginnings of Latin literature; cf. Elliott 2013: 248.

37. Of course, this Ennian line, taken from the speech of the elder T. Manlius Torquatus as he hands his son over to the lictor for execution, might ring a bit ironic in its Ennian context. However, we should remember that the author of the *SHA* who quotes this line from a letter written by Marcus Aurelius (*Avid. Cass.* 5.7) characterizes the verse as *omnibus frequentatum*, "repeated by everyone." This characterization would seem to imply that Ennius was particularly known for this line, which in turn would suggest that Ennius was widely considered a poet who voiced such statements. On this fragment, see Elliott 2007: 52–54 and Goldschmidt 2013: 161–163 and, more generally, ch. 5 on Ennian *exempla* and their reception.

doing, Lucretius not only rejects the traditional Roman fetishization of historical *exempla*, but does so with reference to its most prominent poetic expression in Ennius' *Annales*, and in order to prove his anti-Ennian contention that traditional historiography has no value for us.[38]

Lucretius on the Ennian Past: History and Epicurean Psychology

Lucretius appropriates Ennius' *Annales* at other points in the *DRN* to make the same basic point about historical events and the (lack of) value that they have for us. The procedure is always the same: Lucretius alludes to Ennian language associated with a historical event or personality, but does so without regard for the original context (whatever it may have been) in which these events or personalities appear in the *Annales*. An especially pointed example of this procedure comes from one of Lucretius' arguments for the mortality of the soul in *DRN* 3. Lucretius suggests that since the soul can be divided, along with the limbs of the body, it must be mortal, because whatever is *immortal* must be indivisible. To prove that parts of the soul can be separated from the whole, Lucretius adduces the bizarre example of limbs lopped off in battle that nevertheless continue to move, a phenomenon that indicates that the soul still lives and functions in the amputated limbs (Lucr. 3.642–656):

> *falciferos memorant currus abscidere membra*
> *saepe ita de subito permixta caede calentis,*
> *ut tremere in terra videatur ab artubus id quod*
> *decidit abscisum, cum mens tamen atque hominis vis*
> *mobilitate mali non quit sentire dolorem*
> *et simul in pugnae studio quod dedita mens est:*
> *corpore relicuo pugnam caedesque petessit,*
> *nec tenet amissam laevam cum tegmine saepe*
> *inter equos abstraxe rotas falcesque rapaces,*

---

38. Lucretius may operate similarly at *DRN* 4.710, where, in a bizarre discussion of how lions cannot endure to stare at roosters, he deploys the collocation *gallum noctem*. This may be an allusion to *Ann.* 227 Sk (*Galli . . . noctu*). The Ennian fragment definitely refers to the announcement of the Gauls' arrival inside Rome by the Capitoline geese, and a few lines earlier Lucretius explicitly alludes to this story (4.683). Moreover, the similarity between these two collocations is almost unparalleled outside of Lucretius and Ennius (cf. Caesar, *BG* 3.2.1.3–4 and Verg. *Aen.* 8.657–658). If we are justified in reading this collocation as a Lucretian allusion to Ennius, again Lucretius would seem to disregard any historical value associated with this episode in the *Annales*.

nec cecidisse alius dextram, cum scandit et instat.
inde alius conatur adempto surgere crure,
cum digitos agitat propter moribundus humi pes.
et caput abscisum calido viventeque trunco
servat humi voltum vitalem oculosque patentis,
donec reliquias animai reddidit omnes.

They tell how often scythe-bearing chariots
hot from the confusion of slaughter hack off limbs so suddenly
that the part which falls lopped off from the limbs is seen to twitch on the
  ground,
while the mind and strength of the man
nevertheless is unable to feel pain because of the swiftness of the stroke;
and at the same time because his mind has been surrendered in his zeal for
  the fight,
with the rest of his body he makes for the fight and the slaughter
and often he does not reckon that his left arm has been lost along with
  his shield
and that the wheels have carried it away amongst the horses and ravaging
  scythes;
and another does not realize that his right arm has fallen off, when he climbs
and presses onward. Then another tries to rise when his leg has been lost
while nearby him on the ground the dying foot twitches its toes.
And the head lopped off from a warm and living trunk
preserves on the ground the look of life and the gaping eyes,
until it has given up all the vestiges of the soul.

We should first of all mark that this whole description of the havoc wreaked by the scythe-bearing chariots may be introduced by an Alexandrian footnote, "they tell" (*memorant*, Lucr. 3.642), a fact to which Kenney draws attention in the first edition of his commentary.[39] This verb may serve as a reflexive annotation of the specific allusion to Ennius that many commentators have detected:

et caput abscisum calido viventeque trunco
servat humi voltum vitalem oculosque patentis   (*Lucr. 3.654–655*)

---

39. Kenney 1971: 164; see now Nethercut 2018a on the use of the Alexandrian footnote in Lucretius.

And the head lopped off from a warm and living trunk
preserves on the ground the look of life and the eyes, wide open

oscitat in campis caput a cervice revolsum
semianimesque micant oculi lucemque requirunt   *(Ann. 483–484 Sk)*

the head gapes open-mouthed in the fields, torn from the neck
and the eyes, half-alive, flash and seek the light of day

Presumably allusion has been detected here, because the images in the lines are so similar, given that there are actually almost no verbal similarities between these sets of lines. They share the words *caput* and plural forms of *oculus*, but these are hardly conclusive signifiers of allusion. Even so, the characteristic Ennianisms in Lucretian style permeate this passage, and in much higher frequency than elsewhere in the poem, indicating that Lucretius is writing in a more Ennian way than he does usually.[40] We can also note a potentially Ennian formation in the adjective *falciferos*, "scythe-bearing" (instead of the usual *falcatus-a-um*).[41] These similarities have convinced many scholars that this passage in Lucretius is not only thoroughly and obviously Ennian, but perhaps even more so than we can determine from the evidence now available.[42] Leaving such speculations aside, however, it does seem reasonable to assume, on the basis of the positive evidence I have adduced, that, at the very least, Lucretius intended this passage to come across as Ennian.

---

40. Ennianisms proliferate in this passage at a significantly higher frequency than the average in the poem. The preponderance of verse-final monosyllables (*quod*, 644; *vis*, 645; *est*, 647; *pes*, 653) is an especially Ennian element in this passage, where four such lines occur in the span of fifteen lines (26.67%) far exceeding the frequency of such lines in *DRN* 3 (8.68%) and in the poem as a whole (5.83%).

41. Lucretius adopts a similarly formed adjective *frugiferentis*, "fruit-bearing" (Lucr. 1.3) from Ennius' *frugiferai* (*Ann.* 510 Sk). Skutsch 1985: 605–606 shows that such formulations with an adjective in the first part of *-fer* or *-ger* compounds are uncommon in Latin, but relatively common in Ennius.

42. Skutsch 1985: 645 says that this Lucretian passage was "clearly based on Ennius" (cf. Mayer 1990: 37 and n. 8), and Kenney 2014: 159 also argues that Lucretius "was evidently drawing on Ennius." In drawing this conclusion, Skutsch and Kenney followed scholars such as Heinze 1897: 141, who on the basis of this allusion posited additional Ennian influence elsewhere in the Lucretian passage, specifically suggesting that the phrases "hot from the confusion of the slaughter" (*permixta caede calentes*, Lucr. 3.643), "he makes for the fight and the slaughter" (*pugnam caedesque petessit*, Lucr. 3.648), and "he climbs and presses onward" (*scandit et instat*, Lucr. 3.651) may be derived from Ennius. Similarly, Skutsch 1985: 646 proposes that the Lucretian detail of the arm being cut off together with its shield was mentioned by Ennius.

There seems to be a general consensus that these lines come from Ennius'
account of the Battle of Magnesia in *Annales* 14.[43] Of course, we cannot finally
know the context of this Ennian fragment, and we must be cautious in claiming too
much for its ascription.[44] But it seems almost certain that the Ennian lines come
from a battle scene of some sort.[45] And they seem to have been influential on later
poets. For example, we know from Servius, who provides us with these Ennian lines,
that Vergil adapted them at *Aeneid* 10.384–386; he also tells us that Varro Atacinus
borrowed *Ann.* 483 Sk as it stood, whatever that may mean in reality.[46]

Lucretius, however, seems to have reacted differently from the way other later
poets, such as Vergil, would do, by turning a quite obvious allusion to Ennius'
celebrated account of battlefield chaos into a striking proof of the mortality of
the soul. In addition, at every point in this passage Lucretius undermines any
historical importance this battle scene may have had in Ennius' narrative.[47] For
his part, Lucretius completely elides the fact that this was even a specific battle,
universalizing what was probably a historically-situated confrontation in Ennius.
In fact, the only relevance that the Ennian narrative might have for Lucretius is
that it provides him with a proof that the soul is mortal. Lucretius, therefore,
would appear once again to read history through an Ennian lens, only to reject
in the end any historical value attached by Ennius to this event in the face of
Epicurean psychology.

---

43. Friedrich 1948: 297–299; cf. Skutsch 1985: 644–647 for further bibliography. Kenney
2014: 160 claims that Lucretius' "graphic description is clearly based on lines from Ennius' no
less graphic treatment of the battle of Magnesia." If this does come from the Magnesia narra-
tive, it is pertinent that all other historical accounts regard the use of scythed chariots in this
battle by Antiochus the Great as quite ineffectual, so the emphasis we see in this passage on the
sensational lopping off of limbs and heads would appear to be a specifically Ennian innovation
(Livy 37.39–44 and App. *Syr.* 151–189).

44. Elliott 2013: 102 n. 73.

45. The Ennian fragment to which scholars have argued Lucretius specifically alludes (*Ann.*
483–484 Sk) is not assigned by Servius (*Aen.* 10.396), who cites it, to any specific poem,
let alone to any specific book of the *Annales*. Beginning with Merula 1595: xi, however, who
assigned the fragment to *Annales* 2, most editors have considered this fragment as belonging to
Ennius' epic. Even still, the fragment is usually included with those *sedis incertae*, without any
discussion of possible narrative contexts (e.g., Vahlen 1903: 85).

46. *quem versum ita ut fuit transtulit ad suum carmen Varro Atacinus*, Serv. *Aen.* 10.396. On this
fragment of Varro, see above in chapter 1 (p. 40).

47. If the commentators are correct in ascribing this fragment to the Battle of Magnesia, we
still cannot know what role this would have played in Ennius' narrative, but Magnesia was
undoubtedly a significant battle that paved the way for Roman hegemony over Greece and
Asia Minor (see Gruen 1984: 636–643). Regardless of any hypothetical importance Ennius
may have attached to Magnesia in the *Annales*, Lucretius clearly shows no interest in *any* his-
torical importance Magnesia may have had in the view of Ennius or of anyone else.

Lucretius on the Ennian Past: Pyrrhus of Epirus

Of all the particular historical events narrated in Ennius' *Annales*, none captured Lucretius' imagination more than those associated with Pyrrhus of Epirus. We have already had occasion in the previous chapter to discuss the way in which Lucretius presents his own Epicurus as a sort of foil for Ennius' Pyrrhus.[48] It turns out that the passage in the proem to the *DRN* was programmatic not only for Lucretius' engagement with Ennius as a poet who writes *de rerum natura*, but also as the poet who cast Pyrrhus as an epic hero susceptible of diverse allusive engagements. In *DRN* 5, Lucretius returns to Ennius' Pyrrhus as a foil against which he can articulate his own Epicurean ideas about religion. As a result of this more sustained engagement with Ennian historiography, in the form of a prominent historical antagonist in the *Annales*, Lucretius continues to set up the terms under which his reader is meant to understand the nature of Ennian historiography in the *Annales*, while simultaneously undermining the validity of this very historiographical framework.

In the *Annales*, Ennius appears to have inflected the story of Pyrrhus with many specifically religious elements.[49] For example, Ennius includes in his narrative an episode in which Pyrrhus receives an ambiguous oracle—much like the one that Herodotus' Croesus received—from Delphi (*Ann.* 167 Sk):

> *aio te Aiacida Romanos vincere posse*

> *I declare, son of Aeacus, that you the Romans can defeat*

Cicero, who quotes this fragment, includes it specifically in order to reject the historicity of this prophecy in Ennius on the grounds that "[it] is absent in" all of "the Greek sources" about Pyrrhus (*ista sors inaudita Graecis est, Div.* 2.116). There is good reason to suppose, then, that this prophecy may have been an Ennian innovation.[50]

Similar religious associations are involved when Ennius includes the *devotio* of what appears to be the youngest of the three Decii Mures, as part of a description of the Battle of Asculum, (*Ann.* 191–193 Sk):

---

48. See my discussion in chapter 2 above (pp. 69–70).

49. See Fisher 2014: 92–98 for the role of ritual in the Pyrrhus narrative. See now Taylor 2020a: 79–82 for the discomfort Lucretius' readers might have felt from the juxtaposition of Epicurus and Pyrrhus, especially with respect to religion.

50. Skutsch 1985: 333–334 and Fantham 2006: 555.

> *divi hoc audite parumper:*
> *ut pro Romano populo prognariter armis*
> *certando prudens animam de corpore mitto.*

> *O Gods, listen a moment to this,*
> *how by fighting on behalf of the Roman people in arms,*
> *I deliberately with foresight deliver my soul from my body.*

We must conclude that Ennius introduced this religious element into his narrative of the war with Pyrrhus in direct contradiction of all other independent historical records. Nonius (150.5) ascribes this fragment specifically to *Annales* 6, so that this ought to be the third Decius speaking. The problem, of course, is that the Romans *lost* this battle, even if Pyrrhus' army suffered heavy losses.[51] The only evidence for a successful *devotio* before the Battle of Asculum is Cicero (*Fin.* 2.61; cf. *Tusc.* 1.89), but scholars have long assumed that Cicero follows Ennius himself on this point, given the general similarities between their treatments.[52] Again, it appears that the inclusion of this episode is an Ennian innovation that adds to the religious atmosphere of *Annales* 6 as a whole.

I want to note one final religious innovation in Ennius' Pyrrhus narrative. Ennius may have had Pyrrhus dedicate an epigram to the Temple of Jupiter in Tarentum after the battle of Heraclea (*Ann.* 180–182 Sk):

> *qui antehac*
> *invicti fuere viri, pater optume Olympi,*
> *hos ego vi pugna vici victusque sum ab isdem.*

> *Best father of Olympus,*
> *those men who had never yet been defeated,*
> *I defeated these by force in the fight, but I was defeated by them.*

---

51. Skutsch 1985: 354 suggests on the basis of the very uncertain historical facts surrounding this *devotio*, that one did indeed take place, but that it failed and the third Decius Mus remained alive (see also Fisher 2014: 112–115). Of course, this is a key instance of what Elliott 2013: esp. 7–8 criticizes in Skutsch's method, namely his tendency to prize the *Annales* as a historical source.

52. The present tense of *mitto* suggests that Decius Mus is in the process of performing the *devotio*. Of course, we cannot know the outcome of this *devotio* in the *Annales* narrative. Skutsch suggests that Livy and the majority of historians eliminated this story because it was embarrassing. But it appears that Ennius offered a balanced presentation of Pyrrhus; such a blunder on the Romans' part would contribute to the positive characterization of Pyrrhus we have reason to believe Ennius provided, by de-heroizing his Roman opponent.

The attestation of this fragment is notoriously complicated, and there is no independent evidence that this fragment appeared in the works of Ennius.[53] We ought to be cautious in accepting these lines as part of Ennius' narrative of the war with Pyrrhus, but if editors are correct in ascribing this fragment to *Annales* 6, then we have one more example of an Ennian innovation that contributes to the particularly religious characterization of Pyrrhus.

Regardless of what Ennius may or may not have written in the *Annales* about Pyrrhus and his religiosity, Lucretius' reception of Ennius' Pyrrhus regularly implies that he was a prime representative of the un-Epicurean religious world-view that comes under attack in the *DRN*. Such an attack on the religious world-view was already the primary point of the passage in which Lucretius anoints Epicurus as a latter-day *Graius homo*, who, unlike Ennius' Pyrrhus (Lucretius implies), stood against the destructive force of *religio*, bursting through the *moenia mundi* to bring back to humanity the universal truths that remove humans from the oppression of superstition.

Later in the poem, Lucretius similarly alludes to Ennius' Pyrrhus as a paragon of un-Epicurean religiosity. Lucretius begins Book 5 with a line that closely resembles one from *Annales* 6 and that expresses the difficulty of doing justice to the war with Pyrrhus:

> *Quis potis est dignum pollenti pectore carmen*
> *condere*   *(Lucr. 5.1–2)*

> *Who with mighty mind is able to write a worthy song . . .*

> *Quis potis ingentis oras evolvere belli*   *(Ann. 164 Sk)*

> *Who is able to unfold the huge contours of the war?*

In the proem to *DRN* 5, Lucretius explicitly extols Epicurus' gifts to humanity, chief among which are the truly *divina reperta* (5.13) about the gods themselves (*imortalibu' de divis dare dicta suerit*, 5.53, a line especially filled with Ennianisms, including sigmatic ecthlipsis and a fourfold repetition of word-initial -*d*). As if

---

53. The story explaining Pyrrhus' dedication of this epigram is told by Orosius (4.1.14), and it is almost certainly an invention by one of his sources. Editors have generally followed Lautius in attributing this epigram ultimately to Ennius, assuming that Orosius found it in Livy, who on this hypothesis would have quoted it from Ennius. Lautius' suggestion was published in Cholinus' Mainz edition of Orosius in 1615. For a much more detailed history of the problem, see Skutsch 1985: 344–346.

to hammer home the Ennian aspects of *DRN* 5, Lucretius ends this proem by cross-referencing his description of Ennius' *somnium* (*rerum naturam expandere dictis*, 1.126; *rerum naturam pandere dictis*, 5.54). By beginning this book with an allusion to the beginning of Ennius' narrative of the war with Pyrrhus, Lucretius again implies that his Epicurus offers the correct understanding of religious matters, while Ennius' Pyrrhus (Lucretius implies) stands in as a foil for Epicurus' pronouncements about the gods.

Lucretius develops this juxtaposition of Epicurean theology and Ennius' Pyrrhus later in *DRN* 5. Discussing the origin of *religio*, "religious superstition," in human history, Lucretius offers examples of misunderstood phenomena that humans often impute to hostile divinities. Included in this list is the admiral who prays to the gods when his fleet is taken by a storm (Lucr. 5.1226–1235):

> *summa etiam cum vis violenti per mare venti*
> *induperatorem classis super aequora verrit*
> *cum validis pariter legionibus atque elephantis,*
> *non divom pacem votis adit ac prece quaesit*
> *ventorum pavidus paces animasque secundas,*
> *nequiquam, quoniam violento turbine saepe*
> *correptus nihilo fertur minus ad vada leti?*
> *usque adeo res humanas vis abdita quaedam*
> *opterit et pulchros fascis saevasque secures*
> *proculcare ac ludibrio sibi habere videtur.*

> *Also when the surest strength of the savage wind at sea*
> *sweeps the commander of a fleet over the waters*
> *equally along with his strong legions and elephants,*
> *does he not seek the peace of the gods with vows and*
> *in fear ask through prayer for calm from the winds and favorable breezes,*
> *all in vain, since often caught up in a fierce hurricane*
> *he is borne nevertheless to the shoals of death?*
> *To such an extent does some inscrutable force overwhelm human affairs*
> *and it is seen to tread underfoot and make sport for itself*
> *of the magnificent rods and fierce axes.*

The example used to illustrate Lucretius' main point is significantly overdetermined. It does not deal with a generic sea captain, but one whose fleet carries *elephants* over the sea (Lucr. 5.1228). Picking up on this detail, most commentators have suggested that Lucretius alludes here to Pyrrhus of Epirus, the general who most famously sailed to Italy carrying elephants, and specifically to Ennius' version of the Pyrrhus narrative.[54] This suggestion is bolstered by the fact that Lucretius appears to allude to the Ennian line-ending *atque elephanti* (*Ann.* 236 Sk) with his own *atque elephantis* (5.1228); these are the only two instances of this collocation in all of Latin poetry, and they occur in the same metrical *sedes* in both Ennius and Lucretius.[55] Moreover, the noun "commander" (*induperatorem,* Lucr. 5.1227) may also point to Ennius, as this is an archaism that Ennius used (*Ann.* 78, 322, 347, 577 Sk) in place of the metrically intractable *impĕrātor*.[56] I can add to these observations the fact that this commander has characteristics that would associate him with Odysseus, and that this association may also hint at Ennius' Pyrrhus. Not only is he left unnamed (just like the *Graius homo* passage discussed in the last chapter), but this commander finds himself in a storm at sea, a famous epic-type scene that ultimately finds its origin in Book 5 of the *Odyssey*.

The broader context of this Lucretian allusion to Pyrrhus contributes to our recognition that, in Lucretius' hands, Ennius' Pyrrhus is primarily presented as an example of anti-Epicurean religiosity. The main purpose of the Lucretian passage (Lucr. 5.1194–1240) is to lament humans' susceptibility to religious superstition, a susceptibility that stems from ignorance of what really causes natural phenomena. Traditional religious observance, Lucretius insists, is no piety; piety consists in the contemplation of the universe with an untroubled mind. But it is precisely our inability to confront calmly the more mysterious natural phenomena—the ordered progression of the heavenly bodies, lightning and thunder, violent storms, earthquakes, and so forth—that perpetuates traditional religious attitudes and practices. The *induperator* who confronts the squall with his elephants serves Lucretius as an *exemplum* of profound, if misguided, religiosity, and this admiral exhibits the very sort of traditional religious behavior that Lucretius implies Ennius had innovatively attached to his Pyrrhus. This aspect of Lucretius' argument against religious superstition reflects the fact that Lucretius reads into *Annales* 6 an especially religious characterization of Pyrrhus and the Romans who faced him. Of course, it may be that Ennius himself developed this religious characterization more fully than we can now determine. Again, for my

54. See, e.g., Bailey 1947: 1519, who, as far as I can tell, was the first to make this suggestion, followed by Grimal 1963: 94–95 and Gale 2009: 201, who quite logically suggests that Lucretius specifically follows Ennius' account of the Italian campaign of Pyrrhus.

55. The Ennian fragment is ascribed in all the quoting sources to *Annales* 7, so it almost certainly would have described Hannibal's use of elephants in battle during the Second Punic War (see Skutsch 1985 ad loc). Lucretius, therefore, would appear to conflate the Ennian figures of Pyrrhus and Hannibal here, an indication again that the specifics of Ennius' narrative in the *Annales* are not as important as the fact that the *Annales* provided a narration of the Roman past that Lucretius actively works to undermine in the *DRN*.

56. Skutsch 1985: 227–228.

purposes, it is most important that Lucretius develops this line of reading Ennius in his poem for his own Epicurean purposes, regardless of what may have actually been written in the *Annales*. The main point for Lucretius, after all, is that the *induperator*'s petitionary prayer is fruitless precisely because it is founded on incorrect theology.

I have suggested above that on the basis of the fragments from *Annales* 6, it appears that the Romans who faced Pyrrhus also suffered from excessive religiosity, especially the figure of Decius Mus, who devotes himself before the Battle of Asculum. It is worth noting, then, that this passage in Lucretius about the *induperator* actively confuses the nationality of the commander in question. On the one hand, the line-ending *atque elephantis*, which I suggested alludes to *Ann.* 236 Sk, may actually direct the reader back to Ennius' Hannibal, not Pyrrhus, since this fragment is definitively ascribed to *Annales* 7; unless this is some sort of retrospective description of the Pyrrhus narrative from *Annales* 6, it seems most likely that the elephants mentioned here are those of Hannibal. On the other hand, all other indicators in the Lucretian passage suggest that he is describing a *Roman* ship. Not only does the *induperator* lead legions (*cum . . . legionibus*, Lucr. 5.1228), but Lucretius later mentions how human affairs and power structures are often disrupted despite our best efforts, and he specifically invokes the insignia of Roman power in this context (*pulchros fascis saevasque secures*, Lucr. 5.1234). It is worth noting, too, that we do have evidence for Roman generals bringing elephants back to Rome over the sea, so even that element may suggest a Roman identity for the *induperator*.[57] While I believe the most economical hypothesis is that Lucretius is evoking Ennius' Pyrrhus, he certainly goes to great lengths to condemn by proxy all manner of like-minded generals, regardless of their nationality. And it may even be that he is here condemning all religious behavior featured in Ennius' Pyrrhus narrative, by bringing forward an anonymous Pyrrhus figure who then refuses to conform to any specific national identity. The point for Lucretius is that religiosity is misguided, not that Pyrrhus, and only Pyrrhus, was religious.

Once again, therefore, we witness Lucretius alluding to an element of Ennian historiography, only to question its value, this time on explicitly religious and philosophical grounds. It is important to allow for the possibility that Lucretius completely reads this piety into Ennius' Pyrrhus, and to stress that it is also

---

57. For elephants in Roman triumphs *vel sim.*, see Sen. *Brev. Vit.* 13.3 (presumably Pyrrhus' own elephants?); Livy *per.* 19 (during the First Punic War:); Sen. *Brev. Vit.* 13.8; Plin. *HN* 18.17 (cf. Frontin. *Str.* 1.7.1); Livy 26.21.9 (during the Second Punic War:); and Asc. *Pis.* 14 and Sen. *Brev. Vit.* 13.6 (Pompey the Great). I thank Andrew Riggsby for directing me to these ancient citations.

entirely possible that Ennius' presentation of Pyrrhus' piety (to the extent that there was such a presentation) was neutral, and not laudatory. It is important to allow for this, because, on this view, Lucretius would be developing what may have been in the *Annales* a latent or subsidiary element in the Pyrrhus narrative. After all, Pyrrhus' religious or superstitious behavior did nothing to affect the outcome of his expedition into Italy. And any such behavior he exhibited would stand in direct contradiction to the ancestral impiety associated with his family.[58] So there is every reason to assume that Lucretius is misrepresenting what was in Ennius, even as he is tendentiously developing an element that almost certainly featured in some capacity in Ennius' narrative. Such a procedure is in line with the basic thesis I have been advancing in this chapter, and in this book more generally. The Ennius we encounter in the *DRN* is primarily a distortion that results from Lucretius' own self-interested motivations in articulating an Epicurean perspective of the universe.

Ennian Historiography in Lucretius' Anthropology

This allusion to Ennius' Pyrrhus at *DRN* 5.1226–1235 must also be viewed in the broader context of Lucretius' allusions to the *Annales* throughout the Anthropology, which represent perhaps the most sustained engagement with the *Annales* that we find in the *DRN*. In the context of the Anthropology, Lucretius' reception of Ennius' Pyrrhus must be viewed as part of his emphatic repudiation of teleological historiography. Lucretius implies that, for his purposes, the *Annales* stands in as the defining instantiation of a teleological view of the past. This process begins already with the first line of *DRN* 5, which, as suggested above, alludes directly to the opening of Ennius' narrative of the war against Pyrrhus. Lucretius' substitution of Epicurus for Ennius' Pyrrhus should also be read as another facet in Lucretius' broader revaluation of Ennian historiography, albeit on a much larger scale than what we have explored so far. Ennian historiography, as I have suggested already, gives way, in the hands of Lucretius, to natural historiography. Ennius, in a line from a book that narrated the Roman war with Pyrrhus, asks who has the power to "unroll the huge contours of war." Lucretius, in the first line of a book in which he will narrate almost the entire natural history of the earth, including the prehistory of humankind, asks who is able to write a poem worthy of Epicurus, the discoverer of the truths that Lucretius is about to expound. The reminiscence in line 1 of *DRN* 5 refocuses the reader's attention from the relatively unimportant topic of a single historical war, and from the poet

---

58. As represented above all in Euripides' *Andromache* and Book 2 of Vergil's *Aeneid*.

who wrote about it, to a universally important topic of natural history, and to the philosopher who disclosed the truth of it, not the poet who celebrates the discoverer. As a result, the importance of Epicurus, the protagonist of natural historiography par excellence, eclipses that of the historical protagonist Pyrrhus. If we view these allusions as they progress, we can see how the first appearance of Epicurus in the *DRN* as a *Graius homo* like Pyrrhus culminates in the opening of *DRN* 5, where Lucretius offers Epicurean natural historiography as an alternative to Ennian epic historiography.[59]

One way to assess the claim that Lucretius is effectively making at the beginning of *DRN* 5 with respect to Ennius' *Annales* is by taking Jackie Elliott's suggestion that Ennius begins the *Annales* with Homer's cosmology in the Dream in order to provide a causal prologue to the events of Roman history.[60] When Lucretius offers a systematic cosmology as prelude to his Anthropology in the first half of *DRN* 5, we might read this as an appropriation of this Ennian procedure. The diachronic account of human experience that Lucretius gives in the Anthropology thus takes the place of, and invites comparison with, Ennius' history of the Roman state. Where Ennius focuses on one unique people in fashioning his account of the most significant and powerful human institution of all time, Lucretius instead focuses on the very distant past when there were as yet no nations, and he assumes that his subject is human nature and that it transcends (or predates) national identity. Ennius may depict the Roman national character as evolving; Lucretius seems to treat human development over time as an epiphenomenon that changes while the underlying nature of human life remains the same.[61]

The result of Lucretius' engagement with the *Annales* in the Anthropology, in other words, is an emphatic rejection of the teleological interpretation of the past that scholars, especially Elliott and Fabrizi, have argued characterizes the narrative of the *Annales*.[62] A persuasive argument that has been made by more than one important scholar of the *Annales* does not constitute fact, of course, but nevertheless the *Annales does* appear to be a generally diachronic narrative of Roman history. In the wake of Jackie Elliott's work, we have to confront the

---

59. On the epic narratological aspects of *DRN* 5, see Gale 2004.

60. Elliott 2013: 246.

61. Farrell 1994.

62. Elliott 2013: 292 (cf. ibid.: 284) argues that Ennius' presentation of the past was largely teleological, concluding "that the teleological view [of history] to all intents and purposes trumped the cyclical view, which served its purpose well enough by guaranteeing, on the basis of the past, the significance of the present, Roman moment; in the triumph of that moment, the future was for now untroubling or out of view."

fact that Skutsch's relentlessly chronological reconstruction of the *Annales* is based on almost no actual evidence in our sources for the fragments. Working from Elliott's own list of all the fragments given secure book-attribution, however, it is clear that the *Annales* is *generally* chronological in its treatment of the Roman past:[63] from early mythology to Romulus and Remus in Book 1 (Ilia's Prayer=*Ann.* 58–59 Sk; the she-wolf=*Ann.* 66–68 Sk), to the ascension of Tarquin in Book 3 (*Ann.* 138 Sk), to Pyrrhus in Book 5 (*Ann.* 166 Sk), to the speech of Servilius in Book 7, which one must date to the last half of the 3rd century BCE, regardless of which Servilius is meant (*Ann.* 268–286 Sk), to the consulship (or censorship?) of Tuditanus and Cethegus in the last decade of the 3rd century in Book 9 (*Ann.* 304–308 Sk), to Antiochus' discussion of his conferences with Hannibal in the 190s BCE in Book 13 (*Ann.* 371–373 Sk), and, finally, to the mention of the *Histri* at Ambracia in Book 15 (*Ann.* 398 Sk) and of the Ilyrian king Epulo in Book 16 (*Ann.* 408 Sk). This is all to say that even if we should be wary of the chronological specificity in Skutsch's reconstruction, this does not mean that we cannot be sure that the *Annales* in the broadest strokes narrated Roman history diachronically.

Viewed from the perspective of the wider Greco-Roman tradition, it would be a bizarre aberration if Ennius had not written a diachronic narrative in the *Annales*. Beginning with Homer, every epic poem we have insists on the linear progression of time, even as this linear progression is disrupted by flashbacks and similar devices. To make the point *a fortiori*: even Ovid's *Metamorphoses*, which is the most narratologically disruptive epic in this tradition, reveling in inset narratives, stories within stories, deviant focalizations, and so forth, tells a broadly diachronic story from the cosmogony in the first book to the deification of Julius Caesar and the reign of Augustus, under whose rule the poem was written, in the last book.[64]

Of course, diachrony does not necessarily imply teleology, so we must be careful in how much we read into the *Annales* on the basis of its broadly diachronic narrative. Just as was the case with regard to Elliott's argument about Romanocentrism in the *Annales*, we must be clear that Ennius does not actually say in the fragments of

---

63. Elliott 2013: 308–325.

64. Over one-fourth of the *Metamorphoses* disrupts the diachronic narrative: 3,369 out of the *Metamorphoses*' 11,995 lines: Mercury on Syrinx (1.689–712); the embedded narratives surrounding Apollo's crow (2.542–595); Acoetes' speech to Pentheus (3.582–691); the tales told by the Minyades (4.43–415); the Muse's story to Minerva (5.269–678); Aeacus' narrative of the Plague at Aegina (7.517–660); Cephalus' own tragic history (7.690–862); the embedded narratives at Achelous' house (8.577–589, 590–610, 621–724, 738–878, 9.4–88); Orpheus' song (10.148–739); Daedalion and Chione (11.291–345); the story of Aesacus (11.751–795); the stories told by Nestor (12.182–535, 542–576); the embedded narratives in Ovid's *"Aeneid"* (13.643–674, 681–701, 750–897, 917–965, 14.130–153, 167–440, 464–511); and the Hippolytus-Virbius story (15.492–546).

the *Annales* that the events of the past advanced purposefully to the telos of Roman hegemony. We should not, therefore, treat the arguments of Elliott and Fabrizi as factual, even as their readings do provide a useful way to conceive of the conceptual world of the *Annales* in temporal terms.

Regardless of what Ennius may have actually written in the *Annales*, it is clear that *Lucretius* fundamentally rejects any notion of historical teleology, and that he sets up Ennius' *Annales* as a foil for his articulation of this rejection. Goals and endpoints are not important concepts in Lucretius' conception of the universe. For example, Lucretius repudiates the very idea of teleological development at *DRN* 4.823–857, and his whole discussion of creation and evolution at 5.837–861 is predicated on the idea that there is never a *telos* that determines the function of anything. The key word for Lucretius is utility (*utilitas*, 5.860). In other words, the concept of *utilitas* served Lucretius as a ready-made Epicurean rebuttal to any teleological conception of the past (be it Ennius' or anyone else's), because utility precludes the notion of determinism.

It is against this background that we now can observe that Lucretius fills his discussion of the early life of humans with allusions to the *Annales*. On the one hand, it is important to emphasize that the Anthropology is the single *least* Ennian passage in the *DRN*, exhibiting .17 Ennianisms per line over almost 700 lines (5.771–1457), and this frequency decreases as Lucretius turns specifically to human life and the development of society (.13 per line from 5.1011–1457).[65] On the other hand, the preponderance of identifiable allusions to the *Annales* in the Anthropology is possibly the most concentrated in the entire *DRN*, suggesting that Lucretius here offers his most sustained engagement with the actual text of the *Annales* in his whole poem. The combination of these two considerations may suggest that the Anthropology, which in some sense is one of the most "historiographical" sections of the *DRN*, is also the least Ennian, because in it Lucretius may be trying to present a distinctly non-Ennian, one might even say anti-Ennian, account of the human past.[66] The allusions to the *Annales* we do encounter in the Anthropology are taken from places throughout Ennius' narrative, and are reordered and mixed in sporadically throughout Lucretius' account, thus disrupting the original context of these Ennian fragments. One way to interpret this gesture is to emphasize that Lucretius thus disputes any teleological interpretation of Roman history Ennius may have implied in his diachronic narrative of the Roman past in the *Annales*. Teleology is fundamentally anti-Epicurean, which

---

65. See Appendix 5.

66. The Athenian Plague narrative that ends the poem is likewise one of the most historiographical sections of the *DRN*, but similarly exhibits one of the lowest frequencies of Ennianisms (.17 Ennianisms per line).

necessarily means that historical teleology has no place in the Epicurean cosmos. In using language from the *Annales* to characterize the earliest humans, Lucretius juxtaposes his narration of the ancient past with the events of subsequent Roman history as narrated in the *Annales*. This may imply that Lucretius envisions these events as cyclically recurring, or perhaps simply as constantly occurring, insofar as he represents the events of Ennius' *Annales* as paradoxically reenacting the earlier situation of the first humans. If the same language can describe humans at any given moment in the history of humanity, it is difficult to see how there can be a teleological evolution of any version of human society—or, perhaps, any real evolution, at all.[67]

Lucretius implies that in his Anthropology he is an Ennian poet writing an Ennian poem, but he makes this implication as part of his argument that human progress is an illusion. As part of his discussion of the technological advances in the sphere of agriculture, Lucretius emphasizes the difficulty involved in farming, which is marked by the enduring of hard toil (*durum sufferre laborem*, 5.1359). The line-ending *durum sufferre laborem* looks back both to the difficulty with which metals were extracted from the earth (5.1272) and to the Sisyphean politicians who continuously strive after power (3.999), and so emphasizes the basic difficulty of the human condition in all periods and spheres of activity.[68] This line-ending is taken over from the *Annales* (*post aetate pigret sufferre laborem*, 401 Sk) in a fragment securely ascribed to Book 16 from a (proemial?) passage that appears to discuss Ennius' renewed poetic activity (*laborem*) after taking some time off (*post aetate*).[69] Lucretius thus characterizes the hard work that early humans endure to advance their situation with the same language that he earlier associates, on the one hand, negatively with the human desire for power and, on the other, with Ennius' poetic industry.[70] This nexus of associations implies that the difficult march toward progress for Lucretius' early humans is an Ennian endeavor, but also that the cataloging of this march in poetic form is inherently Ennian. In this way, Lucretius doubles the Ennian associations of his own version of human history by characterizing his own narrative of illusory human progress

---

67. The preceding paragraph is heavily influenced by the arguments in Farrell 1994.

68. Farrell 1994: esp. 91–94.

69. So Skutsch 1985: 565, followed by Flores et al. 2006: 409, who also cite these Lucretian lines as parallels. This collocation is not common (cf. Plaut. *Merc.* 861; Accius. fr. 72; also Ter. *Hec.* 17). Caesar, for example, prefers *laborem ferre* (*BG* 4.2.5.4, 6.31.5.3, 6.31.5.4; *BC* 3.41.5.3). The fact that Lucretius repeats this collocation suggests that he considered it important in some way, presumably because he found it in the *Annales*. See now Goldschmidt 2020: 51–52 for Lucretius' use of the noun *labor* to describe his own poetic productivity.

70. On the connections between farming and music here, see Farrell 1994: 94.

as an alternative to the account of the past presented in the *Annales*, and by asso-
ciating the act itself of narrating this past as an Ennian endeavor. Lucretius thus
implicitly figures himself as an Ennian poet writing an Ennian poem, and as a
result presents the Epicurean Anthropology as a rebuttal to the Ennian *Annales*.

The allusions to the *Annales* in the Anthropology function in three basic ways.
First of all, Lucretius alludes to the *Annales* haphazardly, without what looks like
any larger purpose beyond offering a reminder that his version of human history
is engaging with the version of the past narrated in the *Annales*. In this situa-
tion, Lucretius seems to allude to Ennius as ornamentation to his own narrative,
without any concern for what the original Ennian context may have been. This is
in keeping with his general practice discussed in the other sections of this chap-
ter: Lucretius regularly alludes to Ennian historiography and empties these allu-
sions of any historical significance they may have had in the *Annales*. The point
is to inflect his own narrative of the past with material from the *Annales*, and to
present, in other words, his version of the past as an alternative to the Ennian
past. The vast majority of allusions to the *Annales* in the Anthropology function
this way.[71] The two other effects of allusion to the *Annales* in the Anthropology
are detailed in the next two subsections: Lucretius represents the *Annales* as a foil
for his own discussion of the evolution of human warfare in the Anthropology,
and he alludes to the *Annales* as part of his anti-teleological narrative of progress
in human society as *DRN* 5 reaches its conclusion.

The Theme of Warfare in the Anthropology

Lucretius' account of the development of warfare in human history develops
this characterization of early humans with language taken over from battle scenes
in the *Annales*. Lucretius regularly accesses the Ennian theme of warfare, which
is found scattered throughout the fragments of the *Annales* in many differ-
ent historical contexts, to provide his own anti-teleological account of human
warfare. One conclusion we can draw from this procedure is that Lucretius has
no concern for any specifically Roman associations of the theme of warfare in
the *Annales*, and he certainly undermines any teleological account of Roman
military history that may have been part of Ennius' poem. Lucretius is most
interested in highlighting how little progress characterizes human warfare, even
as time advances.

---

71. For this type of allusion, see *DRN* 5.885=*Ann.* 448 Sk; 5.886=298 Sk; 5.945–7=482 Sk;
5.956=126 Sk; 5.966=562 Sk; 5.975=288 Sk; 5.986=33, 160 Sk; 5.1200=490 Sk; 5.1221=554 Sk;
5.1228=236 Sk; 5.1245=323 Sk; 5.1335=569 Sk; 5.1370–1374=537 Sk; 5.1386=581 Sk; 5.1395=446
Sk; 5.1428=205 Sk; 5.1429=540 Sk; 5.1442=217, 380 Sk.

Lucretius suggests that the origins of war are found in the first hunting expeditions. Ultimately, he connects these first forays in warfare to his later description of human military folly, as wild beasts are sent into the fray with disastrous results. Again Lucretius alludes to the *Annales* in all of these passages. Taken together, then, one can infer that Lucretius articulates a history of human warfare in the Anthropology that is presented in explicitly Ennian terms. Lucretius' point is to emphasize how little advancement there is in the art of war, as the earliest hunts and the more "advanced" battles both feature humans mauled by wild animals.[72] Lucretius describes the earliest hunts at 5.966–968:

> *et manuum mira freti virtute pedumque*
> *consectabantur silvestria saecla ferarum*
> *missilibus saxis et magno pondere clavae*

> *and trusting in the marvelous courage of their hands and feet*
> *they were hunting down the woodland races of beasts*
> *with projectile rocks and the huge weight of a club*

There appears to be a clear allusion here to *Ann.* 562 Sk (*nec metus ulla tenet, freti virtute quiescunt*).[73] The collocation *freti virtute* only appears in these two *loci* and once in Plautus (*Amph.* 212), and it occurs in the same metrical *sedes* in both Ennius and Lucretius. While the context of the Ennian fragment is unknowable, it almost certainly describes some sort of battle scene. A reasonable inference to draw from this allusion, then, is that Lucretius represents the earliest hunting parties as if they were filled with specifically Ennian soldiers headed out to do battle.[74]

---

72. On humans and animals in Lucretius, see generally Saylor 1972; Kenney 1972: 19–23; Schiesaro 1990: 122–133; and Gale 1991. On the connection between hunting and war in Lucretius, see Campbell 2003: 227–231.

73. As transmitted in the manuscripts at Nonius 214.9, the fragment reads *ni metus ulla tenet, rite virtute quiescunt*. Mercier's edition of Nonius in 1614 (149), took note of the textual issues identified by Bentinus in 1526 (*Cornucopiae*, 1305.16), and printed the fragment as we find it in Skutsch's edition of the *Annales*. Skutsch notes that it would be "churlish" to disregard Mercier's corrections, and cites as evidence the Homeric idiom ἠνορέηφι πεποιθώς (*Il.* 4.303; cf. 11.9 and 17.329). If we accept Mercier's restoration of *freti virtute*, which "at a very small cost restores perfect idiom and sense," then Lucretius clearly alludes here to this Ennian fragment, and probably to the Homeric formulae that lie behind it. For further discussion, see Skutsch 1985: 707.

74. On the causal parallels between hunting and war in antiquity, see Ov. *Met.* 15.75–110, which would seem directly to allude to this Lucretian passage and, through window allusion, back to Ennius, Dicearchus (fr. 49 Wehrli), and Porph. *Abst.* 2.20.

Lucretius also appears to characterize later developments in human war-
fare in Ennian language. For example, when he describes the killing of horses
by wild boars that have been sent into battle (*concidere* **atque** *gravi terram*
consternere *casu*, Lucr. 5.1333), he figures the horses in Ennian language as the
trees cut down for a funeral pyre (*fraxinus frangitur* **atque** *abies* **consterni-
tur** *alta*, *Ann.* 177 Sk). A few lines later, Lucretius again describes the battle
zeal of these wild beasts (*effervescere* **cernebant in rebus agundis**, Lucr. 5.1335)
in Ennian language that had presumably been used to describe soldiers in a
battle narrative (*olli* **cernebant** *magnis de* **rebus agentes**, *Ann.* 569 Sk). We
know from Macrobius that the tree-felling fragment comes from *Annales* 6,
and so should have described the gathering of wood for pyres after some battle
in the Romans' war against Pyrrhus. The context of *Ann.* 569 Sk is less cer-
tain, although given that Servius provides this fragment to clarify *Aen.* 12.709
(*inter se coiisse viros et cernere ferro*), one might assume that the Ennian context
also involved a battle scene. Certainly the verb *cernere* is used in that sense
in Ennius (cf. *Ann.* 185 Sk).[75] Regardless of its original context in Ennius,
Lucretius clearly redeploys it to describe a battle scene. By juxtaposing these
two allusions to the *Annales*, Lucretius again generally characterizes the early
life of humans in Ennian terms. But this passage also looks backward to the
origin of war in hunting, and the allusions to the *Annales* that we can identify
in both these passages can be seen as a sort of leitmotiv stringing together
Lucretius' narrative.

The fact that Lucretius frequently alludes to battle scenes taken indiscrimi-
nately from various parts of the *Annales* in his own explanation of the develop-
ment of warfare can be read in two ways. On the one hand, Lucretius accesses
what must have been a frequent theme in Ennius, insofar as Roman military
power was central to its universal domination. But his purpose is not to empha-
size the exceptionalism of Roman power, and certainly not to imply any tele-
ological understanding of Roman hegemony. Rather, Lucretius consistently
emphasizes, on the one hand, the haphazard development of human warfare,
as, for example, a response to the dangers posed by wild animals, and, on the
other, the helplessness of humans when it comes to war, as their best laid plans
still leave them at the mercy of *natura*. Lucretius' conception of human warfare
runs counter to that of Ennius, in that it implies the repetitive nature of human
activity, insofar as Lucretius suggests that all wars in human history, from the
earliest hunts to those narrated in the *Annales*, resemble one another. Lucretius'

---

75. On the possibility of this original context, see Skutsch 1985: 709–710 and Flores et al.
2009: 385.

treatment of warfare suggests that this aspect of history does not develop in a teleological, linear, or cyclical way, but that in some sense nothing ever changes in this domain: Homeric warriors and Roman soldiers of all periods are really no different from primitive humans.

Lucretius on Teleology and Progress

Regardless of how Ennius conceived of the past and its relationship to the present, Lucretius regularly alludes to the *Annales* in the Anthropology in order to articulate his own repudiation of historical teleology. One can read this procedure as Lucretius' (possibly tendentious) insinuation that Ennius has again misunderstood the nature of human progress, as Lucretius again regularly alludes to the *Annales* to emphasize that meaningful progress in human history is illusory.

An illustrative example of this process can be read in Lucretius' descriptions of the habitations, such as they were, of the first humans. Allusions to the *Annales* are worked into the narrative:

> *sed nemora atque* cavos montis *silvasque col*ebant
> *et frutices inter* condebant *squalida* membra
> <u>verbera ventorum vitare</u> imbrisque coacti   (*Lucr. 5.955–957*)

> *but they dwelled in groves and hollow mountains and forests*
> *and amid brushwood they were concealing their rough limbs,*
> *compelled to avoid the beating of the winds and the rains*

> *tum* cava sub monte *late* specus *intus* patebat   (*Ann. 429 Sk*)

> *then a hollow cave was spreading open inside far and wide under*
>   *the mountain*

> *volturus in spineto miserum mandebat homonem:*
> *heu quam crudeli* condebat membra *sepulcro*   (*Ann. 126–127 Sk*)

> *a bird of prey was chewing the wretched man in a thicket*
> *Alas! In how bloody a tomb was he burying his limbs*

The juxtaposition of these two Ennian fragments through compound allusion is combined with other Ennianisms (e.g., the hyper-alliteration of one letter in

three consecutive words (*verbera ventorum vitare*) in these Lucretian lines.[76]
Whatever the original context of *Ann.* 126–127 Sk, Lucretius envisions a differ-
ent scenario as he removes *volturus* from Ennius and applies the phrase *condebant
membra* to the primitive clothing that humans found in nature.[77] Later, Lucretius
alludes to this Ennian fragment again (*viva videns vivo sepeliri viscera busto*, Lucr.
5.993, again with hyper-Ennian alliteration) to describe how the first humans
were ripped away from their makeshift houses and devoured by wild animals. His
point is twofold. First, Lucretius combines different moments from the narra-
tive of the *Annales* to characterize the early life of humans in Ennian language.
Second, as if to underscore the repetitive nature of human experience, Lucretius
later alludes to this very same fragment to emphasize the difficulties faced by early
humans, who, in seeking out shelter from the elements, subjected themselves to
further dangers. The fact that Lucretius appropriates the exact same Ennian pas-
sage to comment on these two moments in the early life of humanity only further
underscores how repetitive the events of the past are. All of this has happened
before, all of this will happen again, and progress is an illusion.

As Lucretius concludes the Anthropology, he details in rapid succession
the achievements that characterize the advancement of human society (*DRN*
5.1416–1457), and his narrative of progress is again filled with allusions to the
Annales. For example, at *DRN* 5.1428–1429, Lucretius alludes in successive lines
to two different Ennian line-endings to describe the elaborate clothing that
humans strive after to their own disadvantage: *signisque ingentibus apta=cum
ingentibus signis* (*Ann.* 205 Sk) and *defendere possit=unus surum Surus ferre,
tamen defendere possent* (*Ann.* 540 Sk). The first allusion at 5.1428 repurposes the
Ennian cosmic setting to describe the decorative weaving of advanced humans.
There is a negative implication here concerning the softness of modern human
life compared to the earlier life that lacked such fineries. The second allusion
immediately contrasts the lowly weapons of the Syrian (*Surus*) in the *Annales*
who only needs one stake (*surum*) to defend himself in battle. Clearly these
Ennian fragments are appropriated into a context that has nothing to do with
how they appeared in the *Annales*, but the narrative Lucretius advances remains
emphatically Ennian in form.

---

76. These are the only collocations of *condere* and *membra*, aside from two later occurrences at
Verg. *Aen.* 10.558 and Sil. *Pun.* 9.99, both of which undoubtedly allude to this Ennian fragment.

77. *Ann.* 429 Sk is securely ascribed to *Annales* 17 by Macrobius, but even Skutsch is stumped as
to the original context. The context of *Ann.* 125–126 Sk is again uncertain, but clearly describes
the consumption of a human body by a vulture. For this reason, Skutsch followed most other
editors in ascribing this fragment to the death of Mettius Fufetius (Skutsch 1985: 276–277; cf.
Flores et al. 2002: 76).

The Ennian characterization of human progress continues later, as Lucretius describes quickly the building of fortifications, the imposition of borders, the invention of sailing, and epic poetry (*velivolis . . . navibus*, 5.1442=*navibus velivolis*, *Ann.* 380 Sk, and *prius actum respicere aetas*, 5.1447=*aetate in agunda*, *Ann.* 374 Sk).[78] Lucretius caps off the Anthropology (and *DRN* 5) by emphasizing the role of *usus* and *experientia* in human progress; these ideas of course stand in direct contradiction to any teleological interpretation of the past (5.1452–1457):

> *usus et impigrae simul experientia mentis*
> *paulatim docuit pedetemptim progredientis*
> *sic unumquicquid paulatim protrahit aetas*
> *in medium ratioque **in luminis** erigit **oras***
> *namque alid ex alio clarescere corde videbant*
> *artibus ad summum donec venere cacumen.*

> *practice and, along with it, the inventiveness of the eager mind*
> *taught them these things gradually, as they made progress step by step,*
> *So, gradually, time brings out each individual thing into our midst,*
> *and reason raises it up into the coasts of light.*
> *For they were seeing that one thing after another grew clear in their heart,*
> *until they came to the topmost pinnacle of the arts.*

Here, at the culmination of his narrative of human advancement, Lucretius employs the Ennian formula *luminis . . . oras* (*Ann.* 109, 135 Sk), which Lucretius has used at various points in his narrative of early human history (Lucr. 5.1455; cf. 5.781 and 5.1389). Of course, Lucretius uses this Ennian phrase many times in the *DRN*, but I suggest that it functions in the Anthropology as a sort of Ennian leitmotif, recurring throughout the narrative to emphasize Lucretius' attempt to present his own history of humanity by appropriating the language of the *Annales*, yet to do so in order to deconstruct the Ennian interpretation of the past. At the end of *DRN* 5, that interpretation is explicitly implied to be the one under attack, and it is one that emphasizes the role of teleology in human history. It is against this interpretation that Lucretius advances the idea of *usus* and *experientia*.

The last two lines of *DRN* 5 similarly involve the *Annales*. In the previous chapter (pp. 67–75, above), I argued that Lucretius' conception of an infinite

---

78. Bailey 1947: 1546 calls Lucr. 5.1442 "perhaps the most desperate textual crux in the poem." For a thorough discussion of the issues, see Murgia 2000. In this example, I think the secure reading of the rare compound adjective *velivolis* in both Lucretius and Ennius is sufficient grounds for seeing an allusion to Ennius here at Lucr. 5.1442.

universe implicitly targets Ennius as an expositor of a cosmos that is centered. This citation involves the powerful demonstration that any cosmology that involves a center must be both finite and, as a result, end up in cataclysm. These arguments are cross-referenced at Lucr. 5.1456 (*namque alid ex alio clarescere corde videbant*=*namque alid ex alio clarescet*, 1.1115). Lucretius alludes in the next line (5.1457) to Ennius' *Annales* (*artibus ad summum donec venere cacumen*=*regni versatum summam venere columnam*, *Ann.* 343 Sk). Whatever the original context may have been, we can say that this Ennian fragment represents the overturning of previous dominion.[79] Lucretius, however, alludes to it to emphasize the highest point to which humanity progresses. Implicit in Ennius is the idea that the highest power (*regni . . . summam . . . columnam*) can be overturned. Lucretius can thus be seen to use Ennius' own idea of political downfall from supreme dominion to describe humanity's highest pinnacle of achievement. Such an allusion to Ennius may inflect Lucretius' praise of human progress with a stark reminder of how transitory any *cacumen* is. This would be in addition to the fact that in the previous line Lucretius incorporates a cross-reference to cosmic cataclysm, thus undermining the stability or permanence of this *cacumen*. It is no accident that the *DRN* as a whole ends with a powerful demonstration of the plague that happens after civilization reaches this pinnacle in Athens.[80] Moreover, given that in this passage Lucretius explicitly identifies *usus* and *experientia mentis* as the primary factors in humanity's rise to its *cacumen*, we may read a further aspect to Lucretius' rejection of any teleological account of these phenomena.[81] As a result, we can appreciate how the allusions to the *Annales* that appear throughout Lucretius' narrative ultimately must be read cumulatively and polemically. Lucretius provides his own counter-narrative to the teleological narrative he reads into the *Annales*, offering an Epicurean version of the human past that emphasizes the anti-teleological nature of human "progress."

Conclusion

On the basis of my analysis above, it appears that Lucretius engages in a program of revision when it comes to the values that inhere in Ennian historiography. This procedure is tendentious because Lucretius insists upon what these values

---

79. This fragment is ascribed by Donatus to *Annales* 10, and therefore probably deals with some moment in the war against Philip. The specific context is unfortunately unknowable.

80. See further Nethercut 2020b.

81. Lucretius often employs *usus* this way in the *DRN* as the idea that refutes teleology (most explicitly at Lucr. 4.822–857; but the idea is implicit also at 3.971, 5.844, and 5.1287).

were while in the very process calling them into question. I began this chapter by discussing the *status opinionis* regarding Ennius' historiographical aims in the *Annales*, and now I want to take a step back, to triangulate my analysis of Lucretius' self-interested presentation of Ennius' historiographical aims with this *status opinionis*. If we follow Jackie Elliott's arguments that one of Ennius' major aims in the *Annales* was to position Rome at the center of the cosmos by constructing Roman history as the culmination of universal history, the Lucretian practice of emptying Ennian historiography of significance would have been quite jarring for the original audience of the *DRN*.[82] It may be that Lucretius specifically targeted Ennius' *Annales* in this way because the ideas that it contained about political *exempla* and the inevitability of Roman hegemony were particularly influential among the Roman elite in the first century BCE. Cicero is, of course, the best evidence for such an Ennian perspective. While it is not clear that he is typical of the period, we certainly do not have any major voice that opposes his conception of the *Annales* before Lucretius. In articulating an Epicurean view of the universe in poetic form, therefore, it was peculiarly advantageous for Lucretius to confront Ennius in the way that I argue he did. Lucretius' revision of the Ennian perspective derives not only from the fact that Epicureanism stands directly opposed to the system of values given poetic form in the *Annales*. More importantly, Ennius apparently made a number of universalizing claims for the significance of his poetic achievement, and these were bound up with the increasingly universalizing claims of Roman ideology during the years when Ennius was writing. In this way, Lucretius' reactionary reception of Ennian historiography provides a window onto potential (anti-)political resonances of the *DRN*, otherwise closed off to us because of the *Annales*' fragmentary state.

On the one hand, then, we have seen that Lucretius is ready to make quite extensive and explicit allusion to Ennius' *Annales*, relying on the reader's ability to recognize that he is doing so; on the other, such allusion appears to involve quite a drastic reorientation of how the reader is meant to respond to what appeared in Ennius. We can see this most clearly in the distortions involved with Lucretius' reception of Ennius' Pyrrhus. Such disruptive allusion turns out to be the primary means through which Lucretius engages with the *Annales*, and in the next chapter I will explore its effect in more general terms, investigating the concept itself of literary affiliation, considering both how Ennius conceives of the process and how Lucretius responds to—and revises—the Ennian perspective.

---

82. Elliott 2013: 233–294.

4

Ennian Poetology and Literary Affiliation in Lucretius

Ennius and The Paradox of Lucretian Poetics

THE PREVIOUS TWO chapters argued that Lucretius tendentiously represents Ennius' *Annales* as a philosophizing epic that narrates a wholly inaccurate account of the cosmos and its history, imputing ideas to the narrative of the *Annales* so that he can then systematically dismantle them. In a similar move, Lucretius' representation of Ennius' poetic persona—and, by extension, his own poetic relationship to this persona—provides for Lucretius a convenient, if constructed, foil for articulating elements of the Epicurean system, and for calling into question the ideas inherent in the poetics he attributes to Ennius' epic. As with Ennian cosmology (chapter 2) and historiography (chapter 3), the representation of "Ennian" poetics in Lucretius tells us more about Lucretius' poem than it ever could about Ennius' *Annales*.

So, on the one hand, my program in this chapter is to do for Lucretius' account of Ennian poetics what I have done for his treatment of Ennian cosmology and history. But, on the other, I must preface this investigation with a warning that the other chapters did not require: targeting the *Annales* via the *De Rerum Natura* brings to the surface an unsettling yet core contradiction in Lucretius' poem. This is, despite the fact that the *DRN*'s content offers a purportedly consistent accounting of the workings of nature, its very form (poetry) undercuts and belies the tenets of its content (Epicurean philosophy). By presenting in Latin hexameters a philosophy whose founder famously denounced poetry, Lucretius both "honeys the cup" of his Epicurean content and introduces a flaw in his plan.[1] This flaw seeds a tension that grows into full-blown paradox

---

1. For Epicurus' hostility to poetry, see Diogenes Laertius 10.121; cf. Asmis 1995.

Ennius Noster: Lucretius and the Annales. Jason S. Nethercut, Oxford University Press (2021). © Oxford University Press. DOI: 10.1093/oso/9780197517697.001.0001.

in practice. The opening lines of the *DRN* provide the most famous instantiation of this paradox, where Lucretius' evocation of Venus to intervene in the world simply does not work on the surface.[2] How can this traditional invocation of an anthropomorphic goddess, a formulaic trapping of poetry, exist in the same universe defined by the content of the poem it graces? Just as Hesiod's Muses boast— or warn—that they can speak truth or *lies that look like truth*, thereby calling into question the reality of Hesiod's claims, Lucretius' poem invokes a goddess that it then undercuts—disproves even—and evokes, both by name and in its modulation of the hexameter, a poet—Ennius—that it ultimately despises.

But does Lucretius go too far? Taking him at his word, his straightforward commitment to Epicureanism would seem to call into question the orthodoxy of his very poetic product, which includes the *content* of his poem, and, as we shall see, Lucretius seems to argue implicitly that, by the logic of Epicureanism, it is impossible for one poem to leave its mark on another. The correct inference to draw from this implicit argument would be that the *DRN* can both allude to the *Annales* and yet remain free of any Ennian associations. Is he wrong?

Yes.

I should state up front, before I get to the business of teasing out these poetic ideas from Lucretius' response to Ennian poetology, that I think Lucretius is entirely wrong when it comes to assessing the reality of literary tradition. Obviously, in a book about the literary affiliations between the *DRN* and the *Annales*, I cannot argue that the *DRN* is free of literary affiliations. Nevertheless, *Lucretius* does not appear to think he is wrong. And, so, rather than just treat this issue as a mistake—which is an option, by the way—and say that Lucretius unintentionally devalues and calls into question his entire literary and poetic pedigree in his attempts to discredit Ennius and his poetology, I think it is worthwhile to imagine that this move might instead be consistent with Epicurean philosophy, and certainly with Lucretius' systematic revision of the *Annales*.

And so, in that spirit, this chapter embraces the form/content tension of the *DRN* by digging deep into those places where Lucretius seems to dismantle the very literary affiliations I and others have shown his poem to emphasize. As we will see, Lucretius' attempts to erase and deny literary history make sense within the context of his larger program of dismantling the cosmic history he implies is narrated in the *Annales*. In the final analysis, Lucretius' deconstruction of the metaphors for literary affiliation that Ennius appears to have deployed represent his most aggressive assault on the thought-world of the *Annales*. Not content

---

2. See now Goldschmidt 2020: 55–57.

to counter the misguided claims about the nature of things that he reads in(to) the *Annales*, Lucretius repudiates the place in literary history that Ennius had claimed for himself and his poem.

Provisional Argumentation and Ennian Poetology

Lucretius' handling of Ennius and the *Annales* follows a pattern established by his invocation and demythologization of Venus, so what is at stake when Lucretius begins his poem with a goddess who cannot exist in the system that his poem explains? Lucretius insists that everything in the universe results from atomic configuration and dissolution, leaving no room for the kind of providential and interventionist divine framework that he adduced by invoking Venus at the opening of the *DRN* and by petitioning that she actively intervene in human affairs. As any reader who understands the basic lessons of Lucretian Epicureanism will recognize, an Epicurean Venus, if one can even exist, certainly cannot do this. And indeed, such readers will have their faith restored by the end of *DRN* 4, where Lucretius reveals that Venus contains no divine or anthropomorphic characteristics, but is simply the sexual drive common to all creatures in nature (*haec Venus est nobis*, 4.1058).[3]

I am not the first to recognize the tension between Lucretius' Venus and "Venus," nor am I the first to argue that this tension manifests the quintessential contradiction between philosophy and poetry inherent to the *DRN*. The most famous engagement with this contradiction dates to the mid-19th century: Patin's so-called *Anti-Lucrèce chez Lucrèce*,[4] which extrapolates from such tensions to argue that there is a constant conflict throughout the *DRN* between two notional authors: "Lucretius the Epicurean," who rejects traditional religious ideas, and "Lucretius the Poet," who makes use of traditional religious imagery. The figure of Venus, on Patin's model, is the most powerful representation of this strife within the *DRN*.[5] Nobody takes Patin's two-author model seriously

---

3. As if to test his reader in the next book, Lucretius returns to the mythological presentation of Venus at 5.737–747, only to insist again later, at 5.1017, that the Epicurean understands Venus to be sexual drive. These instances in *DRN* 5 can be seen to anticipate the "final examination" regarding the fear of death in the Athenian Plague that ends the poem (see Clay 1983: 262).

4. Patin 1868: 117–137; Patin formulated this theory with reference to Cardinal de Polignac's poem *Anti-Lucretius*, which sought to refute the views of Lucretius that conflicted with Christian dogma. See Clay 1983: 234–238 and Johnson 2000: 123–127 for discussion of Patin's theory.

5. See Regenbogen 1961: 363–377 for the most forceful analysis of Venus as evidence of *Anti-Lucrèce chez Lucrèce*.

anymore, myself included, but subsequent scholars, while rejecting his model, nevertheless accept that the two Venuses of the *DRN* represent a contradiction. Even those scholars who assume that inconsistency in Lucretius is the result of interpolation have not suggested that we remove the Venus-proem from the *DRN*, so Venus remains a major problem.[6]

I have suggested elsewhere that this scholarly response to Venus—to see the contradiction between these two models of the goddess as itself a "problem"— has missed the mark. Rather, the procedure that we witness with Venus ought to be understood as a form of what I have called "provisional argumentation," and so represents a major aspect of Lucretius' discursive method throughout the *DRN*.[7] Provisional argumentation is the process whereby Lucretius initially writes within a framework that will be familiar to his readers, but that fundamentally conflicts with the Epicurean system—e.g. he opens his poem with an anthropomorphic deity who resembles other divine figures his readers will have encountered in earlier poetry, or he describes natural phenomena in such a way that he would appear to sympathize with a traditional, un-Epicurean perspective on these phenomena. In this way, Lucretius eases his readers into the hard truths of Epicureanism. The process ends, however, when Lucretius revisits these initial descriptions from an unflinchingly Epicurean perspective. The inconsistent presentation of Venus as goddess and sexual impulse is not a thoughtless mistake, or the result of an unfinished work, but rather is an outstanding example of the provisional argumentation that appears elsewhere in the poem.[8] But while provisional argumentation is prominent in practice, Lucretius never discusses this practice openly at any point, as he does certain other principles of poetics and argumentation, which goes a long way toward explaining why famous inconsistencies such as Venus have been misunderstood for so long.

In this spirit, my goal in the first part of this chapter is to extend the insight regarding the programmatic provisional representation and revision of Venus to

---

6. O'Hara 2007: 56–76 provides a good overview of the issue and offers a nuanced perspective on how we should read the contradictions inherent in Lucretius' Venus. Deufert 1996, followed by Deufert 2017, 2018, and 2019 has advanced the proposition that all inconsistencies in Lucretius are the result of interpolation. Sedley 1998 has based his argument that the *DRN* is unfinished, Books 4–6 still awaiting revision at the time of Lucretius' death, on inconsistencies in the introduction to *DRN* 4 (*contra* O'Hara 2007: 69–74). On the ending of the poem more generally, see P. Fowler 1997.

7. Nethercut 2018b.

8. On provisional argumentation elsewhere in the *DRN*, and, especially concerning the eradication of the fear of death, see Segal 1990. Shearin 2015: 124–140 argues that the linguistic process we witness with Venus' name throughout the *DRN* mirrors the atomic processes at work in the poem.

another passage of obviously programmatic import, 1.117–126, in which Lucretius defines his own position in literary history, particularly with regard to his great predecessors, Homer and, especially, Ennius. The passage comes shortly after the Hymn to Venus, in the proem to the *DRN*, where Lucretius cites a passage apparently from the proem to the *Annales* in which Ennius declares himself to be Homer reborn (Lucr. 1.117–126):

> *Ennius ut noster cecinit, qui primus amoeno*
> *detulit ex Helicone perenni fronde coronam,*
> *per gentis Italas hominum quae clara clueret;*
> *etsi praeterea tamen esse Acherusia templa*
> *Ennius aeternis exponit versibus edens,*
> *quo neque permanent animae neque corpora nostra,*
> *sed quaedam simulacra modis pallentia miris;*
> *unde sibi exortam semper florentis Homeri*
> *commemorat speciem lacrimas effundere salsas*
> *coepisse et rerum naturam expandere dictis.*

> *As our Ennius sang, who first brought down*
> *from lovely Helicon an evergreen garland,*
> *to grow famous throughout the Italian races of men.*
> *Yet Ennius also affirmed that the regions of Acheron exist,*
> *expounding this in immortal verses,*
> *an area to which neither our souls nor bodies flow*
> *but certain likenesses of ourselves, all pale in marvelous ways.*
> *From that place Ennius recalls that the image of Homer, ever-young,*
> *appeared to him and shed salty tears*
> *and began to expound in words on the nature of the universe.*

As discussed in chapter 2, the standard interpretation of this passage is that here Lucretius is announcing his own Homeric and Ennian pedigree, even as he distances himself from the misguided philosophical principles upon which Ennius' own boast are founded.[9] In other words, Lucretius appears to align himself with Ennian poetics, but to reject Ennian philosophy, an alignment that accords with my argument throughout this book that Lucretius' own poetic style is Ennian in

---

9. Presented most directly by Gale 2007a who extends this passage into an analysis of the broader intertextual appropriations in *DRN* 1. On dreams, see now Masi 2020 and Zucca 2020.

many ways.[10] The result is that Lucretius has seemed to be an archaizing poet in the Ennian tradition.

However, my re-evaluation of this traditional interpretation in chapter 1 suggests that Lucretius was *not* the final poet in a continuous tradition, founded by Ennius himself, that remained dominant in Roman poetry until the Neoteric revolution, but rather that Lucretius learned from a few exceptional passages of Accius and other poets how to write in a hyper-Ennian style, and that he employed a version of this style strategically in the *DRN* as part of a deliberate allusive program.[11] Such a view of the matter might seem to entail a relatively modest revision in our understanding of Lucretius' affiliation with Ennius, but in fact this revision calls into question some fundamental and traditional, yet heretofore unquestioned, assumptions about the form, content, and poetics of the *DRN*. To begin with, the standard interpretation that Lucretius' reference to Ennius' Dream of Homer represents the marriage of Ennian style and anti-Ennian psychology may be much too simple.

Given that Lucretius goes to such great lengths to deny the validity of Ennian cosmology and historiography, as documented in the last two chapters, we have every reason to revisit this passage in the *DRN*'s proem. It remains, after all, the most explicit passage regarding Lucretius' relationship to Ennius and the *Annales*. One might wonder, for example, on just what basis Lucretius could be said to align himself as the third in the poetic line of succession from Homer to Ennius, if he rejects the philosophical principle upon which Ennius had established this poetic line? On what basis, once he has disposed of metempsychosis, could Lucretius maintain that such a poetic lineage might exist for Ennius or for himself? At the very least, Lucretius' rejection of Ennian philosophical content would appear to call into question how straightforward his embrace of Ennian poetic form actually is. If in practice Lucretius is *not* simply an "Ennian" poet, as the traditional interpretation of this famous passage implies, then we need to re-evaluate Lucretius' claims about his relationship to Ennius and Homer. Metempsychosis is crucial for this re-evaluation.

As we will see, Lucretius literalizes and then disproves Ennius' claims regarding metempsychosis so thoroughly that he, by easy extension, equally obliterates any notion of literary inheritance or affiliation. But, as any astute reader of Greek or Roman poetry will interject, when Ennius claimed to be Homer reincarnate, he was, more likely than not, merely metaphorically claiming his (very real)

---

10. On Lucretius' Ennian style, see below Appendix 2 and Appendix 5 and Taylor (forthcoming).

11. As I showed in chapter 1, there is reason to be suspicious of any putative Ennian tradition; and, as I show in Appendix 5, Lucretius' style is not uniformly Ennian, as he tends to cluster Ennian characteristics in some passages, while others are relatively free of them.

Somnium. Skutsch (1985: 750) rejects the idea that this image comes from the Dream on the grounds that Persius would not have implied that Ennius ceased to think of himself as Homer while still writing the *Annales*, instead ascribing this fragment to the *Satires*. One could object, of course, that Persius does not imply that Ennius *stops* being Homer; *destertuit* could simply indicate that Ennius speaks this line after he has finished his dream and woken up. In fact, then, this passage from Persius is very good evidence *for* placing this line in the proem to the *Annales*. If this is the case, then we seem to have further confirmation of the connection between the noun *cor* with Ennian metempsychosis. I note in passing that on the basis of the noun *cor* in this passage, Ennius' own assertion that he had *tria corda* (*op. inc.* 1 Sk) may have referred, in addition to his ability to speak three languages (as Gellius would have it: *NA* 17.17), to the three embodiments of his soul: the peacock (*pavone ex Pythagoreo*), Homer (*Maeonides*) and Ennius (*Quintus*).[25]

I return now to Lucretius' reception of Ennius' *cor*. By drawing an association between the soul, the heart, and poetics, Lucretius implies that Ennian metempsychosis is again under attack. In the psychological discourse that he advances in the *DRN*, Lucretius situates the higher faculty of the soul, the *animus*, in the chest. By doing so, Lucretius contradicts every philosophical and medical school in the first century BCE, all of which locate what Lucretius calls the *animus* in the head.[26] Lucretius repeatedly denies that the location of the *animus* is arbitrary (Lucr. 3.788–797=5.132–141), and thus draws repeated attention to this particular aspect of his psychology. Moreover, by insisting that the *animus* is located where the *cor* is, he connects his own ideas about the soul with those of Ennius, further complicating the literary-historical implications of Ennian metempsychosis. For Ennius, metempsychosis and his *cor* are both filled with poetological significance; both metempsychosis and the *cor* are directly related to his self-posturing as a Homeric poet. Lucretius agrees with Ennius to the extent that he combines psychology with the heart, locating the Epicurean *animus* in the *cor*. But by supplanting the Ennian *cor*, with all of its poetic import, with the Epicurean *animus*, once again Lucretius calls into question the philosophical basis of the most distinctive metaphor Ennius uses to represent literary

---

25. On the provenance of the *tria corda* fragment and further bibliography, see Skutsch 1985: 749–750. See now Fisher 2014: 24–26 for a novel interpretation of this fragment. On the peacock and Ennian poetology, see Glauthier 2020.

26. Sedley 1998: 68–72 takes this anomaly as evidence of Lucretius' Epicurean fundamentalism and argues that the poet ignored the discoveries of Alexandrian vivisection in order to parrot the teachings of his master. See now O'Keefe 2020: 182–183 for a nuanced discussion of this issue. Parody may be involved in this section, on which see McOsker 2019.

tradition: the organ of literary metempsychosis, just like all compounds, is subject to atomic dissolution.

By implicitly subverting Ennius' constellation of metaphors for literary appropriation, Lucretius shows once again that Ennius' representation of literary tradition and of the authority he claims as a Homeric poet violate the laws of Epicurean physics. The soul cannot be reborn in the *cor*, because the perpetually dissoluble *animus* already lives there, incapable of *repetentia sui*. Ennian metaphor cannot exist in Epicurean reality.

Up to this point, Lucretius' engagement with the Ennian *cor* looks quite similar to his engagement with any other sort of Ennian material canvassed in this book: Lucretius alludes to Ennius in order to reject what he claims Ennius says. But with respect to Ennian poetology and the *cor*, the same basic paradox that we encountered in the earlier sections of this chapter obtains: Lucretius' deconstruction of Ennius' poetology implicates his own literary relationships. This implication can be seen most famously when Lucretius appropriates the function of Ennius' *cor* into his own poetic manifesto. Here Lucretius pauses after his doxography of earlier natural philosophers to assert his own credentials as both natural philosopher and poet. Widely recognized as one of the most explicit statements regarding poetics in the *DRN*, this passage is filled with terminology that, as I have been arguing in this chapter, Lucretius elsewhere represents as fundamental for Ennian poetics in the *Annales* (Lucr. 1.921–927):[27]

> *nunc age quod superest congnosce et clarius audi.*
> *nec me **animi** fallit quam sint obscura; sed acri*
> *percussit thyrso laudis spes magna **meum cor***
> *et simul incussit suavem **mi in pectus** amorem*
> *musarum, quo nunc instinctus **mente vigenti***
> *avia Pieridum peragro loca nullius ante*
> *trita solo.*

> *Come now, learn what remains and listen more clearly.*
> *Nor do I fail to see **in my mind** how dark are the subjects;*
> *but a great hope has smitten **my heart** with the spur of praise*
> *and at the same time has struck a sweet love of the muses **into my breast**,*
> *goaded on by which now I traverse **with strong mind***
> *the pathless places of the Muses never*
> *trodden before by the foot of anyone.*

---

27. For the presence of Ennius in these lines see Volk 2002: 87–88; cf. Tutrone 2017: 320–322.

literary affiliation and pedigree.[12] By taking Ennius at his word in order to dismantle any literal notion of metempsychosis, and by smuggling in an erasure of the very literary tradition in which he overtly locates his poem, Lucretius presents his greatest paradox of all.

Ennius' Second Punic War and Metempsychosis in the DRN

These issues with metempsychosis and Ennius' *Annales* are not confined to the programmatic passage in Lucretius' proem. Much of *DRN* 3 concerns itself with proving that the soul is mortal and, consequently, unable to implant itself in another body after death. In the course of this book, Lucretius frequently alludes to Ennius' *Annales*, and the poetological associations of metempsychosis that are raised and problematized in the proem persist in these later passages.

In his fullest refutation of metempsychosis, which comes as an illustration of the fact that death is nothing to us, Lucretius asserts that if the atoms of a person's soul were to recombine after death into the exact same form, the reconfigured soul would have no recollection of its previous existence (Lucr. 3.830–869). To illustrate this point, Lucretius adduces the chaos that attended the Second Punic War, and his description makes explicit allusion to Ennius' version (e.g., Lucr. 3.834–835 and *Ann.* 309 Sk; cf. Lucr. 3.836–837 and *Ann.* 82–83 Sk) of the same events (Lucr. 3.830–842):[13]

> *nil igitur mors est ad nos neque pertinent hilum,*
> *quandoquidem natura animi mortalis habetur.*
> *et velut ante acto nihil tempore sensimus aegri,*
> *ad confligendum venientibus undique Poenis,*
> *omnia cum belli trepido concussa tumultu*
> *horrida contremuere sub altis aetheris oris,*
> *in dubioque fuere utrorum ad regna cadendum*
> *omnibus humanis esset terraque marique,*
> *sic, ubi non erimus, cum corporis atque animai*
> *discidium fuerit, quibus e sumus uniter apti,*
> *scilicet haud nobis quicquam, qui non erimus tum,*
> *accidere omnino poterit sensumque movere,*
> *non si terra mari miscebitur et mare caelo.*

---

12. See Gillespie 2010.

13. My discussion in the previous chapter began with this same passage.

Death, then, is nothing to us nor does it matter a jot,
inasmuch as the nature of the soul is held to be mortal.
And, just as in the time that has passed, we felt nothing ill,
when the Carthaginians came from all sides to raise a martial conflict,
when all things shaken by the trembling tumult of war
bristled and shook under the high coasts of the ether,
and they were in doubt to which people's kingdoms
the lot of all humans had to fall both on land and by sea;
in this way, when we will be no more, when there will come
a severance of body and soul out of which we are made one,
you may know that nothing at all will be able to happen to us,
who will not exist at that time, nor arouse our sensation;
not even if the earth will be mixed up with the sea and the sea with the sky.

Lucretius presents here a basic argument against metempsychosis: since we perceive no negative effects from the Second Punic War in the present, obviously we will not experience any ill effects in the future from our current experiences. Death severs our memories.

The allusion to Ennius' narrative of the Second Punic War in this sustained rejection of metempsychosis at 3.830–842 expands the scope of Lucretius' rejection beyond the immediate context. Indeed, Lucretius' incorporation of Ennianisms into his argument against reincarnation here may function to extend his rebuttal not only to metempsychosis broadly conceived, but specifically to Ennius' explanation of the phenomenon in his Dream in the *Annales*. This extension implies, then, that the very notion of literary affiliation may be marked for rejection. At the very least, on the basis of the evidence that we have, we can say that Lucretius appears to be redeploying Ennian language in a rebuttal of Ennian ideas, exactly as we saw him do time and again in the previous two chapters.

Lucretius may be following Ennius' lead in associating literary metempsychosis with the Punic Wars. First of all, Ennius' Punic war narrative seems to have been quite substantial, occupying Books 7–9 of the *Annales*. This central position in the original fifteen-book edition of the *Annales* further reinforces the prominence of this narrative.[14] But Ennius' treatment of the Punic Wars was peculiar, because it handled this conflict disproportionately: Ennius seems

---

14. The *Annales* seems to have existed in a fifteen-book edition for some time. Pliny speaks of Book 16 as an addition (*Q. Ennius . . . sextum decimum adiecit annalem*, *NH* 7.101), and many fragments securely assigned to Book 16 speak of the poet's return to his poem after some inactivity (certainly 401 and 403 Sk, but see 402 and 406 with Skutsch's discussion ad loc.). For the most complete analysis of how the design of the *Annales* influenced the architecture of the *DRN*, see Farrell 2008; cf. Gratwick 1982: 63–66 and Skutsch 1985: 5–6.

to have quickly narrated the First Punic War without much detail, because it had already been treated by Naevius, and Ennius discusses this fact in what appears to have been a major proem that introduces *Annales* 7.[15] In that proem, Ennius also defends himself against those who derided his *Somnium* (*Ann.* 211–212 Sk):

> *nec quisquam sophiam, sapientia quae perhibetur,*
> *in somnis vidit prius quam sam discere coepit.*

> And no one has seen wisdom (sophia), *which is called* sapientia,
> *in dreams before he has begun to learn it.*

The *somnia* mentioned in this fragment must allude in some way back to the Dream of Homer in the proem to *Annales* 1, but now Ennius underscores not his similarity *to* Homer, as he did before, but his difference *from* Naevius.[16] Moreover, he alludes to the *Somnium* of *Annales* 1, but—apparently in response to some critics, either real or imagined—asserts that only a man with his literary culture would be capable of having such a dream.[17]

The logical inference to draw, therefore, is that Ennius here develops the ideas about poetic tradition that he presented earlier in the Dream, perhaps as part of a polemic directed at his rivals and detractors. In other words, the entire basis of Ennius' poetic authority, which we remember is derived from metempsychosis, is at least implicitly brought up again in this proem that introduces

---

15. On this proem, see Suerbaum 1968: 249–295; Williams 1968: 253; Jocelyn 1972: 1017–1020; Gratwick 1982: 62; Skutsch 1985: 366–378; Hinds 1998: 52–63; Habinek 2006; Wiseman 2006; Goldberg 2009: 643–647; Goldschmidt 2013: 55–61, 127–148; and Glauthier 2020: 35–42. The fragments I discuss in the pages that follow are all either explicitly connected to Ennius' Punic War narrative by the sources that quote them, or fall into what Jackie Elliott considers "reasonable modern attributions" to these books of the *Annales* (see, Elliott 2013: 315–319, 324–325, and 329).

16. The pertinent bibliography can be found at Skutsch 1985: 376 and Goldberg 2018: 214–215.

17. Glauthier 2020: 35–42 argues for the relevance of the Dream to the proem to Annales 7 in Ennius' wider poetics and poetology. Ennius appears here to activate the trope of the imaginary critic, the most famous example of which before Ennius was Callimachus' so-called Reply to the Telchines in the proem to the *Aetia*. Callimachus, of course, reworks this trope from earlier literature that goes back at least to Pindar (see Cameron 1995: 185–186). Gratwick 1982: 62 suggests that "here speaks not Homer reincarnated, but the Latin Callimachus." Skutsch 1985: 377 similarly proposes that here we have "a literary argument conducted in the spirit of Alexandria." Most recently, Goldberg 2018: 215 speaks of "evidence for Alexandrian influence on Latin literature at this seminal stage of development." Cf. Conte 2007: 226–229 and Goldschmidt 2013: 55–61.

the Punic War narrative in the *Annales*.[18] We have reason to believe, then, that Lucretius' purpose in singling out Ennius' narrative of the Punic Wars in particular in this argument against metempsychosis takes on a larger and more pointed significance. One could say that the motif of Rome's struggle with Carthage is important to Lucretius not only because it is so intrinsically important in Roman historical consciousness, but also because it appears to have been important in Ennius' *Annales*: Ennius gives it a central position in his poem and connects it to his literary apologetics, which, in turn, were fundamentally informed by his concept of metempsychosis. By alluding to Ennius' version of the Punic Wars in an argument against the possibility of metempsychosis, Lucretius apparently activates Ennius' own poetological discourse surrounding the narration of these wars, mimicking Ennius' own gesture in this passage.

I would suggest, then, that Lucretius' rejection of metempsychosis at the end of *DRN* 3 also involves a rejection of the poetic and literary-historical ideas that inhere in Ennius' Dream. Metempsychosis itself is programmatically associated with Ennius and literary history in the proem to the *DRN*, and when Lucretius revisits the issue in *DRN* 3, he alludes to Ennius again. Lucretius thus forces metempsychosis to be an Ennian phenomenon in his poem. Moreover, because Ennius himself apparently connected his Dream of Homer and literary metempsychosis with his narration of the Punic Wars in the *Annales*, when Lucretius alludes to this very narration of the Punic Wars during a refutation of metempsychosis, he activates the Ennian association of poetics, literary history, and metempsychosis inherent in the *Annales*. One way of looking at this section of *DRN* 3 is to say that Lucretius here develops the attack on Ennian metempsychosis that he initiates in the proem. In order to take proper account of that initial, proemial passage, therefore, we must consider what is at stake in Lucretius' response to Ennian metempsychosis here in *DRN* 3.

Form, Content, and Analogy in the Repudiation of Metempsychosis

Before I explore the implications of this passage, I need to bring in some important and generally accepted ideas in Lucretian scholarship about the relationship between form and content in Epicureanism. This digression will help contextualize Lucretius' response to Ennius' metaphor of literary metempsychosis in the passage from *DRN* 3 that I have been analyzing.

---

18. See now Biggs 2020: 101–104.

Both the *DRN* itself and Philodemus in his treatise *On Poems* posit a fundamental harmony between form and content, a change in the former necessarily affecting the latter.[19] Lucretius agrees with Philodemus' ideas about this harmony, most famously in his atoms-letters analogy (Lucr. 2.1013–1022):

> quin etiam refert nostris in versibus ipsis
> cum quibus et quali sint ordine quaeque locata;
> namque eadem caelum mare terras flumina solem
> significant, eadem fruges arbusta animantis;
> si non omnia sunt, at multo maxima pars est
> consimilis; verum positura discrepitant res.
> sic ipsis in rebus item iam materiai
> [intervalla vias conexus pondera plagas]
> concursus motus ordo positura figurae
> cum permutantur, mutari res quoque debent.

> Indeed even in my verses themselves it makes a difference
> among which other letters and in what order each letter is placed.
> For the same letters signify sky, sea, lands, rivers, sun,
> the same too crops, trees, living creatures;
> if not all, yet by far the greatest part are similar,
> but owing to their position the things sound different.
> So in things themselves likewise when the
> (separating distances, pathways, unions, weights, blows,)
> meetings of matter, its motions, order, position, and shapes
> are changed, things too are bound to change.

By connecting the atoms that make up all the compounds in the universe with the letters that make up all the words in the verses of the *DRN*, Lucretius can be seen to endorse Philodemus' ideas about the relationship between form and content. For Lucretius, form reflects and harmonizes with content.

Also relevant here is an argument that Schiesaro has made about analogy in the *DRN*. For Schiesaro, every analogical model in Lucretius that comprises elements taken over from perceivable reality must necessarily maintain a causal relationship with the generative bodies of nature.[20] The most powerful explanation

---

19. Fundamental is Armstrong 1995. On this analogy, see Volk 2002: 100–105; Noller 2019: 55–106; Frampton 2019: 58–62, 76–82; Nethercut 2020d; and Shearin 2020.

20. Schiesaro 1990: 27–29. On analogy in Lucretius, see also Schrijvers 1978; Garani 2007; Tutrone 2012 (cf. Tutrone 2020: 93–94); and Taub 2012.

of this argument is the passage about the dust-motes in the sunbeam, where Lucretius explains atomic activity that we cannot see by appealing through analogy to the dust-motes that we can see. The frenzied activity of dust reflects for us the frenzied activity of the atoms beneath our ken. More importantly, there is a causal connection involved in this analogy, since the dust we actually see is a visible result of the atomic activity and configuration we cannot see: at some point the invisible becomes visible and behaves the same way that it did before. Schiesaro argues that any analogy that points from the observable to the unobservable must also retain this causal aspect.

Applying Schiesaro's generalization to the letters/atoms analogy, it appears that Lucretius encourages the reader to extrapolate a causal relationship between atomic activity and poetic activity. The shifting of letters, words, and verses is the direct consequence of the shifting of atoms that make up these letters, words, and verses. Taking Lucretius literally, then, form and content are not only inseparable from one another, they are also causally related: any change in poetic form results from the shifting of the atoms that make up the formal aspects of a poem. At the same time this change in poetic form causes a concomitant change in the *res*—i.e., the content—that is signified by these formal aspects.

A note of caution: Philodemus and Schiesaro are potentially at odds with one another. Most obviously, Philodemus does not derive his poetic theory from atomic activity, while Schiesaro does. Philodemus, it appears, views the poet as someone who imposes formal order on the atoms, while Schiesaro's analogical model would seem to imagine that the atoms spontaneously create a poetic *cosmos*, one, in principle, independent of any poet or creator.[21] This tension lies at the heart of the *DRN*, a poem in which atoms haphazardly give rise to the universe, but that is itself the work of an author—Lucretius—who imposes order on his poetic material, according to his own understanding of the universe.

With these ideas about form and content in mind, we can now see that when Lucretius takes aim at belief in metempsychosis at 3.830–861, his inclusion of Ennianisms is even more pointed—targeting poetics in addition to metempsychosis. On the surface, Lucretius disproves the possibility that any reconfiguration of the same soul could be mindful of its previous existence by imagining the dissolution of a given person's soul, the scattering of its atoms, and their eventual recombination (Lucr. 3.854–858). Analogously, however, Lucretius presents the reader with different elements from Ennius' narrative of the Second Punic War that have been separated from their original Ennian thought-world and recombined into a new Epicurean context. In other words, Lucretius shows us in practice within

---

21. Seminal analysis at Volk 2002: 100–105.

the realm of poetry what he puts forward in theory in the realm of psychology. The elements taken from Ennius' narrative of the Second Punic War and recombined into Lucretius' own account of the conflict, even if we understand these elements to be "the same," as, for instance, the same elements form the words *horrida* and *tumultu* in both Ennius' and Lucretius' accounts (Lucr. 3.834–835 and *Ann.* 309 Sk), are nevertheless not "identical" with their former selves, because they lack continuity—*repetentia* in Lucretian terms or, as a modern critic might put it, "poetic memory"—with their former, Ennian instantiation. In this Lucretian passage, the act of appropriation should be seen as fundamentally disruptive: just as the soul cannot survive outside of the body once it has been separated from it (and hence the self must fundamentally dissolve), neither can a text, let alone some smaller portion of a text, survive in separation from its original context.

It would seem, then, that Lucretius' disavowal of metempsychosis carries with it not just a rejection of Ennian psychology, but also a rejection of Ennius' claims about literary tradition. Ennius, of course, claimed a Homeric pedigree for his *Annales*, which he represented as a form of metempsychosis, claiming that Homer's soul had migrated from Homer's body into Ennius' own. Whatever Ennius' intention, Lucretius takes him at his word and literalizes what likely was metaphor in the *Annales*. It is worth stressing, then, that Lucretius is almost definitely misrepresenting Ennius and distorting what he says here. Lucretius' handling of Ennius' representation of literary tradition is primarily a function of this distortion. Ennius probably meant to indicate, in the literal terms of poetic metaphor, that his poem was in the Homeric tradition, but Lucretius is more interested in explicitly denying that Ennius' concept of metempsychosis has any validity. And so, in Lucretius' hands any resemblance between the *Annales* and Homeric poetry is *not* the result of a transfer of souls, whether literal or not. We cannot know for sure what Lucretius thought about literary affiliation, but it cannot be denied that his dismantling of Ennius' claim denies the basis of any affiliation with Homer. According to Lucretius' representation, Ennius' soul is not that of Homer, because Homer's soul dissolved into atoms upon his death. We cannot help but be reminded of Lucretius' letters dissolving into different forms—if Homer's soul dissolved into atoms upon his death, so too, to extend Lucretius' point, do the letters and words of Homer's poems gain new form and content when moved to a new context. Lucretius' teaching insists that even if all of the original atoms had come back together into the very same order that had composed Homer's soul, but this time in Ennius' body, that soul would not be the same as Homer's soul, because it would lack *repetentia sui*. Consequently, the implications for the mechanisms—indeed, the veracity—of literary allusion are drawn into question. Lucretius destroys Ennius' claim with Epicurean truth, but he also touches on questions that continue to plague philologists.

Surely, most readers will wonder, even if Lucretius literalizes and then repudi-
ates the Ennian metaphor of literary metempsychosis, Homeric elements can be
recognized in the *Annales* and Ennian elements in the *DRN*? The answer is yes,
but I believe Lucretius would strongly disagree with me. First of all, the *Annales*,
however much it may seem to resemble Homeric poetry, is obviously not identi-
cal with any Homeric poem, even if we overlook the fact that the *elementa* of
Homeric poetry are Greek letters and those of the *Annales* are Roman letters.
In any case, it is clear that the *Annales*, to the extent that we can consider it a
paraphrasing of Homer, is by Epicurean standards a quite different thing from
the *Iliad* or the *Odyssey*. In the case of Ennius and Lucretius, because both poems
consist of Latin *elementa*, the analogical relationship is perhaps clearer and easier
to understand; and the result is still that the difference between the two poems
is most important. The *Annales* and the *De Rerum Natura* are obviously not
identical; but let us grant that the verbal texture of the latter resembles that of
the former. Lucretius frequently does deploy exactly the same *elementa* in exactly
the same order as Ennius whenever he quotes the *Annales*, paraphrases it, alludes
to it, or writes in what we would consider an Ennian style—these are the very
elementa on which I have rested the majority of my claims in this book. But in
light of his debunking of Ennius' claims to be a Homeric poet, I must infer from
his discussions of the dissolution of souls, both literal and literary, that Lucretius
would have hated this book I have written, inasmuch as I doubt he would agree
with anyone who believed that he, Lucretius, was claiming to be an Ennian poet,
in any terms whatsoever.

The scattering of Ennianisms throughout this argument against metempsy-
chosis underscores—reflects, even—Lucretius' dissolution of Ennius' claim to
literary reincarnation. Moreover, by explicitly rejecting the philosophical prin-
ciple that Ennius invoked to establish the literary tradition with which he aligned
himself, Lucretius calls into question the significance of literary tradition itself
as it is usually conceived and as Ennius clearly conceived of it. If there is no *repe-
tentia nostri* (Lucr. 3.851) when our souls have rematerialized, and if we follow
Lucretius' argument to its logical conclusion, taking as evidence his letters anal-
ogy, then there is no identity or other continuous relationship between similar
configurations of words in poetry, so that the very basis upon which literary tradi-
tion is founded must not really exist. Far from aligning himself with the tradition
entailed by Ennius' Dream of Homer, therefore, Lucretius uses Ennius against
himself to undermine Ennius' claim. Lucretius goes to such lengths to contra-
dict what Ennius says that he calls into question the very possibility of literary
affiliation.

The paradox is obvious: Lucretius frequently alludes to Ennius in ways that
assume that his readership will recognize the appropriation of the *Annales* in the

DRN. Yet Lucretius uses those same allusions to underscore a fundamental rejection of the possibility of literary allusion. Obviously, there is an inconsistency here.

This maneuver may seem disorienting, but the paradox that this kind of argument draws to the surface is not unlike the paradox that faces those who try to make sense of Lucretius' Venus, or of his basic approach to Ennian material. With regard to Venus, Lucretius relies on his readers' experience to interpret Venus in a certain way that they (the readers) will later discover is mistaken. Moreover, as I argued in the previous two chapters, when confronted with cosmological or historiographical material from Ennius, Lucretius relies on his readers' understanding of the way in which he presents this Ennian material in order to undermine the conception of cosmology and history that he has just attributed to Ennius. Similarly, here he relies on the reader to interpret an allusion in a conventional way at first, only later to infer that the conventional understanding of allusive dynamics must be mistaken. Conceived of in this way, Lucretius' lines on Ennian metempsychosis are a powerful affirmation that Lucretius' version of the *Annales* is the only Epicurean version of the *Annales* that exists or can ever exist. It may be that most readers will not extend Lucretius' logic here as far as this, namely to the point that one must conclude that Lucretius is calling into question the very nature of allusion and suggesting that literary affiliation is ultimately impossible. But, at the very least, it is clear that Lucretius is calling into question the historical importance that Ennius ascribes to the Second Punic War and the poetological importance that Ennius ascribed to metempsychosis.

Ennius' cor *and Lucretius'* animus

It would be difficult to stomach Lucretius' assault on allusion that attends his assault on Ennian metempsychosis if that were the only example we could adduce. But the fact is that Lucretius performs the same deconstruction at many other points in the *DRN.* In these cases also, Lucretius goes to such lengths to deny the validity of the claims he imputes to Ennius that he calls into question the validity of his own literary affiliations.

Another of the prominent images that Lucretius implies Ennius had used for his poetic affiliations is the heart or *cor.* Several Ennian passages seem to suggest that Ennius uses the noun *cor* in order both to underscore his place in the epic tradition and to describe the part of the body where literary metempsychosis takes place.[22] First of all, we can observe Ennius deploying the Homeric many-mouths *topos,* in which the poet explains the difficulty of his narrative task by appealing

---

22. On Ennius' use of this noun, see Gowers 2007.

to his own body's inferiority in taking up the challenge; here Ennius translates the Homeric noun ἦτορ with the Latin noun *cor*:[23]

> *Non si lingua loqui saperet quibus, ora decem sint*
> *in me, tum ferro cor sit pectusque revinctum*   (*Ann. 469–470 Sk*)

> *Not if there were ten mouths in me from which my tongue knew how to speak,*
> *nor if my heart and breast were bound up with iron*

> οὐδ᾽ εἴ μοι δέκα μὲν γλῶσσαι, δέκα δὲ στόματ᾽ εἶεν,
> φωνὴ δ᾽ ἄρρηκτος, χάλκεον δέ μοι ἦτορ ἐνείη   (*Il. 2.489–490*)

> *Not even if I had ten tongues, ten mouths,*
> *an unbreakable voice, nor if there were a bronze heart inside of me*

Here Ennius quotes famous lines voiced in the first person by Homer in the *Iliad*. It is hard to imagine a more perfect textual representation of the passing of Homer's soul into Ennius' body as imagined in the proem to the *Annales*.

We have less secure, but just as suggestive, evidence for the connection in the *Annales* between the noun *cor* and literary metempsychosis from Persius.[24] Taken together with the many-mouths *topos*, this evidence also appears to associate the poetic aspects of metempsychosis in Ennius' *Somnium* with the *cor* (*Sat. 6.9–11*):

> *"Lunai portum, est operae, cognoscite, cives."*
> *cor iubet hoc Enni, postquam destertuit esse*
> *Maeonides Quintus pavone ex Pythagoreo.*

> *"Citizens, get to know Luna's port—it's worth the effort!"*
> *So Ennius' heart orders, after he has snored off being*
> *Quintus Maionides, transformed from a Pythagorean peacock.*

Persius represents Ennius' heart as actually speaking, and, moreover, he implicitly—if ironically—connects Ennius' *cor* with the process of metempsychosis by referencing his transformation back into human form. It may even be the case that this fragment should be included as part of Homer's discourse in the

---

23. The bibliography on this *topos* is vast, but see Weinreich 1916–1919: 172–173; Courcelle 1955; Pascucci 1959; Wigodsky 1972: 98–99; Häussler 1976: 322–323; Skutsch 1985: ad loc.; Thomas 1988: at *G* 2.43–44; Farrell 1991: 232–234; and Hinds 1998: 34–47. See above pp. 37–38.

24. Feeney 2016: 187–188 and Glauthier 2020: 33–35, with further bibliography.

Somnium. Skutsch (1985: 750) rejects the idea that this image comes from the Dream on the grounds that Persius would not have implied that Ennius ceased to think of himself as Homer while still writing the *Annales*, instead ascribing this fragment to the *Satires*. One could object, of course, that Persius does not imply that Ennius *stops* being Homer; *destertuit* could simply indicate that Ennius speaks this line after he has finished his dream and woken up. In fact, then, this passage from Persius is very good evidence *for* placing this line in the proem to the *Annales*. If this is the case, then we seem to have further confirmation of the connection between the noun *cor* with Ennian metempsychosis. I note in passing that on the basis of the noun *cor* in this passage, Ennius' own assertion that he had *tria corda* (*op. inc.* 1 Sk) may have referred, in addition to his ability to speak three languages (as Gellius would have it: *NA* 17.17), to the three embodiments of his soul: the peacock (*pavone ex Pythagoreo*), Homer (*Maeonides*) and Ennius (*Quintus*).[25]

I return now to Lucretius' reception of Ennius' *cor*. By drawing an association between the soul, the heart, and poetics, Lucretius implies that Ennian metempsychosis is again under attack. In the psychological discourse that he advances in the *DRN*, Lucretius situates the higher faculty of the soul, the *animus*, in the chest. By doing so, Lucretius contradicts every philosophical and medical school in the first century BCE, all of which locate what Lucretius calls the *animus* in the head.[26] Lucretius repeatedly denies that the location of the *animus* is arbitrary (Lucr. 3.788–797=5.132–141), and thus draws repeated attention to this particular aspect of his psychology. Moreover, by insisting that the *animus* is located where the *cor* is, he connects his own ideas about the soul with those of Ennius, further complicating the literary-historical implications of Ennian metempsychosis. For Ennius, metempsychosis and his *cor* are both filled with poetological significance; both metempsychosis and the *cor* are directly related to his self-posturing as a Homeric poet. Lucretius agrees with Ennius to the extent that he combines psychology with the heart, locating the Epicurean *animus* in the *cor*. But by supplanting the Ennian *cor*, with all of its poetic import, with the Epicurean *animus*, once again Lucretius calls into question the philosophical basis of the most distinctive metaphor Ennius uses to represent literary

---

25. On the provenance of the *tria corda* fragment and further bibliography, see Skutsch 1985: 749–750. See now Fisher 2014: 24–26 for a novel interpretation of this fragment. On the peacock and Ennian poetology, see Glauthier 2020.

26. Sedley 1998: 68–72 takes this anomaly as evidence of Lucretius' Epicurean fundamentalism and argues that the poet ignored the discoveries of Alexandrian vivisection in order to parrot the teachings of his master. See now O'Keefe 2020: 182–183 for a nuanced discussion of this issue. Parody may be involved in this section, on which see McOsker 2019.

tradition: the organ of literary metempsychosis, just like all compounds, is subject to atomic dissolution.

By implicitly subverting Ennius' constellation of metaphors for literary appropriation, Lucretius shows once again that Ennius' representation of literary tradition and of the authority he claims as a Homeric poet violate the laws of Epicurean physics. The soul cannot be reborn in the *cor*, because the perpetually dissoluble *animus* already lives there, incapable of *repetentia sui*. Ennian metaphor cannot exist in Epicurean reality.

Up to this point, Lucretius' engagement with the Ennian *cor* looks quite similar to his engagement with any other sort of Ennian material canvassed in this book: Lucretius alludes to Ennius in order to reject what he claims Ennius says. But with respect to Ennian poetology and the *cor*, the same basic paradox that we encountered in the earlier sections of this chapter obtains: Lucretius' deconstruction of Ennius' poetology implicates his own literary relationships. This implication can be seen most famously when Lucretius appropriates the function of Ennius' *cor* into his own poetic manifesto. Here Lucretius pauses after his doxography of earlier natural philosophers to assert his own credentials as both natural philosopher and poet. Widely recognized as one of the most explicit statements regarding poetics in the *DRN*, this passage is filled with terminology that, as I have been arguing in this chapter, Lucretius elsewhere represents as fundamental for Ennian poetics in the *Annales* (Lucr. 1.921–927):[27]

> *nunc age quod superest congnosce et clarius audi.*
> *nec me **animi** fallit quam sint obscura; sed acri*
> *percussit thyrso laudis spes magna **meum cor***
> *et simul incussit suavem **mi in pectus** amorem*
> *musarum, quo nunc instinctus **mente vigenti***
> *avia Pieridum perago loca nullius ante*
> *trita solo.*

> *Come now, learn what remains and listen more clearly.*
> *Nor do I fail to see **in my mind** how dark are the subjects;*
> *but a great hope has smitten **my heart** with the spur of praise*
> *and at the same time has struck a sweet love of the muses **into my breast**,*
> *goaded on by which now I traverse **with strong mind***
> *the pathless places of the Muses never*
> *trodden before by the foot of anyone.*

---

27. For the presence of Ennius in these lines see Volk 2002: 87–88; cf. Tutrone 2017: 320–322.

These introductory lines of Lucretius' poetic credo suggest that he conceptualizes his *animus* and *mens* as located in his *cor,* which itself is located in his *pectus.* That Lucretius uses the same terms to characterize the Ennian process of literary metempsychosis as he does to contextualize the driving impulse of his own statement of literary purpose reveals how intimately poetics and psychology are connected in Lucretius, just as these concepts also were connected, even if very differently, for Ennius. Conventional accounts of literary history, both ancient and modern, read this sort of imagery as a declaration of belonging to a particular poetic tradition. And indeed, on the surface, Lucretius would appear to be positioning himself within that tradition, even as he establishes his own poetic authority on these terms. At every step, however, Lucretius undermines Ennius' literary-historical claims by complicating or even exposing as baseless the psychological metaphor that Ennius had used. Lucretius uses Ennius against himself in order to assert the impossibility of literary tradition as Ennius conceives of it, and claims for himself, in place of that tradition, complete originality.

Perhaps Lucretius is a good poet but a bad philosopher. The traditional view on these inconsistencies—that Lucretius writes Epicurean philosophy as an Ennian poet—avoids drawing this conclusion by separating Lucretius into poet and philosopher in the same way literary theorists try to separate a poem's form and content. On this view, Lucretius can both reject the philosophical basis of Ennius' conception and nevertheless follow Ennius in agreeing that some such conception of literary tradition does in fact exist. But the fact is that Lucretius undermines the philosophical basis of literary tradition, full stop. He does *nothing* to replace the notion of literary tradition with something that accords with Epicureanism—if anything, the philosophical principles he espouses make it near impossible for such a philosopher-poet to represent himself as a Homeric or Ennian poet.

Provisional argumentation offers us a way to understand Lucretius' poetry and philosophy—his form and his content—as working together. Much as the honey on the cup induces a sick child to drink medicine, Lucretius' "claims" to a poetic authority based on tradition are draws to his readers, inviting them to consider—and reject—poetic authority; this procedure finds an analogy in the way Lucretius' overt stylistic Ennianisms can signal that he is actually demolishing an Ennian claim.

When critics read Lucretius' account of Ennius' Dream as an example of *claiming* literary affiliation, it must logically follow that Lucretius, appealing to a familiar Ennian account of literary succession and criticizing the philosophical basis of that account, but doing so in a poem that looks Ennian in terms of style, must be endorsing the *form* of Ennius' poetry while rejecting the *content* of its authority. This kind of account disintegrates Lucretius into poet and philosopher

in its insistence on separating form from content, even as Lucretius' own phi-
losophy makes it impossible for him to reject Ennius' concept of literary metem-
psychosis while also claiming to be an Ennian poet. Recognizing that Lucretius
often employs this strategy of provisional argumentation, rather than trying to
find ways for both possibilities to be true, we ought to consider the possibility
that, as elsewhere, Lucretius is holding up a "reality" (poetic tradition) to encour-
age reader "buy in," only later to demolish that truth as an illusion. On this view,
Lucretius' declaration of allegiance to the formal principles of Ennius' *Annales* is
a gambit and, ultimately, an illusion. The paradox presents itself again. The para-
dox is the point.

Lucretius on the Water Cycle

The phenomenon I have been discussing in this chapter seems especially dif-
ficult for modern readers to wrap their heads around, perhaps because we are
the byproducts of a culture that often erects rigid boundaries between bodies of
knowledge. For us, "poet" and "philosopher" are completely different categories,
and so we are more comfortable, perhaps, with settling on a formulation that
imagines Lucretius wearing different hats. But, for Lucretius and his readers, the
two roles need not have been so discrete. In fact, the major work of Lucretian
scholarship over the last century has been to insist that poetry and philosophy
work in tandem for Lucretius, thereby banishing the *Anti-Lucrèce* from our dis-
course. Lucretius represents Ennius, Homer, and himself as poets *and* philoso-
phers, so we would do well to take him at his word in these matters and not to
sever poetry and philosophy from one another as we grapple with his representa-
tion of his own work *or* that of his putative forebears.

In this section I adduce one final situation where Lucretius' rejection of Ennian
poetology also appears to suggest that Lucretius' own poetology is Ennian, with
a view toward showing how Lucretius *actually*, practically, does the things poets
usually do to claim poetic affiliation, at the same time as he insists implicitly that
such moves are meaningless. Here, again, the interaction of poetry and philosophy
will be as central as ever.

Perhaps nowhere else is the paradox of Lucretius' representation of Ennian
poetics more pronounced than in Lucretius' discussion of the water cycle (Lucr.
5.261–272), a topic he marks as thoroughly Ennian. Not only does Lucretius
allude to Ennian poetry and deploy Ennian stylistics throughout this passage,
but he also cross-references his own discussion of Ennius' Dream of Homer in
the proem to the *DRN*. For these reasons, Lucretius' water cycle presents itself
as a critical passage in Lucretius' appropriation of Ennian poetics in the *DRN*.

The water-cycle passage appears in *DRN* 5, embedded between analyses of the cyclical conservation first of earth and then of air and fire (Lucr. 5.261–272, N.B. 5.269–272=6.635–638):

> *quod superest, umore novo mare flumina fontes*
> *semper abundare et latices manare perennis*
> *nil opus est verbis: magnus decursus aquarum*
> *undique declarat. sed primum quicquid aquai*
> *tollitur, in summaque fit ut nil umor abundet,*
> *partim quod validi verrentes aequora venti*
> *deminuunt radiisque retexens aetherius sol,*
> *partim quod subter per terras diditur omnis.*
> *percolatur enim virus, retroque remanat*
> *materies umoris et ad caput amnibus omnis*
> *convenit, inde super terras fluit agmine dulci*
> *qua via secta semel liquido pede detulit undas.*

> *Regarding what remains, that the sea, rivers, and springs*
> *are always overflowing with new moisture and that eternal waters seep forth,*
> *there is no need of words to show: the great downrush of waters*
> *on every side proves this. But whatever water is foremost*
> *is taken away and so it happens that the moisture in no way overflows in*
> * the sum,*
> *in part because the strong winds diminish it, sweeping the surfaces of the seas*
> *and so does the heavenly sun as he unweaves their unions with his rays,*
> *in part because it is separated out underneath all the lands.*
> *For the brine is sifted through and the substance of the moisture seeps back,*
> *and it all flows back together at the fountainhead of rivers,*
> *and from there it comes back over the lands with refreshed current,*
> *where the channel once cut away brought the waters in their flowing advance.*

These lines serve as an illustration of the concept of *isonomia* (Lucr. 5.235–305), the idea that there are always atoms available for creation only if atoms are constantly being released from dead or dying compounds. A necessary corollary to the idea of *isonomia* in the *DRN* is that all compounds, regardless of their complexity, are mortal and prone to dissolution. Accordingly, Lucretius argues that the major components of the world—that is, earth, water, air, and fire (in the form of light)—perish and are then re-created, and argues analogically that the earth as a whole must inevitably perish. The water cycle is proof of the mortality of our world.

Lucretius' account of the water cycle is insistently Ennian, replete with allusions throughout the passage (*retroque remanat*, 5.269=*camposque remanant, Ann.* 5 Sk;[28] *fluit agmine dulci*, 5.271=*leni fluit agmine flumen, Ann.* 163 Sk;[29] *verrentes aequora*, 5.266=*verrunt . . . mare, Ann.* 377 Sk;[30] *semper abundare*, 5.262=*semper abundantes, Ann.* 395 Sk;[31] and *tollitur in*, 5.265=*tollitur in, Ann.* 428 Sk).[32] On the basis of these allusions, I infer that Lucretius composed this passage so as to invite his reader to interpret it in an Ennian light, while challenging that same reader to understand its content in terms of Lucretius' Epicurean physics, in the same way as he has been shown to operate throughout this book.

Lucretius connects this passage back to his account of Ennius' Dream in the proem to the *DRN* by prominent verbal echoes that he associates with Ennian poetics. Lucretius begins his exposition of the water cycle with the phrase *latices perennis* (5.262). As part of the description of Ennius' Dream, Lucretius uses the adjective *perennis* as a pun on Ennius' name that marks Ennian poetry for its eternity (*perenni fronde*, 1.118).[33] As if to reinforce this association, Lucretius follows this pun with the collocation *Ennius aeternis* at 1.121. Subsequently, Lucretius uses the adjective *perennis* rarely, and every instance of it would appear to carry the Ennian associations of this first use in the proem. In other words, Lucretius associates the adjective *perennis* programmatically and consistently with Ennius throughout the *DRN*.[34] It seems quite likely, then, in view of the proliferation of

---

28. *Ann.* 5 Sk is a notoriously complicated fragment. All we can say definitively is that it belongs in Book 1 of the *Annales* and describes water in some capacity.

29. These are the only two instances of the collocation in all of Latin literature, aside from a line in Vergil that very clearly is alluding to this Ennian fragment: *leni fluit agmine Thybris, Aen.* 2.782, on which see Goldschmidt 2013: 81–85.

30. We only find *verro* with *mare* in this Ennian fragment and in another Lucretian passage (1.278–279), on which see Merrill 1918: 261. Lucretius' *verro* with *aequora* (5.388, 5.1227, 6.624) worked its effect on subsequent Latin hexameter (see Catull. 64.7; Verg. *G* 3.201, *Aen.* 3.290, 5.778, 8.674; Ov. *Met.* 13.961; Manilius 4.285; and Sil. *Pun.* 14.262–263).

31. The only two instances of this collocation in Latin poetry, aside from a later use in Ovid at *Ib.* 180; twice in prose we find this collocation (Cic. *Tusc.* 2.35.10 and Livy 35.48.7.2).

32. These are the first two examples of this collocation in Latin literature. Again, this phrase proved influential on subsequent Latin hexameter; see Verg. *Aen.* 11.745, 12.462; Statius *Theb.* 5.91; and Sil. *Pun.* 16.319.

33. We know of several passages in which later authors use the adjective *perennis* in ways that seem to involve a pun on Ennius' name, most famously at Catullus 1.10; Horace *Carm.* 3.30.1; and Ovid *Met.* 15.878. Of course, *perennis* is a common epithet of streams, rivers, and other bodies of water (*TLL* 1.A.1, *de aqua*, a.β *fere technice apud iuris consultos*). In the *corpus Ennianum* we also find *amnes perennes* (*V* 12 V). See Gale 2001b.

34. Elsewhere in the *DRN*, *perennis* appears only three other times, once in discussions of the mortality of the soul (3.804), and so implicitly as a rebuttal of the Ennian doctrine of

Ennianisms in the water-cycle passage, that Lucretius uses *perennis* both as a sort of reflexive annotation of the allusions to Ennius that fill his discussion and as a verbal cue for the reader to connect the "perennial waters" in the water cycle with the first use of *perennis* in the *DRN* to describe the poetic authority that Ennius gained by virtue of his Dream in the *Annales*. Ennian poetics and Lucretian water are marked for their "eternity."

Lucretius' use of the verb *manare* and its compounds in the *DRN* also serve to associate the water-cycle passage with Lucretius' account of Ennius' Dream. This verb, of course, forms the basis of explicit allusions to the *Annales* in Lucretius' version of the water cycle (*manare perennis*, 5.262 and *retroque remanat*, 5.268=*camposque remanant, Ann.* 5 Sk). It also may be central to Lucretius' description of Ennius' Dream in DRN 1.[35] If we accept the reading of *permanent* at Lucr. 1.122, then it is clear that Lucretius is connecting his own account of Ennius' Dream to his description of the water cycle: in the one, souls "flow together" (*permanent*), in the other, water "flows (back)" (*manare*, 5.262; *remanat*, 5.269).

Now, scholars have long fretted over the "obstinate crux" at Lucr. 1.122.[36] There Lucretius begins his description of Ennius' Dream, reporting that Ennius maintains that there are *Acherusia templa* (1.120), *quo neque permaneant animae neque corpora nostra* (1.122). In his marginalia, Politian proposed *permanent* instead of *permaneant*, citing as witnesses two late manuscripts; this emendation was adopted by everyone before Lachmann, whose restoration of *permaneant* won general acceptance in most subsequent editions (Goebel, Brieger, and Giussani are notable skeptics concerning *permaneant*). More recently, Skutsch in his edition of the *Annales*, Smith, and Flores have restored *permanent*.

The major argument against *permanent* was succinctly put by Housman in his review of Bailey's first OCT: "as if *corpora* could *permanare*."[37] On the one hand, we must acknowledge that Housman and the others rightly protest this reading with respect to *corpora*, if we are meant to understand the word to describe our physical human bodies. On the other hand, Lucretius regularly uses the noun

---

metempsychosis; once at 5.78 in a heavily Ennian context, marked by allusion to the *Annales* and by heightened Ennian stylistics (see above, pp. 56–57 and pp. 97–98); and finally once in another description of the water cycle that also alludes to Ennius (*fluviique perennes*, 5.463=*amnes perennes, V* 12 V).

35. I thank David Butterfield for discussing this point with me.

36. The quote is from Kenney 2004: 367 in his review of Flores' edition of *DRN* 1–3. In his recent Teubner edition, Deufert 2019 prints *permaneant*, but see Deufert 2018: 8–10 for the most recent discussion of this difficult crux. Rinaldi 2001 and Conte 2013: 69–71 both have endorsed *permanent*.

37. Housman 1900: 368. Bailey, in fact, later was to restore *permaneant* for precisely this reason.

corpora to mean "atoms," and at various points *atoms* definitely can *manare* in the
DRN (2.397, 3.706, 4.622, 5.852, 6.990; cf. 6.916, 6.927). This double valence of *corpora nostra* at 1.122 would be in keeping with Lucretian practice: he often emphasizes the fact that our bodies are made up of "bodies" throughout the *DRN*.[38] The
adjective *nostra* may even hint at the fact that the bodies Lucretius' describes are
his own "Epicurean bodies" or atoms, the only "real" bodies that matter. The use
of the verb *permanent* at 1.122, then, could also serve to draw the reader's attention to how Lucretius smuggles Epicurean doctrine into his account of Ennius'
un-Epicurean dream. The fact that Ennian bodies absolutely cannot *permanare*
should prompt the reader to consider the possibility that Lucretius is undermining
Ennian psychology by presenting it in the language of Epicurean physics.

In any case, we have abundant evidence that *animae* can *manare*. Perhaps
most importantly, Lucretius himself uses *permanare* to describe the activity of
animae (3.698–700):

> *quod si forte putas extrinsecus insinuatam*
> *permanare animam nobis per membra solere,*
> *tanto quique magis cum corpore fusa peribit.*

> *But if by chance you think that the soul's custom is to slither into us from*
>   *outside*
> *and then permeate through our limbs,*
> *all the more will it pass away when spread out in union with the body.*

This passage offers some corroboration of the reading *permanent* at 1.122, because
permanare is used here to describe an incorrect psychological doctrine, just as it
would be doing in Lucretius' account of Ennius' Dream if we read *permanent* at
1.122. Further circumstantial evidence in favor of *permanent* at 1.122 comes from
the fact that ancient etymologists frequently connected *Manes* with *manare*. For
example, at Fest. 114 we find *manes deos deasque . . . ab inferis ad superos emanant*,
and at Paul. Fest. 115 we read *manalem lapidem . . . ostium Orci per quod animae
inferorum ad superos manarent*. Even the editors who reject *permanent* on the
grounds that it is incompatible with *corpora* acknowledge that *permanent* is preferred with respect to *animae*.[39] Despite the crux at 1.122, then, the verb *manare*

---

38. For example, during the Plague of Athens, the proliferation of the noun *corpus* indicates
that the dead Athenian bodies also release their component "bodies" (6.1157; 6.1164; 6.1167;
6.1177; 6.1175; 6.1179; 6.1204; 6.1207; 6.1215; 6.1216; 6.1255; 6.1257; 6.1265; 6.1267; 6.1270;
6.1273; 6.1286).

39. See, e.g., Bailey 1947: ad loc.

both in the *DRN* itself and elsewhere in Roman culture was associated with the soul. On these grounds, at the very least, we are justified in recognizing psychological associations in the water cycle in Lucretius.

In any case, on the basis of the adjective *perennis*, the many allusions to Ennius, and the possible repetition of the root verb *manare*, Lucretius can be seen to connect his description of the water cycle back to his account of Ennius' Dream, suggesting that the insistent Ennianisms in the water-cycle passage should be read as an important component in Lucretius' representation of Ennian poetics in the *DRN*.

Sources of Water and Literary Tradition: Ennius, Callimachus, Empedocles

The content itself of the Lucretian water-cycle passage is a further element in Lucretius' engagement with Ennian poetics, signaling the allusive gesture he is making to Ennius, since water—specifically the flowing of water from some source—was a traditional trope for poetic appropriation. Lucretius activates this trope in the water-cycle passage in order to reassert the misguided ideas he presents in his account of Ennius' Dream: in both passages he takes aim at what he constructs as Ennius' claims about poetic tradition and succession.

This water-source trope had a long history before Lucretius, and this history metapoetically reinforces the power of the trope itself: as each successive poet mobilizes water imagery to figure his relationship to the literary past, the literary past represented by the water trope swells to accommodate the new poet. Hesiod was the first Greek author to speak of holy streams of water as a symbol of poetic inspiration, naming Hippocrene, Permessus, and Olmeus on Helicon as the bathing pools of the Muses.[40] While Hesiod does not explicitly describe himself as inspired by these bodies of water, by bringing in the Muses, he also imports, by extension, the inspiration that they provide.[41] The earliest poet to speak of his own inspiration from holy streams is Pindar, who drinks from Thebe.[42] With Callimachus, however, water becomes a central image for poetic inspiration and aesthetics. As far as we can tell, water seems to derive its symbolic importance for inspiration both from the initiation scene in *Aetia* 1—which is modeled on

---

40. *Theogony* 1–8.

41. Later epigrammatists make this connection explicit. Alcaeus of Messene in the third century BCE (*Anth. Pal.* 7.55) says that Hesiod drank from these pools; Asclepiades (or Archias?) mentions the laurel branch and the inspiring pool of the Hippocrene (*Anth. Pal.* 9.64); Antipater of Thessalonica (*Anth. Pal.* 11.24) mentions the waters of Helicon inspiring Hesiod. See Kambylis 1965: 66–68 and Crowther 1979: 1–2.

42. *Olympian* 6.84–87.

Hesiod's own *Dichterweihe* in the *Theogony*—and from the end of the *Hymn to Apollo* (108–112).[43] Whether Callimachus figured himself as drinking from holy springs or not—a subject hotly debated in the secondary literature—it is clear at least that he represented water as a source of inspiration.[44]

The content of the Lucretian water-cycle passage itself can be seen to activate the metapoetic aspect of the "water source" trope. In addition to the motif of inspiration by the Muses or Apollo, by the Hellenistic era at the latest, sources of inspiration figured as sources of water are understood as analogous both to literary "sources" specifically and to allusive relationships in general.[45] The conceit that Homer was a great ocean of poetry or the fountainhead from which the many diverse poetic rivers took their source, most familiar from its recurrence in Augustan poetry, crystallized in the Hellenistic period probably in the third or second century BCE.[46] That Lucretius, in a context with overtones of literary allusion and succession, connects the discourse of Ennius' Homer—the poet whose ubiquitous influence on poetry of all genres lent credibility to his figuration as the *fons et origo* of all poetry and all genres—with his own version of the water cycle, suggests that he meant to activate for his readers this well-known image. At the same time, the whole convention of Ennius' poetic dream can be traced back to Hesiod via Callimachus. Hesiod was actually the first to associate the Muses with specific sources of water, which, we may thus infer, convey poetic inspiration

---

43. The scholarship here is vast: Reitzenstein 1931: 52–69; Wimmel 1960: 222–237; Kambylis 1965: 98–102; Reinsch-Werner 1976: 6; Crowther 1979: 2–4; Knox 1985: 117–119; Cameron 1995: 363–366; Asper 1997: 109–134; Giuliano 1997; and Fantuzzi and Hunter 2004: 7.

44. As Cameron 1995: 364 makes clear. Part of the debate surrounding Callimachus' water-drinking is the dichotomy between water-drinkers, who were adherents of Callimachean aesthetics, and wine-drinkers, who positioned themselves opposite Callimachus. The scholarship here, once again, is vast. For a good overview, see Knox 1985; Cameron 1995: 366–368; and Asper 1997: 128–134; further bibliography in Albiani 2002.

45. Most relevant here is Callimachus' dream in *Aetia* 1, where the poet seems to have described himself as drinking from the Hippocrene. Since this source of water was associated with Hesiod, and since Callimachus' dream is heavily modeled on Hesiod's own *Dichterweihe* in the *Theogony*, drinking from the Hippocrene is the image Callimachus employs to signal his appropriation of Hesiod; cf. Fantuzzi and Hunter 2004: 7, but see Crowther 1979 and Cameron 1995: 363–366 for skepticism about Callimachus' water-drinking. Bion is similarly described as drinking from Arethusa, whose Sicilian location indicates that he is drawing on Theocritus as a source for his bucolic poetry (Mosch. *Ep. Bion.* 76); cf. Cameron 1995: 364.

46. Brink 1972: 553–556. In the Augustan period, see, e.g., Ovid, *Am* 3.9(8).25–26 and Manilius 2.8–11. This idea was so prominent that the concept of a source poet as an actual source of water was employed with regard to poets other than Homer, most famously by Horace of Pindar at *Epistles* 1.3.10: *Pindarici fontis qui non expalluit haustus?*; cf. *Odes* 4.2.5–24, where Pindar is described as a river rushing down a mountain, and *Sat.* 1.4.11 and 1.10.50–51, where Horace equates Lucilius to a muddy river (see Farmer 2013).

in the proem to his *Theogony*. Lucretius thus activates the "water source" trope by highlighting the fact that in his description of Ennius' Hesiodic dream he characterizes the discourse of the ultimate "source"—Homer—with the same language that he uses later in the water cycle.

So far, then, we have seen that in the water-cycle passage, Lucretius engages with poetological moments from Ennius and Callimachus. But a part of the history of this trope that has been overlooked by scholarship is the perhaps foundational role of Empedocles. This important role of Empedocles is fundamental for Lucretius' version of the water cycle, since this Lucretian passage occurs in what looks like a heavily Empedoclean context in the *DRN*: the water cycle is adduced as an example of how the four Empedoclean elements are conserved through Epicurean *isonomia*.[47] Empedocles' own use of this trope occurs in a programmatic address to the gods at the beginning of *On Nature*, where he asks them to keep the madness of men away from his tongue and allow a pure stream to flow from his hallowed lips (DK 3.1–2):

> ἀλλὰ θεοὶ τῶν μὲν μανίην ἀποτρέψατε γλώσσης,
> ἐκ δ' ὁσίων στομάτων καθαρὴν ὀχετεύσατε πηγήν.

> *But, you gods, turn from my tongue the madness of these men,*
> *and from hallowed lips let a pure fount flow.*

The context in which Sextus cites this passage makes clear that Empedocles is railing against those (τῶν μὲν) who put forward rash opinions without thorough consideration.[48] Empedocles here associates himself with a καθαρὴ πηγή in contrast to his rival(s) who are characterized by μανίη.[49] These considerations suggest a possible Empedoclean precedent for Callimachus' preference at the end of the *Hymn to Apollo* (108–112) for pure water (καθαρὴ λιβὰς, 111–112) from a holy fount (πίδακος ἐξ ἱερῆς, 112).[50] In any case, Empedocles figuring his poetry as a καθαρὴ πηγή suggests that Lucretius may be alluding to Empedocles, in addition to Callimachus and Ennius, especially in the immediate context of the water-cycle analysis in *DRN* 5, given that this passage comes between arguments for the

---

47. Furley 1989: 174–175 argues that this section of the *DRN* proves the Empedoclean association of the four elements throughout Lucretius' poem.

48. Sext. Emp. *Math.* 7.124.

49. Empedocles may be referring here to his poetic rival Parmenides. See further Wright 1995: 157–158, who canvasses the available arguments.

50. I have not found anyone else who has suggested this possibility.

conservation of Empedoclean elements of earth (Lucr. 5.247–260), of air (Lucr. 5.273–280), and of fire, in the form of light (Lucr. 5.281–305).

Concluding his actual discussion of the conservation of (the Empedoclean element) water, Lucretius describes how the pure water from which the salt has been sifted flows back into rivers (Lucr. 5.269–272):

> *percolatur enim virus retroque remanat*
> *materies umoris et ad caput amnibus omnis*
> *convenit, inde super terras fluit agmine dulci*
> *qua via secta semel liquido pede detulit undas.*

> *For the brine is sifted through and the substance of the moisture seeps back,*
> *and it all flows back together at the fountainhead of rivers,*
> *and from there it comes back over the lands with refreshed current,*
> *where the channel once cut away brought the waters in their flowing advance.*

Lucretius refers to the purified water as an *agmen dulce* that flows over the lands into the channels that had carried it before (*via secta semel*). Similarly, Empedocles asks the gods to "create a channel" (ὀχετεύσατε, DK 3.2) from his holy lips for "pure water" (καθαρὴ πηγή, DK 3.2). Lucretius recycles Empedocles' irrigation motif only to strip the image of any metaphorical associations.[51] In the immediate context of the water cycle in the *DRN*, therefore, Lucretius incorporates Empedocles into a web of allusions that includes Ennius and Callimachus. By extending the parameters of his allusion to Ennian poetology to include Callimachus and Empedocles, and by activating the water-source trope to enact this extension, Lucretius underscores the fact that what he is really taking aim at is the entire idea of literary tradition and succession inherent in Ennius' Dream of Homer.

These much broader literary stakes are crystallized already in the repeated passage in which Lucretius affirms his own poetic credentials. We have seen that water is intricately bound up with Callimachus' and Empedocles' own self-positioning in literary history, and that Lucretius associates Ennius with these two poets by connecting the Dream of Homer with a description of the water cycle in the *DRN*. Here again, Lucretius associates himself with Ennius, Callimachus, and Empedocles by virtue of the same water imagery (Lucr. 1.926–930=4.1–5):

---

51. Philip Hardie suggests to me that this removal of metaphorical associations may be analogous to the removal of salt to produce fresh water in the Lucretian passage. In this regard one could suggest that the idea of filtering pure, fresh water out of salt water in the context of window allusion figures a particular relationship between form and content, such that Lucretius "purifies" his allusions of their misguided content, adopting only the "pure water" of their form.

> *avia Pieridum peragro loca nullius ante*
> *tria solo. iuvat integros accedere fontis*
> *atque haurire, iuvatque novos decerpere flores*
> *insignemque meo capiti petere inde coronam,*
> *unde prius nulli velarint tempora Musae.*

> *I wander through the distant regions of the Muses,*
> *trodden before by the foot of no one. It is pleasing to approach inviolate springs*
> *and to drain them down; it is pleasing to pluck new flowers*
> *and to seek out a distinguished garland for my head from a place*
> *whence before the Muses have covered the temples of no one.*

Scholars have taken this passage as evidence for the Callimachean associations of Lucretian poetology. For example, Lucretius' assertion that he walks on untrodden paths resembles what Callimachus says in the *Aetia* prologue. Lucretius may also allude to Ennius' Callimachean claim to poetic originality at the beginning of *Annales* 7 (*Ann.* 208–220 Sk). In these fragmentary lines, Ennius apparently claims that he was the first who dared to ascend the rock of the Muses, much as Lucretius wanders through the previously untrodden regions of the Muses.[52] And Lucretius lays claim, just like Ennius had before him, to a completely original relationship with the Muses in this passage.[53] But, most important for my immediate purposes, Lucretius also says that he tastes of *integros fontis*. On the one hand, this allusion could refer to the end of Callimachus' *Hymn to Apollo*, where the poet expresses his preference for pure water from a holy fount, which itself might be sourced from Empedocles' request to the Muse to allow a pure fount to flow from his mouth. In this prominent passage, Lucretius programmatically asserts his credentials as a Callimachean, Ennian, and an Empedoclean poet by mobilizing the traditional water source trope through the phrase *integros fontis*. Lucretius again implicates his own poetology in his revision of Ennius' claims about literary tradition. And now he also implicates Empedocles and Callimachus.

But though Lucretius goes to such lengths to construct, in traditional ways, his own literary tradition in terms of water, in his description of the water cycle, water is simply water. It is adduced not as a trope for literary affiliation, but as an illustration of *isonomia*, the fundamental physical process in the Epicurean system. For those readers trained to expect provisional argumentation, this revelation that water is *just* water should activate understanding, not confusion.

---

52. On allusion to Ennius in this Lucretian passage, see Volk 2002: 87–88; cf. Tutrone 2017: 320.

53. Fundamental here is Hinds 1998: 52–63.

Again, we can see that Lucretius employs a standard poetic trope to get our attention, only later to strip the metaphor down to its physical components and Epicurean reality. Indeed, earlier in his programmatic statement of poetic affiliation, Lucretius figures himself as an Ennian, Callimachean, and Empedoclean poet by filling his account with allusions to poetological statements by all three of these poetic predecessors and underscoring the allusions by activating the metaphor of the water-source trope. This is a straightforward poetic move, even if decoding the allusions depends on the reader being steeped in the tradition of the water-source trope.

Later in the water-cycle passage, though Lucretius gestures toward aligning himself with Ennius, Callimachus, and Empedocles, he ultimately shows that the metaphorical expressions of poetic affiliation developed by these poets are contradicted by the reality of Epicurean *isonomia*. When Lucretius drinks from the *integros fontes*, we now learn that he receives water that has been purified of all associations. It is not Ennian water, Callimachean water, or Empedoclean water; and so, we should perhaps wonder, it may not even function as a source of inspiration. Lucretius' Muses are implicated in his provisional poetics, just as Venus is; when he drinks from their fountain, what he really gets is a drink of water. At some point he encourages us to understand that. In that sense, his appropriation of earlier poets' water imagery is a way of asserting his radical originality.

Readers are quite ready to accept metaphors in Lucretius *qua* metaphors. The more familiar readers are with how metaphor works in the Greco-Roman literary tradition, the more susceptible they will be toward taking these figures as plausible, or possible, in Lucretius' world.[54] But, really, the lesson of provisional argumentation is that we should be suspicious whenever Lucretius appears to employ a traditional poetic practice in straightforward ways. We have seen him, too many times, literalize metaphors because, in the world of his poem, the physical is primary. So while in Lucretius' poetic tradition water and founts of water stand in for poetic inspiration, an astute reader, keyed into the Lucretian practice of provisional argumentation, will see Lucretius make these moves and instantly start looking for the "correction" regarding the nonmetaphorical reality of water. With respect to the water-source trope, Lucretius suggests that water is miraculously water, given all the metaphors that had to be filtered out to just be water

---

54. Taylor 2020a: 71–112 has now provided a comprehensive study of the instability of Lucretian metaphor, culminating with the following observation which is exactly the point of my arguments in this chapter concerning Lucretius' metaphors for literary affiliation (at 112): "Lucretius' extraordinary metaphorical technique . . . may be said to carry with it certain risks: in its open-endedness, its tendency to employ figurations whose literal meanings are directly at odds with the doctrine they are intended to illuminate, Lucretian metaphor risks contradicting and thereby undermining its own message."

again. The dregs and dross are precisely those bits that most poets actually prize; Lucretius throws it away with both hands, even if, at first, he uses it strategically to capture his reader's attention.

Conclusion

Critics who seek to integrate Lucretius' heroic, "Ennian style" with his practice of disproving the tenets of Ennian philosophy have been content to conclude that Lucretius was comfortable with Ennius as a model in all respects except his Pythagoreanism. But the readings in this chapter suggest that Lucretius does not even endorse Ennian poetics in this relatively straightforward way. Lucretius' treatment of Ennius' metaphors for poetic affiliation undermine the importance of purely poetological claims in the face of Epicureanism: at first, Lucretius appears to endorse the legitimacy of poetological statements, only later to empty them of poetological significance. Ennius' own poetological claims are the main point of access through which Lucretius revises traditional poetology. But, as I have argued, Lucretius creates these paradoxes precisely to get us thinking about what is actually real: Venus is always just the sexual drive in nature; water is always just water. In the end, literary affiliation for Lucretius is a rhetorical enticement with which to introduce his readers to the *vera ratio* of Epicureanism—the honeyed cup strikes again.

Lucretius activates the very same constellation of metaphors (metempsychosis, the *cor*, and water) that he represents Ennius himself as having used to make his claims, but he does so always with the intention of undermining Ennian metaphor by appealing to the physical realities of the universe that form the basis of Epicurean philosophy. The reader is left to conclude that for Lucretius the truths of Epicureanism conflict with much of the Ennian philosophical perspective, implicated in which—because Ennius apparently insisted on their implication—are traditional ideas about poetics and literary tradition. In this way, Lucretius' revisionary appropriation of Ennian poetics mirrors his revisionary appropriation of Ennian cosmology and historiography.

I suggested in the introduction to this chapter that we ought to attempt to make Epicurean sense of any paradoxes found in the *De Rerum Natura* before analyzing them in traditional ways. On that note, I do not think we can say that Lucretius' deconstruction of literary tradition is anything other than concerted—he comes after it in too many different ways. To my mind, the reader who has accepted Lucretius' Epicurean content will forgive him for introducing such paradoxes. But no matter how much Lucretius leans on provisional argumentation to eradicate the possibility of literary influence or affiliation, there will always remain readers who cannot follow him to that place, no matter how much his Epicurean teachings demand that we assent to the truth of what Lucretius implies. In the same way, there will be readers who cannot finally assent to the truth of what Lucretius implies about Venus after her inauguration of the poem. For some, Venus will always retain anthropomorphic attributes, not least because Lucretius himself gives them to her.[55] Similarly, for some, Ennius and the other poets to whom Lucretius alludes will always leave traces of their influence on the *DRN*, not least because Lucretius put those traces there and draws our attention to them.[56]

Perhaps a better way out of this paradox is to recast it in terms of Lucretius' wider engagement with Ennius' *Annales*, about which I have had much to say in this book. It is clear that Lucretius engages with Ennius and the *Annales* more than with any other poet or poem. Ennius' influence permeates the *DRN*, not only in the idiosyncratically Ennian stylistic register that characterizes many of the *DRN*'s lines, but also in the repeated allusions to Ennian language and themes. But the *DRN* is an anti-Ennian poem, precisely because Lucretius represents the *Annales* as a poetic crystallization of the worldview against which Epicureanism stands. And so in the *DRN* there necessarily are traces of Ennius' *Annales* scattered everywhere, like the atoms in our universe, because Lucretius aims to appropriate what is wrong into his account of what is right. An interventionist Venus will always inaugurate the *DRN*, just as allusions to Ennius will always fill its verses. The task Lucretius presents to his readers is to understand these un-Epicurean elements for what they are: stepping-stones on the path toward Epicurean enlightenment.

---

55. Similarly, Taylor 2020b shows how Lucretius' use of first person verbs accommodates both the neophyte and the seasoned Epicurean by incorporating multiple valences into his philosophical discourse.

56. Cf. Burrow 2019: 116: "Lucretius's passage on the meeting between Homer and Ennius also is highly significant for another reason. Despite its overt aim to assail Ennius's mistaken beliefs about his relationship to Homer it actually preserves them."

Conclusion

RECONSTRUCTING LUCRETIUS' *ANNALES*

LET ME END where I began: this has not been a book about Ennius' *Annales*, but about Lucretius' reconstruction of Ennius' *Annales*. I have expanded our understanding of Lucretius' relationship to Ennius well beyond what has been argued traditionally. On my analysis, Lucretius' engagement with Ennius is dynamic and thoroughgoing. Lucretius' ubiquitous Ennian style serves, on the one hand, to signal to the reader that a passage should be read with Ennius in mind and, on the other, to announce a sort of stylistic reflexive annotation of actual allusions to the content of the *Annales*. Such allusions almost always involve a repudiation of philosophical or literary ideas that Lucretius represents as central in the *Annales*. The very ubiquity of Lucretius' Ennian style, however, may on first glance conceal the fact that Lucretius often writes with an insistently *un*-Ennian style, which I have suggested also, via the very absence of Ennian markers, indicates a revision of Ennius' *Annales*.

Lucretius is engaged in a poem-long revision of the entire Ennian value system as he represents it. It appears on my reading, in fact, that the selection of Ennius as a model was made precisely in order to give Lucretius the chance to dismantle thoroughly the values for which he claimed Ennius stood. These values include the importance of history as a poetic subject generally, and especially the cosmic significance of Roman hegemony that finds an analogy in Ennius' quasi-philosophical understanding of literary history. One assumes that we could identify further ways in which Lucretius dismantles the Ennian worldview if we possessed more of the *Annales*. The Ennian values that we witness Lucretius dismantling may even have been intricately connected within the *Annales* itself, although I would not insist on this suggestion. Accordingly, however, I would also suggest that in Lucretius' disruptive approach to Ennius, we may be able to recover aspects of the *Annales* that are closed off to us because of the fragmentary state of Ennius' epic.

Ennius Noster: Lucretius and the Annales. Jason S. Nethercut, Oxford University Press (2021). © Oxford University Press. DOI: 10.1093/oso/9780197517697.001.0001.

In this respect, Ennius' adaptation of Homeric hexameter is part of Lucretius' argument. In other words, Lucretius writes as much like Ennius as possible in order to reveal that Ennius' "Homeric" verse form was not actually Homeric at all. Such a conclusion results from the fact that Lucretius appears to dismantle the very idea of literary affiliation through his reception of the Ennian metaphor of literary metempsychosis. Taken this way, Lucretius can be seen to participate in the same eristic response to the *Annales* that I suggest obtained throughout the epic reception of the *Annales* in the period between Ennius and the *De Rerum Natura*.

As a direct result of Lucretius' engagement with Ennius, I have also raised the possibility that the kind of midcourse correction that is required of the reader of the Venus proem (who must at some point understand that Lucretius was initially presenting Venus in a manner that is incompatible with his basic teachings) should perhaps be extended to other literary aspects of the poem, such as allusion and stylistic affiliation. One major consequence of my study of Ennius' influence on the *DRN* is that we can gauge more fully the extent to which such "provisional argumentation" infuses Lucretius' poetic technique *grosso modo*.

The previous chapters focused uniformly on Lucretius' revision of Ennius' *Annales*—that is, the ways that Lucretius sought to correct or criticize the Ennian worldview. One major consequence of these analyses, however, is that we can now offer a reconstruction of the *Annales* according to Lucretius' reception. I have repeatedly emphasized that this is not a book about Ennius' *Annales*, but for the reader interested in Ennius, I want to offer here a tantalizing look at what could have been the *Annales* and what definitely *is* Lucretius' representation of the *Annales*. In the first chapter of this book, I asked the reader to perform a thought-experiment in which we removed Lucretius from literary history in order to analyze the influence of Ennius on the fragments of later epic poetry without the benefit of Lucretian hindsight. I bookend my study of Lucretius' reception of the *Annales* with another thought-experiment that inverts the terms of my earlier one: What might the *Annales* look like to us, if our *only* witness were Lucretius?

I should stress again that nothing that follows derives necessarily from what Ennius actually wrote in the *Annales*; rather, everything that follows can be recovered from Lucretius' representation of the *Annales* in the *DRN*.

Lucretius' Annales *and Its Afterlife*

Judging from the *DRN*, Ennius offered a diachronic, deeply philosophical account of Roman history that situated Rome at the center of the cosmos. This central position was providentially secured by an interventionist divine machinery that was traditionally encountered in ancient epic beginning with Homer.

Ennius' gods oversaw a fully functioning cosmic apparatus whose presence filled the narrative interstices of the *Annales* with a stable backdrop against which Roman history unfolded. On such a cosmic stage, Roman hegemony was presented teleologically, as the inevitable outcome of universal history.

Various episodes, especially the wars with Pyrrhus and the Carthaginians, occupied prominent positions in Ennius' narrative. Pyrrhus and the Romans he faced were religious zealots. During Pyrrhus' journey west across the Mediterranean, Lucretius implies that Ennius included a storm scene, in which Pyrrhus cried out to the gods to deliver his crew and their elephants to safety. Ennius' Pyrrhus was forged as a conflation of the protagonists of the two Homeric poems, Achilles and Odysseus, and, by virtue of his associations with the traditions of philosophical epic, served as the culminating protagonist of the natural philosophical strain of hexameter poetry. The Punic Wars, dreadfully disruptive, and effecting ruptures in the very fabric of the cosmic mechanism, served Ennius as the pivotal moment when the *telos* of Roman hegemony became manifest in universal history. The Scipiones functioned as cosmic forces, wielding the power of Jupiter for the Romans, who, after the defeat of Carthage, were revealed as the ordained masters of the cosmos. As a result of this newfound *imperium sine fine*, any expansion of Roman power entailed an expansion of the cosmos itself, since Rome was conceived of as coterminous with the wider cosmic mechanism, against which, and as part of which, Ennius presented his historical narrative.

Ennius used the process of metempsychosis to represent himself literally as Homer reborn, information that Homer himself revealed by appearing to Ennius in a dream in which he offered an expansive discourse on natural philosophy. This discourse was explicitly Empedoclean, and Ennius' Homer illustrated the process of reincarnation by appealing to the cyclical existence of the four Empedoclean elements, and especially the water cycle, according to which souls inhabit different bodies, just as water takes on different forms as rain, snow, rivers, and so forth. Ennius clinched this connection through the use of the root verb *manare*, by describing Homer's soul as "flowing upward" from the Underworld, just as water "flows back" to its source as a function of the water cycle. In all of this, Ennius has Homer make extensive use of the water-source trope that figures literary sources as sources of water from which one can drink. This trope was connected back to Empedocles, further reinforcing the general Empedoclean thrust of Ennius' *Somnium*. Moreover, Ennius endowed the human heart, and especially his own heart, with powerful poetic associations. Not only did Ennius locate the reincarnated soul in the heart (reincarnation being a major poetological process in the *Annales*), but Ennius connected this gesture back to Homer via Empedocles and his four elemental substances of which he claimed the soul was constituted.

Lucretius' testimony, it turns out, tells us quite a bit more than we know from independent sources about the specifics of Ennius' narrative of Roman history and the nature of Ennius' claims regarding literary tradition. Of course, as I have emphasized repeatedly in this book, Lucretius' reconstruction of the *Annales* is almost certain to be a drastic distortion of what we would find in Ennius' *Annales* if we had a complete edition to consult. Lucretius' engagement is always primarily a function of his main objective: the positive articulation of Epicurean physics. While the *Annales* must be understood as Lucretius' primary poetic model, it serves Lucretius always as a foil for his Epicurean explanations of various natural phenomena. As a result, we should consider seriously the possibility that all post-Lucretian appropriations of Ennius' epic are similarly tendentious and may even be outright distortions, too. Still, amid Lucretius' many distortions of Ennius' epic, we encounter elements of the *Annales* that find corroboration in other independent sources. Lucretius' *DRN* thus deserves to take its rightful place as the earliest, most serious engagement with Ennius' *Annales* available to us. He would not have the last word on the matter, of course, but it is clear that he left his mark.

APPENDICES

Greek and Roman Hexameter in the Late Republic

Greek Epic Poems, 3rd Century–1st Century BCE

Author	Date (BCE)	Title
Nicaenetus of Samos/ Abdera	3rd c.	*Lyrkos* (historical epic on Caunos; 10 lines preserved, see *Collectanea Alexandrina* 1–2); *Catalogue of Women* (title only)
Cleon of Curion	3rd c.	*Argonautica* (written before Apollonius' poem; title only, but cf. *Supplementum Hellenisticum*, 159–161)
Theolytus of Methymna	3rd c.	*Argonautica* (written before Apollonius; title only; cf. *schol. Apoll. Rhod.* 1.623–626); *Bacchica Epê* (3 lines; see *CA* 9); *Hôroi=Annales?* (possibly the work of a different, later poet; cf. Ath. 11.470b)
Antagoras of Rhodes	3rd c.	*Thebais* (11 books, title only, see *CA* 121); 7 hexameters to Love (allusions to Hesiod's *Theogony*; see *CA* 120)
Diotimus of Adramyttion	3rd c.	*Heracleia* (3 lines; *SH* 181–182)

Author	Date (BCE)	Title
Euphorion of Chalcis	3rd c.	*Thrax* (c. 100 lines; a curse poem); *Curses* (16 lines); *Greater Hippomedon* (c. 10 lines; subject obscure); *Alexander* (title only); *Anius* (1 line); *Apollodorus* (4 lines); *Artemidorus* (1 lines); *Chiliades* (2 lines); *Cletor* (1 line); *Crane* (title only); *Demosthenes* (1 line); *Dionysus* (c. 50 lines); *Dionysus Gaping* (1 line); *Hesiod* (title only); *Histia* (5 lines?); *Hyacinth* (6 lines); *Inachus* (5 lines?); *Lament for Protagoras* (3 lines); *Mopsopia* (5 lines); *Philoctetes* (5 lines); *Polychares* (1 line); *Replies to Theodoridas* (1 line); *Xenios* (title and some *testimonia*); See *CA* 28–58 and *SH* 196–233
Moero of Byzantium	3rd c.	10 hexameters remain on *Mnemosyne* (*CA* 21–22)
Phaestus	3rd c. (?)	*Lacedaemonica (Macedonica?)* (1 line remains; see *CA* 28 and *SH* 316–317)
Theopompus of Colophon	3rd c. (?)	*The Charioteer* (2 lines; see *CA* 28); *Cypria* (?) (title only, perhaps by a different Theopompus; see *SH* 365–366)
Eratosthenes of Cyrene	Mid-3rd c.	*Hermes* (about 30 lines; poem that unites myth with cosmology and other scientific matters; see *CA* 58–63 and *SH* 183–186); other titles include *Anterinys*, *Erigone*, and *Dionysus Gaping* (See *CA* 63–68)
Apollonius of Rhodes	Mid-3rd c.	*Argonautica*; *Canobus* (3 lines); *The Founding of Alexandria* (title only); *The Founding of Caunus* (5 lines); *The Founding of Cnidos* (title only); *The Founding of Naucratis* (6–7 lines); *The Founding of Rhodes* (2 lines); *The Founding of Lesbos* (21 lines); See *CA* 4–8
Agis the Argive	3rd c. (?)	Epic about Alexander the Great (*SH* 6–7)

Author	Date (BCE)	Title
Anaximenes of Lampsacus	3rd c. (?)	Epic about Alexander the Great (*SH* 18)
Crates of Thebes	3rd c.	About 25 hexameters on various subjects, no titles remain (see *SH* 164–168)
Demetrius	3rd c. (?)	Three hexameters remain on the subject of jealousy, though we have no title nor any other information on the author (see *SH* 174)
Hegemon of Alexandria Troas	3rd c. (?)	*Dardanica* (title only); epic on the Leuctrian War (title only); See *SH* 236–237
Hipparchus (not the astronomer)	3rd c. (?)	*Egyptian Iliad* (4 lines; see *SH* 249)
Leschides	mid-3rd c.	wrote epics (no titles; *SH* 250)
Possis of Magnesia	3rd c.	*Amazonis* (at least 3 books, *testimonia* only; *SH* 320)
Zenodotus of Ephesus	3rd c.	Epic (?); *SH* 396
Musaeus of Ephesus	Late 3rd c.	*Perseis* (title only; dedicated to (?) Eumenes and Attalus; see *SH* 274)
Simonides of Magnesia	Late 3rd c.	Epic poem about Antiochus I and the battle against the Galatians (*SH* 349)
Demosthenes of Bithynia	Early 2nd c.	*Bithyniaca* (at least 10 books, only about 10 lines of which survive; see *CA* 25–27)
Rhianus of Crete	Early 2nd c.	*Heracleia* (1 line); *Thessalica* (15 lines); *Achaica* (4 lines); *Eliaca* (2 lines); *Messeniaca* (5 lines); See *CA* 9–18 and *SH* 346–347
Hyperochus of Cumae	2rd c. (?)	*Cumaica* (only *testimonia*); see *SH* 249–250
Idaeus of Rhodes	2nd c. (?)	*Rhodiaca* (title only); See *SH* 250
Phaedimus of Bisanthe	2nd c.	*Heracleia* (1 line; *SH* 316)
Philo the Elder	2nd c.	Around 20 lines of an epic poem on the History of Jerusalem (*SH* 328–331)
Theodotus	Late 2nd c.	Epic poem on Jewish History (c. 45 lines; *SH* 360–365)

Author	Date (BCE)	Title
Nicander of Colophon	Late 2nd c.	***Colophoniaca*** (title only, possibly a prose work); ***Oetaica*** (at least 2 books; 4 lines remain); ***Thebaica*** (at least 3 books; 2 lines remain); ***Sicelia*** (at least 8 books; 2 lines remain); ***Europia*** (at least 5 books; 7 lines remain)
A. Licinius Archias	1st c.	Epic poems (1) on Cimbrian Wars (Cic. *Pro Archia Poeta* 9.19); (2) on War with Mithridates, definitely in Greek (Cic. *Pro Archia Poeta* 9.21; *ad Att.* 1.16.15); (3) on the deeds of Metellus (Cic. *Pro Archia Poeta* 10.25; *ad Att.* 1.16.15)
Thyillus	Mid-1st c.	***Country of the Eumolpidae*** (Cic. *Att.* 1.9.2; *SH* 366)
Menelaus of Aegae	1st c. (?)	***Thebais*** (11 books; historical epic; see *SH* 271–272)
Lyceas the Argive	???	Epic poem on the Argolid (*SH* 257–258)
Pherenicus of Heraclea	???	Epic poet (5 lines, one *testimonium*, no titles; see *SH* 317–318)
Priscus	???	Epic (*SH* 344)
Fragmentary Hexameters	???	*SH* 399–458 (c. 800 badly damaged lines)

Latin Epic Poems Between Ennius and Lucretius

Author	Date (BCE)	Title
Hostius	Late 2nd c.	***Bellum Histricum*** (?) (at least 3 books; probably on the Istrian War of 129 BCE (cf., however, Casali 2006: 591–593); 7 lines remain); for overview see, Vinchesi 1984 and Courtney 1993: 52–55
Accius	Late 2nd c.	***Annales*** (7 or 27 books; subject matter difficult to discern; 12 lines remain); see Courtney 1993: 56–60
Livius Refictus	Late 2nd c.	Anonymous, post-Ennian reworking of Andronicus' *Odissia* into hexameter; 4 lines remain; see Courtney 1993: 45–46

Author	Date (BCE)	Title
Carmen Priami	Late 2nd-c.	Post-Ennian Saturnian epic, which would appear to be a direct, archaizing response to Ennius' introduction of the hexameter into epic; 1 line remains; see Courtney 1993: 44
Furius Antias	Early 1st c.	***Annales***, possibly on the Cimbrian war fought by Catulus; 6 lines remain; see Courtney 1993: 97–98 and Clark (forthcoming)
Gannius (G. Annius?)	1st c. (?)	Hexameter poem in at least 3 books, subject and title unknown; 3 lines remain; see Courtney 1993: 146
Matius (Mattius?)	Early 1st c.	Translation of *Iliad* into Latin hexameters (7 lines remain; see Courtney 1993: 99–102)
Ninnius Crassus	1st c. (?)	Translation of the *Iliad* into Latin hexameters (2 lines remain; see Courtney 1993: 107)
Naevius (not Gn. Naevius)	1st c. (?)	Translation of *Cypria* into Latin hexameters (2 lines remain; see Courtney 1993: 108)
Cicero	Mid-1st c.	***Alcyones*** (2 lines); ***Limon*** (4 lines); ***Thalia Maesta*** (title, subject unclear; 1 line); ***De Consulatu Suo*** (3 books; c. 80 lines remain); ***Marius*** (3 books; 15 lines remain); ***De Temporibus Suis*** (3 books; no lines extant, though some discussion of the subject matter in the letters and subsequent authors; cf. Harrison 1990; Translations of *Iliad* and *Odyssey* into hexameters; see Courtney 1993: 149–178
Julius Caesar	Mid-1st c.	***Limon*** (6 lines; see Courtney 1993: 153)
Furius Bibaculus	Mid-1st c.	***Annales Belli Gallici*** (14 lines remain; perhaps on Julius Caesar's Gallic expedition; at least 11 books originally); see Courtney 1993: 192–200 and Clark (forthcoming)
Varro Atacinus	Mid-1st c.	***Bellum Sequanicum*** (at least 2 books; 1, maybe 2, lines remain; presumably on Julius Caesar's campaign against Ariovistus in 58 BCE); see Courtney 1993: 235–238

Author	Date (BCE)	Title
Sueius	Mid-1st c.	2 hexameters from Book 5 of what is generally agreed to be an epic poem, though we have no title (see Courtney 1993: 116–117)
Volusius	Mid-1st c.	*Annales* (*cacata charta* mentioned by Catullus in *c.* 36; no lines remain)
Hortensius (?)	Mid-1st c.	*Annales* (possibly mentioned alongside Volusius by Catullus in *c.* 95, which, however, is a notoriously difficult crux; no lines remain)

APPENDIX 2

Typology of Ennianisms in Lucretius

THE EVIDENCE IN CHAPTER 1 destabilizes the pervasive notion that the Latin hexametric poetry that intervened between Ennius and Lucretius was all markedly Ennian. There is almost no positive evidence that justifies the conclusion that Ennius' unique style "infected" all, most, or even any Latin writers of this period; we can assume safely that these authors employed their own style most of the time, and that, when they did make use of Ennianisms, they did so in a sophisticated, not a rote, manner. Both of these conclusions— that sustained marked Ennianizing was abnormal, and that concentrated clusters of Ennian elements were used for self-conscious and "refined" reasons—are necessary for my arguments in chapters 2–4. For Lucretius *does* engage with the *Annales* as if infected by Ennius' style. And we have every reason to consider this engagement, even at the atomic level of style, as a significant, rather than an automatic, choice on Lucretius' part.

But what do I mean when I speak of "engagement with Ennius?" Most scholars easily identify Lucretius' distinctive style as Ennian, and assume that Ennius is, to use Conte's terminology, the stylistic *modello codice* for Lucretius. But that is generally where the analysis stops. In this appendix, I will probe further what we mean when we say that the *DRN* has an "Ennian" character. In so doing, I will uncover a *DRN* that is unambiguously Ennian, yet ubiquitously Lucretian. Laying out a typology of Ennianism more broadly here provides an important background for my analysis in chapters 2–4 of this book, where I focus on moments where we can prove that Lucretius deploys words and phrases that derive from the *Annales*, passages in which, again to use Conte's term, Ennius serves Lucretius as *modello esemplare*.

There is no question that the style of the *DRN* makes a general impression that is not dissimilar to that of Ennius' *Annales*. Previous scholarship has focused on evidence that supports the idea that the two poems employ similar styles, offering many affirmations that Lucretius' style is indebted to, or even derived from Ennius.[1] Yet in the majority of cases, such affirmations do not depend on any explicit criteria, save Lucretius' tendency to "archaize."[2] So, for example, Maguinness' widely-cited discussion of Lucretian language and style highlights a few archaizing tendencies:

> [T]o Lucretius, an admirer of Ennius, his real epic precursor in Latin, an archaism redolent of Ennius appeared as the means of creating a style both epic and, in a sense, hierophantic . . . perhaps [archaism] is the one of his qualities of which even his youngest readers are best aware and which they appreciate most. Lines ending in *aquai, animai,* or *materiai* have a grave sonority that in practice is associated with Lucretius alone; the sound of *omnibu' rebus* is something that will never again be heard in Latin poetry except in the last line of the last poem of Catullus.[3]

Maguinness mentions as specifically "Ennian" two archaic usages: the genitive singular ending *-ai* and the suppression of final *-s* after short vowels and before words that begin with a consonant (what Butterfield has called "sigmatic ecthlipsis").[4] Not to discount the significance of these two usages, both of which I discuss below, I want to consider more carefully whether these features are in fact distinctly and specifically Ennian, and I want to consider as well whether there are additional characteristics of Lucretius' style that suggest Ennius. My analysis of what counts as "Ennian" depends on three criteria: whether a given phenomenon was already archaic when Ennius used it, whether it already had a Latin epic pedigree (i.e., in Livius or Naevius) before Ennius used it, and whether Ennius uses it equally in all of his works (i.e., whether it is especially associated with Ennian *epic*). I will return to these questions throughout the discussion that follows, suggesting ultimately that Lucretius' poem is Ennian throughout, and "extra-Ennian" at points.

1. Many important studies of Lucretian style have been written, all offering their own unique perspective on his peculiarities: Holtze 1868; Munro 1886: 2.8–20; Sellar 1889: 384–407; Cartault 1898; Bailey 1947: 72–171; Boyancé 1963: 288–315 (with further bibliography at 343–346); Leonard and Smith 1965: 129–186; Maguinness 1965; Kenney 1971: 14–29 and id. 2007. See Deufert 2017: 204–248 for a comprehensive account of varying orthography in the Lucretian manuscripts. Taylor (forthcoming) offers the most recent analysis of the impact of Ennian Latin on Lucretian style, and his conclusions corroborate much of what I argue in this appendix. See Goldberg (forthcoming) for the most recent analysis of Ennian language.

2. Bailey 1947: 87; Maguinness 1965: 84–85; Leonard and Smith 1965: 32; Kenney 2007: 96.

3. Maguinness 1965: 84–85.

4. Butterfield 2008.

Lucretian and Ennian Poetic Effects
and Morphology

After chapter 1, it will come as no surprise that scholars have long connected the frequent use of alliteration in the *DRN*—what is commonly considered its most Lucretian quality—with Ennius.[5] Rather than just assume that any and all alliteration is meant to signify Ennian style, however, we would do well to remember how Accius used alliteration in his appropriation of Ennius' version of the logging *topos*.[6] There, Accius deploys alliteration to allude to a specific passage of Ennius, not to Ennius' style as a whole. Accius alliterates in his imitation because Ennius does in the original, not because he generally employed a highly alliterative style based generally on that of Ennius. While this precise type of extreme alliteration is found in other fragments of Ennius' *Annales*, Accius, for his part, both simplifies and yet exaggerates the alliteration he found in the lines of the *Annales* to which he alludes by restricting his repetition to one letter at the beginning of multiple successive words. Just as Accius' use of hyper-alliteration in the logging fragment marks his imitation as a potential parody of Ennian style, so too can Lucretius be seen to hyper-Ennianize as a way of marking his allusion to Ennius.

Thankfully, Bailey has already sketched out the development of alliteration in Latin poetry, providing a helpful point of triangulation between the early poets and Lucretius. His conclusion that alliteration is almost nonexistent in Latin epic before Ennius allows us to safely say that its introduction into the genre is an Ennian invention.[7] There are many ways to alliterate, and Ennius shows a marked preference for the repetition of a single letter throughout the line, regularly as the first sound of successive words. We have examples of this being deployed with many letters of the alphabet: e.g., the repetition of *c* in 345 Sk (*nec quom capta capi nec quom combusta cremari*), of *d* in 190 Sk (*dono ducite doque volentibus cum magnis dis*), of *f* in 32 Sk (*accipe daque fidem foedusque feri bene firmum*), of *m* in 620 Sk (*machina multa minax minitatur maxima muris*), of *p* in 548 Sk (*aut permarceret paries percussus trifaci*), and of *t* in 104 Sk (*O Tite, tute, Tati, tibi tanta, tyranne, tulisti*) and 451 Sk (*at tuba terribili sonitu tarantara dixit*). In showing a preference for the type of alliteration that repeats one letter at the beginning of multiple words in a line, Ennius is emulating the alliteration in early Latin that we find in comedy (e.g., Plautus, *Capt.* 769–771; Terence, *Ad.* 134).[8] Ennius rarely alliterates more than one letter, (cf. the logging fragment at 175–179 Sk), which is the sort of alliteration preferred

---

5. On Lucretian alliteration, see Merrill 1892; Bailey 1947: 146–152; and Hendren 2012, with further bibliography at 410 n. 6.

6. See above, pp. 26–30.

7. Bailey 1947: 147–148. This is not to say that alliteration is completely nonexistent before Ennius: we do find the line *scopas atque verbenas sagmina sumpserunt* in Naevius (fr. 2 Strz), but, if anything, this example highlights the relative infrequency of alliteration in Saturnian epic by virtue of its prominence.

8. For comparative data on this type of alliteration in Republican Latin poetry, see Appendix 4.

in the tragic fragments, and not the sort of parodic display we find in Ennius' and Accius' *Annales* (e.g., Pacuvius, fr. 7 and 21 Schierl). Cicero reins in the alliteration of a single letter to two or at the most three successive words (e.g., *Aratea*. 33.224 and 33.227 Soubiran), and prefers the alliteration of two letters, often switching the sound from word-initial position to medial and final consonants (e.g., *Aratea*. 33.304 Soubiran) in what Bailey suggests is a refinement of the "grotesque exaggerations of Ennius."[9]

I have compiled the comparative data on this type of hyper-alliteration in Republican Latin poetry in Appendix 4. To summarize, these data show that alliteration was not prevalent before Ennius. Both the *Annales* and the tragedies are highly alliterative, even as Ennius uses the phenomenon more frequently in tragedy than in his epic. After Ennius, we see a steady, almost linear decline in the deployment of alliteration until Lucretius, who revives it and uses it more frequently than any other Republican poet besides Ennius himself (Table A2.1):

Table A2.1 Alliteration in Republican Latin Poetry

Livius Andronicus	Naevius	Ennius	Plautus	Caecilius Statius	Terence	Accius
2.1% of lines	10.1%	14.0%	11.3%	10.8%	9.88%	10.2%

Pacuvius	Lucilius	Cicero	Catullus	Other Republican Poetry	Lucretius
9.98%	6.82%	6.95%	4.16%	4.63%	12.4%

When it comes to alliteration in the *DRN*, Lucretius appears to occupy a middle ground between the extreme hyper-alliteration we find in Ennius and what we might consider the refinement of the effect in Cicero. Scholars often single out Cicero as a pivotal figure in the development of alliteration, whose restraint points the way towards what one encounters in the Augustan poets (e.g., Verg. *Aen*. 2.209–212 and 5.277–279).[10] The statistical analyses that pepper discussions of Lucretian alliteration show that Lucretius not only alliterates frequently (perhaps more frequently than any other Latin poet, as Bailey 1947, 146–147 would have it), but that his particular penchant is to deploy the alliteration of one letter often in three or more consecutive words, and sometimes in as many as five or six.[11] For example, Merrill applied stringent criteria to the use of alliteration in the *DRN*, concluding that approximately 1,783 of the 7,359 verses—roughly 24% of

9. Bailey 1947: 149.

10. e.g., Bailey 1947: 150.

11. See especially Merrill 1892; Cordier 1939; Deutsch 1939; and Marouzeau 1946.

the poem as a whole—exhibit alliteration.[12] It is important to underscore, however, that according to Merrill's criteria, over three-quarters of Lucretius' lines *do not* contain alliteration. This suggests that, although Lucretius certainly alliterates at times with as much gusto, and in the exact same exaggerated way, as Ennius does (e.g., *non potuit pedibus qui pontum per vada possent*, Lucr. 1.200; *saepe solet scintilla suos se spargere in ignis*, Lucr. 4.606), this exaggerated alliteration occurs sporadically throughout the poem, and very often may be deployed precisely as I have argued Accius deploys this Ennian effect. That is to say, Lucretius likely hyper-alliterates in order to cultivate a hyper-Ennian context that in turn makes the reader think of the *Annales*, and perhaps even of a specific passage of the *Annales*, even if alliteration per se is never the point of such allusions.[13] This reality is borne out by the data I compile in Appendix 4, where we see that such alliteration occurs in the following distribution throughout the *DRN* (Table A2.2):

Table A2.2 Alliteration in the *DRN*

DRN 1	*DRN* 2	*DRN* 3	*DRN* 4	*DRN* 5	*DRN* 6
13.3%	12.8%	11.8%	13.0%	12.9%	10.5%

The difference between Books 1 and 6 is almost 3%, a book-level difference that is mirrored when one consults the actual instances I catalogue in Appendix 5. Even in Book 1, which has the highest rate of this type of alliteration, there are stretches of over 20 lines (e.g., 1.635–656) with no alliteration, while in Book 6 there are stretches where the frequency of alliteration (e.g., 8 instances in 30 lines at 6.848–877) is almost twice as much as the frequency in Book 1. Not only does Lucretius reverse the trend in alliterating much more frequently than any other Republican poet besides Ennius himself, but such alliteration clusters throughout the *DRN*. Cumulatively, then, we are left with the impression that Lucretian alliteration should be seen as a purposefully and recognizably Ennian affectation, and that Lucretius deploys this Ennianism strategically in clusters, rather than inertly throughout his poem.[14]

---

12. According to Merrill's metrics, more than a third (609 out of 1,783 lines) of the alliterative lines in Lucretius involve the repetition of a word-initial sound in at least three consecutive words; this amounts to 8.3% of all lines in the *DRN*. Moreover, extreme cases of hyper-alliteration that involve four, five, or six words are confined, according to Merrill's statistics, to 53 lines. This amounts to less than 1% of all Lucretian lines, and, although he does not provide a comprehensive list for his data set, the examples he does supply come from multiple books in the *DRN*.

13. At 4.606, "the most prolonged" alliteration in the *DRN* (Bailey 1947 ad loc.) may prepare for an allusion to the *Annales* at 4.622 (*manantis corpora suci=manat ex omni corpore sudor*, *Ann.* 417 Sk).

14. Alliteration is not the only pronounced poetic effect employed by Lucretius that has also been seen as Ennian. Tmesis is also considered to be markedly Ennian, on the use of which in the *Annales*, see Skutsch 1985: 66; in Lucretius, see Bailey 1947: 123 and Hinds 1987. Many earlier Lucretian scholars identified the kind of violent tmesis sometimes

When searching for archaisms in Lucretius, we must be careful to differentiate between aspects of Lucretius' language that were in a state of indeterminacy at the time he was writing, and what must have been deliberate archaisms. For example, Lucretius uses some nouns in different declensions where one may find more than one option for the same case ending, such as the ablative form *vasis* from the noun *vas* at 3.434 and 6.231 or the inconsistent use of *-im* and *-em* in the accusative of the third declension i-stem nouns (*frebrim*, 6.656; *puppim*, 4.389; *hostem*, 4.1051; *amnem*, 4.1183); vacillation of this type would appear to represent genuine uncertainty or fluidity in the language at the time Lucretius was writing rather than reflect, in half of such instances, that Lucretius is adopting an archaic form.[15] In other situations, however, Lucretius' bizarre syntax (e.g., the accusative case after verbs that take the ablative (3.940), the genitive of separation (1.1041; 5.840), the adverbial use of the ablative plural of adjectives (3.1069), and (at, e.g., 1.533; 4.1068) the "quasi-passive" use of the gerund) and morphology (e.g., the passive infinitive ending *-ier*, the syncopated perfect infinitive endings *-sse* and *–xe*)

---

encountered in Lucretius as specifically Ennian (e.g., *seque gregari*, Lucr. 1.452 with Hinds 1987; *praeter creditur ire*, 4.388; and *inter quaecumque pretantur*, 4.832). The use of tmesis, however, is not confined to the *Annales*, nor does it appear to have been purified from the Latin poetic repertoire by subsequent poets, as happened with the other Ennianisms I go on to analyze in this appendix. For this reason, I do not think tmesis is a reliably Ennian aspect of Lucretius' poetic style. On the other hand, the tendency to connect Lucretian tmesis with Ennius is likely due to the existence of putative, almost certainly spurious Ennian examples like *saxo cere comminuit brum* (see Skustch 1985: 787–788). No instances of tmesis involving the prefix *inter*, for example, are known to me between Ennius and Lucretius, although see the possible example at Afranius fr. 237: *inter se velitari*. Bailey (1947: 123) again suggests that, as with alliteration, Lucretius represents a middle-point, in this case between the excesses of Ennius and the restraint of Vergil, who restricts tmesis to the separation by *-que* of the prefix *in* (e.g., *Aen.* 10.794–795: *ille pedem referens et inutilis* **inque ligatus** / *cedebat*). The Ennian use of tmesis, however, is never as extreme as what we find regularly in Lucretius, who often separates verbal prefixes with intervening words of many syllables, whereas the Ennian examples only allow one intervening syllable. At points, however, Lucretius does seem to use tmesis as a stylistic annotation of allusion to Ennius. For instance, in Lucretius' explanation of the conservation of the element fire at 5.281–305, we find three examples of tmesis (*inter quasi rumpere*, 5.287; *qua nimbi cumque*, 5.289; *inter quasi rupta*, 5.299) in a passage that also contains an allusion to the *Annales* at 5.295 (*lumina pendentes lychni=lynchorum lumina*, *Ann.* 311 Sk). In general, see Munro 1886 at 1.452, who offers without comment twenty-eight instances of tmesis in Lucretius, though he omits *perque volare* at 4.203.

15. See Bailey 1947: 75–80. That there was real uncertainty regarding the transitional state of Latin, and, thus, that Lucretius represents for us certain aspects of Latin that are in a state of flux, suggests that in some ways, at least, Lucretius' style was more *de rigueur* than archaic. In such instances as these, one can sometimes trace the post-Lucretian evolution of these forms and conclude that ultimately one form became established and the other sticks around as an archaism. For example, by the Augustan period, *febrem* is the default accusative singular, appearing regularly all the way down to Justianian. We do encounter *febrim* in post-Lucretian Latin, but only eight times.

in some cases look to be deliberate archaism.[16] Lucretius' productive deployment of such deliberate archaisms is one of the most innovative aspects of his *Dichtersprache*, but it is not at all clear that such purposeful archaism is specifically Ennian.

We are on somewhat firmer footing for assessing the archaism of Lucretius' coinage of compound adjectives and *hapax legomena*, but it is equally difficult to prove that the abundant examples of such linguistic experimentation are specifically Ennian without independent evidence that Ennius used a particular word in the *Annales* (which occurs only rarely, e.g., *laetificos* 1.193=*laetificum Ann.* 585 Sk). In the end, since we can only really speak about an innovative phenomenon that Lucretius *may* have taken over from Ennius, I will only mention these coinages in passing. While Ennius was the first to introduce compound adjectives into the Latin hexameter, he was not the only Latin poet to use such words, as the tragedians employed them frequently.[17] While Lucretius' penchant for compound adjectives can, on the one hand, be seen as his own innovative contribution, especially given the sheer number of *hapax* compound adjectives that appear in his poem,[18] he is also participating in a tradition of linguistic innovation that Ennius had started for the Latin hexameter.[19] This is not to suggest that Ennius gave rise to a whole tradition of poets, whose epics regularly deployed linguistic innovation as one major stylistic characteristic, but it is fair to assume that the epic poets between Ennius and Lucretius were particularly drawn to Ennius' linguistic innovations as part of their engagement with the *Annales*, as I suggested in chapter 1. Again, such engagement should not be taken as a general feature of post-Ennian hexameter so much as a reliable indicator of occasional imitation of specific Ennian passages or features. As such, we should be prepared to interpret Lucretius' own deployment of *hapax* compound adjectives as a similarly localized phenomenon, meant to evoke an Ennian patina in specific contexts. At the same time, the widespread appearance of such adjectives does provide positive evidence for a more general Ennian stylistic register in Lucretius of the sort that remains unrecoverable in the fragments of hexameter between the *Annales* and the *DRN*; all of this evidence indicates that Lucretius' adoption of a generally Ennian style may have struck his readers as especially novel and pointed.

---

16. Regarding grammar, Bailey 1947: 88–108 is fundamental for understanding which peculiarities are deliberate and which have parallels, especially because he underscores that these very abnormalities are characteristic of Lucretius, and should be attributed to his own innovative use of Latin; cf. Maguinness 1965: 85, who writes that for Lucretius "archaism is then creative, not purely retrospective."

17. In the fragments of Naevius' *BP*, we do find *silvicolae*, fr. 11 Stz. *arquitenens*, fr. 20 Stz. (cf. τοξόφορος Homer *Il.* 21.483 and *Hymn to Apollo* 13, 126) occurs next to *pollens sagittis* (cf. Plautus *Curc.* 114 *vinipollens . . . Liber*; Cicero *Aratea* 73 *sagittipotens*).

18. For lists of Lucretian *hapax legomena*, see Bailey 1947: 137 and Maguinness 1965: 93.

19. Of course, it is important to emphasize, as I do in chapter 1, that, although Ennius is the first Latin hexameter poet, the number of hexameter lines that survive from the period between Ennius and Lucretius is small.

In contrast to alliteration and innovations, the *DRN*'s frequent use of the genitive singular ending *-ai* can confidently be called a deliberate Ennian archaism.[20] This ending is normally confined to nouns, or to adjectives combined with nouns, the latter of which is an emphatically Ennian effect (e.g., *Albai longai, Ann.* 31 Sk, *silvai frondosai, Ann.* 179 Sk, and *terrai frugiferai, Ann.* 510 Sk).[21] Several reasons suggest that the *-ai* ending is a specifically Ennian, and not just a general archaism. First, as this ending does not occur in the fragments of Livius Andronicus or Naevius, and as *-ai* is almost exclusively found in the *Annales*, the only other instance of it occurring in *Medea Exul* (*Medeai*, 223 Jocelyn), Ennius would appear to be the first Latin author to use *-ai* in epic poetry.[22] The use of *-ai*, therefore, would have been especially associated with Ennian *epic*. Second, the fact that the genitive ending *-ae* is encountered frequently in both Lucretius and Ennius, means that *-ai* is not a default choice for either poet. The *-ai* ending, when it occurs, occurs deliberately. Third, *-ai* occurs rarely outside of Ennius in pre-Lucretian poetry. On the handful of occasions where *-ai* does occur between Ennius and Lucretius, the context almost always involves Greek proper names.[23] The data show clearly that this ending was associated with Ennius' *Annales*, gradually disappeared from use in the Republican period, then

---

20. On which, see Bailey 1947: 75–77, who writes that *-ai* is "of all the idiosyncrasies . . . in the *De Rerum Natura* by far the most noticeable" (75). This ending also appears, though somewhat infrequently, in the epigraphical record. See *CIL* 1.366a; 1.443; 1.452; 1.1211; 1.1312; 1.1847; 1.2884; 11.6708.01, .07, and .08. On this material, see Leumann 1977: 419 and Wachter 1987, 464–469. I thank Seth Bernard, Dan-el Padilla Peralta, Andrew Riggsby, and Barnaby Taylor for helpful discussions about these inscriptions.

21. It may also be an emphatically Homeric effect that Lucretius is accessing via Ennius, especially when one considers the rhyme in clausulae found regularly in Homer (e.g., δειλοῖσι βροτοῖσι, *Il.*17.38, 22.31, 22.76, 24.525; *Od.* 11.19, 12.341, 15.408; cf. *Mettoeoque Fufetioeo, Ann.* 120 Sk.). Lucretius' *gelidai stringor aquai* (3.693) is the only example of this doubling in the *DRN*, though we do find *vestis splendorem purpureai* (2.52) and *nigrai noctis ad umbram* (4.537)

22. In the Circe fragment of Livius Andronicus (26 Morel), many scholars have proposed the emendation of *Circai* for *Circae* that is in the MSS. Flores 2011 provides the most helpful discussion on this point, saying, ad loc. that *Circai* was proposed by John Wordsworth in *Fragments and Specimens of Early Latin* (Oxon, 1874), 291, and by Baehrens, according to Lindsay 1893: 318. This reading has been accepted by others, including Pascoli, Warmington, and Ernout. Interestingly, Diehl proposed *Circas,* probably on analogy with *Latonas, Monetas,* and other such genitives, which does tend to remind one that *-as* is the form that Livius uses, not *-ai*.

23. Bailey 1947: 75–76 and Skutsch 1985: 61 both note the ending's rarity in early Latin as compared to Ennius. The ending occurs 54 times in pre-Lucretian poetry: 34 times in Plautus (*Amph.* 359, 367, 821; *Aul.* 121, 295, 305, 372, 540, 797; *Bacch.* 312, 820; *Cas.* 30; *Cist.* 40; *Epid.* 246, 508, 635; *Merc.* 241, 692, 811, 834; *Mil.* 84, 103, 236, 519, 552, 1154; *Poen.* 51, 274, 1045; *Pseud.* 98; *Stich.* 537, 699; *Trin.* 359, 492); 2 times in Terence (*An.* 439; *Heat.* 515); 6 times in Lucilius (135, 164, 226, 304, 993, 1337 Marx); 4 in the dramatic fragments (Titinius 44 Ribbeck; Accius 127, 178, 609 Ribbeck); and 8 in Cicero's poetry (*Aratea* 15.5, 34.58, 34.216, 34.278, 34.324, 34.418 Soubiran; *Ilias* 23.10 Büchner; *Progn.* 4.1 Soubiran). Most of these instances involve Greek proper names, though Bailey lists four instances in Plautus that do not involve proper names (*Aul.* 121, *Stich.* 537, *Poen.* 51, *Mil.* 105), while Skutsch adds two from Terence (*Andr.* 439 and *Haut.* 515). Bailey 1947: 76 also notes that Cicero "made a more restricted use of the

revived again when Lucretius began to use it again, appearing more than three times more frequently than it appeared in Ennius (Table A2.3):

Table A2.3 -ai in Republican Poetry

Livius Andronicus	Naevius	Ennius	Plautus
0% of lines	0%	0.7%	0.16%

Terence	Other Republican Poetry	Cicero	Lucretius
0.03%	0.07%	0.99%	2.3%

Finally, where in Ennius' *Annales -ae* occurs more frequently than *-ai*, Lucretius uses *-ai* more than *-ae* (*-ai* 166 times and *-ae* 153 times).[24] That Lucretius uses *-ai* more frequently than Ennius suggests that he is exploiting deliberately and liberally a feature of archaic Latin that is nevertheless much more common in Ennius than it is in any other earlier poet. The use of this ending in Lucretius, then, likely would have struck his audience as definitely archaic, and very probably as specifically Ennian.[25]

As the data in Appendix 5 show, Lucretius' use of *-ai* mirrors his deployment of word-initial alliteration, as the ending *-ai* tends to cluster, both at the level of the book and at the level of the passage (Table A2.4):

Table A2.4 -ai in the *DRN*

DRN 1	*DRN* 2	*DRN* 3	*DRN* 4	*DRN* 5	*DRN* 6
3.4% of lines	2.6%	3.7%	1.2%	1.4%	2.1%

There are long stretches in which one does not encounter this ending (e.g., no instances for almost 200 lines from 1.726–1.899), and there are examples of intense concentrations of the ending within a few lines (e.g., three instances within 11 lines at 4.69–79). Again, the distribution of *-ai* mirrors that of the other markedly Ennian effects, suggesting that when Lucretius Ennianizes, he does so strategically and in clusters rather than in any sort of inert, reflexive way.

---

termination than either Ennius or Lucretius." Bailey, it turns out, is wrong here with respect to Ennius, but not with respect to Lucretius.

24. The numbers come from Bailey 1947: 76, and are corroborated by Skutsch 1985: 61.

25. Kenney 1971: 22–23 and at Lucr. 3.83 suggests that *-ai* was used freely by Lucretius for metrical and euphonic effect.

Lucretius and Ennian Metrical Effects

I have said already that a lot of the inaccuracies and sweeping generalizations that this book seeks to counter come from scholars' attempts to see an overarching narrative of sharp periodization and straightforward progression for Latin literary history. This tendency is perhaps on no greater display than in the case of the history of Latin hexametric poetry. Metricians write the history of hexameter verse as if there were a linear development from Ennius to Vergil,[26] by necessity figuring Lucretius as a transitional figure who both shows signs of the archaic idiom of Ennius and points forward to the canons of Augustan refinement. Bailey, for example, in his comprehensive treatment of Lucretian style, writes, largely with respect to the coincidence of accent and ictus that, "it is then true, as has often been said, that Lucretius' hexameter stands midway between the naive verses of Ennius and the polished hexameter of the Augustans."[27] Similarly, Maguinness writes of the "common criticism" that assesses Lucretius, "chiefly in respect of language and metre, as a half-way stage between Ennius and Virgil."[28] More recently, Kenney argues that

> the Latin hexameter as Lucretius inherited it was largely the creation of Ennius, and Ennian characteristics such as the elision of final -*s* to create a short open syllable, or readiness, particularly in argumentative passages, to admit "irregular" word-division in the last two feet of the verse, must no doubt have seemed old-fashioned to ears attuned to Ciceronian elegance.

And again that

> there is little evidence of substantial technical advance in the surviving fragments of hexameter poetry from the period between Ennius (d. 169 BCE) and Lucretius (d. c. 55–51 BCE, by the conventional dating).[29]

---

26. The bibliography on the history and the development of the Latin hexameter is vast, but especially helpful analysis can be found in Christ 1879; Hardie 1907; Sturtevant 1919 and 1923; Wilkinson 1940 and 1963: 118–134 and 193–202; Hellegouarc'h 1964; Raven 1965; Pearce 1966; and Duckworth 1969. For a more recent and interpretative discussion of the Latin hexameter, see Morgan 2010: 284–377. On Lucretius' use of the hexameter, still useful are the series of studies by Merrill (1921, 1923, 1924a, 1924b), but see also Büchner 1936 and Duckworth 1969. The most accessible introduction to Lucretian metrics remains Bailey 1947: 109–123.

27. Bailey 1947: 109.

28. Maguinness 1965: 71.

29. Kenney 2007: 96; cf. Quinn 1959: 8: "Lucretius . . . is a better poet than Ennius had been, Cicero, well launched by this date upon his poetic career, was undoubtedly a worse one in his original compositions, though a highly competent translator. Neither, however, did much to change the style of poetry, or to adapt the poetic language and conventions of a hundred years before," and ibid.: 58, "the language of serious poetry, that of epic and tragedy, had really

Kenney's assessment in this piece reworks and expands his own earlier, and still seminal discussion of Lucretian metrics in the introduction to his commentary on *DRN* 3. According to Kenney, Lucretius employs an Ennian lack of enjambment, a technique that he calls the "linear style," as opposed to the more "periodic style," which would find its perfection in the hands of Vergil.[30]

This is not to say that, on some points, we can see a general trajectory from Ennius to Vergil, with Lucretius as a medial point representing the watershed moment when the Latin hexameter would start on the path toward its Vergilian perfection. For example, Bailey shows that Lucretius was an innovator who brought more dactyls into the line, especially in the first foot, and who accordingly discarded the Ennian penchant for a single spondaic word in the first foot.[31] Or take the fact that Lucretius innovates in the use of the diaeresis, incorporating it much more frequently than Ennius had, and, related to this, in his marked preference for a single spondaic word in the fourth foot, which ensured emphatic coincidence in the fourth (and fifth) feet.[32] And so, when it comes to the first four feet at least, the metricians are generally correct to imagine a direct line of development from Ennius, through Lucretius, to Vergil. At the same time, we ought not to overgeneralize about how linear the development of the Latin hexameter was. We know that Cicero's meter was in some ways closer to Vergil's than to either

---

changed very little since the days of Ennius. An effective poetic style (and Ennius' was that) tends, once formed, to persist until its remoteness from living language deprives it of vitality to a degree that is felt to be intolerable and to make it unfit for effective expression of any sincerely felt emotion . . . Catullus keeps, for example, in his more serious writing (in Poems 63 and 64, in the more seriously intended elegies) to that rugged, highly alliterative style which goes back to the very origins of Roman poetry."

30. Kenney 1971: 24–25, following Büchner 1936 and Bailey 1947: 120–123. In any case, Kenney is correct not to overgeneralize, and among many valuable insights regarding Lucretius' use of the hexameter, he includes the nuanced observation that "Ennian" features such as the "linear" or "unperiodic" style are confined more to the technical parts of the *DRN*, rather than the "pathetic" passages. Later, at 28–29, Kenney adds an important caveat regarding "linear" versus "periodic" styles in Lucretius after juxtaposing the two passages of each type, writing that these two examples "have been chosen to represent two extreme cases: an expository passage in a low key is contrasted with a rhetorical harangue highly charged with feeling. Between these extremes there is a wide range of intermediate possibilities; and the analyses have shown that even in these two passages there is no rigid differentiation of style: enjambment occurs in the expository passage, 'linear' writing in the 'pathetic.' Thus there can be no question of a hard-and-fast distinction on stylistic grounds between different types of passage, no application of, so to say, a litmus-paper test, no 'either-or.' " Similarly, he writes (1971: 23) "that Lucretius was technically capable when he wished of writing verse that is 'correct' by Ciceronian or Augustan standards is shown by the observation that in, for example, his famous description of the Sacrifice of Iphigenia (1.80–101), one of the most impassioned pieces of writing in the entire poem, there is not a single 'irregular' verse-ending."

31. Data and discussion at Bailey 1947: 110–111. Duckworth 1969: 37–41 highlights the contribution on this front of Cicero.

32. Bailey 1947: 113.

Lucretius' or Catullus', for example in his preference for diversifying metrical patterns in the first four feet of the line, while Lucretius' preference approximates much more closely to what we find in the *Annales*.[33] Unless Cicero is preternaturally advanced, then Lucretius again appears to be much more deliberately Ennian in his metrical schema than his contemporaries.

When it comes to the metrics of the last two feet, Lucretius approximates much more closely to Ennian practice than to that of Cicero, Catullus, or Vergil, to the point where we can safely consider the metrics of these two feet to be a general Ennian feature of Lucretian versecraft. For example, the use of a five-syllable word to fit the last two feet of the line (e.g., *augurioque*, *Ann.* 73 Sk; *induperator*, *Ann.* 78 Sk; *increpuisti*, *Ann.* 93 Sk; *Egeriai*, *Ann.* 113 Sk; *Fufetioeo*, *Ann.* 120 Sk; *aequiperare*, *Ann.* 133 Sk, etc.) is a relative anomaly in Ennius as compared to subsequent Latin hexameter poets (see Appendix 3 for comparative data):

Table A2.5 Pentasyllabic Line-Endings in Latin Hexameters

Ennius	Lucilius	Cicero	Other Republican Hexameter
3.53% of lines	2.88%	0.70%	0%

Catullus' Hexameter	Lucretius	Vergil	Ovid's *Metamorphoses*
0.63%	4.09%	0.15%	0.03%

Once again, in Table A2.5, we can see Lucretius not just reversing the trend in the use of an Ennian effect, but deploying it more frequently than even Ennius had done. In other words, Lucretius' innovation of using pentasyllabic words in the last two feet of the line represents a deliberate perfection of an Ennian tendency, and a productive one at that. But

---

33. Data found at Duckworth 1969: 37–41. Given the data compiled by Duckworth, Catullan metrics, especially in Poem 64, can confidently be labeled hyper-Ennian: Catullus varies his rhythms significantly less frequently than Ennius does, a monotony that is a feature of Ennian verse and that Cicero and, later, Vergil, would discard. On the one hand, Duckworth 1969: 42–43 has shown that this very monotony is a hallmark of the hexameters of Callimachus, which suggests that this abnormality in Catullan metrics is meant as a purposeful imitation of Callimachean metrics. On the other hand, Catullus, at least in 64, would appear to combine neotericism with purposeful Ennianism in such a way as to confuse the traditional separation of these two categories. For example, Ross 1969, following Norden at *Aen.* 6.55, notes (a) that *pectore ab imo* at 64.125–126 derives from Lucretius 3.57, and (b) Ennius' *effudit voces* (*Ann.* 553 Sk) lies behind the phrase *fudisse voces*. Ross cumulatively suggests we have here "a blend of archaic Ennius and neoteric formality." Similarly, Quinn 1972: 262 writes that "the qualities of Poem 64 are ruggedness and weight; the lines, instead of following one another in breath-taking succession, seem to stride confidently forward one by one, each pausing for our applause before giving place to the next. A very free use of alliteration contributes further to a kind of pastiche of archaic style which is in fact the effect of a highly mannered, self-conscious art, remote from the illusion of primitive simplicity it seeks to create." One is reminded here of Kenney's (1971: 23–25) discussion of Lucretius' "linear" style.

this productivity was not uniform as, again, we can find that a deliberate Ennian effect is not evenly distributed throughout the *DRN* (Table A2.6):

Table A2.6 Pentasyllabic Line-Endings in the *DRN*

DRN 1	*DRN 2*	*DRN 3*	*DRN 4*	*DRN 5*	*DRN 6*
5.82% of lines	7.24%	4.57%	2.10%	2.88%	2.64%

Even in *DRN* 2, where this feature is most frequently used, we find long stretches without a pentasyllabic line-ending (e.g., almost 100 lines from 2.347–440). Likewise, in *DRN* 4, in which Lucretius deploys this effect least frequently, we find passages that contain proportionally more pentasyllabic line-endings than one might expect (e.g., the Bailey paragraph 4.324–336 has 2 in 9 lines, ten times more frequently than in the rest of *DRN* 4).

Relatedly, we can also see Lucretius bucking the trend when it comes to hexameters that end with a single-syllable word (Appendix 3),[34] where, absent Lucretius, we can trace a clear diminishment in the prominence of such monosyllabic line-endings from Ennius to Ovid. These numbers include all monosyllabic line-endings, including those that feature (prod)elision or aphaeresis (e.g., *necesse est* or *fatendum est*). I provide these data comprehensively because even those line-endings that feature such elision appear to appropriate an Ennian innovation. I will handle monosyllabic line-endings that disrupt the coincidence of ictus and accent separately below (Table A2.7):

Table A2.7 Monosyllabic Line-Endings in Latin Hexameters

Ennius	Lucilius	Cicero	Other Republican Hexameter	Catullus' Hexameters
9.15% of lines	6.17%	2.00%	2.25%	4.39%

Lucretius	Vergil	Ovid's *Metamorphoses*
6.4%	1.35%	2.13%

Once again, we find in Lucretius a particularly Ennian effect that was gradually discarded by later poets, although note that in this instance Lucretius does not use this effect quite as frequently as Ennius. And once again—to point out the trend that we have come to expect—when Lucretius does use this Ennianizing effect, it tends to cluster in some passages (e.g., in the arguments for dualism, 6 times in 62 lines at 1.418–482, 5 times in 47 lines at 1.503–550; in his discussion of atomic motion and the dust-motes analogy, 7 times in 62 lines at 2.80–142; or on atomic shapes, 7 times in 35 lines at 4.408–443), even as it can be said to be deployed with some frequency throughout the poem (Table A2.8):

---

34. Obviously, this subject has been widely discussed. See especially Harkness 1910; Bailey 1947: 113–119; Wilkinson 1963; and Skutsch 1985: 49–51.

Table A2.8 Monosyllabic Line-Endings in the *DRN*

DRN 1	DRN 2	DRN 3	DRN 4	DRN 5	DRN 6
5.64% of lines	7.84%	8.96%	7.46%	3.2%	6.0%

Now, as I said above, not all monosyllabic line-endings are equivalent, and Ennius appears to have utilized this effect especially when it would disrupt the coincidence of stress and ictus (i.e., to create a heterodyne line-ending),[35] which is, of course, an almost inevitable consequence of a final monosyllable, but it is worth pointing out that 7% of *all* lines in the *Annales* display this effect, a percentage that similarly decreased in subsequent hexameter poets (Table A2.9):

Table A2.9 Monosyllabic Line-Endings in Latin Hexameters

Ennius	Lucilius	Cicero	Other Republican Hexameter
7.1% of lines	3.29%	0.5%	2.25%

Catullus' Hexameters	Lucretius	Vergil	Ovid's *Metamorphoses*
1.0%	2.3%	0.35%	0.06%

Clearly the use of the verse-final monosyllable to disrupt stress and ictus was a particularly Ennian metrical effect. On the basis of these figures, moreover, it would seem that post-Ennian poets strove to purify the Latin hexameter of this Ennian effect, and, when it does occur, it is reasonable to assume that this is a purposeful Ennianism. At the same time, precisely because this purification was a general trend diachronically, we cannot be certain that all remaining occurrences of the phenomenon necessarily involve Ennius directly or consciously.[36] If it is generally true that the rare occurrences of this feature in Vergil and Ovid suggest an Ennianism, we should consider whether this is also true of the feature in Lucretius. His use of this figure may be no less deliberate than theirs, and its higher frequency in the *DRN* may not be a symptom of him imitating Ennian versecraft unconsciously or reflexively, but rather an indication that he simply does so more often, and that, like Vergil and Ovid, he does so for specific purposes of his own. Moreover, anytime the preponderance of monosyllables in a given passage exceeds the frequency

---

35. On "heterodyne" and "homodyne" lines, see Jackson Knight 1950.

36. In the *Metamorphoses*, for example, while Ovid employs this effect in only 7 of the 11,995 lines (0.06%), the fact that two of the seven total occurrences appear at the beginning of *Met.* 15 in sequential lines (30–31) as part of the introduction to the speech of Pythagoras would indicate that by this gesture Ovid meant to remind readers of the parallel scene in the *Annales* where Homer discourses on natural philosophy (on which, see Hardie 1995).

for the book and/or the poem as a whole, it is fair to say that Lucretius is purposefully Ennianizing. To use an example that I pursued further in chapter 3, four monosyllabic line-endings appear in a span of fifteen lines in Lucretius' description of battle chaos at 3.642–656. The frequency of monosyllables in these lines (26.7%) is higher than in *DRN* 3 as a whole (8.7%) as well as in the *DRN* as a whole (6.2%). It is hard to explain why *DRN* 3 would be more *unconsciously* favorable to final monosyllables than the other books, and, by the same token, why that would be true of this passage other than to entertain the idea that Lucretius means to cultivate an Ennian context here.[37]

Perhaps the most "Ennian" metrical effect that we encounter in Lucretius is the suppression of final -*s* before a short vowel, or sigmatic ecthlipsis.[38] That this effect was an especially Ennian pretension is clear from the fact that while Ennius suppresses final -*s* in 15% of the extant lines of the *Annales*, this percentage decreases dramatically by the time one gets to the poetry of Cicero (1.4% of lines) and also of Lucretius (.6% of lines).[39] As Skutsch (1985, 56) points out regarding this license, "in Lucretius it is much rarer than in Ennius: Ennius has it once in five lines, Lucretius once in 150." It is also important that Lucretius uses the device less frequently than Cicero does, a fact that may reflect the chronological divide between the poetic translations of Cicero's youth and the composition of the *DRN*. After all, Cicero would ultimately disavow the license as *subrusticum*.[40] In any case, this effect likely would have struck Lucretius' reader as especially Ennian, and, given that the uses of sigmatic ecthlipsis tend to cluster in books, it seems to be another Ennian device that Lucretius deploys strategically (Table A2.10):

Table A2.10 Sigmatic Ecthlipsis in the *DRN*

DRN 1	*DRN* 2	*DRN* 3	*DRN* 4	*DRN* 5	*DRN* 6
0.36% of lines	0.51%	0.46%	0.85%	0.48%	0.62%

We find very long stretches of the *DRN* where this feature does not appear (e.g., almost 250 lines, from 5.1198–1444) as well as short passages with many examples (e.g., 5 instances in 18 lines at 4.1018–1035).

---

37. See my discussion in chapter 3, at pp. 91–94.

38. For a thorough discussion of the phenomenon in Lucretius, see Butterfield 2008. See also the recent discussion of the phenomenon in Terence by Pezzini 2015: 193–234.

39. It is assumed, for example, that the only instance of sigmatic ecthlipsis in Catullus occurs in a context that involves literary polemics, and is meant to insinuate that Catullus' opponent is Ennian, that this is bad, and that Catullus himself is, by voicing his opposition to this *subrusticum* effect (Cic. *Orat.* 48.161), a refined Callimachean. See Macleod 1973; Zetzel 1983: 256–257; and Wiseman 1985: 185–186. For the data on sigmatic ecthlipsis in Ennius, see Bailey 1947: 124 and Skutsch 1985: 56.

40. Kenney, 1971: 22: "If Lucretius' style, compared with that of Cicero, seems 'archaic,' that is no more than a summary . . . a well-known example is the practice of eliding final -*s* after a short vowel and before a consonant . . . this usage . . . occurs in Cicero's own earlier poetry, but is discarded in his later work."

Clusters and Anti-Clusters of Ennianisms
in the DRN

Given that all five of the Ennianisms in Lucretius that I have focused on in this appendix have been shown to cluster at various points throughout the *DRN*, only to lie dormant for long stretches elsewhere, it should not surprise us that the same can be said of these Ennianisms in conjunction with one another. In other words, Lucretius can be shown to combine these five effects with one another in clusters throughout his poem, even as it can be shown that long stretches of the *DRN* do not contain a single Ennian effect. I have provided a map of all the Ennianisms in Lucretius in Appendix 5, where I have broken the poem down by Bailey paragraphs to show where such clusters occur. I have defined a cluster there as a passage containing 50% more Ennianisms per ten lines than the average throughout the poem. I have also identified what I call "anti-clusters," or paragraphs in which the frequency of Ennianisms is less than half the average in the rest of the poem. I include here the data in table form (Table A2.11):

Table A2.11 Ennianisms Per Line in the *DRN*

DRN entire	*DRN* 1	*DRN* 2	*DRN* 3
.26 Ennianisms per line	.28	.31	.29

	DRN 4	*DRN* 5	*DRN* 6
	.24	.21	.22

Conclusion

This appendix has offered a typology of what can be considered Ennian effects of language and meter in the *DRN*: (1) hyper-alliteration of a single letter in at least three words in a line or sense-unit, (2) the archaic genitive ending *-ai*, (3) pentasyllabic line-endings, (4) monosyllabic line-endings, and (5) sigmatic ecthlipsis. When Lucretius uses these effects in clusters or in conjunction with one another, I believe that the reader is often prompted by the poet to read that passage with Ennius in mind; this does not always ensure that we can prove from independent evidence that Lucretius is alluding to a specific passage of the *Annales* when he uses these effects. Rather than use this evidence to look for specific Ennian allusions, we would do better to recognize these effects as features of Lucretius' deliberate engagement with Ennius' *Annales* as a stylistic *modello codice*. The fact that these effects are clustered in specific passages suggests that while the *DRN* is consistently "Ennian" according to the criteria I have adduced, it is definitely more "Ennian" in some places, and less so in others.

Comparative Data on Latin Hexameter Line-Endings

Here I have gathered the relevant data on verse-final monosyllables in Lucretius and—for comparison—in all other Republican hexameter, Vergil, and Ovid's *Metamorphoses*.

Verse-Final Monosyllables in Lucretius

DRN 1 (63/1,117): 13 (tua vi), 33 (tuum se), 44 (necesse est), 88 (profusa est),116 (insinuet se), 146 (necesse est), 203 (certa est), 205 (fatendum est), 216 (interemat res), 232 (quae sunt), 245 (materies est), 269 (necesse est), 297 (qui sunt), 302 (necesse est), 304 (potest res), 328 (gerit res), 339 (daret res), 361 (par est), 377 (receptum est), 385 (necesse est), 389 (necesse est), 399 (necesse est), 410 (ab re), 434 (dum sit), 440 (faciet quid), 443 (potest res), 445 (per se), 462 (fatendum est), 465 (videndum est), 485 (potest vis), 504 (reperta est), 506 (necesse est), 508 (tenet se), 511 (inane est), 512 (necesse est), 539 (necesse est), 607 (necesse est), 613 (deminui iam), 621 (quae sunt), 624 (necesse est), 626 (quoniam sunt), 657 (quae sint), 697 (minus sunt), 716 (Empedocles est), 728 (virum vi), 729 (in se), 738 (magis quam), 751 (non quis), 755 (ut qui), 790 (necesse est), 795 (necesse est), 812 (alimur nos), 813 (aliae res), 825 (necesse est), 868 (necesse est), 872 (necesse est), 880 (repulsum est), 893 (docet res), 923 (meum cor), 954 (repertum est), 974 (necesse est), 978 (locet se), 1,049 (necesse est).

5.6 per 100 lines/1 every 17.73 lines.
Range of Frequencies—High: 9 in 100 lines (300–400)/1 every 11.1 lines; Low: 1 in 100 lines (1,000–1,100)/1 every 100 lines.
40/63 preserve the homodyne through elision or because the sixth foot contains two monosyllables. 23/63 create heterodyne.

DRN 2 (92/1,174): 4 (suave est), 16 (ut qui), 36 (cubandum est), 57 (magis quam), 59 (necesse est), 83 (necesse est), 87 (quae sint), 92 (modoque est), 94 (probatum est), 95 (quies est), 123 (potest res), 125 (par est), 177 (quae sint), 185 (sua vi), 193 (putandum est), 231 (necesse est), 241 (per se), 242 (gerat res), 243 (necesse est), 260 (tulit mens), 284 (necesse est), 303 (potest vis), 326 (virum vi), 377 (necesse est), 378 (manu sunt), 412 (organici quae), 416 (recens est), 422 (tibi res), 423 (creata est), 425 (reperta est), 428 (ut quae), 436 (nata est), 437 (Veneris res), 442 (necesse est), 445 (necesse est), 457 (necesse est), 468 (necessum est), 478 (rem quae), 513 (necesse est), 516 (remensum est), 522 (rem quae), 525 (cum sit), 526 (similes sint), 565 (docet res), 578 (secuta est), 586 (in se), 615 (inventi sint), 646 (necesse est), 690 (necesse est), 700 (putandum est), 710 (necessum est), 720 (dissimiles sunt), 721 (necesse est), 725 (necessum est), 751 (necesse est), 757 (principiis est), 774 (quae sint), 791 (variis ex), 799 (propterea quod), 806 (repleta est), 809 (putandum est), 810 (in se), 820 (pariter sunt), 835 (propterea fit), 849 (par est), 861 (necesse est), 865 (necesse est), 868 (quae sunt), 872 (nacta est), 892 (creant res), 896 (quae sint), 900 (nova re), 910 (necesse est), 917 (cum sint), 923 (necesse est), 925 (id quod), 968 (ex se), 975 (auctum est), 984 (ut sit), 998 (adepta est), 1,017 (pars est), 1,018 (discrepitant res), 1,044 (loci sint), 1,046 (velit mens), 1,050 (per se), 1,052 (putandum est), 1,064 (necesse est), 1,069 (confieri res), 1,084 (fatendum est), 1,085 (quae sunt), 1,125 (et dum), 1,156 (ex se).

7.83 per 100 lines/1 every 12.76 lines.
Range of Frequencies=High: 13 in 100 lines (400–500)/1 every 7.69 lines; Low: 2.70 in 100 lines (1,100–1,174)/ 1 every 37.04 lines.
65/92 preserve homodyne through elision or because of two monosyllables in sixth foot. 27/92 create heterodyne.

DRN 3 (98/1,094): 3 (tuis nunc), 8 (equi vis), 17 (geri res), 29 (tua vi), 30 (retecta est), 56 (qui sit), 58 (manet res), 89 (magis quam), 91 (necesse est), 95 (locutum est), 96 (et pes), 100 (faciat nos), 101 (siet mens), 115 (in se), 137 (ex se), 142 (animusque est), 152 (metu mens), 159 (animi vi), 166 (fatendum est), 175 (necesse est), 199 (pro quam), 202 (magis sunt), 204 (necesse est), 209 (loco se), 211 (quies est), 216 (necesse est), 219 (tamen se), 221 (aut cum), 231 (putanda est), 235 (necesse est), 241 (necesse est), 267 (ex his), 278 (creata est), 299 (mens est), 310 (putandum est), 314 (necesse est), 317 (quot sunt), 355 (docuit nos), 413 (peresa est), 424 (res est), 441 (aliqua re), 444 (incohibens sit), 450 (animi vis), 453 (labat mens), 470 (necesse est), 472 (uterque est), 479 (madet mens), 513 (aequum est), 532 (habenda est), 548 (loco quae), 549 (oculi sunt), 578 (necesse est), 583 (animae vis), 585 (loco sunt), 587 (qui sunt), 611 (sua scit), 612 (foret mens), 624 (animai est), 644 (id quod), 645 (hominis vis), 647 (mens est), 653 (humi pes), 667 (simul cum), 668 (putandum est), 686 (putandum est), 688 (putandum est), 690 (docet res), 704 (ex se), 705 (recens in), 718 (ex se), 725 (est ut), 728 (ubi sint), 731 (cum sunt), 764 (equi vis), 766 (necesse est), 790 (animi vis), 798 (necesse est), 802 (putandum est), 806 (necesse est), 812 (inane est), 817 (sunt quae), 819 (habenda est), 840 (erimus tum), 848 (nunc est), 861 (futurum est), 885 (alium se), 926 (putandum est), 934 (ac fles), 936 (in vas), 962 (necesse est), 965 (necesse est), 983 (ferat fors), 995 (oculos est), 1,009 (in vas), 1,038 (quiete est), 1,044 (aetherius sol), 1,050 (mali cum), 1,068 (ut fit).

8.96 per 100 lines/1 every 11.16 lines.
Range of Frequencies=High: 13 in 100 lines (200–300)/1 every 7.69 lines; Low: 4 in 100 lines (300–400)/ 1 every 25 lines.
58/98 preserve homodyne through elision or because there are two monosyllables in the sixth foot. 40/98 create heterodyne.

DRN 4 (96/1,287): 29 (has res), 49 (has res), 51 (nomitanda est), 90 (aliae res), 99 (necesse est), 118 (putandum est), 121 (necessum est), 146 (in res), 148 (ibi iam) 163 (necesse est), 174 (nemo est), 181 (gruum quam), 191 (necesse est), 197 (queant res), 200 (uti lux), 216 (necesse est), 231 (eadem quae), 232 (necesse est), 234 (id nos), 235 (poterit res), 256 (habendum est), 259 (et cum), 263 (aliquae res), 289 (est par), 292 (pars est), 293 (eo quod), 296 (quam sit), 315 (etiam quod), 316 (propterea quod), 317 (ad nos), 342 (hic est), 418 (videre et), 438 (pars est), 484 (orta est), 490 (necesse est), 493 (necesse est), 495 (necesse est), 499 (verum est), 501 (procul sint), 509 (quae sint), 510 (quae sint), 512 (parata est), 516 (necesse est), 520 (necesse est), 521 (orta est), 522 (suam rem), 523 (relicta est), 526 (fatendum est), 535 (et quid), 540 (necesse est), 558 (necesse est), 561 (quae sit), 586 (cum Pan), 603 (dividitur vox), 617 (cibum cum), 634 (amarum est), 636 (differitasque est), 649 (necesse est), 653 (necesse est), 664 (coorta est), 674 (necesse est), 676 (putandum est), 681 (canum vis), 690 (quam res), 694 (ex re), 751 (necesse est), 760 (eum quem), 761 (potita est), 773 (putandum est), 803 (quae sunt), 807 (quae sunt), 837 (creata est), 866 (consequitur rem), 888 (vis est), 910 (gruum quam), 920 (opera sit), 922 (putandum est), 932 (necessum est), 935 (corio sunt), 939 (et cum), 957 (tum se), 961 (intust), 964 (magis mens), 996 (ad se), 1,006 (necessum est), 1,040 (hominis vis), 1,059 (in cor), 1,061 (tamen sunt), 1,142 (inopi sunt), 1,152 (ac vis), 1,162 (merum sal), 1,164 (pudens est), 1,165 (Lampadium fit), 1,166 (non quit), 1,184 (par est), 1,217 (superatum est).

7.45 every 100 lines/1 every 13.41 lines.
Range of Frequencies=High: 15 in 100 lines (500–600)/1 every 6.67 lines; Low: 1.15 in 100 lines/1 every 86.96 lines.
69/96 preserve homodyne through elision or two monosyllables in sixth foot. 27/96 create heterodyne.

DRN 5 (47/1,457): 9 (eam quae), 25 (Arcadius sus), 40 (repleta est), 59 (reperta est), 104 (fidem res), 111 (magis quam), 134 (animi vis), 182 (primum est), 195 (quae sint), 206 (sua vi), 215 (aetherius sol), 226 (aequum est), 229 (adhibenda est), 252 (pedum vi), 267 (aetherius sol), 279 (in res), 281 (aetherius sol), 294 (quae sunt), 319 (ex se), 323 (recipit res), 333 (navigiis sunt), 335 (reperta est), 343 (necesse est), 351 (necessum est), 357 (inane est), 362 (sunt quae), 377 (quae sunt), 389 (aetherius sol), 497 (ut faex),

531 (necesse est), 545 (queant res), 558 (apta est), 563 (animi vis), 581 (necesse est), 620 (causa est), 643 (putandum est), 752 (putandum est), 848 (Veneris res), 855 (necesse est), 858 (mobilitas est), 860 (sua quae), 884 (etiam nunc), 1,047 (notities est), 1,056 (tontoperest re), 1,071 (aut cum), 1,172 (propterea quod), 1,241 (repertum est).

3.23 every 100 lines/1 every 31 lines.
Range of Frequencies=High: 9 in 100 lines (200–300 ; 300–400)/1 every 11.11 lines; Low: 0 in 100 lines (900–1,000; 1300–1,400).
26/47 preserve homodyne through elision or two monosyllables in the sixth foot. 21/ 47 create heterodyne.

DRN 6 (77/1,286): 37 (magis quam), 39 (necesse est), 45 (necesse est), 53 (propterea quod), 71 (deum vis), 87 (utram se), 89 (extulerit se), 139 (docet res), 161 (lapidem si), 166 (moveant res), 167 (si quem), 206 (necessum est), 209 (necesse est), 216 (necesse est), 238 (haec est), 246 (putandum est), 249 (docet res), 262 (putandum est), 272 (necesse est), 279 (sua cum), 288 (fere tum), 299 (tulit vis), 320 (superne est), 325 (se vis), 369 (necesse est), 383 (utram se), 385 (extulerit se), 390 (cumque est), 393 (in re), 402 (eas tum), 414 (necesse est), 432 (ut sit), 448 (necesse est), 458 (coorta est), 534 (quae sint), 541 (putandum est), 560 (premit vis), 582 (cum vis), 620 (loco sol), 663 (mali fert), 665 (putandum est), 693 (sit vis), 697 (fatendum est), 740 (ab re), 780 (quae sint), 781 (homini res), 841 (si qua), 861 (magis quod), 866 (manu sit), 877 (in se), 887 (fieri fons), 896 (quae cum), 898 (in se), 905 (putandum est), 911 (ex se), 917 (prius quam), 922 (necesse est), 936 (sint res), 938 (ad res), 940 (necesse est), 974 (venenum est), 976 (cum sit), 979 (de re), 985 (in se), 1,001 (pelliciat vim), 1,017 (vace fit), 1,029 (in se), 1,054 (ab se), 1,057 (item res), 1,063 (tum fit), 1,076 (operam des), 1,082 (par est), 1,095 (necesse est), 1,101 (nacta est), 1,105 (discrepitant res), 1,130 (necesse est), 1,222 (canum vis).

5.99 every 100 lines/1 every 16.70 lines.
Range of Frequencies=High: 10 in 100 lines (200–300)/1 every 10 lines; Low: 1.16 in 100 lines (1,200–1,286)/1 every 86.21 lines.
48/77 preserve homodyne through elision or two monosyllables in the sixth foot. 29/ 77 create heterodyne.

Total *DRN*: (473/7,415)
6.38 every 100 lines OR 1 every 15.68 lines.
Range of Frequencies=High: 15 in 100 lines (*DRN* 4.500–600)/1 every 6.67 lines; Low: 0 in 100 lines (*DRN* 5.900–1000 and 5.1300–1400).
306/473 (64.7%) of monosyllabic line-endings preserve homodyne. 167/473 (35.3%) create heterodyne.
In other words, 2.3% (167/7,415) of *all* lines in Lucretius disrupt the homodyne in the 6th foot with a monosyllabic line-ending.

Verse-Final Monosyllables in Ennius' Annales

Annales 1 (8/112): 28 (ex se), 85 (foras lux), 87 (exoritur sol), 89 (locis dant), 92 (manu sim), 96 (soliti sunt), 97 (decet rem), 98 (habet sas); *Annales* 2 (0/23); *Annales* 3 (0/12); *Annales* 4 (3/6): 151 (opum vi), 153 (et nox), 155 (Roma est); *Annales* 5 (1/8): 159 (iuvat res); *Annales* 6 (6/41): 165 (homo rex), 186 (ferat Fors), 189 (certum est), 190 (magnis dis), 202 (refert rem), 203 (hominum rex); *Annales* 7 (8/40): 206 (alii rem), 209 (ante hunc), 229 (virum vis), 230 (ibe sos), 232 (hac stat), 238 (paratust), 240 (Venus Mars), 246 (flexa est); *Annales* 8 (5/50): 248 (geritur res), 253 (solida vi), 254 (monuit res), 260 (secuta est), 286 (Servilius sic); *Annales* 9 (2/23): 311 (bis sex), 314 (facit frux); *Annales* 10 (1/30): 342 (potis sint); *Annales* 11 (2/9): 357 (solent sos), 359 (uti des); *Annales* 12 (1/6): 363 (restituit rem); *Annales* 13 (1/6): 372 (meum cor); *Annales* 14 (1/12): 385 (fero sic); *Annales* 15 (0/11); *Annales* 16 (6/26): 405 (opum vi), 415 (interea fax), 419 (oritur nox), 420 (hiems it), 421 (potis sunt), 423 (sit frux); *Annales* 17 (0/11); *Annales* 18 (0/2); *Sedes Incertae* (12/181): 460 (longos per), 465 (equos vi), 466 (termo est), 469 (decem sint), 471 (loqui me), 482 (aquae vis), 560 (gesta est), 566 (sublatae sunt), 585 (laetificum gau), 586 (altisonum cael), 587 (suam do), 591 (pater rex).

Total *Annales* (57/623): 9.15 per 100 lines=9.15% of lines /1 every 10.93 lines.
13/57 (22.8%) preserve homodyne through elision or two monosyllables in the sixth foot. 44/57 (77.2%) create heterodyne.
In other words, 7.1% of *all* lines in the *Annales* disrupt the homodyne in the 6th foot with a monosyllabic line-ending.

Verse-Final Monosyllables in Lucilius' Hexameters (Marx)

60/973=6.2 per 100 lines=6.2% of lines.

21 (pater Mars), 52 (refert res), 62 (Aemilio prae), 86 (tu seis), 117 (hic est) 122 (recipit se), 127 (pervenio nox), 162 (genusque est), 171 (comedit me), 182 (non est), 184 (nolueris cum), 185 (debueris te), 214 (dies sit), 246 (lacerto est), 263 (improbius quem), 266 (vermiculi qui), 267 (qualia sunt), 269 (tuae se), 283 (egomet me), 341 (poema est), 351 (hoc sunt), 364 (atque i), 369 (facies i), 374 (an b), 378 (illi est), 381 (geminat l), 447 (tulit fors), 448 (ingenio sit), 457 (putare et), 469 (agitet me), 483 (ulla est), 494 (vomitum pus), 495 (quid sit), 496 (posterior te), 554 (ac tu), 558 (cum sint), 562 (domi te), 987 (molestum est), 988 (ad te), 990 (inretita est), 1002 (non vis), 1020 (ad te), 1032 (ad rem), 1,036 (quod do), 1,051 (possideas si), 1,074 (dapsilius se), 1,077 (haec est), 1,118 (foro qui), 1,119 (utrique est), 1,140 (cinaedo et), 1,148 (satis sit), 1,175 (altilium lanx), 1,193 (ad se), 1,199 (hoc est), 1,214 (potis sunt), 1,216 (ad te), 1,221 (canes ut), 1,233 (virum se), 1,235 (qui sis), 1,328 (habeat res).

32/60 of these disrupt the homodyne, while the other 28/60 preserve the homodyne. In other words, 3.29% of all hexameters in Lucilius disrupt the homodyne in the 6th foot with a monosyllabic line-ending.

Verse-Final Monosyllables in Cicero

15/747=2.0% of lines.

De Consulatu Suo 10.19 Courtney (perempta est), *Aratea* 7.4 (hac est), 18.1 (repente est), 28.2 (simul pes), 34.58 (Equi vis), 34.65 (curriculo nox), 34.74 (praesto est), 34.153 (ex se), 34.312 (necesse est), 34.339 (relictum est), 34.354 (repulsa est), 34.429 (prae se), 34.448 (Coronae est), 34.463 (umbra est), 34.475 (signipotens nox).

4/15 disrupt the homodyne=26.7%.
In other words, .5% of Cicero's hexameters have a final monosyllable that creates the heterodyne.

Verse-Final Monosyllables in Catullus' Hexameters

35/798=4.39% of hexameters

8/35 disrupt homodyne=22.9%.
8/798 create heterodyne=1.0%.

62.9 (par est), 62.11 (parata est), 62.13 (quod sit), 62.45 (suis est), 62.61 (necesse est), 62.62 (parentum est), 64.119 (lamentata est), 64.301 (aspernata est), 64.315 (opus dens), 66.27 (adepta es), 66.29 (locuta es), 66.63 (deum me), 66.91 (tuam me), 67.9 (nunc sum), 67.43 (quae mi), 68.15 (pura est), 68.19 (mihi mors), 68.33 (apud me), 68.39 (praesto est), 68.41(in re), 68.141 (aequum est), 68.159 (ipso est), 69.7 (valde est), 73.3 (benigne est), 83.5 (est res), 86.5 (tota est), 89.5 (non est), 96.5 (dolori est), 107.5 (refers te), 107.7 (hac res), 110.3 (inimica es), 110.7 (avara est), 111.3 (par est), 112.1 (homo est qui), 115.3 (potis sit).

Verse-Final Monosyllables in Other Republican Epic

2/89=2.2% of lines.

Only 2 examples in 89 lines are found, both of which disrupt the homodyne:

Caesar, *Limon* 3 Courtney (foret vis) and Furius Bibaculus, *Annales Belli Gallici* 10 Courtney (viro vir).

Hostius (0/7), Accius (0/12), Livius Refictus (0/4), Furius Antias (0/6), Gannius (0/3), Egnatius (0/3), Mattius (0/7), Ninius Crassus (0/2), Naevius (0/2), Quintus Cicero (0/20), Caesar (*Limon* 1/6), Furius Bibaculus (1/13), Sueius (0/2), Varro Atacinus (0/2).

Verse-Final Monosyllables in Vergil

Bucolics (13/822)=1.6 per 100 lines OR 1 every 63.23 lines.
1 (0/83); 2 (1/73): 70 (ulmo est); 3 (2/111): 62 (apud me) and 72 (locuta est); 4 (1/63): 63 (cubili est); 5 (1/83): 83 (nec quae); 6 (3/86): 9 (si quis), 11 (ulla est) and 74 (secuta est); 7 (2/70): 35 (at tu) and 43 (anno est); 8 (1/109): 106 (bonum sit); 9 (1/67): 48 (et quo); 10 (1/77): 23 (secuta est).

Georgics (24/2,188)=1.1 per 100 lines/1 every 91.17 lines.
Book 1 (5/514): 181 (exiguus mus), 247 (silet nox), 313 (imbriferum ver), 314 (et cum), 370 (et cum); Book 2 (4/542): 49 (si quis), 103 (quae sint), 272 (multum est), 321 (rapidus sol); Book 3 (10/566): 98 (ventum est), 133 (et cum), 255 (exacuit sus), 358 (nec cum), 391 (dignum est), 428 (et dum), 452 (laborum est), 474 (si quis), 478 (coorta est), 484 (in se); Book 4 (5/566): 6 (si quem), 71 (et vox), 84 (aut hos), 212 (una est), 402 (umbra est)

Aeneid (137/9,895)=1.38 per 100 lines/1 every 72.23 lines.
Book 1 (11/756): 64 (usa est), 65 (hominum rex), 77 (fas est), 105 (aquae mons), 148 (coorta est), 151 (virum quem), 181 (si quem), 386 (dolore est), 601 (ubique est), 603 (si quid), 614 (locuta est); Book 2 (7/804): 163 (ex quo), 170 (deae mens), 217 (et iam), 250 (Oceano nox), 355 (lupi ceu), 648 (hominum rex), 703 (Troia est); Book 3 (9/718): 12 (magnis dis), 151 (qua se), 154 (Apollo est), 320 (locuta est), 375 (deum rex), 390 (ilicibus sus), 463 (amico est), 478 (necesse est), 695 (qui nunc); Book 4 (8/705): 95 (duorum est), 132 (canum vis), 224 (qui nunc), 287 (visa est), 314 (tuam te), 370 (amantem est), 557 (monere est), 613 (necesse est); Book 5 (12/871): 178 (imo est), 224 (magistro est), 372 (qui se), 481 (humi bos), 624 (o gens), 638 (agi res), 679 (Iuno est), 710 (ferendo est), 713 (et quos), 714 (taurum est), 716 (pericli est), 727 (alto est); Book 6 (16/901): 117 (nec te), 133 (cupido est), 173 (dignum est), 189 (locuta est), 325 (turba est), 346 (fides est), 455 (amore est), 459 (ima est), 466 (hoc est), 514 (necesse est), 538 (Sibylla est), 611 (turba est), 719 (putandum est), 737 (necesse est), 845 (ille es), 846 (restituis rem); Book 7 (12/817): 51 (iuventa est), 95 (luco est), 263 (cupido est), 310 (non sunt), 311 (usquam est), 357 (locuta est), 552 (abunde est), 559 (laborum est), 592 (eunt res), 708 (et gens), 784 (supra est), 790 (iam bos); Book 8 (5/731): 43 (ilicibus sus), 71 (unde est), 83 (conspicitur sus), 400 (mens est), 679 (magnis dis); Book 9 (13/818): 5 (locuta est), 57 (atque huc), 131 (adempta est), 175 (tuendum est), 187 (quiete est), 247 (Troia est), 260 (fidesque est), 320 (vocat res), 440 (atque hinc), 490 (de te), 512 (si qua), 532 (opum vi), 723 (agat res); Book 10 (18/908): 2 (hominum rex), 9 (aut hos), 84 (nefandum est), 107 (secat spem), 228 (deum gens), 231 (ut nos), 259 (parent se), 361 (viro vir), 450 (utrique est), 493 (humandi est), 710 (ventum est), 734 (viro vir), 743 (hominum rex), 771 (sua stat), 802 (tenet se), 843 (mali mens), 861 (ulla est), 864 (viam vis); Book 11 (11/914): 3

(mens est), 16 (hic est), 23 (imo est), 151 (dolore est), 164 (nec quas), 170 (et quam), 369 (cordi est), 373 (tibi vis), 429 (et quos), 632 (virum vir), 683 (supra est); Book 12 (15/952): 20 (aequum est), 23 (Latino est), 48 (pro me), 231 (hi sunt), 319 (sagitta est), 360 (qui me), 432 (tergo est), 526 (nunc, nunc), 552 (opum vi), 565 (hac stat), 678 (acerbi est), 739 (ventum est), 755 (inani est), 851 (deum rex), 879 (adempta est).

Total for Vergil (174/12, 905): 1.35 per 100 lines/1 every 74.17 lines.
129/174 monosyllabic lines preserve the homodyne through elision or because the sixth foot contains two monosyllables. Only 45/174 monosyllables create heterodyne.
In other words, roughly one-third of 1% (.35%) of Vergil's lines employ the Ennian effect of disrupting the homodyne in the 6th foot with a monosyllabic line-ending.

Verse-Final Monosyllables in Ovid's Metamorphoses

Book 1 (12/779): 145 (rara est), 239 (imago est), 395 (mota est), 433 (apta est), 452 (quem non), 499 (quae non), 605 (ut quae), 630 (alta est), 638 (voce est), 675 (retenta est), 678 (at tu), 696 (si non); Book 2 (14/875): 57 (fas sit), 189 (non est), 268 (fama est), 278 (locuta est), 347 (questa est), 349 (retenta est), 416 (longa est), 461 (adempta est), 491 (acta est), 520 (nostra est), 611 (secutum est), 674 (novata est), 741 (ausa est), 763 (et quae); Book 3 (18/733): 201 (secuta est), 266 (furto est), 271 (si non), 291 (deorum est), 304 (illo est), 311 (dignum est), 320 (profecto est), 377 (parata est), 417 (unda est), 434 (umbra est), 478 (non est), 612 (isto est), 620 (cupido est), 627 (si non), 653 (rogata est), 654 (vestra est), 681 (cauda est), 728 (nostra est); Book 4 (12/803): 17 (iuventa est), 53 (non est), 132 (haec sit), 167 (orsa est), 233 (querela est), 354 (si quis), 427 (nostra est), 536 (ponto est), 550 (secuta est), 593 (cur non), 654 (nostra est), 696 (ferendam est); Book 5 (24/678): 19 (apta est), 22 (revincta est), 39 (revolsum est), 65 (quo plus), 124 (fixa est), 173 (fixa est), 186 (ultra est), 245 (ira est), 261 (nostro est), 318 (professa est), 333 (non sint), 345 (digna est), 373 (nostra est), 411 (dictum est), 458 (lacerta est), 518 (reperta est), 519 (aut si), 522 (non est), 527 (quantum est), 532 (cautum est), 573 (**sacer fons**), 580 (petita est), 626 (agnae est), 644 (vecta est); Book 6 (14/721): 142 (parva est), 188 (recepta est), 215 (querella est), 255 (et qua), 258 (sagitta est), 293 (caeco est), 309 (saxum est), 331 (ara est), 349 (aquarum est), 512 (repulsa est), 548 (illo est), 586 (tota est), 621 (a! quam), 670 (pluma est); Book 7 (18/865): 12 (hoc est), 299 (senecta est), 310 (aevo est), 339 (prima est), 361 (harena est), 436 (per te), 452 (urbe est), 510 (hoc est), 518 (secuta est), 559 (nec fit), 566 (cura est), 592 (reperta est), 609 (nulla est), 663 (**extulerat sol**), 687 (pudori est), 712 (mens est), 794 (ipso est), 860 (in me); Book 8 (23/884): 45 (amanti est), 55 (quam sim), 65 (in te), 88 (tanta est), 89 (paventem est), 111 (nec te), 130 (patrique est), 131 (digna est), 149 (visa est), 238 (cantu est), 352 (illo est), 359 (**vulnificus sus**), 413 (fixum est), 450 (amorem est), 483 (pianda est), 561 (utroque est), 603 (**aequoreus rex**), 619 (peractum est), 782 (si non), 839 (ipsa est), 862 (a se), 870 (forma est), 879 (novandi est); Book 9 (22/797): 5 (nec tam), 6 (decorum est), 88 (cornu est), 145 (novandum est), 191 (nec mi), 198 (iubendo est), 233 (ministro est), 246 (favore est), 256 (si quis), 259 (visa est), 280 (cui sic), 312 (levata est), 316 (fama est), 385 (non est), 468 (non est), 591 (quae nunc), 619 (secundum est), 676 (sors est), 734 (nulla est), 738 (secuta est), 788 (ipse est), 790 (nam quae); Book 10 (19/739): 26 (ora est), 38 (certum est), 45 (fama est), 57 (relapsa est), 63 (eodem est), 212 (si non), 215 (ai ai), 216 (ducta est), 254 (an sit), 281 (tepere est), 351 (non es), 354 (memorque est), 441 (iussa est), 471 (illa est), 523 (ipso est), 573 (formae est), 597 (meta est), 631 (ore est), 661 (morata est); Book 11 (15/795): 11 (lyraeque est), 109 (facta est), 164 (secuta est), 279 (qui sit), 293 (iam tum), 445 (ipso est), 460 (toto est), 494 (arte est), 543 (relictum est), 550 (imago est), 562 (ore est), 669 (nec me), 706 (si non), 719 (mota est), 743 (solutum est); Book 12 (14/628): 82 (secuta est), 93 (sed qui), 97 (moratum est), 124 (repulsa est), 181 (ullo est), 202 (ne sim), 324 (adacta est), 372 (retenta est), 401 (sic sunt), 428 (maritum est), 434 (perque os), 483 (non sunt), 555 (ferendum est), 618 (hac est); Book 13 (22/968): 15 (sola est), 96 (nostra est), 137 (qua est), 138 (locuta est), 264 (haec sunt), 308 (turpe est), 309 (decorum est), 348 (parta est), 378 (petendum est), 464 (gemenda est), 512 (illa est), 546 (tota est), 569 (ex re), 585 (non est), 593 (hic est), 620 (visum est), 661 (petita est), 715 (nota est), 749 (natam est), 823 (quot sint), 849 (decori est), 858 (ira est); Book 14 (14/851): 21 (herba est), 318 (quae sit), 336 (Pico est), 361 (non sunt), 466 (cremata est), 489 (rerum est), 515 (**semicaper Pan**), 568 (deorum est), 634 (cupido est), 678 (pro quo), 679 (ille est), 725 (carendum est), 841 (promptum est), 851 (Quirino est); Book 15 (15/879): 30 (**abdiderat sol**), 31 (**sidereum nox**), 36 (peracta est), 138 (ciborum est), 184 (relictum est), 205 (ulla est), 208 (ulla est), 288 (nulla est), 368 (origo est), 403 (ferendo est), 454 (illo est), 455 (illa est), 607 (ille est), 664 (secuta est), 867 (piumque est).

Total Numbers for Ovid's *Metamorphoses*:
256/11,995=2.13 per 100 lines/1 every 46.86 lines.

7/256 (2.7%) monosyllabic line-endings disrupt the homodyne; the other 249/ 256 (97.3%) preserve it either through elision or because the 6th foot contains two monosyllables.
In other words, less than one-tenth of 1% (.06%) of all lines in the *Metamorphoses* employ the Ennian metrical effect of disrupting the homodyne in the 6th foot with a monosyllabic line-ending.

Comparative Data on Pentasyllabic Hexameter Line Endings

Ennius, *Annales* (22/623 in Skutsch)=3.5% of lines

8, 73, 76, 78, 93, 113, 120, 133, 184, 197, 304, 317, 322, 347, 398, 412, 447, 510, 549, 554, 577, 590

Lucilius (28/973 in Marx)=2.9% of lines

60, 85, 89, 90, 161, 187, 226, 252, 254, 257, 261, 270, 271, 308, 334, 363, 401, 444, 484, 509, 970, 1,058, 1,064, 1,065, 1,250, 1,283, 1,320, 1,342

Cicero (5/747 in Soubiran)=0.7%

Alcyones 0/2; *Limon* 0/4; *Thalia Maesta* 0/1; *Marius* 0/15; *De Consulatu Suo* 0/89; *Aratea* 5/569 (30.1, 34.24, 34.36, 34.293, 34.388)

Other Post-Ennian Republican Hexameter (0/89)

Hostius (0/7)
Accius (0/12)
Livius Refictus (0/4)
Furius Antias (0/6)
Gannius (0/3)
Egnatius (0/3)
Mattius (0/7)
Ninius Crassus (0/2)
Naevius (0/2)
Quintus Cicero (0/20)
Caesar (*Limon* 0/6)
Furius Bibaculus (0/13)
Sueius (0/2)
Varro Atacinus (0/2)

Catullus (5/798 hexameters)=0.63% of lines

62.8, 64.114, 64.205, 68.105, 97.5

Lucretius (303/7,415 hexameters)=4.1% of lines

DRN 1 (65/1,117): 3, 29, 63, 113, 180, 223, 240, 244, 249, 251, 291, 317, 390, 391, 400, 435, 451, 455, 477, 484, 499, 516, 519, 535, 548, 552, 559, 565, 574, 575, 609, 611, 612, 734, 736, 764, 811, 818, 819, 869, 874, 909, 910, 916, 939, 945, 951, 968, 977, 986, 992, 996, 997, 1,013, 1,017, 1,026, 1,027, 1,030, 1,035, 1,040, 1,043, 1,051, 1,085, 1,109, 1,113

DRN 2 (85/1,174): 11, 26, 42, 44, 52, 62, 89, 100, 124, 127, 134, 135, 142, 145, 157, 161, 167, 169, 183, 200, 234, 266, 281, 292, 294, 297, 304, 346, 441, 450, 459, 498, 507, 508, 527, 529, 531, 544, 551, 562, 568, 569, 571, 573, 584, 587, 666, 671, 684, 706, 712, 722, 735, 737, 761, 762, 792, 818, 866, 878, 885, 899, 914, 919, 922, 936, 941, 942, 947, 948, 963, 969, 980, 1,002, 1,008, 1,009, 1,019, 1,057, 1,065, 1,074, 1,086, 1,138, 1,148, 1,161, 1,162

DRN 3 (50/1,094): 14, 26, 54, 70, 71, 131, 148, 193, 210, 248, 262, 284, 330, 352, 364, 428, 478, 485, 542, 601, 613, 615, 639, 671, 689, 692, 697, 698, 706, 722, 729, 738, 745, 746, 763, 779, 780, 782, 796, 803, 809, 815, 845, 855, 865, 928, 937, 944, 1,028, 1,063

DRN 4 (27/1,287): 14, 20, 25, 70, 258, 271, 278, 328(303), 331(306), 542(551), 555, 594, 628, 667, 668, 697, 776, 791, 824, 854, 943, 1,005, 1,030, 1,145, 1,172, 1,202, 1,210

DRN 5 (42/1,457): 15, 28, 44, 48, 67, 73, 86, 127, 140, 157, 166, 167, 184, 192, 316, 332, 342, 346, 354, 360, 376, 384, 407, 416, 428, 445, 533, 615, 617, 718, 789, 892, 1,022, 1,040, 1,041, 1,109, 1,111, 1,132, 1,320, 1,411, 1,426, 1,453

DRN 6 (34/1,286): 62, 112, 164, 189, 226, 347, 374, 398, 424, 446, 453, 480, 543, 648, 653, 666, 772, 775, 802, 889, 947, 955, 1,032, 1,036, 1,040, 1,066, 1,098, 1,125, 1,133, 1,260, 1,263, 1,275, 1,277, 1,286

Vergil (20/12,905)=0.15% of lines

Bucolics 3.37, 5.73, 8.1, 8.5, 8.62
Georgics 4.336, 4.343, 4.463
Aeneid 1.72, 5.492, 5.826, 6.393, 6.447, 6.483, 6.601, 10.225, 10.413, 11.614, 12.83, 12.363

Ovid's *Metamorphoses* (4/11,995)=0.03% of lines, all of which are transliterations of Greek proper names

Met 6.683, 7.695, 9.283, 15.705

APPENDIX 4

Comparative Data on Alliteration in Republican Latin Poetry

Fragmentary poets' citations come from Ribbeck, unless otherwise noted. These results follow the criteria of Bailey and Merrill and include instances in which at least three words that begin with the same letter occur in the same line. In an attempt to cover the phenomenon as broadly as possible, I have also included examples where three words that begin with the same or adjacent sounds occur in the same line (e.g., $c \ldots c \ldots qu$), as well as examples that involve enjambment over two lines. I have also consulted manuscript variations in order to ensure that these numbers reflect the best editions of the authors represented.

Livius Andronicus: 2/97=2.1% of lines

Odusia: 0/48
Tragedies: 2/41=*Aegisthus* (3=Non. 512M.2), *Andromeda* (18=Non. 62M)
Palliatae: 0/8

Naevius=29/286=10.1% of lines

Bellum Punicum=4/74=5.4% of lines
31.1, 36.1, 41.1, 51.1
Epitaph=2/4
64.1, 64.4
Palliatae=12/138
26a, 33, 53, 67, 76, 84, 90, 92, 93, 106, 110, 112

Praetextae=1/8
6
Tragedies=10/62
13, 17, 28, 29, 34, 35, 36, 44, 45, 46

Ennius=163/1,164=14.0% of lines

Annales (Skutsch's edition)=87/623=14.0% of lines
12, 26, 32, 34, 47, 48, 54, 67, 72, 74–75, 84, 88, 91, 92, 93, 96, 97, 104, 108, 117–118, 126,
133, 143, 154–155, 159, 178, 182, 190, 192, 195, 202, 213, 214, 218, 219, 229, 253, 269, 279,
280–281, 288–289, 298, 307, 309, 310, 314, 323, 332, 333–334, 342, 345, 362, 372, 373,
387, 404–405, 408, 416, 419, 421, 423, 426, 449, 451, 454, 457, 461, 464, 469, 483,
485, 490, 492, 493, 505, 507, 509, 513, 522, 539, 541, 548, 550, 558, 580, 584, 620

Palliatae=0/4
Praetextae=1/6
3

Tragedies=67/402=16.7%
4, 16, 21, 26, 34, 38, 39, 48, 55, 61, 62, 67, 73, 87, 95, 108, 115, 118, 138, 139, 193, 200, 201,
203, 207, 211, 215, 216, 219, 221, 239, 244, 250, 254, 258, 259, 261, 262, 263, 267, 269, 270,
275, 276, 280, 281, 287, 289, 297, 303, 307, 310, 311, 317, 318, 323, 324, 329, 337, 342, 347,
348, 363, 365, 375, 380, 383

Satires=5/70
5, 60, 62, 63, 66

Varia=3/59
18, 32, 42

Plautus: 2444/21,564=11.3% of all lines

Amphitruo: 162/1,146=14.1% of lines
1, 24, 31, 32, 34, 35, 36, 37, 56, 62, 70, 75, 98, 117, 124, 126, 129, 130, 132, 147, 148, 180, 185,
191, 206, 212, 221, 231, 232, 234, 236, 271, 273, 276, 278, 287, 293, 307, 312, 315, 329, 333,

334, 336, 339, 355, 356, 360, 361, 371, 374, 376, 382, 385, 390, 394, 395, 403, 404, 405, 406, 408, 412, 419, 422, 434, 438, 439, 441, 442, 446, 447, 448, 453, 462, 467, 490, 505, 506, 512, 521, 524, 528, 529, 537, 538, 539, 542, 546, 551, 553, 557, 572, 586, 591, 592, 596, 604, 605, 606, 611, 616, 623, 650, 671, 676, 709, 712, 720, 757, 761, 772, 774, 779, 781, 782, 786, 787, 801, 809, 819, 824, 825, 827, 839, 851, 856, 859, 861, 892, 904, 907, 954, 961, 963, 983, 986, 994, 999, 1,002, 1,009, 1,019, 1,028, 1,030, 1,032, 1,049, 1,057, 1,060, 1,062, 1,072, 1,077, 1,078, 1,085, 1,094, 1,101, 1,102, 1,111, 1,114, 1,118, 1,122, 1,124, 1,138

Asinaria: 117/947=12.4% of lines
8, 17, 26, 96, 121, 129, 134, 138, 141, 144, 145, 146, 147, 150, 152, 159, 160, 165, 168, 170, 171, 172, 174, 177, 181, 183, 190, 200, 214, 218, 225, 229, 232, 244, 256, 261, 270, 271, 276, 284, 294, 301, 302, 317, 318, 320, 324, 337, 348, 353, 358, 362, 367, 399, 412, 433, 435, 437, 460, 464, 465, 476, 487, 490, 492, 497, 507, 517, 523, 525, 526, 527, 535, 538, 541, 555, 560, 561, 563, 565, 587, 595, 608, 633, 634, 637, 649, 650, 654, 657, 661, 664, 690, 696, 702, 712, 715, 744, 771, 774, 802, 808, 830, 842, 846, 848, 866, 876, 879, 880, 911, 918, 922, 933, 934, 935, 943

Aulularia: 80/840=9.5% of lines
37, 42, 52, 66, 69, 75, 79, 83, 91, 92, 102, 107, 112, 113, 164, 170, 174, 182, 186, 200, 207, 210, 211, 217, 220, 225, 233, 236, 238, 242, 260, 276, 279, 285, 293, 314, 320, 336, 349, 374, 397, 409, 417, 431, 433, 436, 462, 466, 483, 484, 507, 524, 549, 586, 587, 589, 591, 592, 593, 606, 626, 629, 634, 638, 644, 661, 685, 690, 696, 708, 713, 714, 718, 719, 741, 762, 773, 794, 801, 829

Bacchides: 104/1,211=8.6% of lines
27, 37, 53, 67, 73, 96, 115, 130, 187, 202, 207, 258, 281, 300, 371, 372, 375, 385, 398, 402, 425, 429, 442, 444, 452, 457, 460, 465, 468, 475, 485, 490, 493, 514, 517, 522, 528, 535, 536, 555, 567, 570, 580, 589, 616, 637, 642, 651, 672, 678, 690, 696, 699, 731, 747, 748, 763, 772, 784, 789, 791, 847, 865, 870, 875, 883, 895, 914, 916, 925, 926, 933, 934, 952, 961, 982, 989, 1,000, 1,001, 1,002, 1,004, 1,007, 1,023, 1,027, 1,030, 1,035, 1,043, 1,044, 1,045, 1,049, 1,087, 1,088, 1,097, 1,103, 1,108, 1,127, 1,153, 1,156, 1,157, 1,161, 1,167, 1,174, 1,196, 1,211

Captivi: 110/1,036=10.6% of lines
5, 21, 27, 32, 46, 50, 68, 71, 76, 80, 81, 102, 103, 109, 114, 118, 203, 207, 239, 241, 244, 255, 256, 263, 270, 281, 294, 297, 315, 322, 334, 347, 357, 358, 360, 370, 396, 409, 416, 417, 422, 428, 439, 444, 450, 456, 465, 472, 480, 482, 494, 517, 520, 529, 531, 535, 537, 552, 553, 554, 569, 585, 617, 648, 650, 652, 656, 657, 661, 684, 688, 722, 729, 741, 757, 765,

770, 771, 773, 776, 804, 808, 813, 825, 829, 834, 839, 842, 847, 854, 860, 886, 910, 914, 919, 921, 933, 934, 935, 939, 940, 951, 971, 976, 982, 986, 994, 1,013, 1,020, 1,036

Casina: 104/1,018=10.2% of lines

2, 9, 20, 39, 53, 56, 89, 96, 131, 132, 135, 142, 169, 176, 204, 211, 221, 225, 229, 230, 231, 241, 256, 280, 282, 294, 298, 301, 303, 306, 312, 339, 342, 346, 355, 367, 369, 377, 378, 379, 394, 401, 411, 416, 418, 466, 482, 489, 495, 516, 517, 518, 549, 559, 595, 605, 612, 622, 625, 633, 660, 670, 677, 678, 689, 690, 720, 722, 727, 737, 740, 750, 759, 764, 765, 767, 781, 782, 805, 806, 817, 818, 819, 826, 841, 850, 859, 878, 888, 891, 911, 918, 930, 950, 952, 970, 977, 979, 980, 991, 998, 1,011, 1,015

Cistellaria: 86/787=10.9% of lines

2, 5, 22, 32, 44, 45, 50, 59, 60, 61, 64, 65, 67, 71, 74, 75, 76, 81, 83, 84, 90, 91, 99, 101, 102, 109, 115, 119, 120, 121, 151, 154, 159, 161, 201, 203, 208, 211, 221, 223, 233, 236, 247, 250, 288, 289, 299, 365, 408, 454, 464, 480, 483, 494, 500, 502, 506, 509, 517, 521, 585, 615, 618, 625, 631, 639, 644, 645, 654, 656, 666, 670, 671, 672, 674, 695, 703, 707, 709, 714, 717, 721, 723, 725, 735, 768

Curculio: 78/729=10.7% of lines

7, 24, 28, 40, 55, 74, 85, 88, 102, 103, 117, 121, 140, 148, 156, 163, 164, 166, 169, 173, 179, 184, 185, 193, 202, 212, 222, 252, 262, 282, 297, 304, 316, 317, 321, 329, 352, 355, 362, 384, 385, 388, 398, 409, 414, 419, 423, 456, 458, 469, 473, 484, 503, 505, 506, 509, 510, 512, 513, 516, 521, 564, 571, 572, 573, 576, 579, 596, 599, 602, 610, 613, 626, 640, 663, 708, 711, 713

Epidicus: 94/733=12.8% of lines

2, 17, 29, 38, 49, 51, 52, 60, 61, 74, 78, 88, 113, 119, 125, 130, 134, 140, 142, 159, 162, 180, 202, 228, 229, 233, 256, 270, 272, 286, 288, 328, 333, 336, 344, 346, 350, 358, 359, 360, 364, 373, 383, 415, 419, 433, 478, 480, 486, 489, 494, 507, 519, 526, 536, 537, 541, 543, 546, 547, 548, 550, 553, 554, 558, 567, 575, 576, 586, 588, 590, 592, 594, 607, 616, 637, 638, 649, 651, 658, 661, 667, 675, 676, 679, 680, 681, 700, 705, 707, 710, 718, 723, 724

Menaechmi: 127/1,162=10.9% of lines

1, 25, 34, 54, 82, 113, 114, 115, 116, 132, 151, 176, 192, 202, 212, 224, 248, 252, 268, 294, 296, 302, 319, 338, 361, 383, 386, 400, 403, 404, 423, 426, 441, 448, 454, 458, 461, 469, 487, 504, 510, 530, 571, 582, 585, 590, 591, 602, 603, 608, 609, 610, 613, 614, 624, 627,

635, 639, 647, 657, 665, 671, 675, 676, 677, 681, 689, 705, 731, 743, 750, 754, 755, 758, 776, 777, 778, 779, 783, 794, 796, 802, 804, 805, 812, 813, 823, 824, 826, 827, 831, 842, 844, 849, 861, 895, 897, 904, 906, 912, 914, 917, 918, 921, 941, 957, 977, 983, 998, 1,010, 1,015, 1,026, 1,028, 1,039, 1,041, 1,042, 1,046, 1,068, 1,069, 1,071, 1,076, 1,078, 1,083, 1,090, 1,100, 1,117, 1,125

Mercator: 140/1,026=13.6% of lines

11, 14, 71, 103, 114, 116, 121, 125, 134, 145, 153, 156, 173, 174, 175, 176, 181, 182, 186, 191, 203, 208, 212, 214, 216, 246, 275, 280, 292, 295, 306, 311, 316, 327, 346, 349, 363, 366, 378, 379, 392, 393, 394, 398, 426, 439, 445, 448, 452, 456, 458, 460, 461, 474, 476, 480, 489, 492, 497, 502, 509, 519, 528, 536, 539, 563, 564, 565, 588, 589, 606, 617, 624, 628, 630, 632, 641, 643, 645, 646, 648, 649, 655, 658, 674, 680, 681, 685, 700, 702, 703, 713, 717, 721, 727, 767, 771, 777, 810, 819, 827, 830, 831, 834, 850, 855, 857, 859, 860, 861, 862, 867, 871, 872, 882, 883, 884, 889, 891, 895, 898, 899, 918, 921, 922, 925, 928, 939, 950, 952, 954, 962, 985, 993, 995, 1,012, 1,014, 1,017, 1,018, 1,023

Miles Gloriosus: 191/1,437=13.3% of lines

1, 2, 10, 23, 26, 40, 130, 163, 187, 191, 192, 196, 197, 199, 206, 214, 215, 222, 226, 227, 228, 252, 261, 281, 283, 293, 294, 317, 322, 329, 330, 335, 340, 345, 349, 354, 355, 356, 369, 378, 386, 388, 400, 404, 414, 422, 425, 426, 428, 430, 431, 437, 445, 449, 451, 452, 465, 467, 476, 492, 539, 547, 550, 575, 587, 603, 604, 609, 610, 616, 617, 628, 633, 635, 647, 648, 649, 653, 658, 670, 672, 673, 679, 691, 692, 694, 700, 710, 713, 717, 720, 723, 728, 729, 733, 745, 756, 775, 780, 785, 792, 800, 807, 820, 822, 850, 868, 881, 885, 887, 892, 894, 901, 902, 922, 924, 926, 941, 951, 973, 996, 1,012, 1,014, 1,017, 1,021, 1,037, 1,047, 1,048, 1,051, 1,052, 1,058, 1,061, 1,064, 1,065, 1,070, 1,084, 1,092, 1,113, 1,117, 1,138, 1,140, 1,148, 1,150, 1,156, 1,161, 1,162, 1,173, 1,189, 1,190, 1,205, 1,222, 1,232, 1,233, 1,242, 1,246, 1,255, 1,256, 1,260, 1,261, 1,265, 1,266, 1,274, 1,281, 1,298, 1,306, 1,311, 1,314, 1,315, 1,316, 1,324, 1,330, 1,344, 1,356, 1,358, 1,363, 1,365, 1,374, 1,377, 1,378, 1,383, 1,384, 1,386, 1,389, 1,394, 1,406, 1,407, 1,411, 1,429, 1,430, 1,436, 1,437

Mostellaria: 114/1,181=9.7% of lines

32, 57, 59, 61, 71, 73, 93, 104, 111, 143, 158, 162, 164, 167, 170, 172, 181, 185, 187, 197, 201, 204, 208, 218, 226, 228, 238, 245, 250, 251, 254, 255, 258, 265, 278, 289, 297, 310, 312, 325, 328, 329, 347, 351, 352, 362, 367, 373, 374, 386, 412, 450, 461, 513, 536, 546, 548, 566, 595, 603, 605, 611, 615, 623, 633, 644, 655, 666, 681, 688, 722, 740, 746, 754, 762, 771, 791, 811, 816, 820, 827, 833, 834, 841, 860, 862, 874, 875, 888, 896, 903, 910, 927, 935, 941, 949, 957, 963, 976, 979, 980, 1,049, 1,065, 1,071, 1,075, 1,079, 1,103, 1,107, 1,126, 1,161, 1,165, 1,171, 1,176, 1,177

Persa: 107/858=12.5% of lines

3, 6, 7, 10, 11, 13, 16, 18, 34, 47, 54, 75, 95, 98, 124, 131, 144, 150 171, 183, 202, 207, 228, 232,
233, 235, 238, 246, 259, 264, 267, 270, 272, 280, 282, 291, 292, 296, 311, 331, 346, 350, 351,
361, 366, 377, 383, 387, 391, 398, 418, 427, 447, 450, 480, 533, 536, 547, 552, 577, 578, 579,
587, 592, 600, 608, 610, 615, 621, 623, 636, 638, 647, 650, 663, 667, 674, 682, 690, 709,
720, 730, 741, 750, 753, 757, 761, 769, 773, 777, 783, 785, 786, 787, 792, 796, 810, 815,
825, 834, 837, 842, 844, 846, 847, 852, 854

Poenulus: 143/1,422=10.1% of lines

20, 21, 54, 97, 104, 129, 146, 192, 212, 216, 226, 231, 239, 249, 251, 262, 264, 267, 268, 270,
286, 287, 288, 289, 290, 300, 301, 308, 322, 324, 329, 330, 331, 337, 343, 348, 349, 354, 358,
359, 363, 365, 366, 367, 375, 376, 379, 393, 394, 399, 400, 402, 404, 410, 421, 430, 446,
478, 480, 490, 498, 509, 516, 520, 524, 533, 539, 550, 555, 556, 562, 584, 590, 600, 609,
610, 624, 649, 670, 674, 681, 697, 722, 724, 738, 744, 748, 754, 755, 760, 808, 818,
856, 858, 861, 864, 865, 866, 867, 875, 878, 885, 890, 891, 893, 894, 911, 912, 928, 956,
965, 1,024, 1,025, 1,038, 1,046, 1,063, 1,083, 1,086, 1,120, 1,131, 1,168, 1,188, 1,190, 1,200,
1,201, 1,202, 1,203, 1,210, 1,213, 1,214, 1,216, 1,239, 1,244, 1,250, 1,285, 1,292, 1,295, 1,296,
1,319, 1,324, 1,350, 1,371, 1,414

Pseudolus: 165/1,335=12.4% of lines

4, 20, 22, 34, 52, 93, 94, 109, 121, 126, 134, 145, 155, 164, 168, 169, 170, 175, 177, 180, 181,
208, 209, 218, 226, 229, 234, 235, 236, 239, 240, 242, 243, 246, 256, 265, 267, 269, 276,
279, 291, 299, 307, 339, 344, 345, 359, 368, 372, 373, 398, 408, 426, 433, 479, 492, 509,
517, 521, 524, 542, 543, 555, 589, 592, 596, 608, 615, 630, 632, 636, 644, 657, 659, 663,
683, 689, 695, 696, 700, 703, 704, 705, 709, 715, 727, 729, 737, 741, 743, 744, 748, 770,
784, 800, 810, 811, 815, 819, 854, 858, 860, 861, 863, 877, 881, 885, 889, 908, 912, 914,
915, 937, 939, 940, 942, 943, 948, 958, 965, 976, 982, 989, 1,003, 1,006, 1,044, 1,057,
1,066, 1,068, 1,080, 1,106, 1,112, 1,119, 1,123, 1,124, 1,127, 1,143, 1,164, 1,178, 1,179, 1,183,
1,184, 1,187, 1,203, 1,212, 1,214, 1,220, 1,223, 1,228, 1,230, 1,231, 1,232, 1,243, 1,275, 1,279,
1,286, 1,292, 1,297, 1,301, 1,317, 1,320, 1,323, 1,326, 1,329, 1,330

Rudens: 162/1,423=11.4% of lines

2, 3, 4, 20, 37, 47, 49, 53, 60, 84, 85, 94, 103, 126, 133, 138, 146, 163, 168, 172, 185, 189, 190,
197, 198, 201, 202, 205, 206, 218, 220, 221, 225, 227, 234, 256, 265, 279, 283, 303, 317, 337,
348, 354, 364, 365, 383, 384, 410, 417, 418, 424, 435, 437, 440, 474, 496, 511, 513, 518,
520, 522, 531, 539, 565, 568, 569, 582, 607, 621, 625, 626, 628, 635, 644, 650, 651, 675,
686, 689, 704, 707, 710, 711, 712, 722, 724, 743, 765, 773, 781, 799, 844, 874, 881, 884,

895, 920, 922, 929, 935, 937, 945, 946, 963, 964, 970, 972, 980, 989, 992, 997, 1,002, 1,010, 1,011, 1,017, 1,023, 1,027, 1,045, 1,046, 1,049, 1,052, 1,055, 1,067, 1,070, 1,075, 1,076, 1,089, 1,103, 1,110, 1,113, 1,115, 1,123, 1,131, 1,138, 1,141, 1,150, 1,154, 1,176, 1,179, 1,187, 1,208, 1,212, 1,219, 1,229, 1,262, 1,264, 1,266, 1,271, 1,272, 1,274, 1,281, 1,312, 1,314, 1,331, 1,338, 1,391, 1,394, 1,398, 1,399, 1,401, 1,412

Stichus: 87/775=11.2% of lines
6, 11, 33, 53, 58, 62, 72, 77, 85, 93, 94, 97, 100, 101, 105, 109, 112, 120, 124, 127, 133, 142, 156, 206, 209, 210, 222, 273, 275, 280, 298, 301, 302, 303, 316, 321, 333, 339, 351, 365, 369, 388, 394, 400, 404, 419, 420, 426, 441, 455, 469, 482, 500, 503, 505, 517, 521, 527, 528, 534, 544, 549, 552, 580, 587, 591, 598, 602, 608, 609, 614, 626, 658, 673, 680, 687, 692, 693, 705, 708, 709, 741, 742, 749, 755, 765, 771

Trinummus: 136/1,189=11.4% of lines
32, 33, 41, 50, 64, 68, 71, 84, 91, 104, 140, 156, 162, 185, 191, 205, 241, 244, 249, 260, 267, 281, 285, 286, 287, 294, 297, 309, 312, 315, 316, 324, 328, 339, 345, 347, 348, 349, 360, 364, 378, 395, 417, 423, 430, 442, 476, 487, 490, 498, 509, 526, 566, 577, 590, 605, 628, 636, 642, 658, 661, 666, 669, 676, 681, 691, 698, 720, 741, 755, 786, 801, 821, 829, 832, 837, 839, 850, 855, 861, 867, 871, 877, 879, 886, 893, 903, 916, 917, 922, 923, 929, 930, 945, 949, 953, 960, 972, 973, 978, 985, 992, 1,004, 1,009, 1,011, 1,015, 1,020, 1,029, 1,032, 1,045, 1,051, 1,064, 1,073, 1,083, 1,087, 1,088, 1,094, 1,096, 1,102, 1,109, 1,113, 1,123, 1,124, 1,142, 1,146, 1,148, 1,150, 1,153, 1,154, 1,155, 1,163, 1,167, 1,169, 1,173, 1,186, 1,189

Truculentus: 121/968=12.5% of lines
1, 44, 46, 51, 60, 70, 106, 117, 129, 130, 132, 147, 152, 161, 198, 202, 206, 212, 217, 221, 232, 236, 245, 253, 259, 264, 265, 287, 303, 353, 387, 389, 410, 414, 431, 443, 447, 451, 453, 466, 471, 474, 484, 487, 488, 493, 501, 509, 511, 527, 528, 537, 544, 546, 553, 554, 560, 569, 570, 572, 576, 578, 588, 595, 608, 615, 618, 635, 662, 698, 699, 704, 706, 707, 708, 721, 723, 724, 726, 727, 732, 755, 756, 769, 773, 775, 782, 786, 789, 805, 812, 813, 820, 822, 823, 825, 831, 832, 855, 856, 861, 862, 863, 865, 873, 879, 880, 890, 910, 913, 918, 926, 927, 937, 940, 948, 950, 951, 957, 958, 959

Vidularia: 2/110=1.8% of lines
62, 102

Fragments (Leo's edition): 14/231=6.1% of lines
Acharistio: 1.1, *Caecus*: 5.1, 8.1, *Carbonaria*: 1.1, *Colax*: 2.1, 2.2, *Cornicula*: 6.2, *Nervolaria*: 7.1, *Sittelitergus*: 2.1, *Incertae Fabulae*: 12.1, 17.1, 19.1, 28.1, 88.1

Terence: 602/6,093=9.88% of lines

Andria: 98/1,000=9.8% of lines

45, 74, 76, 80, 82, 153, 159, 164, 170, 175, 178, 184, 193, 194, 213, 249, 251, 262, 276, 282, 293, 297, 302, 305, 310, 323, 340, 351, 354, 361, 367, 380, 383, 384, 399, 402, 408, 426, 430, 431, 449, 467, 470, 477, 486, 489, 498, 502, 503, 519, 526, 536, 543, 575, 611, 612, 614, 615, 623, 631, 635, 641, 646, 666, 671, 680, 685, 687, 691, 692, 693, 699, 705, 706, 743, 768, 788, 798, 802, 820, 860, 862, 864, 871, 882, 886, 903, 905, 906, 914, 943, 947, 954, 956, 957, 964, 973, 979

Heauton Timoroumenos: 117/1,067=10.97% of lines

26, 33, 37, 43, 56, 57, 129, 188, 189, 192, 193, 200, 206, 209, 220, 222, 223, 224, 230, 244, 248, 251, 255, 267, 274, 277, 290, 297, 317, 318, 322, 331, 348, 358, 379, 383, 388, 396, 397, 401, 443, 452, 456, 468, 469, 473, 479, 484, 485, 486, 511, 549, 555, 562, 563, 591, 594, 617, 619, 620, 625, 626, 640, 650, 666, 687, 692, 696, 700, 701, 707, 719, 735, 736, 742, 745, 746, 748, 764, 770, 787, 789, 791, 796, 808, 814, 815, 820, 848, 867, 885, 889, 894, 896, 901, 919, 930, 931, 935, 937, 939, 941, 944, 947, 973, 975, 977, 987, 1,000, 1,008, 1,014, 1,022, 1,026, 1,032, 1,039, 1,044, 1,054

Eunuchus: 108/1,094=9.87% of lines

1, 18, 37, 46, 65, 76, 96, 97, 130, 144, 182, 194, 195, 197, 211, 216, 227, 228, 237, 243, 258, 271, 273, 294, 307, 310, 318, 319, 340, 346, 354, 374, 382, 400, 445, 479, 482, 485, 508, 511, 518, 521, 549, 551, 555, 558, 559, 563, 567, 577, 598, 604, 605, 607, 613, 628, 632, 650, 651, 680, 687, 688, 714, 722, 725, 727, 735, 737, 742, 745, 760, 761, 770, 772, 774, 775, 777, 780, 786, 793, 795, 798, 799, 800, 804, 810, 849, 858, 894, 943, 951, 959, 961, 965, 968, 969, 992, 997, 1,007, 1,010, 1,025, 1,036, 1,047, 1,055, 1,067, 1,069, 1,081, 1,094

Phormio: 97/1,055=9.2% of lines

1, 27, 76, 95, 96, 98, 110, 138, 166, 171, 185, 186, 187, 188, 193, 207, 208, 211, 232, 248, 254, 256, 273, 303, 316, 320, 321, 334, 344, 345, 347, 367, 369, 382, 385, 398, 400, 402, 430, 439, 466, 470, 478, 496, 500, 507, 510, 512, 518, 519, 527, 539, 541, 543, 546, 554, 584, 614, 636, 643, 645, 662, 692, 693, 704, 711, 722, 723, 726, 728, 750, 755, 771, 785, 792, 803, 806, 833, 841, 852, 863, 872, 873, 935, 941, 943, 976, 998, 1,005, 1,014, 1,016, 1,022, 1,023, 1,029, 1,033, 1,036, 1,050

Hecyra: 89/880=10.1% of lines

10, 24, 35, 53, 74, 77, 110, 112, 119, 133, 139, 152, 155, 159, 160, 204, 205-6, 220, 229, 230, 239, 269, 271, 276, 300, 306, 320, 323, 337, 350, 353, 355, 363, 397, 439, 440,

446, 451, 461, 483, 493, 513, 516, 517, 531, 532, 536, 538, 561, 566, 567, 572, 573, 575, 582, 584, 588, 594, 595, 605, 606, 610, 614, 637, 639, 656, 699, 703, 727, 728, 734, 739, 742, 753, 769, 776, 779, 793, 794, 808, 813, 822, 829, 834, 849, 851, 853, 863, 877

Adelphoe: 93/997=9.3% of lines

1, 21, 34, 67, 84, 90, 104, 134, 141, 148, 174, 177, 186, 193, 206, 215, 222, 262, 267, 271, 275, 283, 290, 297, 301, 304, 321, 323, 324, 333, 335, 339, 346, 352, 357, 361, 380, 388, 411, 412, 423, 473, 514, 528, 534, 543, 548, 552, 553, 556, 566, 590, 598, 605, 607, 623, 637, 656, 658, 670, 671, 691, 702, 705, 727, 743, 761, 765, 774, 789, 798, 803, 825, 840, 851, 860, 865, 866, 879, 881, 883, 890, 893, 898, 923, 931, 932, 940, 945, 946, 956, 979, 996

Caecilius Statius: 32/295=10.8% of lines

1, 4, 10, 39, 48, 70, 73, 91, 114, 116, 130, 144, 145, 149, 172, 175, 185, 190, 191, 193, 199, 204, 206, 209, 215, 235, 262, 263, 265, 266, 269, 278

Accius: 80/785=10.2% of lines

Annales: 1/10=10% of lines
4.1

Carmina: 1/32=3.1% of lines
10.2

Praetextae: 3/41=7.3% of lines
6, 9, 39

Tragedies: 75/702=10.7% of lines
9, 16, 17, 19, 23, 32, 36, 37, 81, 82, 83, 85, 90, 96, 104, 109, 127, 150, 164, 175, 195, 200, 201, 223, 229, 232, 245, 266, 271, 288, 294, 302, 314, 316, 322, 326, 343, 355, 361, 365, 366, 393, 394, 414, 433, 434, 437, 443, 444, 445, 451, 453, 460, 494, 504, 517, 519, 520, 541, 552, 554, 557, 566, 573, 576, 580, 587, 591, 601, 607, 628, 630, 635, 647, 661

Pacuvius: 44/441=9.98% of lines

Praetextae: 2/5=40% of lines
1, 5

Tragedies: 42/436=9.6% of lines

12, 25, 30, 39, 44, 46, 53, 54, 79, 82, 86, 99, 117, 129, 136, 144, 156, 167, 173, 186, 205, 212,
  246, 251, 276, 292, 298, 319, 320, 324, 325, 327, 330, 333, 337, 375, 385, 389, 390, 396,
  412, 413

Lucilius (Marx's edition): 94/1,378=6.82% of lines

5, 61, 119, 132, 180, 191, 193, 199, 200, 203, 214, 219, 233, 234, 242, 243, 267, 282, 291, 292,
  296, 304, 332, 340, 350, 357, 360, 387, 419, 447, 449, 481, 499, 507, 515, 520, 529, 551,
  558, 581, 597, 603, 605, 611, 621, 622, 624, 626, 629, 663, 667, 681, 685, 692, 702, 713,
  716, 728, 729, 730, 747, 811, 854, 872, 878, 884, 890, 901, 929, 960, 969, 976, 993, 996,
  997, 1020, 1028, 1069, 1082, 1085, 1120, 1147, 1165, 1205, 1229, 1248, 1266, 1293, 1297,
  1330, 1332, 1337, 1340, 1368

Cicero (Soubiran's edition): 61/878=6.95% of lines

Hexameters: 57/747=7.6% of lines

Aratea: 3.1, 8.2, 16.2, 27.1, 33.1, 34.5, 34.13, 34.16, 34.38, 34.53, 34.69, 34.71, 34.73, 34.91,
  34.103, 34.106, 34.127, 34.131, 34.169, 34.172, 34.218, 34.224, 34.227, 34.251, 34.259,
  34.263, 34.264, 34.298, 34.309, 34.314, 34.315, 34.323, 34.340, 34.350, 34.356, 34.363,
  34.364, 34.365, 34.376, 34.381, 34.393, 34.410. 34.415, 34.428, 34.432, 34.437,
  34.462, *Prognostica:* 3.3, 5.3, *De Consulatu Suo:* 7, 18, 22, 24, 26, 56, 65, *Iliad:* 14

Other meters: 4/131=3.1% of lines
Translation of Aeschylus: 1/32 (33.1)
Translation of Sophocles: 1/50(34.23)
Translation of Euripides: 2/33 (40.4, 42.5)
Other Translations: 0/16

Catullus: 95/2,281=4.16% of lines

2.7, 7.2, 11.6, 12.15, 15.18, 16.13, 17.6, 17.18, 17.20, 23.2, 25.1, 29.1, 30.5, 40.1, 42.5, 42.7, 43.2,
  44.1, 44.3, 44.5, 45.5, 45.15, 52.2, 61.165, 61.214, 62.28, 62.33, 62.46, 62.63, 63.6, 63.9,
  63.10, 63.22, 63.78, 63.79, 63.86, 63.91, 64.1, 64.28, 64.53, 64.92, 64.101, 64.147, 64.156,

64.202, 64.222, 64.241, 64.259, 64.261, 64.262, 64.278, 64.282, 64.287, 64.293, 64.297, 64.320, 64.350, 64.351, 65.19, 66.19, 66.24, 66.47, 66.61, 66.83, 67.18, 67.26, 68.17, 68.30, 68.48, 68.49, 68.81, 68.97, 68.98, 68.139, 69.7, 70.1, 72.3, 73.2, 78b.3, 84.5, 86.3, 87.3, 88.4, 89.2, 89.3, 91.9, 94.1, 95.5, 95.9, 98.4, 103.1, 104.1, 110.4, 114.5, 115.8

Other Republican Poetry (all from Courtney's The Fragmentary Latin Poets*): 20/432=4.63% of lines*

Carmen Priami (0/1)
Pompilius (0/2)
Hostius (2/9)=1, 2
Livius Refictus (0/4)
Valerius Soranus (0/3)
Quinctius Atta (0/1)
Valerius Aedituus (2/10)=1, 3
Catulus (0/10)
Loreius Tiburtinus (0/4)
Porcius Licinius (3/27)=1.3, 3.3, 4.3
Volcacius Sedigitus (1/15)=1.4
Furius Antias (1/6)=3
Mattius (1/21)=8
Ninius Crassus (0/2)
Naevius (1/2)=2
Papinius (0/4)
Manilius (0/7)
Sueius (3/17)=1.3, 5, 7
Laevius (1/100)=12.8
Sevius Nicanor (0/2)
Pompeius Lenaeus (0/3)
Gannius (1/3)=2
Egnatius (0/4)
Quintus Cicero (1/20)=19
Tullius Laurea (0/10)
Terentius Varro (0/4)
Mucius Scaevola (0/1)
Caesar (0/7)
Furius Bibaculus (1/34)=10
Licinius Calvus (1/24)=6.2

Helvius Cinna (0/20)
Cornificius (0/5)
Ticida (0/3)
Memmius (0/1)
Volumnius (0/1)
Varro Atacinus (1/45)=16.1

Lucretius (918/7,415)=12.4%

DRN 1 (149/1,117=13.3%): 15, 16, 24, 28, 40, 41, 47, 59, 64, 68, 72, 86, 87, 88, 89, 106, 110, 119, 121, 122, 129, 143, 144-145, 158, 163, 167, 168, 169, 177, 200, 201, 202, 206, 216, 219-220, 221, 234, 250, 257, 266, 271, 278, 285-286, 288, 302, 307-308, 338-339, 341, 347, 356, 361, 371, 374, 387, 388, 398, 403, 411, 425, 436-437, 446, 449, 456, 480, 482, 483, 484, 500, 505, 508, 510, 517, 518, 521, 522, 529, 536, 538, 544, 548, 562, 566, 568, 574, 575, 586, 588, 594, 599, 600, 607, 609, 621, 626, 629, 634, 657, 675, 684, 687, 697, 699, 725, 726, 735, 739, 743, 749, 751, 763, 775, 781, 794, 799, 800, 803-804, 812, 813, 814, 829, 848, 857, 859, 861, 873, 900, 903, 904, 909, 921, 934, 937, 948, 950, 979, 1,000, 1,010, 1,012, 1,014, 1,022, 1,024, 1,043, 1,057, 1,058, 1,077, 1,080, 1,085, 1,091, 1,114

DRN 2 (150/1,174=12.8%): 4, 17, 30, 34, 37, 38, 44, 64, 65, 72, 77, 80, 95, 100, 104, 108, 114, 116, 130, 133, 136, 140, 145-146, 147, 157, 160, 166, 172, 190, 193, 226, 230, 235, 250, 258, 267, 280, 281, 283, 285, 288, 296, 298, 310, 315, 322, 324, 350, 352, 358, 372, 390, 414, 416, 424, 439, 452, 460, 463, 465, 478, 481, 486, 516, 522, 524, 538, 559, 560, 563, 566, 578, 582, 587, 593, 596-597, 598, 603, 606, 618, 619, 625, 626, 632, 635, 637, 643, 649, 654, 679, 681, 684, 704, 708, 712, 715-716, 732, 733, 734, 736, 749, 755, 776, 791, 793, 802, 808, 817, 820, 822, 826, 829-830, 837, 838, 842, 845, 848, 851, 852-853, 859, 871, 881, 905, 906, 912, 914-915, 930, 936, 947-948, 955-956, 964, 965, 989, 996, 1,001, 1,003, 1,008, 1,010, 1,014, 1,023, 1,028-1,029, 1,030, 1,046-1,047, 1,059, 1,092, 1,093, 1,144, 1,151, 1,168, 1,172

DRN 3 (129/1,094=11.8%): 1, 4, 5, 6, 19, 25, 43, 47, 54, 71, 121, 144, 145, 146, 147, 152, 169, 197, 199, 201, 209, 212, 218, 223, 226, 231, 238, 246, 275, 278, 294, 322, 324, 343, 345-346, 348, 349, 350, 365, 375, 378, 383, 390, 403, 419-420, 440, 441, 443, 445-446, 448, 456, 462, 467, 483, 484, 494, 498, 500-501, 508, 529, 533, 552, 553, 557, 579, 582, 585, 601, 603, 611, 631, 661, 662, 665-666, 682, 700, 705, 709, 710, 731, 740, 743, 746, 747, 759, 763, 769, 787, 794, 807, 808, 814, 816, 817, 823, 824, 826, 830, 834-835, 842, 845, 846, 852, 855-856, 857, 873, 874, 875, 883, 888, 925, 926, 959, 963, 969, 983, 986, 990-991, 994, 1,022, 1,029, 1,040, 1,043-1,044, 1,046, 1,048-1,049, 1,055, 1,058, 1,083, 1,091

DRN 4 (167/1,287=13.0%): 9, 12, 23, 27, 31, 44, 48, 51, 53, 61-62, 63, 69, 94, 100, 111, 113, 119, 120, 128, 130, 131, 150, 152, 155, 158, 165, 171, 181, 187, 193, 194, 211, 212-213, 221, 222,

232, 250, 259, 283, 313, 318, 327, 334, 340, 342, 347, 350, 353, 360, 368, 384, 385, 394, 400, 439, 449, 453-454, 456-457, 458-459, 460, 463, 466, 471, 472, 475, 493, 494, 501, 522-523, 526, 544, 578, 581, 598, 606, 608, 630, 631, 654, 659-660, 668, 690, 697, 712, 714, 725, 730, 748, 753, 760, 767, 779, 783, 789, 790, 802, 804, 808, 809, 825, 827, 832, 843, 851-852, 859, 861, 884, 888, 894, 899, 902, 910, 915, 935-936, 939, 940, 941, 950, 954, 958, 966, 980, 981, 983, 988, 995, 1,009-1,010, 1,011, 1,020, 1,032, 1,040, 1,041, 1,043, 1,061, 1,065, 1,071, 1,074, 1,092, 1,102, 1,117, 1,118, 1,138, 1,140, 1,157, 1,159, 1,169, 1,176, 1,193, 1,201-1,202, 1,205, 1,209, 1,220, 1,222, 1,230, 1,231, 1,232, 1,237, 1,240, 1,244, 1,249, 1,252, 1,259, 1,280, 1,281, 1,283, 1,284, 1,286-1,287

DRN 5 (188/1,457=12.9%): 1, 5, 8, 11, 12, 18, 24, 36, 43, 50-51, 53, 56, 60, 62, 63, 65, 80, 85, 86, 88, 94, 96, 97, 112, 114, 117, 118, 124, 126, 128, 131, 138, 143, 162, 187, 191, 204, 217, 220, 251, 256, 257, 266, 277, 295-296, 302, 310, 323, 333, 334, 335, 352, 353, 359, 361, 362, 372, 380-381, 392-393, 411, 420, 422, 426, 441-442, 449, 452, 454, 465, 466, 468, 471, 479, 480, 482, 498, 509, 511, 533, 545, 547, 551, 562, 564, 575, 582, 586, 593, 594, 600-601, 619, 654, 661, 679, 682, 696, 702, 707, 718, 719, 736, 737, 752, 757, 772, 775, 778, 779, 784, 788, 792, 796, 801-802, 805, 843, 850, 856, 857, 864, 869, 881, 882, 891, 892-893, 901, 904, 909, 914, 920, 926, 930, 931-932, 935, 938, 939, 950, 951, 957, 961, 963, 964, 969, 974, 977, 989, 993, 995, 1,004, 1,009, 1,011, 1,027, 1,035, 1,058, 1,112, 1,116, 1,126, 1,137, 1,147, 1,158, 1,163, 1,185, 1,193, 1,200, 1,219, 1,226, 1,229-1,230, 1,242, 1,244, 1,245, 1,248, 1,251, 1,252, 1,257, 1,270, 1,309, 1,313, 1,315, 1,316-1,317, 1,327, 1,333, 1,343, 1,380, 1,391, 1,413, 1,432, 1,437, 1,444, 1,447, 1,453

DRN 6 (135/1,286=10.5%): 5, 19, 23, 44, 46, 47, 54-55, 61, 62, 64, 72, 85, 88, 92-93, 95, 96, 101, 115, 123, 127, 135, 137, 182, 195, 196, 213, 217-218, 243, 247, 252, 255, 256, 270, 276, 284, 302, 307-308, 318, 338, 350-351, 362, 368, 386, 390, 391, 421, 433, 462, 490, 494, 501, 508, 521, 527, 534, 540, 545, 565, 571, 576, 588, 589, 608, 615, 631, 645, 652, 679, 681, 719-720, 741, 757, 771, 773, 777, 789, 814, 826, 829, 846, 848-849, 852, 854, 857, 859, 862, 873, 877, 879, 882, 896, 914, 918, 920, 928, 936, 937, 942, 951, 954, 956-957, 967, 969, 976, 992, 995, 1,018, 1,021, 1,059, 1,075, 1,084, 1,091, 1,096, 1,107, 1,110, 1,122, 1,123, 1,157, 1,159, 1,169, 1,183, 1,188, 1,236, 1,240, 1,248, 1,251, 1,254-1,255, 1,260-1,261, 1,264, 1,267, 1,269, 1,272, 1,274, 1,276, 1,285

A Comprehensive Map of Ennianisms in Lucretius

Alliteration (508 lines with repetition of word-initial sound at least three times *per Merrill*; my numbers are: 149 (*DRN* 1) + 150 (*DRN* 2) + 129 (*DRN* 3) +167 (*DRN* 4) + 188 (*DRN* 5) + 135 (*DRN* 6) = 918, see Appendix 4)

-ai (169 (Bailey only lists 166)=36 (*DRN* 1) + 30 (*DRN* 2) +40 (*DRN* 3) + 15 (*DRN* 4) + 21 (*DRN* 5) +27 (*DRN* 6) = 169)

pentasyllable (65 (*DRN* 1) + 85 (*DRN* 2) + 50 (*DRN* 3) + 27 (*DRN* 4) + 42 (*DRN* 5) + 34 (*DRN* 6) = 303, see Appendix 3)

monosyllable (63 (*DRN* 1) + 92 (*DRN* 2) + 98 (*DRN* 3) + 96 (*DRN* 4) + 47 (*DRN* 5) + 77 (*DRN* 6) = 473, see Appendix 3)

sigmatic ecthlipsis (41 in MSS [32 legitimate *per Butterfield*]=4 (*DRN* 1) + 6 (*DRN* 2) + 5 (*DRN* 3) +11 (*DRN* 4) + 7 (*DRN* 5) + 8 (*DRN* 6) = 41)

TOTAL: 1,904 Ennianisms in 7,415 lines=.26 Ennianisms per line=2.6 Ennianisms per 10 lines

Map of Ennianisms by Paragraph in Bailey

Clusters of 3.9 Ennianisms per 10 lines (higher than 50% more than the average) are in bold.

Anti-clusters of lower than 1.3 Ennianisms per 10 lines (less than half the average) are in bold and italics.

***Bailey paragraphs that are significantly higher or lower than the frequency of Ennianisms in each individual book are marked with three ***.

90/274 Bailey paragraphs in the poem have abnormally high or low frequency of Ennianisms=roughly one-third of Bailey paragraphs deviate significantly from the average. 11 Bailey paragraphs have **zero** Ennianisms in them. Longest continuous stretches of poem without any Ennianisms (anti-clusters): 38 lines (5.1,270–1,309), 36 lines (5.1,343–1,380), and 33 lines (6.1,188–1,222).

DRN *1*

317 Ennianisms in 1,117 lines=.28 per line=2.8 per 10 lines; 7 Bailey paragraphs with exceptionally high frequency of Ennianisms; 5 Bailey paragraphs with exceptionally low frequency of Ennianisms; 12/38 Bailey paragraphs with abnormal frequency of Ennianisms; Longest anti-cluster is 18 consecutive lines (1.1,058–1,077) without any Ennianisms

1. 1.1–61 (alliteration: 1.15; 1.16; 1.24; 1.28; 1.40; 1.41; 1.47; 1.59; -ai: 1.29; 1.41; pentasyllable: 1.3; 1.29; monosyllable: 1.13; 1.33; 1.44=15 Ennianisms in 61 lines=.25 per line=2.5 per 10 lines)

2. 1.62–79 (alliteration: 1.64; 1.68; 1.72; pentasyllable: 1.63=4 Ennianisms in 18 lines=.22 per line=2.2 per 10 lines)

3. 1.80–101 (alliteration: 1.86; 1.87; 1.88; 1.89; -ai: 1.84; 1.85; monosyllable: 1.88=7 Ennianisms in 22 lines=.32 per line=3.2 per 10 lines)

4. 1.102–135 (alliteration: 1.106; 1.110; 1.119; 1.121; 1.122; 1.129; -ai: 1.112; pentasyllable: 1.113; monosyllable: 1.116=9 Ennianisms in 34 lines=.26 per line=2.6 per 10 lines)

5. 1.136–145 (alliteration: 1.143; 1.144-145=2 Ennianisms in 10 lines=.2 per line=2 per 10 lines)

6. 1.146–158 (alliteration: 1.158; monosyllable: 1.146= 2 Ennianisms in 13 lines=.15 Ennianisms per line=1.5 Ennianisms per 10 lines)

7. 1.159–214 (alliteration: 1.163; 1.167; 1.168; 1.169; 1.177; 1.200; 1.201; 1.202; 1.206; -ai: 1.212; sigmatic ecthlipsis: 1.159; 1.186; pentasyllable: 1.180; monosyllable: 1.203; 1.205=15 Ennianisms in 56 lines=.27 Ennianisms per line=2.7 per 10 lines)

8. 1.215–264 (alliteration: 1.216; 1.219-220; 1.221; 1.234; 1.250; 1.257; -ai: 1.249; 1.251; pentasyllable: 1.223; 1.240; 1.244; 1.249; 1.251; monosyllable: 1.216; 1.232; 1.245=16 Ennianisms in 50 lines=.32 per line=3.2 per 10 lines)

9. 1.265–328 (alliteration: 1.266; 1.271; 1.278; 1.285–286; 1.288; 1.302; 1.307–308; -ai: 1.283; 1.285; 1.307; pentasyllable: 1.291; 1.317; monosyllable: 1.269; 1.297; 1.302; 1.304; 1.328=17 Ennianisms in 64 lines=.27 Ennianisms per line=2.7 per 10 lines)

10. 1.329–369 (alliteration: 1.338–339; 1.341; 1.347; 1.356; 1.361; monosyllable: 1.339; 1.361=7 Ennianisms in 41 lines=.17 per line=1.7 per 10 lines)

11. 1.370–397 (alliteration: 1.371; 1.374; 1.387; 1.388; pentasyllable: 1.390; 1.391; monosyllable: 1.377; 1.385; 1.389=9 Ennianisms in 28 lines=.32 per line=3.2 per 10 lines)

***12. 1.398–417 (alliteration: 1.398; 1.403; 1.411; -ai: 1.404; 1.406; 1.415; pentasyllable: 1.400; monosyllable: 1.399; 1.410=9 Ennianisms in 20 lines=.45 per line=4.5 per 10 lines)**

13. 1.418–448 (alliteration: 1.425; 1.436–437; 1.446; pentasyllable: 1.435; monosyllable: 1.434; 1.440; 1.443; 1.445=8 Ennianisms in 31 lines=.26 per line—2.6 per 10 lines)

14. 1.449–482 (alliteration: 1.449; 1.456; 1.480; 1.482; -ai: 1.453; pentasyllable: 1.451; 1.455; 1.477; monosyllable: 1.462; 1.465=10 Ennianisms in 34 lines=.29 per line=2.9 per 10 lines)

15. 1.483–502 (alliteration: 1.483; 1.484; 1.500; pentasyllable: 1.484; 1.499; monosyllable: 1.485=6 Ennianisms in 20 lines=.30 per line=3.0 per 10 lines)

***16. 1.503–550 (alliteration: 1.505; 1.508; 1.510; 1.517; 1.518; 1.521; 1.522; 1.529; 1.536; 1.538; 1.544; 1.548; -ai: 1.516; pentasyllable: 1.516; 1.519; 1.535; 1.548; monosyllable: 1.504; 1.506; 1.508; 1.511; 1.512; 1.539=23 Ennianisms in 48 lines=.48 per line=4.8 per 10 lines)**

17. 1.551–583 (alliteration: 1.562; 1.566; 1.568; 1.574; 1.575; -ai: 1.552; 1.565; pentasyllable: 1.552; 1.559; 1.565; 1.574; 1.575=12 Ennianisms in 33 lines=.36 per line=3.6 per 10 lines)

18. 1.584–598 (alliteration: 1.586; 1.588; 1.594; -ai: 1.586=4 Ennianisms in 15 lines=.27 per line=2.7 per 10 lines)

***19. 1.599–634 (alliteration: 1.599; 1.600; 1.607; 1.609; 1.621; 1.626; 1.629; 1.634; pentasyllable: 1.609; 1.611, 1.612; monosyllable: 1.607; 1.613; 1.621; 1.624; 1.626=16 Ennianisms in 36 lines=.44 per line=4.4 per 10 lines)**

*****20. 1.635–644 (0 Ennianisms)***

*****21. 1.645–689 (alliteration: 1.657; 1.675; 1.684; 1.687; -ai: 1.659; monosyllable: 1.657=6 Ennianisms in 45 lines=.13 per line=1.3 per 10 lines)***

22. 1.690-704 (alliteration: 1.697; 1.699; monosyllable: 1.697=3 Ennianisms in 15 lines=.2 per line=2.0 per 10 lines)

23. 1.705–733 (alliteration: 1.725; 1.726; -ai: 1.725; monosyllable: 1.716; 1.728; 1.729=6 Ennianisms in 29 lines=.21 per line=2.1 per 10 lines)

24. 1.734–762 (alliteration: 1.735; 1.739; 1.743; 1.749; 1.751; pentasyllable: 1.734; 1.736; monosyllable: 1.738; 1.751; 1.755=10 Ennianisms in 29 lines=.34 per line=3.4 per 10 lines)

25. 1.763–781 (alliteration: 1.763; 1.775; 1.781; pentasyllable: 1.764=4 Ennianisms in 19 lines=.21 per line=2.1 per 10 lines)

26. 1.782–802 (alliteration: 1.794; 1.799; 1.800; monosyllable: 1.790; 1.795=5 Ennianisms in 21 lines=.24 per line=2.4 per 10 lines)

27. 1.803–829 (alliteration: 1.803-804; 1.812; 1.813; 1.814; 1.829; **pentasyllable: 1.811; 1.818; 1.819; monosyllable: 1.812; 1.813; 1.825=11 Ennianisms in 27 lines=.41 per lines=4.1 per 10 lines)**

28. 1.830–874 (alliteration: 1.848; 1.857; 1.859; 1.861; 1.873; sigmatic ecthlipsis: 1.838; pentasyllable: 1.869; 1.874; monosyllable: 1.868; 1.872=10 Ennianisms in 45 lines=.22 per line=2.2 per 10 lines)

***29. 1.875–896 (monosyllable: 1.880; 1.893= 2 Ennianisms in 22 lines=.09 per line=0.9 per 10 lines)*

30. 1.897–920 (alliteration: 1.900; 1.903; 1.904; 1.909; -ai: 1.900; 1.916; pentasyllable: 1.909; 1.910; 1.916=9 Ennianisms in 24 lines=.38 per line=3.8 per 10 lines)

31. 1.921–950 (alliteration: 1.921; 1.934; 1.937; 1.948; 1.950; pentasyllable: 1.939; 1.945; monosyllable: 1.923=8; Ennianisms in 30 lines=.27 per line=2.7 per 10 lines)

***32. 1.951–957 (-ai: 1.951; 1.953; pentasyllable: 1.951; monosyllable: 1.954=4 Ennianisms in 7 lines=.57 Ennianisms per line=5.7 Ennianisms per 10 lines)**

33. 1.958–1,001 (alliteration: 1.979; 1.1,000; -ai: 1.984; 1.986; 1.997; sigmatic ecthlipsis: 1.978; pentasyllable: 1.968; 1.977; 1.986; 1.992; 1.996; 1.997; monosyllable: 1.974; 1.978=14 Ennianisms in 44 lines=.32 Ennianisms per line=3.2 Ennianisms per 10 lines)

***34. 1.1,002–1,007 (0 Ennianisms)*

***35. 1.1,008–1,051 (alliteration: 1.1,010; 1.1,012; 1.1,014; 1.1,022; 1.1,024; 1.1,043; -ai: 1.1,016; 1.1,017; 1.1,035; 1.1,041; 1.1,047; 1.1,051; pentasyllable: 1.1,013; 1.1,017; 1.1,026; 1.1,027; 1.1,030; 1.1,035; 1.1,040; 1.1,043; 1.1,051; monosyllable: 1.1,049=22 Ennianisms in 44 lines=.5 Ennianisms per line=5.0 Ennianisms per 10 lines)**

***36. 1.1,052–1,082 (alliteration: 1.1,057; 1.1,058; 1.1,077; 1.1,080=4 Ennianisms in 31 lines=.13 per line=1.3 per 10 lines)*

37. 1.1,083–1,113 (alliteration: 1.1,085; 1.1,091; -ai: 1.1,113; pentasyllable: 1.1,085; 1.1,109; 1.1,113=6 Ennianisms in 31 lines=.19 per line=1.9 per 10 lines)

***38. 1.1,114–1,117 (alliteration: 1.1,114; -ai: 1.1,116=2 Ennianisms in 4 lines=.5 per line=5.0 per 10 lines)**

DRN 2

363 Ennianisms in 1,174 lines=.31 per line=3.1 per 10 lines; 15 Bailey paragraphs with exceptionally high frequency of Ennianisms; 4 Bailey paragraphs with exceptionally low frequency of Ennianisms; 19/45 Bailey paragraphs with abnormal frequency of Ennianisms; Longest anti-cluster is 25 lines (2.200–225) without any Ennianisms.

1. 2.1–61 (alliteration: 2.4; 2.17; 2.30; 2.34; 2.37; 2.38; 2.44; -ai: 2.52; sigmatic ecthlipsis: 2.53 *bis*; pentasyllable: 2.11; 2.26; 2.42; 2.44; 2.52; monosyllable: 2.4; 2.16; 2.36; 2.57; 2.59=20 Ennianisms in 61 lines=.33 per line=3.3 per 10 lines)

2. **2.62–2.79 (alliteration: 2.64; 2.65; 2.72; 2.77; -ai: 2.62; 2.79; pentasyllable: 2.62=7 Ennianisms in 18 lines=.39 per line=3.9 per 10 lines).**

3. **2.80–141 (alliteration: 2.80; 2.95; 2.100; 2.104; 2.108; 2.114; 2.116; 2.130; 2.133; 2.136; 2.140; -ai: 2.89; 2.124; 2.127; pentasyllable: 2.89; 2.100; 2.124; 2.127; 2.134; 2.135; monosyllable: 2.83; 2.87; 2.92; 2.94; 2.95; 2.123; 2.125= 27 Ennianisms in 62 lines=.44 per line=4.4 per 10 lines)**

4. 2.142–166 (alliteration: 2.145–146 ; 2.147 ; 2.157; 2.160; 2.166; -ai: 2.142; pentasyllable: 2.142; 2.145; 2.157; 2.161=10 Ennianisms in 25 lines=.40 per line=4.0 per 10 lines)

5. 2.167–183 (alliteration: 2.172; sigmatic ecthlipsis: 2.175; -ai: 2.167; pentasyllable: 2.167; 2.169; 2.183; monosyllable: 2.177=7 Ennianisms in 17 lines=.41 per line=4.1 per 10 lines)

6. 2.184–215 (alliteration: 2.190; 2.193; pentasyllable: 2.200; monosyllable: 2.185; 2.193=5 Ennianisms in 30 lines=.17 per line=1.7 per 10 lines)

***7. 2.216–224 (0 Ennianisms)*

8. 2.225–250 (alliteration: 2.226; 2.230; 2.235; 2.250; -ai: 2.249; pentasyllable: 2.234; monosyllable: 2.231; 2.241; 2.242; 2.243=10 Ennianisms in 26 lines=.38 per line=3.8 per 10 lines)

9. 2.251–293 (alliteration: 2.258; 2.267; 2.280; 2.281; 2.283; 2.285; 2.288; -ai: 2.266; 2.281; pentasyllable: 2.266; 2.281; 2.292; monosyllable: 2.260; 2.284=14 Ennianisms in 43 lines=.33 per line=3.3 per 10 lines)

***10. 2.294–2.307 (alliteration: 2.296; 2.298; -ai: 2.294; 2.302; 2.304; pentasyllable: 2.294; 2.297; 2.304; monosyllable: 2.303=9 Ennianisms in 14 lines=.64 per line=6.4 per 10 lines)**

11. 2.308–332 (alliteration: 2.310; 2.315; 2.322; 2.324; monosyllable: 2.326=5 Ennianisms in 25 lines=.2 per line=2.0 per 10 lines)

***12. 2.333–380 (alliteration: 2.350; 2.352; 2.358; 2.372; pentasyllable: 2.346; monosyllable: 2.377; 2.378=7 Ennianisms in 48 lines=.15 per line=1.5 per 10 lines)

***13. 2.381–397 (alliteration: 2.390=1 Ennianism in 17 lines=.06 per line=0.6 per 10 lines)*

***14. 2.398–407 (0 Ennianisms)*

15. 2.408–443 (alliteration: 2.414; 2.416; 2.424; 2.439; pentasyllable: 2.441; monosyllable: 2.412; 2.416; 2.422; 2.423; 2.425; 2.428; 2.436; 2.437; 2.442=14 Ennianisms in 36 lines=.38 per line=3.8 per 10 lines)

16. 2.444–477 (alliteration: 2.452; 2.460; 2.463; 2.465; sigmatic ecthlipsis: 2.462; pentasyllable: 2.450; 2.459; monosyllable: 2.445; 2.457; 2.468=10 Ennianisms in 34 lines=.29 per line=2.9 per 10 lines)

17. 2.478–521 (alliteration: 2.478; 2.481; 2.486; 2.516; -ai: 2.490; pentasyllable: 2.498; 2.507; 2.508; monosyllable: 2.478; 2.513; 2.516=11 Ennianisms in 44 lines=.25 per line=2.5 per 10 lines)

***18. 2.522–568 (alliteration: 2.522; 2.524; 2.538; 2.559; 2.560; 2.563; 2.566; ai: 2.527; 2.529; 2.544; 2.562; pentasyllable: 2.527; 2.529; 2.531; 2.544; 2.551; 2.562; 2.568; monosyllable: 2.522; 2.525; 2.526; 2.565=22 Ennianisms in 47 lines=.47 per line=4.7 per 10 lines)**

19. 2.569–580 (alliteration: 2.578; pentasyllable: 2.569; 2.571; 2.573; monosyllable: 2.578= 5 Ennianisms in 12 lines=.42 per line=4.2 per 10 lines)

20. 2.581–599 (alliteration: 2.582; 2.587; 2.593; 2.596–597; 2.598; pentasyllable: 2.584; 2.587; monosyllable: 2.586=8 Ennianisms in 19 lines=.42 per line=4.2 per 10 lines)

21. 2.600–660 (alliteration: 2.603; 2.606; 2.618; 2.619; 2.625; 2.626; 2.632; 2.635; 2.637; 2.643; 2.649; 2.654; monosyllable: 2.615; 2.646; 14 Ennianisms in 61 lines=.23 per line=2.3 per 10 lines)

22. 2.661–699 (alliteration: 2.679; 2.681; 2.684; -ai: 2.663; 2.666; pentasyllable: 2.666; 2.671; 2.684; monosyllable: 2.690=9 Ennianisms in 39 lines=.23 per line=2.3 per 10 lines)

23. 2.700–729 (alliteration: 2.704; 2.708; 2.712; 2.715–716; pentasyllable: 2.706; 2.712; 2.722; monosyllable: 2.700; 2.710; 2.720; 2.721; 2.725=12 Ennianisms in 30 lines=.4 per line=4.0 per 10 lines)

24. 2.730–747 (alliteration: 2.732; 2.733; 2.734; 2.736; -ai: 2.735; 2.737; pentasyllable: 2.735; 2.737=8 Ennianisms in 18 lines=.44 per line=4.4 per 10 lines)

25. 2.748–756 (alliteration: 2.749; 2.755; monosyllable: 2.751=3 Ennianisms in 9 lines=.33 per line=3.3 per 10 lines)

26. 2.757–794 (alliteration: 2.776; 2.791; 2.793; pentasyllable: 2.761; 2.762; 2.792; monosyllable: 2.757; 2.774; 2.791=9 Ennianisms in 38 lines=.24 per line=2.4 per 10 lines)

27. 2.795–809 (alliteration: 2.802; 2.808; monosyllable: 2.799; 2.806; 2.809=5 Ennianisms in 15 lines=.33 per line=3.3 per 10 lines)

***28. 2.810–816 (monosyllable: 2.810=1 Ennianism in 7 lines=.14 per line=1.4 per 10 lines)

***29. 2.817–825 (alliteration: 2.817; 2.820; 2.822; pentasyllable: 2.818; monosyllable: 2.820=5 Ennianisms in 9 lines=.56 per line=5.6 per 10 lines)**

30. 2.826–833 (alliteration: 2.826; 2.829–830; sigmatic ecthlipsis: 2.830=3 Ennianisms in 8 lines=.38 per line=3.8 per 10 lines)

31. 2.834–841 (alliteration: 2.837; 2.838; monosyllable: 2.835=3 Ennianisms in 8 lines=.38 per line=3.8 per 10 lines)

32. 2.842–864 (alliteration: 2.842; 2.845; 2.848; 2.851; 2.852–853; 2.859; monosyllable: 2.849; 2.861=8 Ennianisms in 23 lines=.35 per line=3.5 per 10 lines)

33. 2.865–885 (alliteration: 2.871; 2.881; pentasyllable: 2.866; 2.878; 2.885; monosyllable: 2.865; 2.868; 2.872=8 Ennianisms in 21 lines=.38 per line=3.8 per 10 lines)

34. **2.886–930 (alliteration: 2.905; 2.906; 2.912; 2.914-915; 2.930; -ai: 2.899; sigmatic ecthlipsis: 2.930; pentasyllable: 2.899; 2.914; 2.919; 2.922; monosyllable: 2.892; 2.896; 2.900; 2.910; 2.917; 2.923; 2.925=18 Ennianisms in 45 lines=.4 per line=4.0 per 10 lines)**

35. 2.931–943 (alliteration: 2.936; pentasyllable: 2.936; 2.941; 2.942=4 Ennianisms in 13 lines=.31 per line=3.1 per 10 lines)

36. 2.944–962 (alliteration: 2.947-948; 2.955-956; pentasyllable: 2.947; 2.948=4 Ennianisms in 19 lines=.21 per line=2.1 per 10 lines)

***37. **2.963–972 (alliteration: 2.964; 2.965; -ai: 2.963; pentasyllable: 2.963; 2.969; monosyllable: 2.968=6 Ennianisms in 10 lines=.6 per line=6.0 per 10 lines)**

38. 2.973–990 (alliteration: 2.989; monosyllable: 2.975; 2.984; pentasyllable: 2.980=4 Ennianisms in 18 lines=.22 per line=2.2 per 10 lines)

***39. **2.991–1,022 (alliteration: 2.996; 2.1,001; 2.1,003; 2.1,008; 2.1,010; 2.1,014; -ai: 2.1,002; 2.1,019; pentasyllable: 2.1,002; 2.1,008; 2.1,009; 2.1,019; monosyllable: 2.998; 2.1,017; 2.1,018=15 Ennianisms in 32 lines=.47 per line=4.7 per 10 lines)**

40. 2.1,023–1,047 (alliteration: 2.1,023; 2.1,028-1,029; 2.1,030; 2.1,046-1,047; monosyllable: 2.1,044; 2.1,046=6 Ennianisms in 25 lines=.24 per line=2.4 per 10 lines)

***41. **2.1,048–1,066 (alliteration: 2.1,059; -ai: 2.1,057; 2.1,063; 2.1,065; pentasyllable: 2.1,057; 2.1,065; monosyllable: 2.1,050; 2.1,052; 2.1,064=9 Ennianisms in 19 lines (.47 per line=4.7 per 10 lines)**

42. 2.1,067–1,076 (pentasyllable: 2.1,074; monosyllable: 2.1,069=2 Ennianisms in 10 lines=.2 per line=2.0 per 10 lines)

43. 2.1,077–1,089 (pentasyllable: 2.1,086; monosyllable: 2.1,084; 2.1,085=3 Ennianisms in 13 lines=.23 per line=2.3 per 10 lines)

44. *2.1,090–1,104 (alliteration: 2.1,092; 2.1,093=2 Ennianisms in 15 lines=.13 per line=1.3 per 10 lines)*

***45. 2.1,105–1,174 (alliteration: 2.1,144; 2.1,151; 2.1,168; 2.1,172; pentasyllable: 2.1,138; 2.1,148; 2.1,161; 2.1,162; monosyllable: 2.1,125; 2.1,156=10 Ennianisms in 70 lines=.14 per line=1.4 per 10 lines)

DRN 3

322 Ennianisms in 1,094 lines=.29 per line=2.9 per 10 lines; 7 Bailey paragraphs with exceptionally high frequency of Ennianisms; 3 Bailey paragraphs with exceptionally

low frequency of Ennianisms; 10/39 Bailey paragraphs with abnormal frequency of Ennianisms; Longest anti-cluster is 20 lines without any Ennianisms (3.557–578).

1. **3.1–30 (alliteration: 3.1; 3.4; 3.5; 3.6; 3.19; 3.25; pentasyllable: 3.14; 3.26; monosyllable: 3.3; 3.8; 3.17; 3.29; 3.30=13 Ennianisms in 30 lines=.42 per line=4.2 per 10 lines)**

2. 3.31–93 (alliteration: 3.43; 3.47; 3.54; 3.71; sigmatic ecthlipsis: 3.52; -ai: 3.83; pentasyllable: 3.54; 3.70; 3.71; monosyllable: 3.56; 3.58; 3.89; 3.91=13 Ennianisms in 63 lines=.21 per line=2.1 per 10 lines)

3. 3.94–135 (alliteration: 3.121; -ai: 3.131; pentasyllable: 3.131; monosyllable: 3.95; 3.96; 3.100; 3.101; 3.115=8 Ennianisms in 42 lines=.19 per line=1.9 per 10 lines)

4. **3.136–160 (alliteration: 3.144; 3.145; 3.146; 3.147; 3.152; -ai: 3.150; pentasyllable: 3.148; monosyllable: 3.137; 3.142; 3.152; 3.159=11 Ennianisms in 25 lines=.44 per line=4.4 per 10 lines)**

5. 3.161–176 (alliteration: 3.169; -ai: 3.161; monosyllable: 3.166; 3.175=4 Ennianisms in 16 lines=.25 per line=2.5 per 10 lines)

6. 3.177–230 (alliteration: 3.197; 3.199; 3.201; 3.209; 3.212; 3.218; 3.223; 3.226; -ai: 3.193; pentasyllable: 3.193; 3.210; monosyllable: 3.199; 3.202; 3.204; 3.209; 3.211; 3.216; 3.219; 3.221=19 Ennianisms in 54 lines=.35 per line=3.5 per 10 lines)

7. 3.231–257 (alliteration: 3.231; 3.238; 3.246; -ai: 3.254; sigmatic ecthlipsis: 3.257; pentasyllable: 3.248; monosyllable: 3.231; 3.235; 3.241=9 Ennianisms in 27 lines=.33 per line=3.3 per 10 lines)

8. 3.258–322 (alliteration: 3.275; 3.278; 3.294; 3.322; -ai: 3.303; pentasyllable: 3.262; 3.284; monosyllable: 3.267; 3.278; 3.299; 3.310; 3.314; 3.317=13 Ennianisms in 65 lines=.20 per line=2.0 per 10 lines)

9. 3.323–349 (alliteration: 3.324; 3.343; 3.345–346; 3.348; 3.349; -ai: 3.341; 3.344; pentasyllable: 3.330=8 Ennianisms in 27 lines=.30 per line=3.0 per 10 lines)

10. 3.350–358 (alliteration: 3.350; pentasyllable: 3.352; monosyllable: 3.355=3 Ennianisms in 9 lines=.33 per line=3.3 per 10 lines)

11. 3.359–369 (alliteration: 3.365; pentasyllable: 3.364=2 Ennianisms in 11 lines=.18 per line=1.8 per 10 lines)

12. 3.370–395 (alliteration: 3.375; 3.378; 3.383; 3.390; -ai: 3.380; 3.392=6 Ennianisms in 26 lines=.23 per line=2.3 per 10 lines)

13. 3.396–416 (alliteration: 3.403; -ai: 3.396; 3.397; 3.399; 3.406; monosyllable: 3.413=6 Ennianisms in 21 lines=.29 per line=2.9 per 10 lines)

14. 3.417–424 (alliteration: 3.419–420; monosyllable: 3.424=2 Ennianisms in 8 lines=.25 per line=2.5 per 10 lines)

15. 3.425–444 (alliteration: 3.440; 3.441; 3.443; -ai: 3.427; pentasyllable: 3.428; monosyllable: 3.441; 3.444=7 Ennianisms in 20 lines=.35 per line=3.5 per 10 lines)

16. **3.445–458 (alliteration: 3.445–446; 3.448; 3.456; -ai: 3.455; monosyllable: 3.450; 3.453= 6 Ennianisms in 14 lines=.43 per line=4.3 per 10 lines)**

17. 3.459–525 (alliteration: 3.462; 3.467; 3.483; 3. 484; 3.494; 3.498; 3.500–501; 3.508; -ai: 3.498; 3.499; pentasyllable: 3.478; 3.485; monosyllable: 3.470; 3.472; 3.479; 3.513=16 Ennianisms in 67 lines=.24 per line=2.4 per 10 lines)

18. 3.526–547 (alliteration: 3.529; 3.533; -ai: 3.536; pentasyllable: 3.542; monosyllable: 3.532=5 Ennianisms in 22 lines=.23 per line=2.3 per 10 lines)

***19. 3.548–557 (alliteration: 3.552; 3.553; 3.557; monosyllable: 3.548; 3.549=5 Ennianisms in 10 lines=.5 per line=5.0 per 10 lines)**

***20. 3.558–579 (alliteration: 3.579; monosyllable: 3.578=2 Ennianisms in 22 lines=.09 per line=0.9 per 10 lines)*

21. 3.580–614 (alliteration: 3.582; 3.585; 3.601; 3.603; 3. 611; -ai: 3.580; pentasyllable: 3.601; 3.613; monosyllable: 3.583; 3.585; 3.587; 3.611; 3.612=13 Ennianisms in 35 lines=.37 per line=3.7 per 10 lines)

***22. 3.615–623 (pentasyllable: 3.615=1 Ennianism in 9 lines=.11 per line=1.1 per 10 lines)*

23. 3.624–633 (alliteration: 3.631; -ai: 3.624; monosyllable: 3.624=3 Ennianisms in 10 lines=.3 per line=3.0 per 10 lines)

24. 3.634–669 (alliteration: 3.661; 3.662; 3.665-666; -ai: 3.638; 3.656; pentasyllable: 3.639; monosyllable: 3.644; 3.645; 3.647; 3.653; 3.667; 3.668=12 Ennianisms in 36 lines=.33 per line=3.3 per 10 lines)

25. 3.670–678 (-ai: 3.670; pentasyllable: 3.671=2 Ennianisms in 9 lines=.22 per line=2.2 per 10 lines)

***26. 3.679–712 (alliteration: 3.682; 3.700; 3.705; 3.709; 3.710; -ai: 3.693; 3.693; pentasyllable: 3.689; 3.692; 3.697; 3.698; 3.706; monosyllable: 3.686; 3.688; 3.690; 3.704; 3.705=17 Ennianisms in 34 lines=.5 per line=5.0 per 10 lines)**

27. 3.713–740 (alliteration: 3.731; 3.740; -ai: 3.713; pentasyllable: 3.722; 3.729; 3.738; monosyllable: 3.718; 3.725; 3.728; 3.731=10 Ennianisms in 28 lines=.36 per line=3.6 per 10 lines)

28. 3.741–775 (alliteration: 3.743; 3.746; 3.747; 3.759; 3.763; 3.769; pentasyllable: 3.745; 3.746; 3.763; monosyllable: 3.764; 3.766=11 Ennianisms in 35 lines=.31 per line=3.1 per 10 lines)

29. 3.776–783 (pentasyllable: 3.779; 3.780; 3.782=3 Ennianisms in 8 lines=.38 per line=3.8 per 10 lines)

***30. 3.784–829 (alliteration: 3.787; 3.794; 3.807; 3.808; 3.814; 3. 816; 3.817; 3.823; 3.824; 3.826; -ai: 3.809; pentasyllable: 3.796; 3.803; 3.809; 3.815; monosyllable: 3.790; 3.798; 3.802; 3.806; 3.812; 3.817; 3.819=22 Ennianisms in 46 lines=.48 per line=4.8 per 10 lines)**

***31. 3.830–869 (alliteration: 3.830; 3.834-835; 3.842; 3.845; 3.846; 3.852; 3.855-856; 3.857; -ai: 3.838; 3.855; 3.859; pentasyllable: 3.845; 3.855; 3.865; monosyllable: 3.840; 3.848; 3.861=17 Ennianisms in 40 lines=.43 per line=4.3 per 10 lines)**

32. 3.870–893 (alliteration: 3.873; 3.874; 3.875; 3.883; 3.888; monosyllable: 3.885=6 Ennianisms in 24 lines=.25 per line=2.5 per 10 lines)

***33. 3.894–911 (sigmatic ecthlipsis: 3.905=1 Ennianism in 18 lines=.06 per line=0.6 per 10 lines)*

34. 3.912–930 (alliteration: 3.925; 3.926; -ai: 3.928; 3.930; pentasyllable: 3.928; monosyllable: 3.926=6 Ennianisms in 19 lines=.32 per line=3.2 per 10 lines)

35. 3.931–977 (alliteration: 3.959; 3.963; 3.969; -ai: 3.956; pentasyllable: 3.937; 3.944; monosyllable: 3.934; 3.936; 3.962; 3.965=10 Ennianisms in 47 lines=.21 per line=2.1 per 10 lines)

36. 3.978–1,023 (alliteration: 3.983; 3.986; 3.990–991; 3.994; 3.1,022; -ai: 3.989; 3.1,007; monosyllable: 3.983; 3.995; 3.1,009=10 Ennianisms in 46 lines=.22 per line=2.2 per 10 lines)

37. 3.1,024–1,052 (alliteration: 3.1,029; 3.1,040; 3.1,043–1,044; 3.1,046; 3.1,048–1,049; sigmatic ecthlipsis: 3.1,025; 3.1,038; pentasyllable: 3.1,028; monosyllable: 3.1,038; 3.1,044; 3.1,050=11 Ennianisms in 29 lines=.38 per line=3.8 per 10 lines)

38. 3.1,053–1,075 (alliteration: 3.1,055; 3.1,058; pentasyllable: 3.1,063; monosyllable: 3.1,068=4 Ennianisms in 23 lines=.17 per line=1.7 per 10 lines)

39. 3.1,076–1,094 (alliteration: 3.1,083; 3.1,091; -ai: 3.1,077; 3.1,084; 3.1,093=5 Ennianisms in 19 lines=.26 per line=2.6 per 10 lines)

DRN 4

316 in 1,287 lines=.246 per line=2.46 per 10 lines; 6 Bailey paragraphs with exceptionally high frequency of Ennianisms; 5 Bailey paragraphs with exceptionally low frequency of Ennianisms; 11/45 Bailey paragraphs with abnormal frequency of Ennianisms; Longest anti-cluster without any Ennianisms is 19 lines (4.418–438 and 4.1,118–1,138).

1. 4.1–25 (alliteration: 4.9, 4.12, 4.23; pentasyllable: 4.14; 4.20; 4.25=6 Ennianisms in 25 lines=.24 per line=2.4 per 10 lines)

2. 4.26–44 (alliteration: 4.27; 4.31; 4.44; monosyllable: 4.29=4 Ennianisms in 19 lines=.21 per line=2.1 per 10 lines)

***3. 4.45–53 (alliteration: 4.48; 4.51; 4.53; monosyllable: 4.49; 4.51=5 Ennianisms in 9 lines=.56 per line=5.6 per 10 lines)*

4. 4.54–109 (alliteration: 4.61–62; 4.63; 4.69; 4.94; 4.100; -ai: 4.69; 4.78; 4.79; pentasyllable: 4.70; monosyllable: 4.90; 4.99=11 Ennianisms in 56 lines=.20 per line=2.0 per 10 lines)

5. 4.110–128 (alliteration: 4.111; 4.113; 4.119; 4.120; 4.128; monosyllable: 4.118; 4.121=7 Ennianisms in 19 lines=.37 per line=3.7 per 10 lines)

6. 4.129–142 (alliteration: 4.130; 4.131=2 Ennianisms in 14 lines=.14 per line=1.4 per 10 lines)

7. 4.143–175 (alliteration: 4.150; 4.152; 4.155; 4.158; 4.165; 4.171; monosyllable: 4.146; 4.148; 4.163; 4.174=10 Ennianisms in 33 lines=.30 per line=3.0 per 10 line)

8. 4.176–215 (alliteration: 4.181; 4.187; 4.193; 4.194; 4.211; 4.212–213; -ai: 4.211; monosyllable: 4.181; 4.191; 4.197; 4.200=11 Enniansims in 42 lines=.26 per line=2.6 per 10 lines)

9. 4.216–238 (alliteration: 4.221; 4.222; 4.232; monosyllable: 4.216; 4.231; 4.232; 4.234; 4.235=8 Enniansms in 23 lines=.35 per line=3.5 per 10 lines)

10. 4.239–268 (alliteration: 4.250; 4.259; pentasyllable: 4.258; monosyllable: 4.256; 4.259; 4.263=6 Enniansims in 20 lines=.3 per line=3.0 per 10 lines)

11. 4.269–323 (alliteration: 4.283; 4.313; 4.318; pentasyllable: 4.271; 4.278; monosyllable: 4.289; 4.292; 4.293; 4.296; 4.315; 4.316; 4.317= 12 Enniansims in 55 lines=.22 per line=2.2 per 10 lines)

***12. 4.324–336 (alliteration: 4.327; 4.334; pentasyllable: 4.328 (4.303); 4.331 (4.306) =4 Enniansims in 9 lines=.44 per line=4.4 per 10 lines)

13. 4.337–352 (alliteration: 4.340; 4.342; 4.347; 4.350; monosyllable: 4.342=5 Enniansims in 16 Lines=.31 per line=3.1 per 10 lines)

14. 4.353–363 (alliteration: 4.353; 4.360=2 Enniansims in 11 lines=.18 per line=1.8 per 10 lines)

***15. 4.364–378 (alliteration: 4.368=1 Ennianism in 15 lines=.07 per line=0.7 per 10 lines)

16. 4.379–468 (alliteration: 4.384; 4.385; 4.394; 4.400; 4.439; 4.449; 4.453–454; 4.456–457; 4.458–459; 4.460; 4.463; 4.466; sigmatic ecthlipsis: 4.466; monosyllable: 4.418; 4.438=15 Enniansims in 90 lines=.17 per line=1.7 per 10 lines)

17. 4.469–521 (alliteration: 4.471; 4.472; 4.475; 4.493; 4.494; 4.501; sigmatic ecthlipsis: 4.493; monosyllable: 4.484; 4.490; 4.493; 4.495; 4.499; 4.501; 4.509; 4.510; 4.512; 4.516; 4.520; 4.521=19 Enniansims in 53 lines=.36 per line=3.6 per 10 lines)

***18. 4.522–523 (alliteration: 4.522–523; monosyllable: 4.522; 4.523=3 Enniansims in 2 lines=1.5 per line=15 per 10 lines)

19. 4.524–548 (alliteration: 4.526; 4.544; -ai: 4.537; pentasyllable: 4.542 (4.551); monosyllable: 4.526; 4.535; 4.540=7 Enniansims in 25 lines=.28 per line=2.8 per 10 lines)

20. 4.549–594 (alliteration: 4.578; 4.581; pentasyllable: 4.555; 4.594; monosyllable: 4.558; 4.561; 4.586=7 Enniansims in 46 lines=.15 per line=1.5 per 10 lines)

21. 4.595–614 (alliteration: 4.598; 4.606; 4.608; monosyllable: 4.603=4 Enniansims in 20 lines=.2 per line=2.0 per 10 lines)

***22. 4.615–632 (alliteration: 4.630; 4.631; -ai: 4.616; 4.618; 4.624; pentasyllable: 4.628; monosyllable: 4.617=7 Enniansims in 18 lines=.39 per line=3.9 per 10 lines)

23. 4.633–672 (alliteration: 4.654; 4.659–660; 4.668; pentasyllable: 4.667; 4.668; monosyllable: 4.634; 4.636; 4.649; 4.653; 4.664=10 Enniansims in 39 lines=.26 per line=2.6 per 10 lines)

24. 4.673–686 (monosyllable: 4.674; 4.676; 4.681=3 Enniansims in 14 lines=.21 per line=2.1 per 10 lines)

25. 4.687–705 (alliteration: 4.690; 4.697; pentasyllable: 4.697; monosyllable: 4.690; 4.694=5 Enniansims in 19 lines=.26 per line=2.6 per 10 lines)

26. 4.706–721 (alliteration: 4.712; 4.714; -ai: 4.713=3 Ennianisms in 16 lines=.19 per line=1.9 per 10 lines)

***27. 4.722–748 (alliteration: 4.725; 4.730; 4.748=3 Ennianisms in 27 lines=.11 per line=1.1 per 10 lines)*

28. 4.749–776 (alliteration: 4.753; 4.760; 4.767; pentasyllable: 4.776; monosyllable: 6.751; 6.760; 6.761; 6.773=8 Ennianisms in 28 lines=.29 per line=2.9 per 10 lines)

29. 4.777–817 (alliteration: 4.779; 4.783; 4.789; 4.790; 4.802; 4.804; 4.808; 4.809; pentasyllable: 4.791; monosyllable: 6.803; 6.807=11 Ennianisms in 41 lines=.27 per line=2.7 per 10 lines)

***30. 4.818–822 (0 Ennianisms)*

31. 4.823–857 (alliteration: 4.825; 4.827; 4.832; 4.843; 4.851–852; -ai: 4.847; pentasyllable: 4.824; 4.854; monosyllable: 4.837=9 Ennianisms in 35 lines=.26 per line=2.6 per 10 lines)

32. 4.858–876 (alliteration: 4.859; 4.861; monosyllable: 4.866= 3 Ennianisms in 19 lines=.16 per line=1.6 per 10 lines)

***33. 4.877–906 (alliteration: 4.884; 4.888; 4.894; 4.899; 4.902; -ai: 4.888; monosyllable: 4.888=7 Ennianisms in 20 lines=.35 per line=3.5 per 10 lines)

34. 4.907–928 (alliteration: 4.910; 4.915; -ai: 4.920; 4.925; monosyllable: 4.910; 4.920; 4.922=7 Ennianisms in 22 lines=.32 per line=3.2 per 10 lines)

***35. 4.929–961 (alliteration: 4.935–936; 4.939; 4.940; 4.941; 4.950; 4.954; 4.958; -ai: 4.944; 4.959; pentasyllable: 4.943; monosyllable: 4.932; 4.935; 4.939; 4.957; 4.961=15 Ennianisms in 33 lines=.45 per line=4.5 per 10 lines)*

36. 4.962–1,036 (alliteration: 4.966; 4.980; 4.981; 4.983; 4.988; 4.995; 4.1,009–1,010; 4.1,011; 4.1,020; 4.1,032; sigmatic ecthlipsis: 4.1,018; 4.1,022; 4.1,028; 4.1,035; 4.1,035; pentasyllable: 4.1,005; 4.1,030; monosyllable: 4.964; 4.996; 4.1,006=20 Ennianisms in 75 lines=.27 per line=2.7 per 10 lines)

37. 4.1,037–1,057 (alliteration: 4.1,040; 4.1,041; 4.1,043; monosyllable: 4.1,040=4 Ennianisms in 21 lines=.19 per line=1.9 per 10 lines)

38. 4.1,058–1,072 (alliteration: 4.1,061; 4.1,065; 4.1,071; monosyllable: 4.1,059; 4.1,061=5 Ennianisms in 15 lines=.33 per line=3.3 per 10 lines)

***39. 4.1,073–1,120 (alliteration: 4.1,074; 4.1,092; 4.1,102; 4.1,117; 4.1,118=5 Ennianisms in 48 lines=.10 per line=1.0 per 10 lines)*

***40. 4.1,121–1,140 (alliteration: 4.1,138; 4.1,140=2 Ennianisms in 20 lines=.1 per line=1.0 per 10 lines)*

41. 4.1,141–1,191 (alliteration: 4.1,157; 4.1,159; 4.1,169; 4.1,176; sigmatic ecthlipsis: 4.1,152; pentasyllable: 4.1,145; 4.1,172; monosyllable: 4.1,142; 4.1,152; 4.1,162; 4.1,164; 4.1,165; 4.1,166; 4.1,184=14 Ennianisms in 51 lines=.27 per line=2.7 per 10 lines)

42. 4.1,192–1,208 (alliteration: 4.1,193; 4.1,201–1,202; 4.1,205; sigmatic ecthlipsis: 4.1,204; 4.1,208; pentasyllable: 4.1,202=6 Ennianisms in 17 lines=.35 per line=3.5 per 10 lines)

43. 4.1,209–1,232 (alliteration: 4.1,209; 4.1,220; 4.1,222; 4.1,230; 4.1,231; 4.1,232; pentasyllable: 4.1,210; monosyllable: 4.1,217=8 Ennianisms in 24 lines=.33 per line=3.3 per 10 lines)

44. 4.1,233–1,277 (alliteration: 4.1,237; 4.1,240; 4.1,244; 4.1,249; 4.1,252; 4.1,259; sigmatic ecthlipsis: 4.1,268=7 Ennianisms in 45 lines=.16 per line=1.6 per 10 lines)

***45. 5.1,278–1,287 (alliteration: 4.1,280; 4.1,281; 4.1,283; 4.1,284; 4.1,286–1,287=5 Ennianisms in 10 lines=.5 per line=5.0 per 10 lines)**

DRN 5

305 Ennianisms in 1,457 lines=.21 per line=2.1 per 10 lines; 5 Bailey paragraphs with exceptionally high frequency of Ennianisms; 16 Bailey paragraphs with exceptionally low frequency of Ennianisms; 21/56 Bailey paragraphs with abnormal frequency of Ennianisms; Longest anti-clusters=38 lines (5.1,270–1,309) and 36 lines (5.1,343–1,380).

***1. 5.1–54 (alliteration: 5.1; 5.5; 5.8; 5.11; 5.12; 5.18; 5.24; 5.36; 5.43; 5.50–51; 5.53; -ai: 5.28; pentasyllable: 5.15; 5.28; 5.44; 5.48; monosyllable: 5.9; 5.25; 5.40=19 Ennianisms in 54 lines=.35 per line=3.5 per 10 lines)

***2. 5.55–90 (alliteration: 5.56; 5.60; 5.62; 5.63; 5.65; 5.80; 5.85; 5.86; 5.88; -ai: 5.67; pentasyllable: 5.67; 5.73; 5.86; monosyllable: 5.59=14 Ennianisms in 36 lines=.39 per line=3.9 per 10 lines)**

3. 5.91–109 (alliteration: 5.94; 5.96; 5.97; monosyllable: 5.104=4 Ennianisms in 19 lines=.21 per line=2.1 per 10 lines)

***4. 5.110–145 (alliteration: 5.112; 5.114; 5.117; 5.118; 5.124; 5.126; 5.128; 5.131; 5.138; 5.143; pentasyllable: 5.127; 5.140; monosyllable: 5.111; 5.134=14 Ennianisms in 36 lines=.39 per line=3.9 per 10 lines)**

***5. 5.146–155 (0 Ennianisms)*

6. 5.156–194 (alliteration: 5.162; 5.187; 5.191; pentasyllable: 5.157; 5.166; 5.167; 5.184; 5.192; monosyllable: 5.182= 9 Ennianisms in 39 lines=.23 per line=2.3 per 10 lines)

7. 5.195–234 (alliteration: 5.204; 5.217; 5.220; -ai: 5.208; monosyllable: 5.195; 5.206; 5.215; 5.226; 5.229=9 Ennianisms in 40 lines=.23 per line=2.3 per 10 lines)

***8. 5.235–246 (-ai: 5.235=1 Ennianism in 12 lines=.08 per line=0.8 per 10 lines)*

***9. 5.247–260 (alliteration: 5.251; 5.256; 5.257; -ai: 5.251; monosyllable: 5.252=5 Ennianisms in 14 lines=.36 per line=3.6 per 10 lines)

10. 5.261–272 (alliteration: 5.266; -ai: 5.264; monosyllable: 5.267=3 Ennianisms in 12 lines=.25 per line=2.5 per 10 lines)

***11. 5.273–280 (alliteration: 5.277; monosyllable: 5.279=2 Ennianisms in 18 lines=.11 per line=1.1 per 10 lines)*

12. 5.281–305 (alliteration: 5.295–296; 5.302; monosyllable: 5.281; 5.294=4 Ennianisms in 25 lines=.16 per line=1.6 per 10 lines)

13. 5.306–317 (alliteration: 5.310; pentasyllable: 5.316=2 Enniansms in 12 lines=.17 per line=1.7 per 10 lines)

***14. 5.318–323 (alliteration: 5.323; monosyllable: 5.319; 5.323= 3 Ennianisms in 6 lines=.5 per line=5.0 per 10 lines)**

***15. 5.324–350 (alliteration: 5.333; 5.334; 5. 335; pentasylable: 5.332; 5.342; 5.346; mono-syllable: 5.333; 5.335; 5.343=9 Ennianisms in 27 lines=.33 per line=3.3 per 10 lines)

***16. 5.351–379 (alliteration: 5.352; 5.353; 5.359; 5.361; 5.362; 5. 372; -ai: 5.354; pentasyllable: 5.354; 5.360; 5.376; monosyllable: 5.351; 5.357; 5.362; 5.377=14 Ennianisms in 29 lines=.48 per line=4.8 per 10 lines)**

17. 5.380–415 (alliteration: 5.380–381; 5.392–393; 5.411; -ai: 5.407; pentasyllable: 5.384; 5.407; monosyllable: 5.389=7 Ennianisms in 36 lines=.19 per line=1.9 per 10 lines)

***18. 5.416–431 (alliteration: 5.420; 5.422; 5.426; -ai: 5.416; 5.418; 5.431; penta-syllable: 5.416; 5.428=8 Ennianisms in 16 lines=.5 per line=5.0 per 10 lines)**

19. 5.432–448 (alliteration: 5.441–442; pentasyllable: 5.445=2 Ennianisms in 17 lines=.12 per line=1.2 per 10 lines)

20. 5. 449–494 (alliteration: 5.449; 5.452; 5.454; 5.465; 5.466; 5.468; 5.471; 5.479; 5.480; 5.482; sigmatic ecthlipsis: 5.456; -ai: 5.449=12 Ennianisms in 46 lines=.26 per line=2.6 per 10 lines)

21. 5.495–508 (alliteration: 5.498; monosyllable: 5.497=2 Ennianisms in 14 lines=.14 per lines=1.4 per 10 lines)

22. 5.509–533 (alliteration: 5.509; 5.511; 5.533; pentasyllable: 5.533; monosyllable: 5.531=5 Ennianisms in 25 lines=.2 per line=2.0 per 10 lines)

23. 5.534–563 (aliteration: 5.545; 5.547; 5.551; 5.562; -ai: 5.557; monosyllable: 5.545; 5.558; 5.563=8 Ennianisms in 30 lines=.27 per line=2.7 per 10 lines)

24. 5.564–591 (aliteration: 5.564; 5.575; 5.582; 5.586; monosyllable: 5.581=5 Ennianisms in 28 lines=.18 per line=1.8 per 10 lines)

25. 5.592–613 (alliteration: 5.593; 5.594; 5.600–601; -ai: 5.602=4 Ennianisms in 22 lines=.18 per line=1.8 per 10 lines)

26. 5.614–649 (alliteration: 5.619; pentasyllable: 5.615; 5.617; monosyllable: 5.620; 5.643=5 Ennianisms in 36 lines=.14 per line=1.4 per 10 lines)

27. 5.650–655 (alliteration: 5.654=1 Ennianism in 6 lines=.17 per line=1.7 per 10 lines)

***28. 5.656–679 (alliteration: 5.661; 5.679=2 Ennianisms in 24 lines=.08 per line=0.8 per 10 lines)**

29. 5.680–704 (alliteration: 5.682; 5.696; 5.702=3 Ennianisms in 25 lines=.12 per line=1.2 per 10 lines)

30. 5.705–750 (alliteration: 5.707; 5.718; 5.719; 5.736; 5.737; -ai: 5.713; 5.720; 5.726; 5.739; pentasyllable: 5.718= 10 Ennianisms in 46 lines=.22 per line=2.2 per 10 lines)

31. 5.751–771 (alliteration: 5.752; 5.757; monosyllable: 5.752=3 Ennianisms in 21 lines=.14 per line=1.4 per 10 lines)

***32. 5.772–782 (alliteration: 5.772; 5.775; 5.778; 5.779=4 Ennianisms in 11 lines=.37 per line=3.7 per 10 lines)

33. 5.783–820 (alliteration: 5.784; 5.788; 5.792; 5.796; 5.801–802; 5.805; pentasyllable: 5.789=7 Ennianisms in 38 lines=.18 per line=1.8 per 10 lines)

34. 5.821–836 (sigmatic ecthlipsis: 5.824; 5.825=2 Ennianisms in 16 lines=.13 per line=1.3 per 10 lines)

35. 5.837–854 (alliteration: 5.843; 5.850; monosyllable: 5.848=3 Ennianisms in 18 lines=.17 per line=1.7 per 10 lines)

36. 5.855–877 (alliteration: 5.856; 5.857; 5.864; 5.869; monosyllable: 5.855; 5.858; 5.860=7 Ennianisms 23 lines=.30 per line=3.0 per 10 lines)

37. 5.878–924 (alliteration: 5.881; 5.882; 5.891; 5.892–893; 5.901; 5.904; 5.909; 5.914; 5.920; pentasyllable: 5.892; monosyllable: 5.884=11 Ennianisms in 47 lines=.23 per line=2.3 per 10 lines)

38. 5.925–987 (alliteration: 5.926; 5.930; 5.931–932; 5.935; 5.938; 5.939; 5.950; 5.951; 5.957; 5.961; 5.963; 5.964; 5.969; 5.974; 5.977; sigmatic ecthlipsis: 5.936; -ai: 5.946=17 Ennianisms in 63 lines=.27 per line=2.7 per 10 lines)

39. 5.988–1,010 (alliteration: 5.989; 5.993; 5.995; 5.1,004; 5.1,009=5 Ennianisms in 23 lines=.22 per line=2.2 per 10 lines)

40. 5.1,011–1,027 (alliteration: 5.1,011; 5.1,027; pentasyllable: 5.1,022=3 Ennianisms in 17 lines=.18 per line=1.8 per 10 lines)

***41. 5.1,028–1,090 (alliteration: 5.1,035; 5.1,058; pentasyllable: 5.1,040; 5.1,041; monosyllable: 5.1,047; 5.1,056; 5.1,071=7 Ennianisms in 63 lines=.11 per line=1.1 per 10 lines)

***42. 5.1,091–1,104 (-ai: 5.1,099=1 Ennianism in 14 lines=.07 per line=0.7 per 10 lines)

43. 5.1,105–1,135 (alliteration: 5.1,112; 5.1,116; 5.1,126; -ai: 5.1,124; pentasyllable: 5.1,109; 5.1,111; 5.1,132=7 Ennianisms in 31 lines=.23 per line=2.3 per 10 lines)

44. 5.1,136–1,160 (alliteration: 5.1,137; 5.1,147; 5.1,158=3 Ennianisms in 25 lines=.12 per line=1.2 per 10 lines

45. 5.1,161–1,193 (alliteration: 5.1,163; 5.1,185; 5.1,193; sigmatic ecthlipsis: 5.1,164; monosyllable: 5.1,172=5 Ennianisms in 33 lines=.15 per line=1.5 per 10 lines)

46. 5.1,194–1,240 (alliteration: 5.1,200; 5.1,219; 5.1,226; 5.1,229–1,230; sigmatic ecthlipsis: 5.1,197=5 Ennianisms in 47 lines=.11 per line=1.1 per 10 lines)

47. 5.1,241–1,280 (alliteration: 5.1,242; 5.1,244; 5.1,245; 5.1,248; 5.1,251; 5.1,252; 5.1,257; 5.1,270; monosyllable: 5.1,241=9 Ennianisms in 60 lines=.15 per line=1.5 per 10 lines)

***48. 5.1,281–1,296 (0 Ennianisms)

***49. 5.1,297–1,307 (0 Ennianisms)

50. 5.1,308–1,349 (alliteration: 5.1,309; 5.1,313; 5.1,315; 5.1,316–1,317; 5.1,327; 5.1,333; 5.1,343; pentasyllable: 5.1,320=8 Ennianisms in 42 lines=.19 per line=1.9 per 10 lines)

***51. 5.1,350–1,360 (0 Ennianisms)

***52. 5.1,361–1,378 (0 Ennianisms)

***53. 5.1,379–1,435 (alliteration: 5.1,380; 5.1,391; 5.1,413; 5.1,432; pentasyllable: 5.1,411; 5.1,426=6 Ennianisms in 57 lines=.11 Ennianisms per line=1.1 per 10 lines)*

54. 5.1,436–1,439 (alliteration: 5.1,437=1 Ennianism in 4 lines=.25 per line=2.5 per 10 lines)

***55. 5.1,440–1,447 (alliteration: 5.1,444; 5.1,447; sigmatic ecthlipsis: 5.1,445=3 Ennianisms in 8 lines=.38 per line=3.8 per 10 lines)

56. 5.1,448–1,457 (alliteration: 5.1,453; pentasyllable: 5.1,453=2 Ennianisms in 10 lines=.2 per line=2.0 per 10 lines)

Anthropology (5.771–1,457)=116 Ennianisms in 687 lines=.17 Per lines=1.7 per 10 lines

Development of Human Life (5.925–1,457)=82 Ennianisms in 533 lines=.15 per line=1.5 per 10 lines

Origins and Evolution of Civilization (5.1,011–1,457)=60 Ennianisms in 447 lines=.13 per line=1.3 per 10 lines

DRN *6*

281 Ennianisms in 1,286 lines=.22 per line=2.2 per 10 lines; 6 Bailey paragraphs with exceptionally high frequency of Ennianisms; 11 Bailey paragraphs with exceptionally low frequency of Ennianisms; 17/51 Bailey paragraphs with abnormal frequency of Ennianisms; Longest anti-cluster without any Ennianisms=33 lines (6.1,188–1,222).

1. 6.1–42 (alliteration: 6.5; 6.19; 6.23; sigmatic ecthlipsis: 6.29; monosyllable: 6.37; 6.39=6 Ennianisms in 42 lines=.14 per line=1.4 per 10 lines)

***2. 6.43–95 (alliteration: 6.44; 6.46; 6.47; 6.54–55; 6.61; 6.62; 6.64; 6.72; 6.85; 6.88; 6.92–93; 6.95; sigmatic ecthlipsis: 6.51; pentasyllable: 6.62; monosyllable: 6.45; 6.53; 6.71; 6.87; 6.89=19 Ennianisms in 53 lines=.36 per line=3.6 per 10 lines)

3. 6.96–120 (alliteration: 6.96; 6.101; 6.115; sigmatic ecthlipsis: 6.98; pentasyllable: 6.112=5 Ennianisms in 25 lines=.2 per line=2.0 per 10 lines)

4. 6.121–131 (alliteration: 6.123; 6.127=2 Ennianisms in 11 lines=.18 per line=1.8 per 10 lines)

***5. 6.132–159 (alliteration: 6.135; 6.137; monosyllable: 6.139=3 Ennianisms in 28 lines=.11 per line=1.1 per 10 lines)*

6. 6.160–172 (pentasyllable: 6.164; monosyllable: 6.161; 6.166; 6.167=4 Ennianisms in 13 lines=.31 per line=3.1 per 10 lines)

7. 6.173–203 (alliteration: 6.182; 6.195; 6.196; sigmatic ecthlipsis: 6.195; pentasyllable: 6.189=5 Ennianisms in 31 lines=.16 per line=1.6 per 10 lines)

***8. 6.204-218 (alliteration: 6.213; 6.217-218; monosyllable: 6.206; 6.209; 6.216=5 Ennianisms in 15 lines=.33 per line=3.3 per 10 lines)

9. **6.219–238 (pentasyllable: 6.226; monosyllable: 6.238=2 Ennianisms in 20 lines=.10 per line=1.0 per 10 lines)**

10. 6.239–245 (alliteration: 6.243=1 Ennianism in 7 lines=.14 per line=1.4 per 10 lines)

11. 6.246–294 (alliteration: 6.247; 6.252; 6.255; 6.256; 6.270; 6.276; 6.284; monosyllable: 6.246; 6.249; 6.262; 6.272; 6.279; 6.288=13 Ennianisms in 49 lines=.27 per line=2.7 per 10 lines)

12. 6.295–299 (monosyllable: 6.299=1 Ennianism in 5 lines=.2 per line=2.0 per 10 lines)

13. 6.300–308 (alliteration: 6.302; 6.307–308=2 Ennianisms in 9 lines=.22 per line=2.2 per 10 lines)

14. 6.309–322 (alliteration: 6.318; monosyllable: 6.320= 2 Ennianisms in 14 lines=.14 per line=1.4 per 10 lines)

15. **6.323–345 (alliteration: 6.338; monosyllable: 6.325=2 Ennianisms in 23 lines=.09 per line=0.9 per 10 lines)**

16. 6.346–356 (alliteration: 6.350–351; pentasyllable: 6.347=2 Ennianisms in 11 lines=.18 per line=1.8 per 10 lines)

17. 6.357–378 (alliteration: 6.362; 6.368; pentasyllable: 6.374; monosyllable: 6.369=4 Ennianisms in 20 lines=.2 per line=2.0 per 10 lines)

18. 6.379–422 (alliteration: 6.386; 6.390; 6.391; 6.421; pentasyllable: 6.398; monosyllable: 6.383; 6.385; 6.390; 6.393; 6.402; 6.414=11 Ennianisms in 44 lines=.25 per line=2.5 per 10 lines)

19. 6.423–450 (alliteration: 6.433; pentasyllable: 6.424; 6.446; monosyllable: 6.432; 6.448=5 Ennianisms in 28 lines=.18 per line=1.8 per 10 lines)

20. 6.451–494 (alliteration: 6.462; 6.490; 6.494; pentasyllable: 6.453; 6.480; monosyllable: 6.458=6 Ennianisms in 44 lines=.14 per line=1.4 per 10 lines)

21. **6.495–526 (alliteration: 6.501; 6.508; 6.521; -ai: 6.497=4 Ennianisms in 32 lines=.13 per line=1.3 per 10 lines)**

***22. 6.527–534 (alliteration: 6.527; 6.534; monosyllable: 6.534=3 Ennianisms in 8 lines=.38 per line=3.8 per 10 lines)

***23. 6.535–556 (alliteration: 6.540; 6.545; -ai: 6.535; 6.540; 6.550; pentasyllable: 6.543; monosyllable: 6.541=7 Ennianisms in 21 lines=.33 per line=3.3 per 10 lines)

24. 6.557–576 (alliteration: 6.565; 6.571; 6.576; monosyllable: 6.560=4 Ennianisms in 20 lines=.20 per line=2.0 per 10 lines)

25. 6.577–607 (alliteration: 6.588; 6.589; -ai: 6.580; 6.586; 6.591; 6.598; monosyllable: 6.582=7 Ennianisms in 31 lines=.23 per line=2.3 per 10 lines)

26. 6.608–638 (alliteration: 6.608; 6.615; 6.631; sigmatic ecthlipsis: 6.618; -ai: 6.614; 6.633; monosyllable: 6.620=7 Ennianisms in 31 lines=.23 per line=2.3 per 10 lines)

27. **6.639–646 (alliteration: 6.645=1 Ennianism in 8 lines=.13 per line=1.3 per 10 lines)**

28. 6.647–679 (alliteration: 6.652; 6.679; -ai: 6.650; 6.652; 6.679; pentasyllable: 6.648; 6.653; 6.666; monosyllable: 6.663; 6.665=10 Ennianisms in 33 lines=.30 per line=3.0 per 10 lines)

29. 6.680–702 (alliteration: 6.681; -ai: 6.693; monosyllable: 6.693; 6.697=4 Ennianisms in 23 Lines=.17 per line=1.7 per 10 lines)

****30. 6.703–711 (0 Ennianisms)*

****31. 6.712–737 (alliteration: 6.719–720=1 Ennianism in 26 lines=.04 per line=0.4 per 10 lines)*

****32. 6.738–768 (alliteration: 6.741; 6.757; monosyllable: 6.740=3 Ennianisms in 31 lines=.10 per line=1.0 per 10 lines)*

****33. 6.769–780 (alliteration: 6.771; 6.773; 6.777; -ai: 6.774; pentasyllable: 6.772; 6.775; monosyllable: 6.780=7 Ennianisms in 12 lines=.58 per line=5.8 per 10 lines)*

34. 6.781–817 (alliteration: 6.789; 6.814; -ai: 6.800; 6.809; 6.814; pentasyllable: 6.802; monosyllable: 6.781=7 Ennianisms in 37 lines=.19 per line=1.9 per 10 lines)

35. 6.818–829 (alliteration: 6.826; 6.829= 2 Ennianisms in 12 lines=.17 per line=1.7 per 10 lines)

****36. 6.830–847 (alliteration: 6.846; monosyllable: 6.841=2 Ennianisms in 18 lines=.11 per line=1.1 per 10 lines)*

****37. 6.848–878 (alliteration: 6.848–849; 6.852; 6.854; 6.857; 6.859; 6.862; 6.873; 6.877; -ai: 6.854; 6.863; 6.872; 6.874; monosyllable: 6.861; 6.866; 6.877=15 Ennianisms in 31 lines=.48 per line=4.8 per 10 lines)*

****38. 6.879–905 (alliteration: 6.879; 6.882; 6.896; sigmatic ecthlipsis: 6.893; -ai: 6.890; 6.897; pentasyllable: 6.889; monosyllable: 6.887; 6.896; 6.898; 6.905=11 Ennianisms in 27 lines=.41 per line=4.1 per 10 lines)*

39. 6.906–916 (alliteration: 6.914; monosyllable: 6.911=2 Ennianisms in 11 lines=.18 per line=1.8 per 10 lines)

****40. 6.917–920 (alliteration: 6.918; 6.920; monosyllable: 6.917=3 Ennianisms in 4 lines=.75 per line=7.5 per 10 lines)*

41. 6.921–935 (alliteration: 6.928; monosyllable: 6.922=2 Ennianisms in 15 lines=.13 per line=1.3 per 10 lines)

****42. 6.936–958 (alliteration: 6.936; 6.937; 6.942; 6.951; 6.954; 6.956–957; sigmatic ecthlipsis: 6.943; pentasyllable: 6.947; 6.955; monosyllable: 6.936; 6.938; 6.940=12 Ennianisms in 23 lines=.52 per line=5.2 per 10 lines)*

43. 6.959–978 (aliteration: 6.967; 6.969; 6.976; sigmatic ecthlipsis: 6.972; monosyllable: 6.974; 6.976=6 Ennianisms in 20 lines=.3 per line=3.0 per 10 lines)

44. 6.979–997 (alliteration: 6.992; 6.995; monosyllable: 6.979; 6.985=4 Ennianisms in 19 lines=.21 per line=2.1 per 10 lines)

45. 6.998–1,041 (alliteration: 6.1,018; 6.1,021; pentasyllable: 6.1,032; 6.1,036; 6.1,040; monosyllable: 6.1,001; 6.1,017; 6.1,029=8 Ennianisms in 44 lines=.18 per line=1.8 per 10 lines)

46. 6.1,042–1,064 (alliteration: 6.1,059; monosyllable: 6.1,054; 6.1,057; 6.1,063=4 Ennianisms in 23 Lines=.17 per line=1.7 per 10 lines)

47. 6.1,065–1,089 (alliteration: 6.1,075; 6.1,084; -ai: 6.1,072; pentasyllable: 6.1,066; monosyllable: 6.1,076; 6.1,082=6 Ennianisms in 35 lines=.17 per line=1.7 per 10 lines)

48. 6.1,090–1,137 (alliteration: 6.1,091; 6.1,096; 6.1,107; 6.1,110; 6.1,122; 6.1,123; pentasyllable: 6.1,098; 6.1,125; 6.1,133; monosyllable: 6.1,095; 6.1,101; 6.1,105; 6.1,130=13 Ennianisms in 48 lines=.27 per line=2.7 per 10 lines)

****49. 6.1,138–1,229 (alliteration: 6.1,157; 6.1,159; 6.1,169; 6.1,183; 6.1,188; -ai: 6.1,153; monosyllable: 6.1,222=7 Ennianisms in 92 lines=.08 per line=0.8 per 10 lines)*

50. 6.1,230–1,251 (alliteration: 6.1,236; 6.1,240; 6.1,248; 6.1,251; -ai: 6.1,239=5 Ennianisms in 22 Lines=.23 per line=2.3 per 10 lines)

*****51. 6.1,252–1,286 (alliteration: 6.1,254–1,255; 6.1,260–1,261; 6.1,264; 6.1,267; 6.1,269; 6.1,272; 6.1,274; 6.1,276; 6.1,285; pentasyllable: 6.1,260; 6.1,263; 6.1,275; 6.1,277; 6.1,286=14 Ennianisms in 35 lines=.40 per line=4.0 per 10 lines)**

Works Cited

Adamik, B. (2014) "Zur Prosodie, Metrik und Interpretation von Catulls Carmen 116," *WS* 127: 151–164.

Aicher, P. J. (1989/90) "Ennian Artistry: *Annals* 175–79 and 78–83 (Sk.)," *CJ* 85: 218–224.

Albiani, M. G. (2002) "Ancora su 'bevitori d'acqua' e 'bevitori di vino' (Asclep. XLV, Hedyl. V G.-P.)," *Eikasmos* 13: 159–164.

Armstrong, D. (1995) "The Impossibility of Metathesis: Philodemus and Lucretius on Form and Content," in D. Obbink, (ed.) *Philodemus and Poetry: Poetic Theory and Practice in Lucretius, Philodemus, and Horace*, Oxford, 210–232.

Asmis, E. (1995) "Epicurean Poetics," in D. Obbink (ed.) *Philodemus and Poetry: Poetic Theory and Practice in Lucretius, Philodemus, and Horace*, Oxford, 15–34.

Asmis, E. (2020) "A Tribute to the Hero: Marx's Interpretation of Epicurus in his Dissertation," in O'Rourke (2020a), Cambridge, 241–258.

Asper, M. (1997) *Onomata Allotria: Zur Genese, Struktur und Funktion poetologischer Metaphern bei Kallimachos*, Stuttgart.

Atack, C. (2019) "Tradition and Innovation in the *Kosmos*-Polis Analogy," in P. Horky (ed.) *Cosmos in the Ancient World*, Cambridge, 164–187.

Baier, T. (2008) "Marullus und Lukrez," in E. Lefèvre and E. Schäfer (eds.) *Michael Marullus: Ein Grieche als Renaissancedichter in Italien*, Tübingen, 217–227.

Bailey, C. (1947) *Titi Lucreti Cari "De Rerum Natura" Libri Sex*, Oxford.

Bakker, F. (2016) *Epicurean Meteorology: Sources, Method, Scope and Organization*, Leiden.

Bakker, F. (2018) "The End of Epicurean Infinity: Critical Reflections on the Epicurean Infinite Universe," in F. Bakker, D. Bellis, and C. Palmerino (eds.) *Space, Imagination, and the Cosmos from Antiquity to the Early Modern Period*, Cham, 41–67.

Barchiesi, A. (1995) "Figure dell'intertestualità nell' epica romana," *Lexis* 13: 49–67.

Batstone, W. W. (1996) "The Fragments of Furius Antias," *CQ* 46: 387–402.

Biggs, T. (2015) "Review of Fisher 2014, Goldschmidt 2013, and Elliott 2013," *AJP* 136: 713–719.

Biggs, T. (2020) "Allegory and Authority in Latin Verse-Historiography," in Damon and Farrell (2020), Cambridge, 91–106.

Bignone, E. (1929) "Ennio ed Empedocle," *RFIC* 57: 10–30.

Bignone, E. (1945) *Storia della letteratura latina*, vol. 2, Florence.

Boyancé, P. (1963) *Lucrèce et l'Épicurisme*, Paris.

Breed, B. and A. Rossi (eds.) (2006) "Ennius and the Invention of Roman Epic," special issue, *Arethusa* 39.3.

Brink, C. O. (1972) "Ennius and the Hellenistic Worship of Homer," *AJP* 93: 547–567.

Brown, A. (2010) *The Return of Lucretius to Renaissance Florence*, Cambridge, MA.

Brown, B. K. M. (2016) *The Mirror of Epic: The Iliad and History*, Berrima.

Brown, R. D. (1982) "Lucretius and Callimachus," *ICS* 7: 77–97.

Buchheit, V. (1971) "Epikurs Triumph des Geistes," *Hermes* 99: 303–323.

Büchner, K. (1936) *Beobachtungen über Vers und Gedankengang bei Lukrez* (*Hermes* Einzelschriften 1), Wiesbaden.

Buffière, F. (1956) *Les mythes d'Homère et la pensée grêcque*, Paris.

Buglass, A. (2019) "Lucretius' Journey to the Underworld: Poetic Memory and *allegoresis*," in R. Falconer and M. Scherer (eds.) *A Quest for Remembrance: The Underworld in Classical and Modern Literature*, New York, 61–86.

Burkert, W. (1972) *Lore and Science in Ancient Pythagoreanism*, Cambridge, MA.

Burrow, C. (2019) *Imitating Authors: Plato to Futurity*, Oxford.

Butterfield, D. (2008) "Sigmatic Ecthlipsis in Lucretius," *Hermes* 136: 188–205.

Cameron, A. (1995) *Callimachus and His Critics*, Princeton.

Campbell, G. (2003) *Lucretius on Creation and Evolution: A Commentary on "De Rerum Natura" Book Five, Lines 772–1104*, Oxford.

Cartault, A. G. C. (1898) *La Flexion dans Lucrèce*, Paris.

Casali, S. (2006) "The Poet at War: Ennius on the Field in Silius' Punica," in Breed and Rossi (2006), 569–593.

Catto, B. (1988–1989) "Venus and Natura in Lucretius," *CJ* 84: 97–104.

Christ, W. (1879) *Metrik der Griechen und Römer*, Leipzig.

Clark, J. H. (2015) "Review of Elliott 2013," *Histos* 9: I–VIII.

Clark, J. H. (forthcoming) "How Many Furii Poetae? The Hexameter Fragments Reconsidered," *PLLS* 18.

Clarke, K. (2008) *Making Time for the Past: Local History and the Polis*, Oxford.

Clausen, W. V. (1987) *Vergil's "Aeneid" and the Tradition of Hellenistic Poetry*, Berkeley.

Clay, D. (1983) *Lucretius and Epicurus*, Ithaca.

Cole, S. (2006) "Cicero, Ennius, and the Concept of Apotheosis at Rome," in Breed and Rossi (2006), 531–548.

Commager, H. S. (1957) "Lucretius' Interpretation of the Plague," *HSCP* 62: 105–118.

Conte, G. B. (1966) "Hypsos e diatriba nello stile di Lucrezio," *Maia* 18: 338–368.

Conte, G. B. (1986) *The Rhetoric of Imitation: Genre and Poetic Memory in Virgil and Other Latin Poets*, ed. and trans. C. Segal, Ithaca.

Conte, G. B. (1994a) *Genres and Readers: Lucretius, Love Elegy, Pliny's Encyclopedia*, Baltimore.

Conte, G. B. (1994b) *Latin Literature: A History*, Baltimore.

Conte, G. B. (2007) *The Poetry of Pathos: Studies in Vergilian Epic*, Oxford.

Conte, G. B. (2013) *Ope Ingenii: Experiences of Textual Criticism*, Berlin.

Cordier, A. (1939) *L'Allitération Latine: Le procédé dans l'Énéide de Vergile*, Paris.

Courcelle, P. (1955) "Histoire du cliché virgilien des cent bouches (Georg. II, 42-44 = Aen. VI, 625–627," *REL* 33: 231–240.

Courtney, E. (1993) *The Fragmentary Latin Poets*, Oxford.

Coxon, A. H. (1986) *The Fragments of Parmenides*, Assen.

Crierlaard, J. P. (1995) "Homer, History and Archeology: Some Remarks on the Date of the Homeric World," in J. P. Crierlaard (ed.) *Homeric Questions*, Amsterdam, 201–288.

Crowther, N. B. (1979) "Wine and Water as Symbols of Inspiration," *Mnemosyne* 32: 1–11.

Damon, C. and J. Farrell (eds.) (2020) *Ennius' "Annals": Poetry and History*, Cambridge.

Damon, C. (2020) "Looking for auctoritas in Ennius' Annals," in Damon and Farrell (2020), Cambridge, 125–146.

Davies, M. (2015) *The Theban Epics*, Cambridge, MA.

Dench, E. (2005) *Romulus' Asylum: Roman Identities from the Age of Alexander to the Age of Hadrian*, Oxford.

Deufert, M. (1996) *Pseudo-Lukrezisches im Lukrez: Die unechten Verse in Lukrezens "De rerum natura,"* Berlin.

Deufert, M. (1999) "Lukrez und Marullus: Ein kurzer Blick in die Werkstatt eines humanistischen Interpolators," *RhM* 142: 210–223.

Deufert, M. (2017) *Prolegomena zur editio teubneriana des Lukrez* (Untersuchungen zur antiken Literatur und Geschichte 124), Berlin.

Deufert, M. (2018) *Kritischer Kommentar zu Lukrezens "De rerum natura,"* Berlin.

Deufert, M. (2019) *Titus Lucretius Carus "De Rerum Natura" Libri VI*, Berlin.

Deutsch, R. (1939) *The Pattern of Sound in Lucretius*, Diss. Bryn Mawr.

Diels, H. (1956) *Doxographi Graeci*, Berlin (reprint of 1879 edition).

Donahue, H. (1993) *The Song of the Swan: Lucretius and the Influence of Callimachus*, Lanham, MD.

Duckworth, G. (1969) *Vergil and Classical Hexameter Poetry*, Ann Arbor.

Edmunds, L. (2001) *Intertextuality and the Reading of Roman Poetry*, Baltimore.

Elliott, J. (2007) "The Voices of Ennius' *Annales*," in Fitzgerald and Gowers (2007), 38–54.

Elliott, J. (2010) "Ennius as Universal Historian: The Case of the *Annales*," in P. Liddel and A. T. Fear (eds.) *Historiae mundi: Studies in Universal History*, London, 148–161.

Elliott, J. (2013) *Ennius and the Architecture of the Annales*, Cambridge.

Elliott, J. (2015) "The Epic Vantage Point: Roman Historiographical Allusion Reconsidered," *Histos* 9: 277–311.

Fabrizi, V. (2012) *Mores veteresque novosque: Rappresentazioni del passato e del presente di Roma negli Annales di Ennio*, Pisa.

Fabrizi, V. (2020) "History, Philosophy, and the *Annals*," in Damon and Farrell (2020), Cambridge, 45–62.

Fantham, E. (2006) "'Dic si quid potes de sexto annali': The Literary Legacy of Ennius' Pyrrhic War," in Breed and Rossi (2006), 549–568.

Fantuzzi, M. and R. Hunter (2004) *Tradition and Innovation in Hellenistic Poetry*, Cambridge.

Farmer, M. (2013) "Rivers and Rivalry in Petronius, Horace, Callimachus, and Aristophanes," *AJP* 134: 481–506.

Farrell, J. (1988) "Lucretius, *DRN* 5.44 *insinuandum*," *CQ* 38: 179–185.

Farrell, J. (1991) *Vergil's* Georgics *and the Traditions of Ancient Epic: The Art of Allusion in Literary History*, Oxford.

Farrell, J. (1994) "The Structure of Lucretius' 'Anthropology,'" *MD* 33: 81–95.

Farrell, J. (2005) "Intention and Intertext," *Phoenix* 59: 98–111.

Farrell, J. (2008) "The Six Books of Lucretius' *De Rerum Natura*: Antecedents and Influence," *Dictynna* 5: 115–139.

Farrell, J. (2014) "Philosophy in Vergil," in M. Garani and D. Konstan (eds.) *The Philosophizing Muse: The Influence of Greek Philosophy on Roman Poetry*, Cambridge, 61–89.

Farrell, J. (2020) "Was Memmius a Good King?," in O'Rourke, D. (2020a), Cambridge, 219–240.

Feeney, D. (1991) *The Gods in Epic: Poets and Critics of the Classical Tradition*, Oxford.

Feeney, D. (1999) "*Mea tempora*: Patterning of Time in Ovid's *Metamorphoses*," in P. Hardie, A. Barchiesi, and S. Hinds (eds.) *Ovidian Transformations: Essays on Ovid's Metamorphoses and its Reception*, Cambridge, 13–30.

Feeney, D. (2007) *Caesar's Calendar: Ancient Time and the Beginnings of History*, Berkeley.

Feeney, D. (2016) *Beyond Greek: The Beginnings of Latin Literature*, Cambridge, MA.

Finley, M. (1954) *The World of Odysseus*, New York.

Fisher, J. (2014) *The "Annals" of Quintus Ennius and the Italic Tradition*, Baltimore.

Fitzgerald, W. and E. Gowers (eds.) (2007) *Ennius Perennis: The "Annals" and Beyond*, Cambridge Philological Society, Cambridge.

Flores, E. (2002) *Titus Lucretius Carus: "De Rerum Natura." Edizione critica con introduzione e versione. Volume Primo (Libri I–III)*, Naples.

Flores, E. (2011) *Livi Andronici Odusia: Introduzione, edizione critica e versione italiana*, Naples.

Flores, E. et al. (2002) *Quinto Ennio, "Annali" Vol. II: Libri I–VIII. Commentari*, Naples.

Flores, E. et al. (2006) *Quinto Ennio, "Annali" Vol. IV: Libri IX–XVIII. Commentari*, Naples.

Flores, E. et al. (2009) *Quinto Ennio, "Annali" Vol. V: Frammenti de collocazione incerta. Commentari*, Naples.

Foster, E. (2009) "The Rhetoric of Materials: Thucydides and Lucretius," *AJP* 130: 367–399.

Fowler, D. (1997) "On the Shoulders of Giants: Intertextuality and Classical Studies," *MD* 39: 13–34.

Fowler, D. (2000a) "The Didactic Plot," in M. Depew and D. Obbink (eds.) *Matrices of Genre: Authors, Canons, and Society*, Cambridge, MA, 205–219.

Fowler, D. (2000b) "Philosophy and Literature in Lucretian Intertextuality," in *Roman Constructions: Readings in Postmodern Latin*, Oxford, 138–155.

Fowler, P. (1997) "Lucretian Conclusions," in D. Roberts, F. Dunn and D. Fowler (eds.) *Classical Closure: Reading the End in Greek and Latin Literature*, Princeton, 112–138.

Frampton, S. (2019) *Empire of Letters: Writing in Roman Literature and Thought from Lucretius to Ovid*, Oxford.

Friedländer, P. (1941) "Pattern of Sound and Atomistic Theory in Lucretius," *AJP* 62: 16–34.

Friedrich, W. H. (1948) "Ennius-Erklärungen," *Philologus* 97: 277–301.

Furley, D. (1970) "Variations on Empedocles in the Proem of Lucretius," *BICS* 17: 55–64.

Furley, D. (1989) *Cosmic Problems: Essays on Greek and Roman Philosophy of Nature*, Cambridge.

Gale, M. (1991) "Man and Beast in Lucretius and the *Georgics*," *CQ* 41: 414–426.

Gale, M. (1994) *Myth and Poetry in Lucretius*, Cambridge.

Gale, M. (2000) *Virgil on the Nature of Things: The "Georgics," Lucretius, and the Didactic Tradition*, Cambridge.

Gale, M. (2001a) *Lucretius and the Didactic Epic*, London.

Gale, M. (2001b) "Etymological Wordplay and Poetic Succession in Lucretius," *CP* 96: 168–72.

Gale, M. (2004) "The Story of Us: A Narratological Analysis of Lucretius' *De Rerum Natura*," in M. Gale (ed.) *Latin Epic and Didactic Poetry: Genre, Tradition and Individuality*, Swansea, 49–71.

Gale, M. (2005) "*Avia Pieridum loca*: Tradition and Innovation in Lucretius," in M. Horster and C. Reitz (eds.) *Wissensvermittlung in dichterischer Gestalt*, Stuttgart, 175–191.

Gale, M. (2007a) "Lucretius and Previous Poetic Traditions," in Gillespie and Hardie (2007), 59–75.

Gale, M. (ed.) (2007b) *Oxford Readings in Classical Studies: Lucretius*, Oxford.

Gale, M. (2009) *Lucretius: "De Rerum Natura" V*, Aris and Phillips.

Gale, M. (2013) "Piety, Labour, and Justice in Lucretius and Hesiod," in Lehoux, Morrison, and Sharrock (2013), 25–50.

Galzerano, M. (2018) "*Machina mundi*: significato e fortuna di una iunctura da Lucrezio alla tarda antichita'," in *Bollettino Di Studi Latini* 48: 10–34.

Galzerano, M. (2019) *La fine del mondo nel De rerum natura di Lucrezio*, Berlin.

Garani, M. (2007) *Empedocles Redivivus: Poetry and Analogy in Lucretius*, New York.

Geddes, A. G. (1984) "Who's Who in Homeric Society?," *CQ* 34: 17–36.

Gee, E. (2016) "Dogs, Snakes and Heroes: Hybridism and Polemic in Lucretius' *De Rerum Natura*," in S. Oakley and R. Hunter (eds.) *Latin Literature and its Transmission: Papers in Honour of Michael Reeve*, Cambridge, 108–141.

Gee, E. (2020) "The Rising and Setting Soul in Lucretius, *De Rerum Natura* 3," in O'Rourke (2020a), 195–215.

Gellar-Goad, T. H. M. (2018) "Lucretius' Personified Natura Rerum, Satire, and Ennius' *Saturae*," *Phoenix* 72: 143–160.

Gellar-Goad, T. H. M. (2020) *Laughing Atoms, Laughing Matter: Lucretius' De Rerum Natura and Satire*, Ann Arbor.

Gigon, O. (1978) "Lukrez und Ennius," in O. Gigon (ed.) *Lucrèce*, Vandoeuvres, 167–196.

Gildenhard, I. (2003) "The 'Annalist' before the Annalists: Ennius and his *Annales*," in U. Eigler et al. (eds.) *Formen römischer Geschichtsschreibung von den Anfängen bis Livius: Gattungen, Autoren, Kontexte*, Darmstadt, 93–114.

Gildenhard, I. (2016) "Review of Elliott 2013," *Gnomon* 88: 510–512.

Gillespie, S. (2010) "Literary Afterlives: Metempsychosis from Ennius to Jorge Luis Borges," in P. Hardie and H. Moore (eds.) *Classical Literary Careers and Their Reception*, Cambridge, 209–225.

Gillespie, S. and P. Hardie (2007) *The Cambridge Companion to Lucretius*, Cambridge.

Giuliano, F. M. (1997) "οὐδ᾽ ἀπὸ κρήνης πίνω: Ancora poetica della brevitas?," *MD* 38: 153–173.

Glauthier, P. (2020) "Hybrid Ennius: Cultural and Poetic Multiplicity in the *Annals*," in Damon and Farrell (2020), Cambridge, 25–44.

Goldberg, S. (1995) *Epic in Republican Rome*, Oxford.

Goldberg, S. (2005) *Constructing Literature in the Roman Republic: Poetry and Its Reception*, Cambridge.

Goldberg, S. (2009) "Review of Flores et al.," *Paideia* 64: 637–655.

Goldberg, S. (2018) *Fragmentary Republican Latin: Ennius*, Cambridge, MA.

Goldberg, S. (2020) "Ennius and the *fata librorum*," in Damon and Farrell (2020), Cambridge, 169–187.

Goldberg, S. (forthcoming) "The Language of Early Latin Epic," in J. Adams, A. Chahoud, and G. Pezzini (eds.) *Early Latin: Constructs, Diversity, Reception*, Cambridge.

Goldschmidt, N. (2013) *Shaggy Crowns: Ennius' Annales and Virgil's Aeneid*, Oxford.

Goldschmidt, N. (2015) "Review of Elliott 2013," *JRS* 105: 424–425.

Goldschmidt, N. (2020) "Reading the 'Implied Author' in Lucretius' De Rerum Natura," in O'Rourke (2020a), Cambridge, 43–58.

Goodyear, F. R. D. (1972) *The "Annals of Tacitus," Books 1–6, Edited with a Commentary, Volume 1: Annals 1.1–54*, Cambridge.

Gowers, E. (2007) "The *cor* of Ennius" in Fitzgerald and Gowers (2007), 17–37.

Gratwick, A. S. (1982) "Ennius' *Annales*," in P. Easterling and E. J. Kenney (eds.) *The Cambridge Companion to Classical Literature*, vol. 2: *Latin Literature*, E. J. Kenney and W. V. Clausen (eds.), Cambridge, 60–76.

Grimal, P. (1963) "Lucrèce et son public," *REL* 41: 91–100.

Gruen, E. (1984) *The Hellenistic World and the Coming of Rome*, 2 vols., Berkeley.

Habinek, T. (2006) "The Wisdom of Ennius," in Breed and Rossi (2006), 471–488.

Haimson Lushkov, A. (2020) "Livy's Ennius," in Damon and Farrell (2020), Cambridge, 211–227.

Hanses, M. (forthcoming) "Page, Stage, Image: Confronting Ennius with Lucretius' *De Rerum Natura*," in G. Davis and S. Yona (eds.) *Epicurus in Rome*, Cambridge.

Hardie, P. (1986) *Virgil's "Aeneid": Cosmos and Imperium*, Oxford.

Hardie, P. (1995) "The Speech of Pythagoras in Ovid *Metamorphoses* 15: Empedoclean *Epos*," *CQ* 45: 204–214.

Hardie, P., V. Prosperi, and D. Zucca (2020) *Lucretius Poet and Philosopher: Backgrounds and Fortunes of De Rerum Natura*, Berlin.

Hardie, W. R. (1907) "A Note on the History of the Latin Hexamter," *Journal of Philology* 30: 266–279.

Harkness, A. G. (1910) "The Final Monosyllable in Latin Prose and Poetry," *AJP* 31: 154–174.

Harrison, S. J. (1990) "Cicero's 'De Temporibus Suis': The Evidence Reconsidered," *Hermes* 118: 455–463.

Harrison, S. J. (2002) "Ennius and the Prologue to Lucretius *DRN* 1 (1.1–148)," *LICS* 1.4: 1–13.

Häussler, R. (1976) *Das historische Epos der Griechen und Römer bis Vergil*, Heidelberg.

Havelock, E. A. (1958) "Parmenides and Odysseus," *HSCP* 63: 133–143.

Heinze, R. (1897) *T. Lucretius Carus "De rerum natura," Buch III*, Leipzig.

Hellegouarc'h, J. (1964) *Le Monosyllabe dans l'hexamètre latin: Essai de métrique verbale*, Paris.

Hendren, G. (2012) "Woven Alliteration in the *De Rerum Natura*," *CJ* 107: 409–421.

Hershbell, J. P. (1972) "Parmenides and *Outis* in *Odyssey* 9," *CJ* 68: 178–180.

Herzog, R. and P. L. Schmidt (eds.) (2002) *Handbuch der Lateinischen Literatur der Antike. Erster Band: von den Anfängen bis Sullas Tod*, Munich.

Hinds, S. (1987) "Language at the Breaking Point: Lucretius 1.452," *CQ* 37: 450–453.

Hinds, S. (1998) *Allusion and Intertext: Dynamics of Appropriation in Roman Poetry*, Cambridge.

Hollis, A. (2007) *Fragments of Roman Poetry c. 60 BC–AD 20*, Oxford.

Holtze, F. W. (1868) *Syntaxis Lucretianae Lineamenta*, Leipzig.

Housman, A. E. (1900) "Review of *Lucreti de rerum natura libri sex, recognovit brevique adnotatione critica instruxit Cyrillus Bailey. Oxonii, e typographeo Clarendoniano. No Date. Pp. 248*," *CR* 14: 367–368.

Hug, T. (1852) *Q. Ennii Annalium Librorum VII–IX sive de Bellis Punicis Fragmenta*, Bonn.

Hunter, R. (1993) *The Argonautica of Apollonius: Literary Studies*, Cambridge.

Hutchinson, G. O. (2001) "The Date of De Rerum Natura," *CQ* 51: 150–162.

Inwood, B. (2001) *The Poem of Empedocles: A Text and Translation with an Introduction*, Toronto.

Jackson Knight, W. F. (1950) *Accentual Symmetry in Vergil*, Oxford.

Jocelyn, H. D. (1972) "The Poems of Quintus Ennius," *ANRW* 1.2: 987–1026.

Johnson, W. R. (2000) *Lucretius and the Modern World*, London.

Kambylis, A. (1965) *Die Dichterweihe und ihre Symbolik*, Heidelberg.

Kennedy, D. F. (2013) "The Political Epistemology of Infinity," in Lehoux, Morrison, and Sharrock (2013), 51–68.

Kennedy, D. (2020) "Plato and Lucretius on the Theoretical Subject," in O'Rourke (2020a), Cambridge, 259–281.

Kenney, E. J. (1970) "Doctus Lucretius," *Mnemosyne* 23: 366–392.

Kenney, E. J. (1971) *Lucretius, "De Rerum Natura" Book III*, Cambridge.

Kenney, E. J. (1972) "The Historical Imagination of Lucretius," *G&R* 19: 12–24.

Kenney, E. J. (2004) "Review, *Lucretius I–III. E. Flores: Titus Lucretius Carus: "De Rerum Natura." Edizione critica con introduzione e versione. Volume primo (Libri I–III), Naples*," *CR* 54: 366–370.

Kenney, E. J. (2007) "Lucretian Texture: Style, Metre, and Rhetoric in the *De Rerum Natura*," in Gillespie and Hardie (2007), 92–110.

Kenney, E. J. (2014) *Lucretius: "De Rerum Natura" Book III*, 2nd ed., Cambridge.

Kim, L. (2010) *Homer between History and Fiction in Imperial Greek Literature*, Cambridge.

King, J. (1985) "Lucretius the Neoteric," in W. Calder, U. Goldsmith, and P. Kenevan (eds.) *Hypatia: Essays in Classics, Comparative Literature and Philosophy Presented to Hazel E. Barnes on Her Seventieth Birthday*, Boulder, 27–43.

Kleve, K. (1990) "Ennius in Herculaneum," *CErc* 20: 5–16.

Knox, P. (1985) "Wine, Water, and Callimachean Polemics," *HSCP* 89: 107–119.

Knox, P. (1999) "Lucretius on the Narrow Road," *HSCP* 99: 275–287.

Krebs, C. B. (2013) "Caesar, Lucretius and the dates of *De Rerum Natura* and the *Comentarii*," *CQ* 63: 772–779.

Kristeva, J. (1969) "Word, Dialogue and Novel" (ch. 4), in *Sémeiôtiké: Recherches pour une sémanalyse*, Paris.

Kronenberg, L. (2019) "The Light Side of the Moon: A Lucretian Acrostic (*LUCE*, 5.712–15) and Its Relationship to Acrostics in Homer (*LEUKÊ, IL.* 24.1–5) and Aratus (*LEPTÊ, PHAEN.* 783–87)," *CP* 114: 278–292.

Kvičala, J. (1906) "Enniana II," *Z. für die öst. Gym.* 57: 97–120

Lamberton, R. (1986) *Homer the Theologian: Neoplatonist Allegorical Reading and the Growth of the Epic Tradition*, Berkeley.

Leen, A. (1984) "The Rhetorical Value of the Similes in Lucretius," in D. Bright and E. Ramage (eds.) *Classical Texts and Their Traditions: Studies in Honor of C. R. Trahman*, Chico, CA, 107–123.

Lehoux, D., A. Morrison, and A. Sharrock (2013) *Lucretius: Poetry, Philosophy, Science*, Oxford.

Leo, F. (1913) *Geschichte der römischen Literatur*, Berlin.

Leonard, W. E. and S. B. Smith (1965) *Titus Lucretius Carus "De Rerum Natura" Libri Sex*, 2nd ed., Madison.

Leumann, M. (1977) *Lateinische Laut- und Formen-Lehre*, Munich.

Lindsay, W. M. (1893) "The Saturnian Meter," *AJP* 14: 139–170, 305–334.

Long, A. A. and D. N. Sedley (1987) *The Hellenistic Philosophers*, Cambridge.

Lück, W. (1932) *Die Quellenfragen im 5 und 6 Buch des Lukrez*, Breslau.

Lyne, R. O. A. M. (1978) "The Neoteric Poets," *CQ* 28: 167–187.

Macleod, C. W. (1973) "Catullus 116," *CQ* 23: 304–309.

Maggiali, G. (2008) "Ennio in Catullo 15: Dall'apoteosi alla rhaphanidosis," *Paideia* 63: 157–161.

Maguinness, W. S. (1965) "The Language of Lucretius," in D. Dudley (ed.) *Lucretius*, London, 69–93.

Marouzeau, J. (1946) *Traité de stylistique latine*, Paris.

Martindale, C. (1993) *Redeeming the Text: Latin Poetry and the Hermeneutics of Reception*, Cambridge.

Marx, F. (1927) "De Lucretii prosodia Enniana, Indog." *Forsch* 45: 191–195.

Masi, F. (2020) "Lucretius on the Mind–Body Relation: The Case of Dreams," in Hardie, Prosperi, and Zucca (2020), 43–60.

Mastandrea, P. (2008) "Mamurra 'ennianista': Catullo 115 e dintorni," in P. Arduini et al. (eds.) *Studi offerti ad Alessandro Perutelli*, Rome, 175–190.

Mayer, R. (1990) "The Epic of Lucretius," *PLLS* 6: 35–43.

McOsker, M. (2019) "Head-Fake: Two Jokes in Lucretius 3.136–150," *CQ* 69: 903–904.

Merrill, W. A. (1892) "Alliteration in Lucretius," *TAPA* 23: ix–x.

Merrill, W. A. (1918) *Parallelisms and Coincidences in Lucretius and Ennius*, Berkeley.

Merrill, W. A. (1921) *Lucretius and Cicero's Verse*, Berkeley.

Merrill, W. A. (1923) *The Lucretian Hexameter*, Berkeley.

Merrill, W. A. (1924a) *The Characteristics of Lucretius' Verse*, Berkeley.

Merrill, W. A. (1924b) *The Metrical Technique of Lucretius and Cicero*, Berkeley.

Merula, P. (1595) *Q. Enni Annalium LIBB. XIIX Fragmenta*, Leiden.

Montiglio, S. (2011) *From Villain to Hero: Odysseus in Ancient Thought*, Ann Arbor.

Morenval, A. (2017) *Le tout et l'infini dans le "De rerum natura" de Lucrèce*, Amsterdam.

Morgan, L. (2010) *Musa Pedestris: Metre and Meaning in Roman Verse*, Oxford.

Morgan, L. and B. Taylor (2017) "Memmius the Epicurean," *CQ* 67: 528–541.

Morris, I. (1986) "The Use and Abuse of Homer," *CA* 5: 81–138.

Morrison, A. D. (2020) "Arguing Over Text(s): Master-Texts vs. Intertexts in the Criticism of Lucretius," in O'Rourke (2020a), Cambridge, 157–176.

Mourelatos, A. (1970) *The Route of Parmenides: A Study of Word, Image and Argument in the Fragments*, New Haven.

Munro, H. A. J. (1886) *T. Lucreti Cari "De Rerum Natura" Libri Sex*, Cambridge.

Murgia, C. E. (2000) "'The Most Desperate Textual Crux' in Lucretius-5.1442," *CP* 95: 304–317.

Murley, C. (1947) "Lucretius, *De Rerum Natura*, Viewed as Epic," *TAPA* 78: 336–346.

Murrin, M. (1980) *The Allegorical Epic: Essays in Its Rise and Decline*, Chicago.

Nelis, D. (1992) "Demodocus and the Song of Orpheus: (Ap. Rhod. Arg. I, 496–511)," *MH* 49: 153–170.

Nelis, D. (2000) "Apollonius Rhodius and the Traditions of Latin Epic Poetry," in M. Harder, R. Regtuit, and G. Wakker (eds.) *Apollonius Rhodius (Hellenistica Groningana 4)*, Leuven, 85–103.

Nethercut, J. S. (2014) "Ennius and the Revaluation of Traditional Historiography in Lucretius' *De Rerum Natura*," in J. Ker and C. Pieper (eds.) *Valuing the Past in the Greco-Roman World*, Leiden, 435–461.

Nethercut, J. S. (2017) "Empedocles' 'Roots' in Lucretius' *De Rerum Natura*," *AJP* 138: 85–105.

Nethercut, J. S. (2018a) "The Alexandrian Footnote in Lucretius' *De Rerum Natura*," *Mnemosyne* 71: 75–99.

Nethercut, J. S. (2018b) "Provisional Argumentation and Lucretius' Honeyed Cup," *CQ* 68: 523–533.

Nethercut, J. S. (2019) "History and myth in Graeco-Roman epic," in C. Reitz and S. Finkmann (eds.) *Structures of Epic Poetry. Volume I: Foundations*, Berlin, 193-211.

Nethercut, J. S. (2020a) "How Ennian Was Latin Epic Between the Annals and Lucretius?," in Damon and Farrel (2020), Cambridge, 188–210.

Nethercut, J. S. (2020b) "*Urbs/Orbis*: Urban Cataclysm in Lucretius' *De Rerum Natura*," in V. Closs and E. Keitel (eds.) *Urban Disasters and the Roman Imagination*, Berlin, 115–130.

Nethercut, J. S. (2020c) "Callimachus, Lucretius and Didactic Elements in Vergil's *Aeneid*-Proem," *CP* 115: 727-736.

Nethercut J. S. (2020d) "Lucretian Echoes: Sound as Metaphor for Literary Allusion in DRN 4.549–594," in O'Rourke (2020a), Cambridge, 124–139.

Nisbet, R. G. M. and N. Rudd (2004) *A Commentary on Horace: Odes Book III*, Oxford.

Noller, E. M. (2019) *Die Ordnung der Welt: Darstellungsformen von Dynamik, Statik und Emergenz in Lukrez' "De Rerum Natura,"* Heidelberg.

Norden, E. (1916) *Ennius und Vergilius*, Leipzig.

Norden, E. (1927) *Aeneis Buch VI*, 3rd ed., Stuttgart.

O'Hara, J. J. (2007) *Inconsistency in Roman Epic: Studies in Catullus, Lucretius, Vergil, Ovid and Lucan*, Cambridge.

O'Keefe, T. (2020) "Lucretius and the Philosophical Use of Literary Persuasion," in O'Rourke (2020a), Cambridge, 177–194.

O'Rourke, D. (ed.) (2020a) *Approaches to Lucretius: Traditions and Innovations in Reading the "De Rerum Natura,"* Cambridge.

O'Rourke, D. (2020b) "Infinity, Enclosure and False Closure in Lucretius' *De Rerum Natura,"* in O'Rourke (2020a), Cambridge, 103–123.

Otis, B. (1964) *Virgil: A Study in Civilized Poetry,* Oxford.

Pascucci, G. (1959) "Ennio, Ann., 561–6 vs 2 e un tipico procedimento di ΑΥΞΗΣΙΣ nella poesia Latina," *SIFC* 31: 79–99.

Pasoli, E. (1970) "Ideologia nella poesia: Lo stile di Lucrezio," *L&S* 5: 367–386.

Pasquali, G. (1942) "Arte Allusiva," *L'Italia che Scrive* 25: 185–187.

Patin, M. (1868) *Études sur la poésie latine,* Paris.

Pavlock, B. (2013) "Mentula in Catullus 114 and 115," *CW* 106: 595–607.

Pearce, T. (1966) "The Enclosing Word Order in the Latin Hexameter," *CQ* 16: 140–171, 298–320.

Pezzini, G. (2015) *Terence and the Verb "To Be" in Latin,* Oxford.

Piazzi, L. (2008) "*Velut aeterno certamine:* immaginario epico-eroico nel *De rerum natura* di Lucrezio," in R. Uglione (ed.) *Atti del convegno nazionale di studi "Arma virumque cano . . .": L'epica dei Greci e dei Romani: Torino, 23–24 aprile 2007,* Alexandria, 103–117.

Pullig, H. (1888) *Ennio quid debuerit Lucretius,* Diss. Phil. Hal.

Quinn, K. (1959) *The Catullan Revolution,* Melbourne.

Quinn, K. (1972) *Catullus: An Interpretation,* London.

Ramelli, I. L. E. (2014) "Valuing Antiquity in Antiquity by Means of Allegoresis," in J. Ker and C. Pieper (eds.) *Valuing the Past in the Greco-Roman World,* Leiden, 485–507.

Raven, D. S. (1965) *Latin Metre,* London.

Rebeggiani, S. (2019) "Roman Agamemnon: Political Echoes in the Proem to Lucretius' *De Rerum Natura,"* *Mnemosyne* 73: 441–463.

Reeve, M. D. (1980) "The Italian Tradition of Lucretius," *Italia medioevale e umanistica* 23: 27–48.

Regenbogen, O. (1961) "Lukrez: Seine Gestalt in seinem Gedicht," in *Kleine Schriften,* Munich, 296–386.

Reinsch-Werner, H. (1976) *Callimachus Hesiodicus: Die Rezeption der hesiodischen Dichtung durch Kallimachos von Kyrene,* Berlin.

Reitzenstein, E. (1931) "Zur Stiltheorie des Kallimachos," in *Festschrift R. Reitzenstein,* Leipzig, 23–69.

Rinaldi, M. (2001) "Per la storia di un verso lucreziano (*De Rerum Natura* 1, 122)," *MD* 46: 171–182.

Ross, D. O. (1969) *Style and Tradition in Catullus,* Cambridge, MA.

Ross, D. O. (1987) *Virgil's Elements: Physics and Poetry in the Georgics,* Princeton.

Roy, S. (2013) "Homeric Concerns: A Metapoetic Reading of Lucretius, *De Rerum Natura* 2.1–19," *CQ* 63: 780–784.

Sallmann, K. (1968) "Epische Szenen bei Lukrez," *C&M* 29: 75–91.

Sauron, G. (2019) "The Architectural Representation of the *Kosmos* from Varro to Hadrian," in P. Horky (ed.) *Cosmos in the Ancient World*, Cambridge, 232–246.

Saylor, C. F. (1972) "Man, Animal, and the Bestial in Lucretius," *CJ* 67: 306–316.

Schanz, M. (1890) *Geschichte der römischen Litteratur bis zum Gesetzgebungswerk des Kaisers Justinian*, vol. 1, Munich.

Schiesaro, A. (1990) *Simulacrum et Imago: Gli Argomenti Analogici nel "De Rerum Natura,"* Pisa.

Schiesaro, A. (2007) "Lucretius and Roman Politics and History," in Gillespie and Hardie (2007), 41–58

Schiesaro, A. (2014) "*Materiam superabat opus*: Lucretius Metamorphosed," *JRS* 104: 73–104.

Schrijvers, P. H. (1970) *Horror ac Divina Voluptas: Études sur la Poétique et la Poésie de Lucrèce*, Amsterdam.

Schrijvers, P. H. (1978) "Le regard sur l'invisible: étude sur l'emploi de l'analogie dans l'oeuvre de Lucrèce," in O. Gigon (ed.) *Lucrèce*, Vandoeuvres, 77–114. Trans. M. Gale in Gale (2007b), Oxford, 255–288.

Schrijvers, P. H. (1999) *Lucrèce et les sciences de la vie* (*Mnemosyne*, Suppl. 186), Leiden.

Sciarrino, E. (2015) "Review of Elliott 2013," *CR* 65: 423–425.

Sedley, D. N. (1998) *Lucretius and the Transformation of Greek Wisdom*, Cambridge.

Sedley, D. N. (2003) "Lucretius and the New Empedocles," *LICS* 2.4: 1–12; also online at www.leeds.ac.uk/classics/lics.

Segal, C. (1990) *Lucretius on Death and Anxiety: Poetry and Philosophy in "De Rerum Natura,"* Princeton.

Sellar, W. Y. (1889) *Roman Poets of the Republic*, Oxford.

Shearin, W. (2015) *The Language of Atoms: Performativity and Politics in Lucretius' "De Rerum Natura,"* Oxford.

Shearin, W. (2019) "The Deep-Sticking Boundary Stone: Cosmology, Sublimity, and Knowledge in Lucretius' *De Rerum Natura* and Seneca's *Naturales Quaestiones*," in P. Horky (ed.) *Cosmos in the Ancient World*, Cambridge, 247–269.

Shearin, W. (2020) "Saussure's cahiers and Lucretius' elementa: A Reconsideration of the Letters-Atoms Analogy," in O'Rourke (2020a), Cambridge, 140–153.

Sherratt, E. (1990) "'Reading the Texts': Archeology and the Homeric Question," *Antiquity* 64: 807–824.

Skutsch, O. (1985) *The Annals of Quintus Ennius*, Oxford.

Snodgrass, A. M. (1974) "An Historical Homeric Society?," *JHS* 94: 114–125.

Stoddard, K. (1996) "Thucydides, Lucretius and the end of the *De Rerum Natura*," *Maia* 48: 107–128.

Sturtevant, E. H. (1919) "The Coincidence of Accent and Ictus in the Roman Dactylic Poets," *CP* 14: 373–385

Sturtevant, E. H. (1923) "Harmony and Clash of Accent and Ictus in the Latin Hexameter," *TAPA* 54: 51–73.

Suerbaum, W. (1968) *Untersuchungen zur Selbstdarstellung älterer römischer Dichter, Livius Andronicus, Naevius, Ennius*, Hildesheim.

Suerbaum, W. (1995) "Der Pyrrhos-Krieg in Ennius' *Annales* VI im Lichte der ersten Ennius-Papyri aus Herculaneum," *ZPE* 106: 31–52.

Taub, L. C. (2012) "Physiological Analogies and Metaphors in Explanations of the Earth and the Cosmos," in M. Horstmanshoff, H. King, and C. Zittel (eds.) *Blood, Sweat, and Tears: The Changing Concepts of Physiology from Antiquity into Early Modern Europe*, Leiden, 41–63.

Taylor, B. (2016) "Rationalism and the Theatre in Lucretius," *CQ* 66: 140–154.

Taylor, B. (2020a) *Lucretius and the Language of Nature*, Oxford.

Taylor, B. (2020b) "Common Ground in Lucretius' De Rerum Natura," in O'Rourke (2020a), Cambridge, 59–79.

Taylor, B. (forthcoming) "Lucretius and Early Latin," in J. Adams, A. Chahoud, and G. Pezzini (eds.) *Early Latin: Constructs, Diversity, Reception*, Cambridge.

Thomas, R. F. (1982) "Catullus and the Polemics of Poetic Reference (64.1-018)," *AJP* 103: 144–164.

Thomas, R. F. (1986) "Virgil's *Georgics* and the Art of Reference," *HSCP* 90: 171–198.

Thomas, R. F. (1988) *Virgil Georgics*, 2 vols. (Cambridge Greek and Latin Classics), Cambridge.

Timpanaro, S. (2005) *Contributi di filologia greca e latina*, Florence.

Townend, G. (1965) "Imagery in Lucretius," in D. Dudley (ed.) *Lucretius*, 95–114, London.

Trinacty, C. (2020) "Memmius, Cicero, and Lucretius: A Note on Cic. *Fam.* 13.1," *CQ* 70.

Tutrone, F. (2012) "Between Atoms and Humours: Lucretius' Didactic Poetry as a Model of Integrated and Bifocal Physiology," in M. Horstmanshoff, H. King, and C. Zittel (eds.) *Blood, Sweat, and Tears: The Changing Concepts of Physiology from Antiquity into Early Modern Europe*, Leiden, 83–102.

Tutrone, F. (2017) "Granting Epicurean Wisdom at Rome: Exchange and Reciprocity in Lucretius' Didactic (*DRN* 1.921-950)," *HSCP* 109: 275–337.

Tutrone, F. (2020) "Coming to Know Epicurus' Truth: Distributed Cognition in Lucretius' *De Rerum Natura*," in O'Rourke (2020a), Cambridge, 80–100.

Vahlen, J. (1903) *Ennianae Poesis Reliquiae*, Leipzig.

Verbrugghe, G. P. (1989) "On the Meaning of *Annales*, On the Meaning of Annalist," *Philologus* 133: 192–230.

Vinchesi, M. A. (1984) "Il *Bellum Histricum* di Ostio, epos storico ennianeggiante," in V. Tandoi (ed.) *Disiecta Membra Poetae I*, Foggia, 35–59.

Volk, K. (2002) *The Poetics of Latin Didactic: Lucretius, Vergil, Ovid, Manilius*, Oxford.

Volk, K. (2010) "Lucretius' Prayer for Peace and the Date of the "De Rerum Natura"" *CQ* 60: 127–131.

Wachter, R. (1987) *Altlateinische Inschriften: Sprachliche und epigrahische Untersuchungen zu den Dokumenten bis etwa 150 v. Chr.*, Bern.

Wakefield, G. (1813) *T. Lucreti Cari "De Rerum Natura" Libri Sex*, 4 vols., with annotations by Richard Bentley, Glasgow.

Weinreich, O. (1916–1919) "Religiöse Stimmen der Völker," *Archiv für Religionswissenschaft* 19: 158–173.

West, D. A. (1969) *The Imagery and Poetry of Lucretius*, Edinburgh.

West, D. A. (1970) "Virgilian Multiple-Correspondence Similes and Their Antecedents," *Philologus* 114: 262–275.

Wigodsky, M. (1972) *Vergil and Early Latin Poetry* (*Hermes* Einzelschriften 24), Wiesbaden.

Wilkinson, L. P. (1940) "The Augustan Rules for Dactylic Verse," *CQ* 34: 30–43.

Wilkinson, L. P. (1963) *Golden Latin Artistry*, Cambridge.

Williams, G. W. (1968) *Tradition and Originality in Roman Poetry*, Oxford.

Wimmel, W. (1960) *Kallimachos in Rom: Die Nachfolge seines apologetischen Dichtens in der Augusteerzeit*, Wiesbaden.

Wiseman, T. P. (1985) *Catullus and His World: A Reappraisal*, Cambridge.

Wiseman, T. P. (2006) "Fauns, Prophets, and Ennius' *Annales*," in Breed and Rossi (2006), 513–529.

Wreschniok, R. (1907) *De Cicerone Lucretioque Ennii imitatoribus*, Diss. Phil. Vratisl.

Wright, M. R. (1995) *Empedocles: The Extant Fragments*, London.

Zetzel, J. E. G. (1983) "Catullus, Ennius, and the Poetics of Allusion," *ICS* 8: 251–266.

Zetzel, J. E. G. (2007) "The Influence of Cicero on Ennius," in Fitzgerald and Gowers (2007), 1–16.

Zucca, D. (2020) "Lucretius and the Epicurean View that 'All Perceptions Are True,'" in Hardie, Prosperi, and Zucca (2020), 23–42.

Index of Passages

Index of Topics